D0015689

HUBERTINE AUCLERT
The French Suffragette

HUBERTINE AUCLERT
The French Suffragette

Steven C. Hause

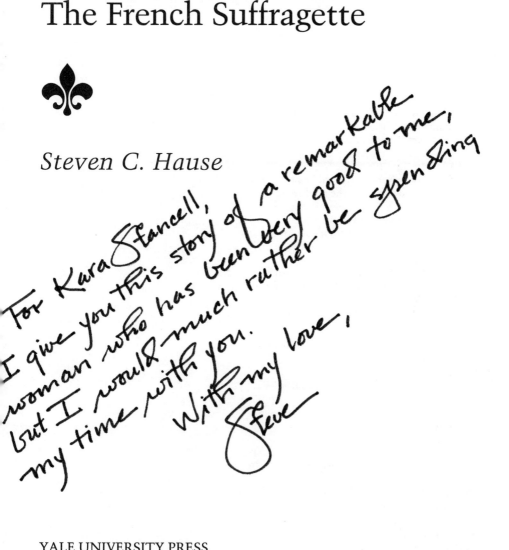

For Kara Stancell,
I give you this story of a remarkable
woman who has been very good to me,
but I would much rather be spending
my time with you.
With my love,
Steve

YALE UNIVERSITY PRESS
New Haven and London

Copyright © 1987 by Yale University.
All rights reserved.
This book may not be reproduced, in whole or in
part, in any form (beyond that copying permitted by
Sections 107 and 108 of the U.S. Copyright Law and
except by reviewers for the public press), without
written permission from the publishers.

Designed by Susan P. Fillion
and set in Trump Medieval type by Keystone
Typesetting Co., Orwigsburg, Pennsylvania.

Printed in the United States of America by
Edwards Brothers, Inc., Ann Arbor, Michigan.

Library of Congress Cataloging-in-Publication Data
Hause, Steven C., 1942–
    Hubertine Auclert : the French suffragette.

    Bibliography: p.
    Includes index.
    1. Auclert, Hubertine.   2. Suffragettes—
France—
Biography.   3. Women—Suffrage—France—
History.
I. Title.
JN2954.H37 1987   324.6'23'0924 [B]   87–2120
ISBN 0–300–03845–3 (alk. paper)

*The paper in this book meets the guidelines for
permanence and durability of the Committee on
Production Guidelines for Book Longevity of the
Council on Library Resources.*

10 9 8 7 6 5 4 3 2 1

To the memory of my brother, **Sheldon Kendall Hause** (*1946–1981*),
a biochemist, killed before he could publish a book too.

Contents

Contents   viii

Tables

Illustrations

Following page 111

Abbreviations

Used in both the text and the notes:

CNFF	Conseil national des femmes françaises
IWSA	International Woman Suffrage Alliance
LFDF	Ligue française pour le droit des femmes
SFIO	Section française de l'internationale ouvrière
UFF	Union fraternelle des femmes
UFSF	Union française pour le suffrage des femmes

Used only in the notes:

AD	Archives départmentales
AHR	*American Historical Review*
AN	Archives nationales
APP	Archives du Préfecture de Police
BHVP	Bibliothèque historique de la ville de Paris
BMD	Bibliothèque Marguerite Durand
DdPF	*Dictionnaire des parlementaires français* (1789–1889)
DF	Droit des femmes
DPF	*Dictionnaire des parlementaires français* (1889–1940)
DMO	*Dictionnaire biographique du mouvement ouvrier français*
FHS	*French Historical Studies*
FRS	Fédération républicaine socialiste
HR/RH	*Historical Reflections/Réflexions historiques*
JMH	*Journal of Modern History*

JO	*Journal officiel*
PWSFH	*Proceedings of the Western Society for French History*
SF	*Suffrage des Femmes*
TR/TR	*Third Republic/Troisième Republique*

Acknowledgments

I began the acknowledgments to my first book by thanking two senior professors at the University of Missouri-St. Louis for their confidence in me at the beginning of my career. Neal Primm and Ed Fedder deserve more than that single public thank-you. As a *hastatus* in the legion of new Ph.D.'s that poured into American universities in the late 1960s and early 1970s, I survived Caesar's decimation through tenure evaluation by the narrowest of margins. And I watched while very talented friends were less fortunate. Some administrators believed that I would never publish anything worthy of UMSL, and it is due solely to the strong support of Neal and Ed that I am not today an attorney, or a journalist, or a denizen of Harry Hope's establishment. I thank those *triarii* for saving my academic life.

My gratitude is also large for those whose confidence in my work extended to the financial support for European research. The national granting agencies turned down my applications again, although I asked only for a historian's expenses, not a businessman's. Instead of the foundations, I thank the University of Missouri-St. Louis which gave me the financial aid without which this book would not exist. I have received consistent and generous research support from UMSL. My thanks for travel and photocopying money, as well as the released time in which to write, go to the Department of History, the Center for International Studies, the Office of Research Administration, the dean's office of the College of Arts and Sciences, and the Weldon Spring fund. Their support was particularly important because the state of Missouri

xiii

pays most researchers wages calculated to usher them unceremoniously out of the middle class.

I am also indebted to many librarians and archivists in France for assisting my work. Most of the essential materials on Auclert's life are located in the Bibliothèque historique de la ville de Paris and in the Bibliothèque Marguerite Durand; the staff in both places helped me greatly. Special thanks are due to the staff at the archives of the Prefecture of Police, who made working there a pleasure, and to two individuals: Charles Uthéza of the Section d'outre mer at Aix-en-Provence, who spent hours of his time tracking down information on Antonin Lévrier and on Auclert's years in Algeria; and Gonzague Delacour of the Departmental Archives of Allier, whose knowledge of local records produced the evidence about Auclert's family and background. I hope someday to understand France well enough to comprehend the assorted regulations I have encountered, particularly those concerning photocopying.

Many colleagues contributed to the improvement of this book. Karen Offen and Pat Bidelman read portions of my first draft and gave me the benefit of their deep knowledge of the woman question in France. Charles Sowerwine and Jolyon Howorth similarly shared their superior grasp of French socialism. Susan Hartmann and Marcia Dalbey helped me grope toward understanding Auclert as a person. Anne R. Kenney collaborated with me in my original research on French suffragism and added much to its merits (but she met another and phfft, she was gone). Marilyn Boxer, Linda Clark, Claire Moses, and Michelle Perrot gave me many ideas about Auclert in helpful conversations. My thanks are also due to others who have studied Auclert: Pat Bidelman, who provided me with a xerographic copy of Auclert's diary when it had been lost at the BHVP; and Beth Lindquist and Edith Taïeb, who shared their writings and their thoughts on Auclert. Bob Nye and Karen Offen provided me with the remarkable document from *L'Escrime*. Of all of my colleagues, I owe the most to Joan Scott, who has the best critical mind that I have ever encountered—perceptive, demanding, and supportive.

I also wish to acknowledge the help that I received in the course of seminars, colloquia, and lectures. There is an active seminar and colloquium program among the faculty at UMSL, and many colleagues aided me with questions during my presentations to the Department of History, the Center for International Studies, the Department of Modern Foreign Languages, and the Social Science Colloquium. I received similar benefits from presenting papers to the Society for French Historical Studies, the Western Society for French History, and the Berkshire Conference on the History of Women. Special recognition is due Barrie Ratcliffe and the participants in his stimulating seminar on biography at the Western Society for French History. My thanks also go to those who asked probing questions at the University of Missouri—Kansas City, where I delivered the Weldon Spring Humanities Seminar lecture, and at the University of Montana, where I spoke with the support of the University of Montana Foundation.

Among those workers who are too frequently left anonymous, I want to thank the secretaries who helped me in the preparation of this book. Richie Martin came to my aid with her exceptional skills when work at UMSL began to swamp my research, and I appreciate it immensely. Mary Hines and Helen Binko, of the Center for International Studies at UMSL, typed and retyped my work with remarkable good cheer and efficiency.

Finally, more personal thanks go to those who sustained me in many places and many ways during the research and writing of this book. First, to my parents, who have come to accept (with only an occasional shaking of the head) that my travel too often takes me to research centers rather than to them. Next, to those who made those travels more pleasant: to Brenda Gardner (and the happy memories of J. D., dead far too young), who showed such gracious European hospitality; to Jack and Marcia Schnedler, the most remarkable travelers that I know, still teaching me how to enjoy it; to Tony and Sonia O'Donnell, who commented that I must have been drunk the last time I wrote acknowledgments; to Harry Fritz, who invited me to discuss Auclert at the University of Montana and made that trip a delight, even if he never sent me the photographs; to those whose friendship continues to make Paris my second home—Lorna Lennon, Sandra Moore, Anne Perotin, Yvonne Pettett, Michel Rieutord, and Bob Walshe; and to Dr. Prisnon, of Hornu, Belgium, and his family, who showed exceptional hospitality to the victim of an automobile accident. At home, to Mark Burkholder, whose nights at Whalen's have taught me much about energetic dedication to research; to Jerry Cooper, Chuck Korr, and Roland Champagne, constant challenges to my backhand; to John Works and Ron Munson, stimulating companions. Most of all, to Kathy Walterscheid for being Kathy Walterscheid, and to Lance LeLoup for being my lifeline.

My closing thanks go the staff of the Yale University Press: to Chuck Grench, the senior editor who first interested me in the Press and then encouraged me over several years of preparation; to Cynthia Wells, the production editor who directed the conversion of a manuscript into a book; and especially to Stella Hackell, the freelance manuscript editor who brought such superb skills to my manuscript that I took notes to remind myself of her advice.

Introduction

L ate on a spring afternoon in 1908, a stout woman dressed in widow's black marched forcefully past the doorman at a Parisian polling place, Her strong eyes and determined features persuaded voters to withdraw from her path. Hubertine Auclert, sixty years old and the founder of the women's suffrage movement in France, strode to the plain table where pollwatchers nodded as men deposited paper ballots in a wooden box. Those officials sat motionless at the sight of a woman in the sanctum sanctorum of masculine politics. One retained enough composure to gasp, "Sacrilege!" Another remembered Auclert as stilling them, as if she were the Medusa. They watched as she seized the ballot box, regarded it thoughtfully, and then hurled it to the floor. As the contents of "that urn of lies" spread at her feet, Auclert denounced the "unisexual suffrage" of the French republic, then stamped on the evidence of it. The police arrested her a few moments later.

Auclert had become the French Suffragette, a title that she proudly accepted in her subsequent trial.[1] She had earned that identity, before the word existed, during a militant career which had begun in the mid-1870s. Auclert had created the women's suffrage movement in

1. The London press coined the term *suffragette* a few months earlier and clearly employed it as a patronizing and diminutive label. The term did not remain pejorative, however, because the militant suffragists described by it cleverly appropriated the term to capitalize on the publicity that it had generated. The Pankhursts even named their periodical *The Suffragette*. Auclert responded in the same way because she also recognized an opportunity for publicity and did not object to notoriety.

France almost single-handedly, through her organizations Droit des femmes (Women's Rights) and Suffrage des femmes (Women's Suffrage). She had founded and edited the first suffragist newspaper in France, *La Citoyenne* (The Citizeness), personally providing most of its financing and writing. She had led marches in the streets, and she had wrestled with policemen. She had taken her cause to the established political parties, winning the theoretical support of socialists as early as 1879 and being rebuffed by the governing radical republicans as late as 1907. She had made lecture tours of the provinces, submitted dozens of petitions to the government, and written impassioned articles for newspapers across the entire political spectrum. And now, in the twilight of her career, she chose to make a vehement demonstration, hoping to create enough publicity to arouse the timid (both politicians and feminists).

Eighty years after Auclert's protest and trial, French women have four decades of electoral experience and little memory of Auclert. There is no rue Hubertine Auclert honoring her in Paris, although two dozen of the men with whom she negotiates in this book have received that recognition. There is certainly no French coin bearing her likeness. In fact, there is not even a biography of Auclert in French. At the time of the research for this book, no one at the historical museum in her birthplace, Allier, knew her name. Yet it is reasonable to compare Auclert to Elisabeth Cady Stanton or Susan B. Anthony in the United States, to Millicent Fawcett or the Pankhursts in Britain. Auclert won fewer victories than her better-remembered contemporaries, but it was no small accomplishment to create a women's suffrage movement in nineteenth-century France—in the face of public derision, political hostility, feminine apathy, and even feminist opposition. Nonetheless, the French began to forget Auclert in her own lifetime. When a large suffrage movement developed at the beginning of the twentieth century, Auclert's personality and attitudes reduced her to a secondary position; she was a suffragette among bourgeois moderates. Her death in 1914 made the front pages of many Parisian newspapers, but as a historical item: she died as the leader of a few dozen militants on the fringe of a movement numbering thousands of women. Her lifelong dedication to women's rights received little recognition beyond a small tablet outside her former residence on the rue de la Roquette. The recent resurgence of French feminism has stimulated new interest in Hubertine Auclert, including a television program devoted to her. She earned, and will undoubtedly receive, much more attention.

This biography examines both Auclert and her career. It is thus a story with two interwoven strands: the personal and the political. Auclert's public career is necessarily the dominant theme of the story. Her politics made her famous and generated the evidence that permits this book. The former theme, her private life, is more difficult to trace.

Auclert kept an extremely intimate diary for several years during the 1880s, and she had a lifelong habit of jotting down her thoughts and feelings (*pensées*) on scraps of paper. These important sources, combined with her correspondence, fragmentary autobiographical sketches, frequent newspaper interviews, a revealing short portrait by her sister, records of police investigations, and a careful reading of her voluminous works permit a close look at the person. The personal side of the story carries especial importance because there are many histories of masculine politics in modern France and many biographies of its practitioners, but few detailed studies of the individual women who sought to join them. Thus, even limited information about the personal development that led Auclert to politics, about her inner struggles over the appropriateness of marriage, about her feelings of lonely martyrdom, or about her consideration of suicide illuminate French politics with a different light.

The interpretations presented here can be stated briefly. The term *republican feminism* summarizes Auclert's political career.[2] Beginning in her youth during the authoritarian Second Empire, she considered the republic to be the ideal form of government, and she never deviated from that conviction. She carefully named her newspaper *La Citoyenne;* this title summarized her ambition of full and equal republican citizenship for women. Auclert used the republic as the lens through which to examine all questions. When she considered herself a socialist, she envisioned a "republican socialism"; when she lived in Algeria and criticized French colonialism, she advocated a form of "republican colonialism," in which Algerians would be assimilated into the republic. Auclert's feminism developed within the same ideal republicanism. The route to the equality of the sexes lay in the participation of women in the republic; women's suffrage must be the first step. The hostility of republican politicians did not daunt her; it merely proved that the Third Republic was not yet a "true republic." Republican feminism would change that.

Auclert's feminism included much more than the political rights with which she insisted that women must start. She indicated the

2. Strictly speaking, it may be anachronistic to employ the terms *feminism* or *feminist* before the 1890s. An undocumented tradition exists that Fourier coined the term *féminisme* in the early nineteenth century, but the advocates of equal rights for women did not begin employing that term, or the construction *féministe*, until the 1880s. It will be seen below that Hubertine Auclert claimed to have popularized these terms, but she apparently exaggerated her role. Auclert was nonetheless one of the first to adopt the labels. She began to call herself a *féministe* at least as early as 1882 (see chapter 5). Other studies are needed to determine if any woman anywhere preceded her; Karen Offen has begun to explore this in the French setting, Nancy Cott among American feminists. For consistency, both terms are used throughout this book.

breadth of her concern with the term *integral feminism,* claiming that she omitted no question that affected women. Hence, she wrote and spoke on a tremendous range of subjects (see appendix 1) and deserves to be remembered as a feminist as well as a suffragist. Indeed, Auclert may have been the first woman in any country to use the term *feminist* to describe herself.

The person beneath the tough public carapace is more difficult to summarize briefly. No attempt at formal psychobiography is made in this book. Readers interested in that genre will immediately recognize their starting point: Auclert fits the personality type known in the descriptive literature as a revolutionary ascetic.[3] Instead of categorizing and psychoanalyzing, I have tried to use all of the evidence known to me to depict the subtle contours and nuances of her personality. Thus, her portrait is drawn here with the inconsistencies and contradictions that appear in the evidence. Auclert will be seen rebelling against authority, yet behaving as an authoritarian; insisting upon personal independence, yet craving private companionship and seeking political alliances; confident and aggressive in her politics, yet describing herself as timid and insecure; sometimes flexible and opportunistic, but simultaneously dogmatic and uncompromising.

The foremost characteristic of Auclert's personality stressed in this biography is her self-image as a "martyr" (her own word, along with

---

3. Those wishing to explore the possibilities of psychobiography in this case can profitably begin by looking at the literature on the revolutionary personality. See Bruce Mazlish, *The Revolutionary Ascetic: Evolution of a Personality Type* (New York, 1976); E. Victor Wolfenstein, *The Revolutionary Personality: Lenin, Trotsky, Gandhi* (Princeton, 1967). These are useful despite the fact that neither Mazlish nor Wolfenstein studied female revolutionary ascetics and the further problem that there is too little evidence on Auclert's childhood to apply Erik Erikson's model of childhood development, which Wolfenstein employs; Harold Lasswell, *Psychopathology and Politics* (1930; reprint, New York: Viking, 1962), is somewhat dated and embarrassingly insensitive to women in politics (for which, see p. 124). For the initial reexamination of this literature for its application to women, see Marie M. Mullaney, "Gender and the Socialist Revolutionary Role, 1871–1921: A General Theory of the Female Revolutionary Personality," *HR/RH* 11 (1984):99–151, although she explicitly excludes radical middle-class women ("specifically the suffrage movement") like Auclert. For interesting hints from older social and psychological theory, see Freud's *Group Psychology and the Analysis of the Ego* (1921); despite the obvious problems of applying Freud to a feminist, it provides some of the key concepts, like politicians having "few libidinal ties," that subsequent commentators have stressed.

Serious psychobiographical study of women like Auclert must obviously go beyond such descriptive labels as "revolutionary ascetic" or even "female revolutionary ascetic." I have limited myself to a direct portrait of the dynamics of Auclert's life. It is essential to understand the equilibrium between the private person and the public figure, rather than to present an old-fashioned political biography with private curtains pulled; my qualifications, however, are not those necessary for a direct psychobiography.

pariah, outcast, and *déclassée*). Her sense of martyrdom began to develop in her youth; it became pronounced when she confronted the frustrations of trying to change Parisian politics. Auclert used this self-image to assimilate both political setbacks and her personal problems, to understand her experiences and her feelings. Simultaneously, a second basic characteristic propelled her onward: she possessed an exceptionally strong will. This appears at times as stubbornness, at times as dedication. When she chose feminism as the outlet for her determination—when she found her "faith," in her terms—she persisted with almost fanatical self-righteousness. As she recorded in her diary, she was "pushed by I know not what implacable devil."[4] Her will—to continue, to succeed—enabled Auclert to endure for forty years despite the suffering that she felt both in public (such as the ridicule she faced as a woman trying to compete in the male-dominated world of politics) and in private (such as an unhappy love life that made her "cry" in her diary).

Behind the interpretations of Auclert's career and the explanations of her private life stands another theme of this book: biography is important precisely because it describes the intersection between the individual and her epoch. One must analyze the struggle for women's rights (as I attempted in *Women's Suffrage and Social Politics*) through the formative characteristics of a society—legal traditions, religious beliefs, collective mentalities, political organization, economic development, social issues.[5] Biography enriches this analysis by examining the interplay between a feminist career and a woman's life. The living dialectic between historic role and human existence provides a perspective not otherwise available. In the life of Hubertine Auclert, one sees unhappiness mixed with idealism. Such a dialectic should clarify her politics and amplify the larger experience of the French struggle for women's rights.

4. Auclert's diary, which provides some of the most important evidence of this book, survived in the Auclert Papers which were given to the Bibliothèque historique de la de Paris (hereafter BHVP) as part of the extremely rich Bouglé Collection. This diary cannot presently be located at the BHVP, apparently because of misfiling. Patrick K. Bidelman first used this document in preparing his doctoral dissertation, and he reproduced several dramatic portions of it in his *Pariahs Stand Up! The Founding of the Liberal Feminist Movement in France, 1858–1889* (Westport, Conn., 1982), pp. 147–54. Bidelman fortunately preserved a xerographic copy of the complete diary, and he generously provided me with a copy of it. I have made an enlargement of this copy and deposited it at the BHVP to permit researchers to use it until the original can be located. The entry quoted here is for March 2, 1884 (hereafter cited thus: Diary, 2 March 1884, Auclert Papers).

5. See Steven C. Hause with Anne R. Kenney, *Women's Suffrage and Social Politics in the French Third Republic* (Princeton, 1984), esp. pp. 248–81.

CHAPTER ONE

From a Provincial Convent to Parisian Feminism, 1848–1872

The Allier is a narrow river about 250 miles long. It rises in the mountains of the Massif Central and flows northward to join the Loire. En route, it passes through the ancient province of Bourbonnais, to which it gives the republicanized name of the modern department of Allier. This is not a wealthy area. Throughout the nineteenth century, Allier remained a rural department, less densely populated than most departments in a rural country. Its agriculture had been stagnant since the Middle Ages, providing a comfortable living only to the few landed proprietors who possessed large holdings.[1]

The cadastral records of Allier survive for the period beginning in the late eighteenth century. They indicate that the Auclert (sometimes Auclaire or Auclerc) family had been among the more prosperous landowners of western Allier since before the French revolution. Police records confirm this impression. They describe the Auclerts as "an honorable family," later as "an excellent family, enjoying a certain affluence." The Auclert properties were located in the village of Tilly and in neighboring sections of the commune of Saint-Priest-en-Murat,

1. Hilda Ormsby, *France: A Regional and Economic Geography,* 2d ed. (London, 1964), pp. 45–55; André Leguai, *Histoire du Bourbonnais,* 2d ed. (Paris, 1974), pp. 109–11. See also the economic maps in Jean Vidalenc, *La Société française de 1815 à 1848: Le Peuple des campagnes* (Paris, 1970), pp. 371–78, and glimpses of life in Allier in Eugen Weber, *Peasants into Frenchmen: The Modernization of Rural France, 1870–1914* (Stanford, 1976), for example, pp. 43, 105, 161. According to the census of 1891, Allier had a population density of 151 per square mile, compared to a national rate of 187.

approximately twenty-five kilometers east of Montluçon. Jean-Baptiste, the Auclert paterfamilias of the mid-nineteenth century, owned sixty-eight arpents (about seventy acres) of land there, divided into seventy-six parcels of meadow, pasturage, and farmland which contained five separate residences. Tax records reveal that Jean-Baptiste was one of eighty-two proprietors in his canton to provide the state with one hundred francs of revenue per year. Under the restrictive electoral laws of the Orleanist monarchy (1830–1848), this made him one of only 421 voters in his arrondissement.[2]

It is difficult to restore human features to the skeletons buried in such public records. One may surmise that Jean-Baptiste Auclert's seventy acres provided him with a life of relative ease—in the context of an early nineteenth-century village of fewer than fifty persons, located in a commune whose chief town and several villages held barely a thousand. His tenant farmers and the neighboring peasants with small holdings may have faced starvation during the severe agricultural crises of the late eighteenth and early nineteenth centuries; Auclert, however, maintained a large house with several servants and no worries about daily bread. When 80 to 90 percent of the men of Allier were marking their marriage certificates with an *X*, Jean-Baptiste signed with the flourish of the educated class. He was, in short, a wealthy peasant and one of those important figures whom the French call "local notables."[3]

Not surprisingly, Jean-Baptiste Auclert became mayor of Tilly and served the commune of Saint-Priest-en-Murat in several official capacities, including adjunct mayor. But he was not one of the "landlords and stockholders" whose dominance Karl Marx considered characteristic of the French monarchy of the 1840s. Jean-Baptiste Auclert was a republican in an epoch when that term indicated the radical left wing of French politics. The family had a Jacobin tradition and republican loyalties dating from the 1790s. They owed part of their wealth and security to the purchase of nationalized lands from the revolutionary government. In the early nineteenth century, the Auclerts formed part of the new elite of well-to-do republican property owners in provincial France—a caste of local notables at odds with the ancient landowning aristocracy and its monarchical government.

2. Matrice cadastrale des propriétés foncières. Saint-Priest-en-Murat. Folios 302, 303, 314; Cadastre-registre; plans cadastrales; Liste générale du jury; and *Annuaire de l'Allier*, Archives départmentales (hereafter AD), Allier. Police reports, 11 August 1879, September 1880, and 22 April 1910, Dossier Hubertine Auclert, Bª 885, Archives du Préfecture de Police, Paris (hereafter Dossier Auclert, APP).

3. Leguai, *Histoire du Bourbonnais*, pp. 94–95; Paul-M. Bouju et al., *Atlas historique de la France contemporaine, 1800–1965* (Paris, 1966), p. 171, map 352; Actes de mariage, Arrondissement de Montarault, 2E 192/G, 11 May 1835, AD-Allier; Etat nominatif des habitants, Saint-Priest-en-Murat, 6M 502, 1836–1851, AD-Allier.

Jean-Baptiste Auclert did not serve the monarchy. He assumed office after the revolutionaries of 1848 had ousted King Louis-Philippe and proclaimed a Second Republic. The western portion of Allier had experienced especially depressed agricultural conditions in the late 1840s and now became a bastion of rural radicalism. Consequently, Allier also became a center of the political repression of radicalism begun by moderate republicans and redoubled during the Second Empire established after Louis Napoleon's coup d'état in 1851. Arrests in Allier soon placed the department near the top of the prefectural lists for anti-republican activity. Jean-Baptiste Auclert, a well-known republican in a small place, became a victim of the Bonapartist purges in 1852. He escaped imprisonment or deportation apparently because the prefect concentrated his efforts on more urban areas than the commune of Saint-Priest-en-Murat. His dismissal from office, however, intensified his Jacobinism. Thereafter, Jean-Baptiste declined to serve the authoritarian empire. His children grew up in a household that understood the republican revolution as the basis of their prosperity and prominence and the republic as the ideal government. They also had in their father a model for adhering to unpopular political principles, for opposing authoritarianism, and for openly disagreeing with the established power.[4]

While historical detective work can give a few glimpses of the life even of an obscure man like Jean-Baptiste Auclert, it is significantly more difficult to make public records speak of his wife, Marie Chanudet. The evidence that is useful for Jean-Baptiste—census, tax, police, and cadastral records—locates Marie only in terms of her father. *He* was a landed proprietor, apparently much like the Auclerts, in the neighboring arrondissement of Montmarault. Of Marie herself, little evidence exists. This silence, of course, speaks loudly of the situation of French women of her generation. The French civil law, codified under Napoleon Bonaparte in 1804, followed the traditions of Roman law and denied women the rights of citizenship. Those rights, like the documen-

---

4. Registres, 2E 260/G, AD-Allier. There is a large literature on the revolution in the provinces and on the repression of republicanism. See especially the detailed treatment of Allier in Thomas R. Forstenzer, *French Provincial Police and the Fall of the Second Republic: Social Fear and Counterrevolution* (Princeton, 1981), pp. 270–73. There is suggestive data on the disturbances in R. Gossez, "Carte des troubles en 1846–1847," *Bibliothèque de revolution de 1848* 19 (1956):1, and good data on arrests in Roger Price, *The French Second Republic: A Social History* (Ithaca, 1972), pp. 291–95. See also John M. Merriman, *The Agony of the Republic: The Repression of the Left in Revolutionary France, 1848–1851* (New Haven, 1978), esp. pp. 108 and 121; Howard Machin, "The Prefects and Political Repression: February 1848 to December 1851," and Vincent Wright, "The Coup d'état of December 1851: Repression and the Limits to Repression," both in Roger Price, ed., *Revolution and Reaction: 1848 and the Second French Republic* (London, 1975), pp. 280–302 and 303–33; Howard C. Payne, *The Police State of Louis Napoleon Bonaparte, 1851–1860* (Seattle, 1966).

tary record of Marie Chanudet's life, were stated in terms of women's fathers or husbands. A married woman, for example, did not control her own wealth. She could not witness a document, enroll in a university, file a paternity suit, vote in an election, serve as legal guardian for children, own a newspaper, join a trade union, sue for divorce, or hold any of dozens of different jobs.[5]

Marie Chanudet had one moment when her name filled several documents: in the late spring of 1835, when she married Jean-Baptiste Auclert. An examination of that moment is revealing. The Napoleonic Code paid careful attention to marriage. An entire chapter specified the technical requirements of residence, posting the banns, and parental (that is, paternal) consent. Among the stipulations was the requirement (Article 75) that an officer of the state read to the prospective couple, before witnesses, a statement on the formalities of marriage. This included the full text of articles from the code "On Marriage" and "Concerning the Respective Duties and Rights of the Spouses." Only after hearing and accepting Articles 212–226 could Marie wed Jean-Baptiste. By accepting Article 213, she agreed that "the wife owes obedience to her husband." Subsequent articles specified ways in which the law would treat her as a minor, unable to act without her husband's authorization. Other articles, not read to the couple, covered such matters as his power over their children. By signing the marriage contract, Marie Chanudet prepared to leave the home of one proprietor and take her property to the home of another proprietor.[6]

Jean-Baptiste and Marie Auclert had seven children between 1836 and 1850. Two sons were born in quick succession, followed by five daughters over eighteen years. The wealth of the family meant that the children need not labor in a family wage economy, and all of them could receive a formal education. The eldest son, Théophile, was expected ultimately to manage the family property, and did so from Jean-Baptiste's death in 1861 until his own, half a century later. He also assumed the duties of a local notable and served a long term as mayor of Saint-Priest-en-Murat. The other son, Prosper, was established as a manufac-

5. For an introduction to the situation of women in nineteenth-century France, see Claire G. Moses, *French Feminism in the Nineteenth Century* (Albany, 1984); Bidelman, *Pariahs Stand Up!*, esp. pp. 3–32; James F. McMillan, *Housewife or Harlot: The Place of Women in French Society, 1870–1940* (New York, 1981), esp. pp. 9–75; Karen Offen, "Aspects of the Woman Question During the Third Republic," *TR/TR* 3–4 (1977): 1–19; Theodore Zeldin, *France, 1848–1945* (Oxford, 1973–1977), 1:343–62; Hause with Kenney, *Women's Suffrage and Social Politics*, esp. pp. 3–27.

6. *Le Code civil. Textes antérieures et version actuelle. Edition à jour au 30 juin 1981* (Paris, 1981), pp. 34–35 (Articles 63–76 of 1803), 86 (Articles 212–26 of 1803); Contrats de mariage, 20 April 1835, 3Q 59/19 and Actes de mariage, Arrondissement de Montmarault, 11 May 1835, 2E 192/G, AD-Allier.

turer of candles at Montmarault. The eldest daughters, Eugénie and Delphine, were provided with appropriate dowries, married, and left Tilly. And none of the family would be remembered had not the fifth child, Hubertine, born in 1848, become one of the most notorious women of her generation by founding the women's suffrage movement in France.[7]

Marie-Anne-Hubertine Auclert spent her early childhood in the house where she was born, with her parents, two younger sisters, Rosalie and Marie, two orphaned nieces of Jean-Baptiste, and four domestic servants—the household accounting for 20 percent of the population of Tilly. The bucolic life left a lasting impression on her; georgics lingered in her writing after forty years of living in Paris. So did pastoral metaphors: her feminist ideas were ripening fruit; French women were sheep who needed the right shepherd to lead them to rich political pastures. According to the recollections of her sister Marie (who was closest to Auclert throughout her life), the future militant displayed precocious intelligence and a strong will but grew up as a typical girl of her class and epoch. She played with dolls, learned to embroider, learned the lessons of parsimonious management, and generally "acquired all the qualities of an accomplished mistress of the household."[8]

Although the evidence is limited, it seems clear that Auclert enjoyed a happy and privileged childhood, growing up somewhat indulged, if not spoiled. Her health was good. She enjoyed her country surroundings. The family prospered, and she suffered no material deprivation. They retained their prominent status, and she grew up with the self-confidence and security of a child of the local notable. The Auclerts also remained attentive to politics, although the extent of Jean-Baptiste's activity after 1852 is unknown. They valued education and sent their children to boarding schools. In short, Auclert grew up more conscious of the world beyond her *pays* than one would expect in a French farm family of the 1850s. Because of the difference in age between Auclert and her siblings and their early departure for school, Auclert also spent

7. Registres de naissances, Saint-Priest-en-Murat, 2E 260/G; Actes de décès, Saint-Priest-en-Murat, 2E 260/11; Registre de recette, Déclarations des mutations, 3Q 6160; Matrice cadastrale des propriétés foncières, Saint-Priest-en-Murat, AD-Allier. To understand the family in the economic context of the epoch, see the discussion of the family wage economy in Louise A. Tilly and Joan W. Scott, *Women, Work, and Family* (New York, 1978), pp. 9–60.

8. Etat nominatif des habitants, Saint-Priest-en-Murat, 1851–1872, 6M 502, AD-Allier; Marie Chaumont, "Hubertine Auclert," preface to Hubertine Auclert, *Les Femmes au gouvernail* (Paris, 1923), pp. 1–2. The examples of Auclert's metaphors are from the title page of *Les Femmes au gouvernail* and from her essay "Les Françaises ont une docilité de brebis qui surprend même les bergers," in Auclert, *Le Vote des femmes* (Paris, 1908), p. 207. There are many more illustrations in the Auclert Papers, a subseries of the Bouglé Collection at the BHVP; see especially Cartons 6, 8, and 11.

her childhood as the oldest child at home, playing with two younger sisters. Her sense of leadership and authority, so strong in adulthood, must have emerged at this time.

THE ROUTE TO REBELLION

Two events disturbed the tranquility of Auclert's privileged youth: her relocation to a convent school and the death of her father. The evidence concerning these experiences is again scanty and sometimes contradictory. Her family apparently enrolled her as a residential pupil at the convent of the Dames de l'enfant Jésus in Montmirail (Allier) at the age of nine, and she received eight years of formal education before leaving school at sixteen, in 1864.[9] Jean-Baptiste died in 1861 while she was away from home.

Auclert initially reacted to convent schooling with hostility.[10] She did not wish to go, and she apparently resisted with the subbornness and the resistance to authority that characterized her later behavior. Auclert soon adapted to the convent, however, and found it to be an appealing home. She became a devout pupil, although the nuns thought her too independent and willful; no incidents are known, but she presumably showed them some of the truculence with which she had greeted the diktat from her parents that she enroll.

Auclert made an emotional commitment to the church as a student and developed her youthful identity in her piety. She told interviewers in later years that at school she had "the most ardent faith." Police investigations of her background reached the same conclusion: "She attracted notice by her piety." Auclert's childhood religiousness was so strong that she emulated the nuns who taught her. Contemporaries saw this in the adult suffragist. Many commented that, despite comfortable wealth, Auclert's dress, home, and habits revealed the austerity of the convent. Such asceticism characterizes many radicals, but in Auclert's

9. Different accounts name Saint-Maur and the Dames trinitaires (both in Montluçon) and the Dames de l'enfant Jésus (in Montmirail). See *La France,* 23 May 1880; clippings in Auclert Papers, Carton 1; police report, 19 April 1910, Dossier Auclert, APP. The confusion apparently results from two sources. Auclert never referred to the specific convent, leading authors to speculate; she also entered a convent briefly for a second time, after the death of her mother, and that convent has been confused with the location of her schooling.

10. *Le Gaulois,* 20 September 1880. A copy of this article (and many of the other articles cited here) can be found in the Auclert Papers, Carton 1; another is in the Dossier Auclert, APP (also a source of many clippings). The same account appears in several places, most recently in Hubertine Auclert, *La Citoyenne: Articles de 1881 à 1891,* ed. Edith Taïeb (Paris, 1982), p. 7.

case the church shaped this trait first and vividly. "Her entire personality," wrote one newspaperman, "exhales the aroma of the seminary and the convent." This was not a notion concocted by a hostile reporter. Auclert described herself in similar terms; some feminists called her (behind her back) "the Jesuit".[11]

Her piety, admiration of the nuns who taught her, and acceptance of the conventual life persuaded Auclert that a religious life called her too. In 1864, at sixteen, she sought to join the Sisters of Charity of St. Vincent de Paul upon the completion of her schooling. That order rejected her. Why would the church reject an intelligent and devout pupil? A later police investigation of Auclert reported that "her superiors found her too mystical and even a little crazy [*folle*]." She echoed this explanation in a newspaper interview in which she described getting into trouble at the convent over her beliefs: she cherished the primitive Christianity of the first centuries after Christ as an egalitarian society. One interviewer characterized her image of Christianity as "a sort of republican communism"—presumably leavened with some of her father's Jacobinism. In that account, Auclert used the same words that the police investigator reported from Allier thirty years later; the nuns told her, "You are a little crazy." This seems a plausible answer from the Sisters of Charity; for most of the nineteenth century, monarchists unsympathetic to egalitarianism guided their order. The daughter of a purged republican, the advocate of a radical Christianity, could be rejected.[12]

After this traumatic experience, Auclert left the convent and returned to the family home in Tilly. Acording to the census records of 1866, she resided with her widowed mother, Marie, in the home of her brother Théophile, with his wife, Josephine, and two servants. Her younger sisters, Rosalie (then fifteen) and Marie (thirteen), boarded at the convent as Auclert had. The death of her father and the departure of her sisters significantly altered Auclert's family relations, especially with her mother and eldest brother, both of whom now shaped her character and her future.[13]

Hurt, confused, and angered by the church's rejection of her, Auclert turned to her mother for support. Madame Auclert, forty-nine years old

11. *Le Figaro*, 1 January 1881 (quotation); *Le Gaulois*, 20 September 1880; *La Lumière*, 16 February 1935; *La France*, 23 May 1880; Arria Ly to Auclert, 17 June 1913, Auclert Papers, 3/337; police report, 19 Arpil 1910, Dossier Auclert, APP. See also Bidelman, *Pariahs Stand Up!*, p. 108; Bidelman speculates that Auclert acquired "the martyr-like attitude that characterized her campaign" at the convent.

12. Etat nominatif des habitants, Saint-Priest-en-Murat, 1866, 6M 502, AD-Allier; police report, 19 April 1910, Dossier Auclert, APP; *Le Gaulois*, 20 September 1880; Adrien Dansette, *Religious History of Modern France* (London, 1961), 1:141, 290.

13. Etat nominatif des habitants, Saint-Priest-en-Murat, 1866, 6M 502, AD-Allier.

and three years a widow in 1864, suffering from ill health and her difficult transition in life, welcomed the companionship of her teenaged daughter. Thus, Auclert recalled in 1894, "I became for my mother more than a child, a friend." She considered her mother to have been an important source of her egalitarianism: Madame Auclert was "a bit of a socialist without knowing it." Auclert illustrated this assertion with simple recollections. Her earliest memory was of eating bread and jam with enthusiasm. Then, in a scene duplicated in many homes, her mother explained that poor children rarely tasted such treats. Auclert claimed that this made a profound impression on her. She answered, "Well, I don't want to eat preserves if all other children can't have them too." In a more distinctive illustration from her postconvent years, Auclert praised her mother for "preaching by example." The plight of unwed mothers troubled Madame Auclert. Pregnancies outside marriage were common in Allier; in Saint-Priest-en-Murat during the 1850s, they had accounted for as much as 25 percent of all births. Auclert recalled that peasants had "very great contempt" for unwed mothers and "would have let them die, on the side of the road, without aiding them." Marie Chanudet defied this attitude and taught her daughter to help these women. Whenever possible, she found work for them, usually employing them to sew for her household.[14]

The intimacy between Auclert and her mother during the mid-1860s shaped the future feminist's thoughts in another way, through discussion of the problems of marriage. Auclert recorded this only obliquely, noting that her mother shared "certain confidences" to explain that she "had not been absolutely happy" in marriage. Whatever her mother divulged had a sharp impact on Auclert, who remembered the conversations for the rest of her life. It is possible that the problem involved wife-beating, not an uncommon occurrence in rural France during the nineteenth century; this was a world in which folk wisdom held that "women and omelets are never beaten enough." There is evidence that Auclert worried about such violence as a young woman. Marie reported her sister's concern with a husband's turning violent and striking his wife. Among Auclert's papers there remains a note stating that one of the origins of Auclert's feminism was "the brutality of man towards woman, *for whom my childhood was terror-stricken.*" One cannot accuse Jean-Baptiste Auclert of wife-beating on such slender evidence. One can, however, combine Auclert's valid fear of masculine violence within marriage with her mother's confession of some significant prob-

14. *La Libre parole*, 2 June 1894; *Le Gaulois*, 20 September 1880; Registre de naissances, Saint-Priest-en-Murat, 1839–1862, 2E 260/G, AD-Allier. For a discussion of the importance of mother-daughter relations in shaping the personality of revolutionary women, see Mullaney, "Gender and the Socialist Revolutionary Role, 1871–1921."

lem in her marriage, and thereby understand how the young woman began to formulate objections to the legal submission of women to men. It is not surprising, therefore, to discover Auclert's assertion that her mother's confidences "developed in me the germ of rebellion and independence."[15]

Auclert's new relationship with her brother produced the same rebelliousness and desire for independence in a different way. After Jean-Baptiste's death in 1861, Théophile became the head of the family under French law and exercised paternal authority over Auclert. He administered a dramatic shock to her when their mother died in 1866. Théophile returned her to the now-despised convent as a "paying resident." He lodged her with a different order, in Montluçon, but that hardly mattered. Auclert had resisted entering the convent as a child, but she had adapted well; as a young adult, she hated it without reservation. Auclert later recalled her reentry into a convent with anguish: "After the death of my mother, I was locked up [*enfermée*] in a convent as a pensioner, and I had great fear, on entering there, of being obliged to leave behind my beautiful ideas of independence and liberty." She was, however, no longer a young supplicant. Her natural determination and boldness emerged, and Auclert made the first shrewd demonstration of her career. As she described it, "In order to forestall this [loss of freedom] I hastened to make a public showing of these ideas [about feminine independence], to the great amazement of the religious, who trembled at them, in terror for my future." Auclert did not stay long in the convent.[16]

THE ROUTE TO FEMINISM

Hubertine Auclert's journey from a convent in Allier in 1866 to the feminist organizations of Paris in 1873 merits a careful examination. What led her to leave home? Why did she turn to politics? Once in politics, why did she choose to enter the feminist movement? The context for answering such questions is clear. The young woman who returned from the convent in 1866 had begun to search for her adult identity; the woman who joined the feminist movement in 1873 had found it. The components of this identity crisis, and thus of her decisions, can be found in the sketch of her youth drawn above.

15. *La Libre parole,* 2 June 1894. For the life of peasant wives, see Tilly and Scott, *Women, Work, and Family,* pp. 9–60; Weber, *Peasants into Frenchmen,* pp. 171–75 and p. 528 n. 13. (quotation). Chaumont, "Hubertine Auclert," p. 2; note by Auclert, Auclert Papers, 14/46 (italics added).

16. *La Libre parole,* 2 June 1894.

One should begin by noting that Auclert experienced a markedly different transition into adulthood from most women in mid-nineteenth-century France. Choices common for other women were not applicable or not acceptable to her: neither a job nor the church, neither her home nor a marriage, would resolve Auclert's search for identity.

A job, or training for an occupation, provided no answer because she did not need it. No economic pressure weighed upon Auclert; she could choose a life that involved no gainful employment. Jean-Baptiste's will gave her economic security for life if she managed her inheritance carefully. Given Auclert's parsimonious instincts and her satisfaction in the ascetic life, this posed no problem. Her inheritance did not make Auclert rich, but it made her independent. Thus, circumstances did not oblige her to seek an occupation; she could contemplate stimulating forms of nonpaying employment.

The church likewise did not contain the answer, for obvious reasons. At sixteen, Auclert thought that her identity was in religion, but the church told her that it was not. The young woman who searched for her identity in her late teens and early twenties had already rejected Christianity. Her subsequent anticlericalism remained with her for life. It contributed directly to her choice of a career by leading to association with like-minded people when she had arrived in Paris. Furthermore, it will be seen that Auclert's conventual experience played a great role in shaping her decision to devote herself to feminism. But the fact remains simple: the church did not offer her a vocation.

Staying in the home where she had grown up was also not an option for Auclert. She might have chose to remain with her parents, especially her mother, but they had died. The brother and sister-in-law who now controlled that home gave her no choice. She scarcely knew this man who had been absent in her childhood. He and his wife preferred to live alone, and they did so, childless, for life. Auclert's younger sisters quickly married and left. When she gave no indication of following their example, Théophile dispatched her to the convent, where she certainly did not desire to stay. For the remainder of her life, Auclert described herself as an "orphan," and by this she may have meant more than being parentless.[17] Thus, even if she had been temperamentally suited to growing old at home (and she was not), the option did not exist.

Marriage, the choice made by Rosalie, by Marie, and by thousands of other women in Auclert's situation, was not an acceptable alternative. For want of suitors, it may not have been an option at all. Auclert received several proposals of marriage in later years, the evidence of which remains in her papers; none of her autobiographical sketches or

17. For illustrations of the term *orphan,* see Chaumont, "Hubertine Auclert," p. 5; autobiographical fragment, Auclert Papers, 14/61.

biographical interviews mention such proposals in Allier. Even if marriage had been a possibility then, Auclert probably would have rejected it as she did many times in the next twenty years. Her experiences had conditioned her toward autonomy. She had already decided, in seeking to enter a religious order, that she was comfortable with (or preferred) the celibate life. Auclert's conversations with her mother reinforced this sentiment by focusing upon unhappiness in marriage.

While the traditional choices of job, church, home, or marriage gave Auclert insufficient direction in finding her way, it should also be noted that her personality facilitated nontraditional choices. One can only deduce the salient features of her character from the surviving evidence, but these traits constitute a strong person. She had acquired self-confidence and a sense of leadership from the socioeconomic status of her family and from her position within that family. Her strong will and stubbornness are obvious in Marie's recollections of their childhood, in the church's criticism of her days in the convent, and in her adult life.

Other aspects of Auclert's character contributed to her choice of politics and feminism. During her years in Montmirail, Auclert acquired a strong sense of dedication and sacrifice. She admired the women who had chosen celibacy and self-denial in the service of their beliefs and for the benefit of others. Auclert learned from her parents how to channel other-directedness into independent activity; her fondness for the story of her mother's aid to unwed mothers illustrates both the service to others and the independence in performing it. Auclert sought a vocation that combined those of her mother and her mother superior. This might have led her toward philanthropy, education, or social welfare and reform movements. Other aspects of her youth are needed to explain why politics, and especially feminist politics, attracted her more than other careers, serving in the Red Cross, for example.

The most obvious fact in this explanation is that Auclert grew up in a political family. She observed her father and her brother holding political office—Théophile served as mayor of Saint-Priest-en-Murat and of Tilly during the liberal empire of the 1860s. Seventy years of Jacobin tradition in her family created an idealized sense of the Republic and service to it. The model of Jean-Baptiste's political life must have made a profound impression on his daughter. His criticism of monarchy and unwillingness to serve it, his support of the revolution of 1848 and service to the ensuing Second Republic, and his conflict with authority in 1851–1852 and subsequent removal from office sound remarkably like Auclert's own career. It must have been easy for a child to see the heroic in Jean-Baptiste and to cherish the republican ideals that he had served. That Jacobin republicanism complemented the egalitarianism that Auclert learned from her mother. Whatever the extent of political discussion in their daily life, the Auclert family prepared their daughter to find politics respectable and rewarding; if an opportunity arose for her to serve French republicanism, it could hardly be surprising that she accepted it.

Given this background, the experience in Auclert's youth that it is critical to understand is her education in the convent of Montmirail. That story is greater than its elements that are important *prima facie*— formal education, exposure to Catholic virtues, rejection of vocation, and loss of religion. Her years with the Dames de l'enfant Jésus should also be recognized as an empowering experience that enabled her to make the transition from thinking of republican politics as admirable to believing that women could take an active role in such politics. Why? Because she spent them into a community of women that provided her with a range of female role models. She saw women as authority figures, decision makers, and administrators, women who could manage the spiritual, economic, and political spheres. The child who went to Montmirail with a strong will and sense of leadership, and the student who proposed to spend her life in a convent, must have identified herself with the strong leaders she encountered rather than with the role of submissive pupil. Her known behavior there—her defiant, independent thought that made her seem "crazy" to her elders—underscores the empowering nature of this experience: she did not learn to submit herself, she learned to assert herself. Auclert assimilated her experience of a highly structured, authoritarian environment in a paradoxical way. She learned to project herself as an authority figure like those whom she desired to join. And she developed this image of women in general and herself in particular by reinforcing her habit of challenging external authority.

Auclert's leadership in her subsequent political career bore the imprint of this formative experience. She acted with a religious, dogmatic certainty. She sought to lead with the authority of a mother superior, and she did so with the self-righteousness of a true believer attacking the heathen. Indeed, feminism became a secular religion for Auclert, and she frequently showed this in her choice of religious metaphors. She acknowledged that she was "as attached to my ideas as to a religion." Sincere feminists became "apostles," their beliefs, "the faith." Those "coreligionists" who joined her in challenging authority were "martyrs." Such imagery extended to messianic leadership, and she even compared her situation to the life of Jesus. Little wonder that journalists found "the aroma of the convent" around her.

Auclert's conventual experience also enriched her developing ideology. The Jacobin egalitarianism that she drew from her parents became mixed with her Christian morality. She had found an egalitarianism in primitive Christianity, in its sensitivity to the needs of the oppressed, in the lessons of the Beatitudes and the Sermon on the Mount. Hence, the same Christian teachings that led to Auclert's rejection from holy orders also led to the other-directedness of her political gospel.

Even Auclert's rejection of Christianity shaped her political development. As she reflected on her years of "ardent faith," she concluded that Christianity treated men and women differently, both in theology, where women were considered "the devil's gateway" because of the original sin of Eve, and in daily life, where women were expected to obey. Thus Auclert's later writings frequently blamed the church for its role in the subjection of women. She heaped scorn on Paul, Tertullian, and canon law for assigning to women a position in life inferior to that of men. "Christianity," Auclert wrote in a biographically revealing passage, "offers the woman a deceptive charm. It does not give her the equality dreamt of. The woman has been duped by Christianity. . . . The religion is opposed to the liberation of the woman, with its dogma of the fall." This reaction to Catholicism intersected another tenet of the French republican credo that Auclert had inherited, anticlericalism. Many sources of Auclert's thinking were clear in a letter she published at age twenty-five proclaiming the urgency of freeing women from "the pernicious influence" of "superstition." She also demanded the expulsion of the Jesuits from France and called for the closing of all convents in France. Convents, she said, were "only a refuge offered to laziness and demoralization."[18]

All of this background did not yet make Hubertine Auclert a feminist. It strongly predisposed her toward politics and gave her a basis for embracing feminism. Auclert, of course, later tried to portray herself as a feminist from childhood. In her memories and in Marie's report, Auclert claimed that "almost from birth I have been a rebel agaist the devastation [*écrasement*] of women."[19] This understandable exaggeration only strengthens the argument that the origins of Auclert's republican feminism can be seen in her youth. Her decision to go to Paris and join the women's movement still required a few developments in the period after 1868: the financial independence that enabled her to leave home; the continuing political growth in the turbulent years at the end

18. Several of Auclert's sharpest comments on the church can be found in her notes in the folder "Femmes et cléricalisme," Auclert Papers, Carton 6; the examples used here are from 6/53, 6/59, and from an untitled essay, 6/39. Auclert to Richer, published in *L'Avenir des femmes*, 4 January 1874; open letter by Auclert, *Le Petit Parisien*, 1 June 1877; *Séances du congrès ouvrier socialiste de France*, 3d session, Marseille, 20–31 October 1879 (Marseille, 1879), p. 804; *La Libre parole*, 2 June 1894. For an examination of the connections between French feminism and anticlericalism, see Richard J. Evans, "Feminism and Anticlericalism in France, 1870–1922," *Historical Journal* 25 (1982):947–52.

19. Chaumont, "Hubertine Auclert," p. 2; *La Lumière*, 16 February 1935.

of the Second Empire and the beginning of the Third Republic; and the triggering experience that excited her interest in the Parisian movement and motivated her to leave Allier.

THE ROUTE TO PARIS

Financial independence came first and most easily. In 1869, when Auclert turned twenty-one, her father's will provided her with an independent fortune. Jean-Baptiste had divided his lands among his wife and children, leaving Hubertine twenty-six parcels of land which included two separate residences. The income from this estate assured her of a comfortable life, even without her childhood frugality and conventual austerity. As those became lifetime habits (she wrote many of her works on mere scraps of paper, such as envelopes), Auclert was unquestionably secure.[20]

It is difficult to determine precisely how wealthy Auclert was. She never needed to take a husband or a job, yet she was not so rich that she could personally finance large political activities. Press and police reports on Auclert used vague terms. "It is said that she is rich, or at least very comfortable," ran a typical newspaper report. Auclert preferred the significant term "independent," telling interviewers that she had an independent fortune or that she was an independent orphan. Her sister described her in the same terms.[21] It is probable that her inheritance was worth approximately sixty thousand francs, producing two to three thousand francs of income per annum.[22] Police investigations of 1876 and 1910 estimated her fortune at sixty thousand francs, and that amount is very close to her estate probated in 1914. It will be seen that Auclert lived in Paris according to the prudent bourgeois principle of spending only her income and rarely touching her capital. Inflation never became a problem for her. Hence, the consistency between earlier estimates and her known estate is plausible. The annual income from her sixty thousand francs is also difficult to ascertain. A police investigation of 1877 put it at three thousand francs. Her will, however,

20. Registre de recette, Déclarations des mutations par décès, Saint-Priest-en-Murat, 17 March 1862, 3Q 6160; Matrice cadastrale des propriétés foncières, Saint-Priest-en-Murat, Folio 568, AD-Allier.

21. *Le Petit méridional,* 1880 clipping, Auclert Papers, Carton 1; *La France,* 23 May 1880; Auclert to Jeanne Schmahl, June 1895, Auclert Papers, 14/61; Chaumont, "Hubertine Auclert," p. 5; autobiographical fragment, c. 1894, Auclert Papers, 14/58.

22. Using mean exchange rates given in *The Statesman's Yearbook,* 60,000 francs in the late nineteenth century was equal to approximately $12,000 or £2,400. J. Scott Keltie, ed., *The Statesman's Yearbook. Statistical and Historical Annual of the States of the World* (London, 1891), pp. 495, 1078.

shows that her investments in 1914 were very conservative and yielded closer to two thousand at that date.[23]

How rich was a young woman living in Paris with two to three thousand francs each year? Not very, though she was certainly among the privileged. It is more accurate to describe Auclert's condition as comfortable, secure, and independent. A more precise answer becomes a matter of class standards. Two thousand francs surpassed the average annual wages of skilled workingmen in the Paris region in the early 1870s. It was still higher than that figure in the late 1890s. A government survey of 1893, for example, reported that male cabinetmakers (among the highest-paid workers) in the department of the Seine earned daily wages of 7.1 francs, and male chemical workers (among the lowest-paid), 4.85 francs. This converts to a *maximum* annual wage of 1,400 to 2,100 francs. A rough calculation for the early 1870s provides a range of 1,100 to 1,700 francs. This, of course, was in a society that understood a man's wages to be family wages. A working woman seeking to support herself with similar skills earned half the wages of a man—a maximum of 600 to 800 francs in the early 1870s, 750 to 1,000 in the 1890s. And if one looks outside Paris, such wages fall by 30 to 65 percent.[24]

Auclert, with no family to support and with austere personal habits, certainly possessed a privileged financial position, easily within the range of bourgeois comfort in the 1870s. She was rich from the perspective of a single working woman who labored sixty hours per week to obtain one-third of Auclert's unearned income. But Auclert was hardly rich in comparison to the wealthy women of the *grande bourgeoisie* or of the old nobility. Maria Deraismes, a leader of the women's movement when Auclert arrived in Paris, was rich. She inherited from her father, a wholesale merchant, stocks and bonds yielding fifty to seventy-five thousand francs per annum—that is, an annual income equal to Au-

23. Police reports of 21 September 1876, 11 August 1877, 22 July 1878, and 19 April 1910, Dossier Auclert, APP; Déclaration de mutation par décès, Succession d'Hubertine Auclert (her will), 18 April 1914 (déclaration 189), Ministère des finances, Archives des directions de l'enregistrement, Place St. Sulpice.

24. These are rough figures, for purposes of comparison. They are drawn from the report of the Office du travail covering the years 1891–1893: *Salaires et durée du travail dans l'industrie française* (Paris, 1893), 1:355, as reproduced by Madeleine Guibert in *Les Femmes et l'organisation syndicale avant 1914. Présentation et commentaires de documents . . .* (Paris, 1966), p. 18, table 2. These data are in the form of average daily wages. The ranges given above are predicated upon a maximum of 300 working days per year. The ranges estimated for the early 1870s are extrapolations, computed by using the data on money wages in industry in B. R. Mitchell, ed., *European Historical Statistics, 1750–1970* (London, 1975), p. 185, table C4. This table provides an index for Parisian wages, with 1901 as a base of 100; scant nineteenth-century figures give 1873 = 73, 1896 = 92. Figures given above for the early 1870s are *estimated* at 79.3 percent of Guibert's data for the 1890s; they are reliable only as a relative indicator.

clert's entire capital. And the Duchess d'Uzès, one of the most fascinating converts to feminism in the 1890s, was unmistakably rich. Widowed young, she controlled an income so staggering that her shares alone produced 2.8 million francs in a single year, and she could joke about how cheap it was to buy a general and minister (Boulanger). D'Uzès's campaign contributions in the by-elections of 1888 alone mounted to five hundred thousand francs; by some accounts, her financing of Boulangism exceeded three million—fifty times Auclert's total fortune.[25]

Despite her material independence after 1869, Auclert stayed in Allier until 1873. Meanwhile, her republicanism continued to develop. Those years, of course, were tremendously important in shaping the political attitudes of the entire French nation. During the late 1860s the emperor of France, Napoleon III, continued to relax the authoritarianism of his regime. This attempt to create a "liberal empire" permitted Théophile Auclert to resume the family's traditional political role by serving as mayor. The new political environment permitted more openly contested elections, and with that came a revival of French republicanism, as seen in Léon Gambetta's Belleville Program of 1869. Given the republican tradition of Auclert's family, it may be assumed that these trends did not escape discussion when Théophile entered politics.

Auclert's precise reaction to the liberal empire is unknown, but it is clear that the national climacteric of 1870–1871 profoundly affected her. When Prussia invaded France in the summer of 1870, the disasters of the war awakened several strong feelings in her. The first was nationalism, a powerful component of Jacobin republicanism. Her wartime patriotism was reinforced by the marriage of her sister Delphine to an army officer. Auclert carried the sentiments of 1870 throughout her life. Her militant feminism and left-wing republicanism never lost their Jacobin nationalism. Her idealism led to the espousal of many pacifist beliefs, but such feelings were secondary when a German army stood on French soil. Instead, Auclert's altruism found its wartime expression in seeking to aid the suffering. Like subsequent leaders of the women's movement, such as Sarah Monod, Auclert volunteered for the ambulance service. According to her sister, Auclert wanted most to care for the wounded. The Red Cross administered this service, however, and it

25. Maria Deraismes, *Ce que veulent les femmes: Articles et conférences de 1869 à 1891*, ed. Odile Krakovitch (Paris, 1980), p. 8; Bidelman, *Pariahs Stand Up!*, pp. 75–76; Jean Puget, *La Duchesse d'Uzès*, 2d ed. (Uzès, 1972), p. 10; the Duchesse d'Uzès, *Souvenirs* (Paris, 1939), pp. 81–107; Dossier Duchesse d'Uzès, Bibliothèque Marguerite Durand (hereafter BMD); Frederic H. Seager, *The Boulanger Affair: Political Crossroads of France, 1886–1889* (Ithaca, 1969), p. 151.

was insufficiently developed in Allier to provide this opportunity. Undeterred, Auclert found an active role by volunteering to aid the victims of a smallpox epidemic that accompanied the Franco-Prussian War.[26]

In addition to stimulating her patriotism and idealistic activism, the war of 1870 excited Auclert's political enthusiasm. Following the defeat of Napoleon III's army at Sedan, Parisian republicans proclaimed the end of his empire and the formation of a Third Republic. The Jacobin republicanism of the new government's leaders, especially Gambetta, greatly appealed to Auclert. Her precise reaction to the next events of "the terrible year" of 1870–1871 is unclear. In January 1871, the victorious German army forced the capitulation of Paris through a protracted siege. In February, French elections chose a national government dominated by monarchists to negotiate terms of peace with Germany. In March, revolutionaries in Paris and other cities formed radical governments known as the Commune, determined to defy both the Germans and the new French government. Civil war followed. The monarchist government, located at Versailles, suppressed the Commune of Paris in a week of tragic fratricide during May 1871. The government then executed or sentenced to penal transportation thousands of communards. There is no direct evidence of Auclert's reaction to the Commune during 1871, but one can surmise that she was sympathetic to it. During the late 1870s, while it remained a controversial issue in French politics, Auclert defended the communards, particularly the women. She joined a committee to aid those in exile, attended numerous celebrations of the Commune, and organized a petition campaign in favor of amnesty. This put her on the left wing of French feminism, most of whose leaders had opposed the Commune.[27]

The events of 1869–1871 thus constituted a critical stage in Auclert's education in national politics. Like so many people of her generation, her feelings then never left her political thoughts. She remained a republican of 1870, even when republican politicians opposed her ideas. She had found, as she told Marie, "my two idols: my *patrie* and my republic."[28] Her humanitarianism, her militancy, and her nationalism endured. All that remained was to find the appropriate outlet.

Hubertine Auclert found the feminist movement in 1872. Women's rights organizations had begun to revive during the last years of the

26. Chaumont, "Hubertine Auclert," p. 3; police report, 19 April 1910, Dossier Auclert, APP.

27. For Auclert's procommunard activities, see chapter 3. For the role of women during the Commune, see Edith Thomas, *The Women Incendiaries* (London, 1967). For the Commune and the feminist movement, see Moses, *French Feminism in the Nineteenth Century*, pp. 189–196.

28. Chaumont, "Hubertine Auclert," p. 4.

liberal empire. The principal architects of this reawakening were Deraismes and Léon Richer, a liberal republican journalist and notary. Richer had been writing articles expressing republican, anticlerical sentiments when he began to defend the rights of Julie Daubié, the first woman to obtain a bachelor's degree in France. In 1868, following Napoleon III's liberalization of restrictive imperial laws on the press and public meetings, several feminists—led by Deraismes, André Léo, Paule Mink, and Olympe Audouard—began to call for equal rights for women. Deraismes quickly became the most respected speaker advocating their cause. Léo, meanwhile, organized a small association of women, the Société de revindication des droits de la femme, whose members included Deraismes, Mink, Louise Michel, and Eliska Vincent. In 1869, with the financial backing of Deraismes, Richer founded a weekly review, *Le Droit des femmes*, to publicize the claims of the movement. A few months later, in early 1870, Richer and Deraismes created another feminist organization, the Association pour le droit des femmes. It attracted an astonishing range of members, from the moderate liberal Mme Jules Simon to the revolutionary Elie Reclus. Léo's organization soon merged with the larger and better-funded association led by Deraismes and Richer. By the summer of 1870 the group was strong enough to organize a public banquet to celebrate its progress. It took place a few days before the declaration of war.[29]

The Franco-Prussian War and the Commune disrupted the women's movement and divided its adherents. The most militant women, especially those from working-class backgrounds, supported or participated in the Commune. Michel was transported to New Caledonia, Mink driven into exile. Feminists of more moderate allegiances, usually from middle-class backgrounds, favored a republic but opposed the Commune. Deraismes and Richer both did so, and they were the leaders who remained active in 1871. Their temperaments, class attitudes, and conclusions about 1871 led them to insist upon the caution that characterized feminism in late nineteenth-century France. Thus, for example,

29. For a general introduction to the previous history of French feminism, see Maïte Albistur and Daniel Armogathe, *Histoire du féminisme français: Du moyen âge à nos jours* (Paris, 1977). For the feminist revival of the 1860s, see Moses, *French Feminism in the Nineteenth Century*, pp. 173–89 and Bidelman, *Pariahs Stand Up!* and idem, "Maria Deraismes, Léon Richer, and the Foundation of the French Feminist Movement, 1866–1878," *TR/TR* 3–4 (1977):20–73. Sources for this period include a small collection of Richer Papers in the Bouglé Collection, BHVP; dossiers on Deraismes, Richer, and others at both the BHVP and the BMD; police files on Deraismes and Mink, B^a 1031 and B^a 1178, APP; Ministry of the Interior files on Richer's review, Dossiers de la presse parisienne, F18 399/4, Archives nationales (hereafter AN). For Reclus, see Marie Fleming, *The Anarchist Way to Socialism: Elisée Reclus and Nineteenth-Century European Anarchism* (London, 1979), p. 244.

when Richer resumed the publication of his review after the war, he discreetly moderated its title, from the pronouncement of women's rights to *L'Avenir des femmes* (Women's Future).

The Parisian feminist movement captured Auclert's attention in June 1872 when Richer organized another banquet, which he advertised as the first great public meeting for the emancipation of French women. Approximately 150 supporters attended, including a dozen dignitaries from the Parisian press and Parisian politics, such as Alfred Naquet, the republican deputy from Vaucluse who later sponsored legislation to reestablish divorce in France, and Victor Schoelcher, who had drafted the decree of 1848 that abolished slavery in the French colonies. The celebrants heard speeches by Richer and Deraismes, but the highlight of the evening was the reading of letters of support from notable public figures such as Victor Hugo, George Sand, Ernest Legouvé, and Louis Blanc. Hugo's letter received the most attention. And, according to her own oft-repeated testimony, it was this letter that convinced Auclert to go to Paris.

Victor Hugo bluntly described the position of French women as that of slaves: "It is sad to say, that there are still slaves in today's civilization. The law uses euphemisms. Those whom I call slaves, it calls minors; these minors according to the law and slaves according to reality, are women. . . . Women cannot own, they are outside the legal system, they do not vote, they do not count, they do not exist. There are citizens, THERE ARE NOT CITIZENESSES. This is a violent fact; it must cease." Hugo concluded by saying that he wished to shake Richer's hand for his efforts. He did not realize it, but his words also shook Hubertine Auclert's mind.[30]

The echoes of Hugo's words, as Auclert later put it, even reached the Bourbonnais. Richer and Hugo had "put hope in the feminine heart." Auclert immediately decided to go "to Paris to fight for the liberty of my sex." There are no citizenesses? She would become *la citoyenne.* She had no doubt, as she often told reporters and attested herself, that her reading and reflecting upon Hugo's letter was the turning point of her life. "In quoting our great poet," she wrote in *Le Vote des femmes* (1908), "the press awakened among the despoiled the idea of equity and, one year later, I was not the sole conscript who went a hundred leagues to enroll herself in the feminist army." The struggle for women's rights brought together the experiences and thoughts of her youth, and it

---

30. See reports of the banquet in *L'Avenir des femmes* during 1872, especially the July issue, which includes the text of Hugo's letter to Richer, 8 June 1872; Moses, *French Feminism in the Nineteenth Century,* pp. 194–95. For Hugo's feminism, see Nicole Savy, "Victor Hugo féministe," *Pensée* 245 (1985):5–18.

would dominate the remainder of her life. As a friend said at her burial, she had discovered "her religion."[31]

Auclert was an independent woman, in spirit as well as income, and she simply refused to let her brother dissuade her from traveling her hundred leagues. Théophile capitulated to her insistence and accepted the fact that she could live respectably with their sister Delphine Paradis and her husband, now a retired officer, in Paris. So Hubertine Auclert, like the Allier River, headed north to richer soil.

31. Auclert, "L'Homme des femmes," *Le Radical*, 13 November 1899 (first quotation); Auclert to Jeanne Schmahl, June 1895, Auclert Papers, 14/61 (second quotation); speech, "Sur la tombe de Léon Richer," ibid., 6/53; autobiographical fragment, ibid., 14/58; Jane Misme, "De Maria Deraismes à Maria Vérone," *Minerva*, 19 October 1923; Auclert, *Le Vote des femmes*, pp. 102–03 (third quotation); Chaumont, "Hubertine Auclert," p. 4; *La Lumière*, 16 February 1935; *Le Gaulois*, 20 September 1880; *La Libre parole*, 2 June 1894; *L'Evenement*, 14 April 1914, quoting Kauffmann at Auclert's burial.

CHAPTER TWO

Apprenticeship and Rebellion in French Feminism, 1873–1878

F rench feminism was a small and fragile political movement when Hubertine Auclert arrived in Paris in 1873 to join Richer's group. The two Parisian feminist leagues—Léo's Société pour la revindication des droits de la femme and Richer's Association pour le droit des femmes—had together fewer than two hundred members, of whom over one hundred fifty belonged to the association, and a combined treasury of less than five thousand francs. Less than 10 percent of the membership attended each meeting, so they did not strain their meeting hall—Richer's apartment between the Gare du Nord and the Gare de l'Est. These small discussion groups received minimal public attention and exerted little political influence. The voice of the movement, *L'Avenir des femmes*, was in debt and losing more money with each issue; Richer soon abandoned weekly for monthly publication.[1]

The endurance and expansion of this movement must be attributed to the dedication of Léon Richer and Maria Deraismes. Richer gave more than his sitting room. He presided over the association until 1878 and pressed its program on his friends in journalism and politics. He edited *L'Avenir des femmes*, often completing it by writing articles under

1. Richer's reports to the general assemblies of the association in September 1872 and January 1874 both claimed a membership of approximately 150. Léo's society had fewer than 50 members. By 1874, Richer's treasury totaled 3,450 francs. *L'Avenir des femmes*, 1 February 1874; police report, 3 May 1875, Dossier Maria Deraismes, Bᵃ 1031, APP; Bidelman, *Pariahs Stand Up!*, pp. 97–98; Moses, *French Feminism in the Nineteenth Century*, pp. 178–89.

three names (his own, "Georges Bath," and "Jeanne Mercoeur"). In 1872–1873 he published his sixth and seventh books on the woman question: *Le Livre des femmes* and *Le Divorce.* Deraismes contributed both her wealth and her health. Without the former, Richer's journal and association probably would have folded. She gave of the latter until it was broken; she organized many of the activities of the association, wrote for *L'Avenir des femmes,* and lectured regularly until a severe attack of chronic emphysema forced her to stop for a few years.[2]

To portray Richer's and Deraismes' feminist program and political action as moderate and cautious would be accurate, but it would be insufficient for an understanding of their importance to the history of human rights. Few of their contemporaries thought of them as timid conservatives. As French feminism expanded in the next generation, militants led by Auclert pushed past them in both aspirations and tactics. But in 1873 such radicalism was scarcely possible. Richer and Deraismes were acting in the aftermath of a revolution which had been violently repressed. Their most militant associates were in exile or in prison. The men who had crushed the Commune still held power in France; they held opinions hostile to democracy, favoring the reestablishment of a monarchy. The government of the National Assembly harassed radical groups, and Richer's association faced the constant threat of being outlawed. Seen in this context, the policy of Richer and Deraismes in 1873 was a realistic reading of the objective political facts. Furthermore, their feminist aspiration for equality represented a vast social revolution for which the French nation was not prepared. Men and women alike knew little and supported less of their program. A handful of dedicated feminists had no prospect of winning complete emancipation (or public backing for the idea) at a single stroke. As John Stuart Mill argued in *The Subjection of Women* (1869)—written while Mill was living in southern France in the 1860s—"it must be remembered, also, that no enslaved class ever asked for complete liberty at once."[3]

The program that emerged from these considerations has best been summarized as *la politique de la brèche*—a policy of making breaches one by one in the fortress of masculine domination, rather than assaulting it frontally.[4] The great majority of French feminists during the Third

2. Léon Richer, *Le Livre des femmes* (Paris, 1872); Richer, *Le Divorce: Projet de loi . . .* (Paris, 1873). For more on Richer and Deraismes, see the works of Bidelman and Moses and the introduction by Odile Krakovitch to Deraismes, *Ce que veulent les femmes,* pp. 7–36.

3. John Stuart Mill, *The Subjection of Women* (1869), reprinted in Alice S. Rossi, ed., *Essays on Sexuality: John Stuart Mill and Harriet Taylor Mill* (Chicago, 1970), p. 140. The quotation appears in the middle of chapter 1, in the discussion of resistance to the rule of force; see also pp. 214–15 for the same argument.

4. The term "the policy of the breach" was used occasionally by French feminists but

Republic accepted this evolutionary, reformist route to sexual equality. They hailed the wisdom of Richer and Deraismes, as Jane Misme, a feminist journalist, did half a century later: "With eminent common sense, they introduced what we call the tactic of the 'breach', to which feminism directly owes all of the success that it has obtained until now. They perceived, among the reforms to claim, the least ripe, the most shocking for public opinion . . . [and] they excluded them from their program."[5]

The objectives of this program were still numerous, as one would expect from the extent of the subjection of women. Richer focused on the civil and criminal codes. *L'Avenir des femmes* printed, on the inside cover of each issue, a column listing over a dozen statements of French law, matched with a column of corresponding feminist objectives: the right to file paternity suits (*recherche paternité*) and otherwise to aid sexually exploited women; the equal sharing of paternal authority within the family; the abolition of the husband's control over the property and earnings of his wife; the end of the legal double standard concerning adultery; the acceptance of a woman's testimony in civil and public law; and the legalization of divorce. Richer placed the greatest stress upon regaining the right of divorce, abolished in 1816, and he contributed significantly to the adoption of the Naquet Law of 1884.[6] Deraismes agreed with Richer that the feminist revolution "cannot be obtained *en bloc*," and she supported his list of goals. "It is necessary that we order our priorities," she told the feminist banquet of 1872, "and that we limit our demand to civil rights." She had had an exceptional education, including the classics, and emphasized the equal education of women in laic schools as the starting point.[7]

What was missing in this program? Hubertine Auclert was to answer: political rights. Both Richer and Deraismes advocated enfranchisement, but only as a theoretical ideal to be sought in the future. In Auclert's criticism, women must abandon the patient policy of the breach, of asking men for civil rights. Instead, they must demand the vote, then use that leverage to oblige men to grant them full equality. This idea

---

owes its reestablishment to Bidelman's distinction between the strategies of *la brèche* and *l'assaut*. See *Pariahs Stand Up!*, chs. 3 and 4; Moses, *French Feminism in the Nineteenth Century*, p. 189.

5. Misme, "De Maria Deraismes à Maria Vérone."

6. A translation of the program of *L'Avenir des femmes* in January 1876 is found as appendix A in Bidelman, *Pariahs Stand Up!*, pp. 203–5. See also Richer's signed articles (such as 1875–1876 on marital authority), his books, the Dossiers Richer at the BMD and the BHVP, and the Richer Papers, BHVP.

7. The texts of many of her speeches on education can be found in her dossier at the BMD; reports of them are in her dossier at the APP. The speech of 9 June 1872 is reprinted in Deraismes, *Ce que veulent les femmes*, pp. 121–25.

seemed terribly radical in the 1870s. Leave it to the future, Deraismes argued: "This will be the business of our nieces."[8] Even they balked at Auclert's extremism.

There were other omissions in the feminist agenda. Aside from calling for the property rights of married women, there was no attention to economic rights. This, of course, revealed the class basis of the feminist movement: it was essentially a bourgeois phenomenon. The right of women to job training, equal access to employment, unionization, and equal pay for equal work were secondary issues to most feminists of the 1870s. And Richer and Deraismes strenuously opposed any hint of collectivism. Deraismes was, after all, a bourgeois *grande dame* of great wealth and property. She and Richer were social radicals because they dreamt of a democratic republic, not a social democracy. This policy exacerbated the historic division between the socialist women's movement, which gave relatively little support to ameliorative reforms within a bourgeois society, and the bourgeois feminist movement. Auclert became a central figure in this debate too, by seeking to forge a socialist-feminist alliance in the late 1870s.[9]

Among the other responses to Richer's program, one should also note the perspective of some militant feminists of the next generation: in addition to political and economic rights, his program ignored sexual rights. Richer demanded *recherche paternité* and attacked the system of regulated prostitution. Few French feminists of 1873, however, advocated sexual emancipation, in the sense either of freedom of action (such as free love and trial marriage) or of control of reproduction (such as sex education, birth control, and abortion). The attitude of Maria Deraismes was typical: she linked women's rights to a defense 'of the family, in which women were to be equals. Hence she attacked free love. In addition to being a sincere conviction, this support of the family was

8. Ibid, p. 122.

9. For the relationship between feminism and socialism in France, see the works of Charles Sowerwine and Marilyn J. Boxer, especially Sowerwine's *Sisters or Citizens? Women and Socialism in France Since 1876* (Cambridge, 1982); "The Organization of French Socialist Women, 1880–1914," *HR/RH* 3 (1976):3–24; "Women and the Origins of the French Socialist Party," *TR/TR* 3–4 (1977):104–27; "Le Groupe féministe socialiste, 1899–1902," *Le Mouvement social* 90 (1975):87–120; "Workers and Women in France before 1914: The Debate over The Couriau Affair," *JMH* (1983):411–41; and Boxer's "Socialism Faces Feminism in France, 1879–1913," Ph.D. diss., University of California at Riverside, 1975; "Socialism Faces Feminism: The Failure of Synthesis in France, 1879–1914," in Marilyn Boxer and Jean H. Quataert, eds., *Socialist Women: European Socialist Feminism in the Nineteenth and Early Twentieth Centuries* (New York, 1978), pp. 75–111; "When Radical and Socialist Feminism Were Joined: The Extraordinary Failure of Madeleine Pelletier," in Jane Slaughter and Robert Kern, eds., *European Women on the Left: Socialism, Feminism, and the Problems Faced by Political Women, 1880 to the Present* (Westport, Conn. 1981), pp. 51–74.

good politics because the overwhelming majority of French women shared that attitude. Any other policy in the early 1870s would have alienated most potential converts to feminism.[10]

The same political caution that shaped the program of *L'Avenir des femmes* characterized the tactics of Richer and Deraismes. They did not hide their republicanism; indeed, it can be argued that the defense of the republic preceded women's rights for them. This republicanism jeopardized their movement. The conservative "government of moral order" of Marshal MacMahon (1873–1877) required prior authorization for public lectures, regulated the press under Bonapartist legislation, and used the police to keep track of dissidents, including prominent feminists). If this were insufficient, the government could disband organizations it considered seditious under the Law of Associations. Such harassment conditioned feminist moderation. Fear was probably a factor in Richer's changing the name of his journal from *Le Droit des femmes* to *L'Avenir des femmes* in 1871, a course he soon followed with the name of the association: the Association pour le droit des femmes became the Association pour l'avenir des femmes before settling in 1875 on the title Société pour l'amélioration du sort de la femme (hereafter, Amélioration).[11]

Was it excessively timid of Richer to remove the mere mention of rights (*droit*) from the names of his organization and publication in favor of a promised future (*avenir*)? Militants such as Auclert were soon to scoff at this action, and in the late 1870s, when republicans controlled the government, Richer resumed using *droit*, a word of sound republican connotations. Under MacMahon, those connotations made Richer's fears credible. In 1873, the government forbade some feminist lectures—notably one by Olympe Audouard, who had earned notoriety for a book entitled *Guerre aux hommes* (*War on Men*, 1866) and had twice had journals banned by the government. The Minister of the Interior, Marc-Thomas de Goulard (right-center, Hautes-Pyrénées), ruled that such talks were "only a pretext for the assembly of numerous women who are too emancipated" and that the theories presented were "subversive, dangerous, and immoral." This threat was sufficient to persuade Richer and Deraismes to cancel their feminist congress planned for 1873. But they were already marked. When Louis Buffet (right-center, Vosges) formed a cabinet in 1875, he banned Amélioration.[12] It is not

10. See the discussion in Moses, *French Feminism in the Nineteenth Century*, pp. 181–84.

11. The name of the group reached its final form a few years later; for the changes, see table 2.1. The merger of Amélioration with the remnants of Léo's Société pour la revindication des droits de la femme produced the Société pour l'Amélioration du sort de la femme et la revindication de ses droits, referred to as Amélioration throughout the text.

12. Léon Richer, "Silence aux femmes!", *L'Avenir des femmes*, 16 March 1873. For

surprising, therefore, that the feminist movement which Auclert joined in 1873 was typified by tactical caution. Indeed, the militant claims that she later advanced, and the tactical flair with which she advanced them, were possible partly because moderates had sustained the movement until the climate of opinion changed.

APPRENTICESHIP IN FEMINISM AND REPUBLICANISM,
1873–1876

Hubertine Auclert had convinced her family that it would be respectable for her to move to Paris if she stayed with her older sister Delphine and her husband, a retired army captain. Auclert did so for a few months, but she had no intention of allowing either Théophile or Captain Paradis to dictate her behavior. Instead, she contacted Richer and directed her life to his feminist association. According to Marie, they found her "quite sociable" and immediately accepted her into their inner circle. The statutes of Richer's association provided for a central committee of eighteen members, one-third elected each year for a three-year term. Given that only ten to twelve people attended the regular meetings of the association, diligent new members had few difficulties in entering the leadership. Thus, within a few months of her arrival in Paris, Auclert was named to fill a vacancy on the *comité*, on the recommendation of Maria Deraismes. Then, at the general assembly of the association in January 1874, she was elected to a full term and to the office of librarian. This placed her in an inner circle composed of Richer (president), Madame Richer (treasurer), Deraismes, Anna Feresse-Deraismes, Maria's older sister, and Louis Jourdan, the director of *Le Siècle*. Less than a year away from the village of Tilly, she had become one of the two dozen most prominent feminists in Paris. The police reached the same conclusion and established a file on her early in 1875.[13]

Auclert thrived in her new environment, finding for the first time the autonomy she craved. Early in 1874 she decided to stay in Paris and sold her property in Allier to Théophile, accepting part of the payment in cash and part in two interest-bearing notes. She invested this in municipal bonds issued by the city of Paris, which produced an estimated income of three thousand francs. Auclert then proclaimed her independence by searching for her own apartment. The Richers found her one, in

more on Audouard, see Maïte Albistur and Daniel Armogathe, eds., *Le Grief des femmes: Anthologie de textes féministes du second empire à nos jours* (Paris, 1978), 2:28–33; Bidelman, *Pariahs Stand Up!*, pp. 40–41, 58. For the ban on Amélioration, ibid., p. 96.

13. Police report, 21 September 1876, Dossier Auclert, APP; Chaumont, "Hubertine Auclert," p. 5; *L'Avenir des femmes*, 1 February 1874; *La Libre parole*, 2 June 1894.

the same building in which they lived and the association met, on the rue des Deux-Gares. Her apartment was large, comfortable, and appropriately bourgeois. It cost five hundred francs per annum—well beyond the reach of working women. She did not devote her considerable remaining income, however, to furnishing her home with the accoutrements of bourgeois propriety. The asceticism of the convent remained with her, and she rejected middle-class comforts just as she rejected traditional roles for women. Journalists who visited Auclert commented on her spartan sense of comfortable lodgings. She preferred to reinvest her income or allocate it to the library that she now kept.[14]

The office of librarian suited Auclert. She had intelligence and commitment but little knowledge of feminism. Its history and doctrines had not penetrated the conventual curriculum. She was drawn to politics, but, by her own admission, she "was very ignorant about politics." Now she had a rare opportunity for self-education. The keeper of one of the few feminist collections in France, she had the money to expand it as her taste dictated, the guidance of the two foremost feminists in the land, and a life unencumbered by daily toil or family duty. Auclert recorded in an autobiographical fragment that the study of the woman question consumed her energy for the next three years. Her life was "tranquil and of a perfect simplicity; nothing irregular, nothing adventurous; the existence of a recluse."[15]

Little evidence survives about Auclert's daily life as she made the transition into adulthood during these early months in Paris. The sun of her childhood had set, and Auclert greeted that fact with quiet exhilaration. She gave to feminism the dedication and the sacrifice that she had learned in Montmirail and tried to offer to the church—a commitment that she later expected from her own followers, to their mutual frustration. Her sacrifices included social life outside the movement; this isolation was to trouble her in the future. In her twenties, the fires of enthusiasm and confidence burnt brightly: she could and would change the world. She found a consequent joy in devoting to the cause the "existence of a recluse." Later, when years of such sacrifice without victory took their toll, Auclert would begin to experience the loneliness of an anchorite as well as the consecration.

During her years of study, Auclert continued her close collaboration with Richer and Deraismes. Although she subsequently split from them, she always remembered them as "my masters." She later crit-

---

14. Matrice cadastrale des propriétés foncières, Saint-Priest-en-Murat, Folio 568, AD-Allier; police reports, 11 August 1877 and 30 January 1881, Dossier Auclert, APP.

15. *La Libre parole,* 2 June 1894 (first quotation); autobiographical fragment, Auclert Papers, 14/58; Auclert to Jeanne Schmahl, June 1895, ibid., 14/61; Auclert to the editor, *La France,* 23 May 1880; (second quotation); *La Lumière,* 16 February 1935.

icized Richer for his limited program, but she also esteemed him as "a modern knight who gave combat for the French pariah." In 1874, she was his student. In January of that year, she began to publish an occasional letter in *L'Avenir des femmes,* the first published writings of a prolific career (see appendix 1). She first exhorted the women of France to support the journal and its director, the "indefatigable apostle of our cause." Subsequent letters embraced Richer's program but tried to enlarge it by inserting a call for equal wages for working women. Encouraged by this beginning, she tackled the daily press. When Buffet closed Amélioration, some papers seized the opportunity to make feminist-baiting jokes about "unnatural" women. Auclert rebutted one of them, the monarchist *Journal de Paris,* in a sarcastic letter to the editor inquiring what was so unnatural about seeking justice. Richer reprinted these letters and named Auclert secretary of *L'Avenir des femmes,* whose staff meetings (with guests) at a local restaurant filled the gap opened by the outlawing of Amélioration.[16]

During her years of apprenticeship and study, Auclert shared republicanism with Richer and Deraismes as well as feminism. Her Jacobin sentiments made her significantly more radical than they were, but she gratefully accepted their efforts to introduce her to Parisian political circles. She learned firsthand about many components of the republican movement—anticlericalism, which she found congruent with her childhood experience; free thought (on which Richer was a voluminous author) as an alternative to Christianity; Freemasonry (in which Richer had long been active, and of which Deraismes was to become the first woman member) as a nexus of extraparliamentary republicanism; and laic education (a passionate interest of Deraismes) as a cornerstone of the republican future.

She also learned about the pressure groups that fueled republican enthusiasm and about the political press that fired French discourse. She met and took the measure of young deputies and those who aspired to be deputies; she learned to be comfortable at a new level of society and quickly grasped that women could fill the same roles. And she began to form a network of contacts, especially in the world of republican journalism. Amélioration provided her with an entree to *Le Siècle,* the voice of moderate republicanism. Auclert then established connections with radical republican journalists—especially with Auguste Vacquerie, editor of *Le Rappel,* and with the group of radicals (including Henri Rochefort) that created *La Lanterne* in 1877. She quickly realized

16. Autobiographical fragment, Auclert Papers, 14/58 (first quotation); speech, "Sur la tombe de Léon Richer," ibid., 6/53; Auclert, "L'Homme des femmes," *Le Radical,* 13 November 1899 (second quotation); *L'Avenir des femmes,* 4 January 1874 (third quotation) and 2 May 1875; *Journal de Paris,* 14 May 1875.

that her republicanism was more compatible with the Hugoist radicalism of *Le Rappel* than with the Simonian moderation of *Le Siècle.*

Auclert's republicanism permeated her feminism. One of her first
public political acts, in 1875, was to circulate a petition calling upon the
electorate to create a "truly republican republic" that would apply "our
immortal principles of 1789." By that shibboleth, Auclert meant equality. As she said in a speech in Lille in 1880, the republic was "the
government of equality. . . . It will truly exist only when it has proclaimed the equality of all . . . and when I speak of equality, I mean it
complete and entire." This republican equality, of course, meant feminist equality. As Auclert explained, in the rural metaphor of her youth:
"To cultivate roses, one must have a special soil, a particular exposure.
It is the same with ideas. To make feminine emancipation flourish, the
Republic is the favorable terrain." Auclert's feminism remained republican feminism throughout her life. The Third Republic simply was
not a "true republic," because it governed "nine million adult women
who form a nation of slaves within a nation of free men." Moderates had
to learn that "the republican idea excludes an aristocracy of sex, just as it
excludes an aristocracy of caste."[17]

Auclert's radicalism led her away from Richer and Deraismes. In this
she illustrates a generational difference. Richer and Deraismes had
formulated their republicanism under the Second Empire, alongside
Jules Simon and the men of *Le Siècle* (then known as "the *moniteur* of
the opposition"). They proceeded slowly in 1875 because the years had
taught them the frailty of the republic. Auclert knew such matters
intellectually, indirectly. She came to the republic filled with the ineffa-
ble promise and certitude of youth. Her first thought was not to protect
the infant Third Republic but to expect it to grow faster. So she thought
nothing of criticizing the institution. "She sometimes fires on republican troops," wrote one surprised journalist.[18] There was a message to
Richer and Deraismes in Auclert's republicanism: their apprentice
might also fire on fellow feminists.

THE FOUNDATION OF LE DROIT DES FEMMES, 1876–1878

Auclert's years of apprenticeship ended when she concluded that she
was more revolutionary than her mentors, that "Maria Deraismes and
the others went too slowly in their claims." Richer seemed too "irrita-

---

17. Taïeb, preface to Hubertine Auclert, *La Citoyenne*, p. 38 (first quotation); Auclert,
Les Femmes au gouvernail, pp. 15–16 (second quotation); Auclert, *Pensées*, Auclert
Papers, 8/129 (third quotation); *L'Avenir des femmes*, October 1877 (last quotations).

18. *Le Gaulois*, 20 September 1880.

ble, authoritarian" when presented with new ideas; "he never tolerated the enlargement of his program." Branding Richer "authoritarian" represented Auclert's ultimate insult; it made him an amalgam of the emperor who purged her father, the nuns who spurned her application, and the brother who sent her back to the convent. This naturally spurred her rebelliousness. Auclert realized that she was an "impatient neophyte," an "undisciplined disciple," but she could not sit quietly. The government provided her with an opportunity to leave Deraismes and Richer by outlawing Amélioration in 1875. Within weeks, Auclert and an "avant-garde of the *irreductibles*" left Amélioration to create a more militant league.[19]

Hubertine Auclert was not the first young feminist to balk at the caution of Richer and Deraismes (see table 2.1). Julie Daubié, Richer's first disciple, had done the same. Daubié, a primary school teacher in Lyons, became the first *bachelière* in France after completing the examinations of the Faculty of Lyons in 1862. She further demonstrated her exceptional abilities by winning a literary prize awarded by the Academy of Lyons for her book *La Femme pauvre du XIXe siècle*. Nonetheless, obtaining her university diploma required a long bureaucratic wrangle with the Ministry of the Interior, a fight which Richer publicized. Daubié subsequently joined the Parisian feminist movement, became a licenciée-ès-lettres (in 1871), began preparations for a doctorate, and argued with Richer about political rights for women. When revolutionaries proclaimed the republic in September 1870, she went to the town hall of her arrondissement of Paris to register to vote. Denied registration, Daubié decided to devote herself to women's suffrage. She split with Richer and Deraismes early in 1871 and founded her own group, variously called the Association pour le suffrage des femmes and the Association pour l'émancipation de la femme. This group, not Auclert's, was the first French organization devoted to women's suffrage. The history of French suffragism might have been very different had Daubié not died in 1874 at the age of 50 without organizing a suffrage movement.[20]

A more acrimonious defection involved Céleste Hardouin, the flamboyant head of a Parisian pension for young women. Her rupture with Richer resulted from both a personality conflict and a political dispute. Unlike Daubié and Auclert, Hardouin did not press Richer to champion

19. *La Libre parole*, 2 June 1894 (first quotation); Auclert, "L'Homme des femmes," *Le Radical*, 13 November 1899 (other quotations); Auclert, *Le Vote des femmes*, p. 103.

20. Julie Daubié, *La Femme pauvre au XIXe siècle* (Paris, 1866); Richer, *La Femme libre*, p. 255; Auclert, *Le Vote des femmes*, pp. 103–4; note on Daubié, Auclert Papers, 13/8; *L'Avenir des femmes*, 1 November 1874; Albistur and Armogathe, eds., *Le Grief des femmes*, 2:23–28, reprinting an excerpt from *La Femme pauvre*; Bidelman, *Pariahs Stand Up!*, pp. 38–39; Moses, *French Feminism in the Nineteenth Century*, pp. 175–76.

TABLE **2.1. Parisian Feminist Leagues in the 1870s**

Name	Founded	Leader(s)	Publication	Program	Membership
Société pour la revindication des droits de la femme	1866	Léo	none	moderate	c. 25
Association pour le droit des femmes; later, Association pour l'avenir des femmes; Société pour l'amélioration du sort de la femme; Société pour l'amélioration du sort de la femme et la revindication de ses droits	1870	Richer, Deraismes	*L'Avenir des femmes*	moderate	c. 150
Association pour l'émancipation de la femme; also, Association pour le suffrage des femmes	1871	Daubié	none	militant	—
Ligue française pour l'amélioration du sort des femmes	1876	Hardouin	none	socialist	—
Société le droit des femmes; later, Société pour le suffrage des femmes	1876	Auclert	none	militant	c. 150

political rights. Indeed, she derided Auclert for hopeless utopianism, starting a long-standing feud. Hardouin stood far to the left of Richer; she defended the communards, although in those circles it was suspected that she was a police informer. When she left Richer in 1875 to found her own short-lived group, Hardouin taunted him by adopting virtually the same name as the banned Amélioration: the Ligue française pour l'amélioration du sort des femmes. Richer then disassociated himself from Hardouin and her league.[21]

Seen against this pattern of militants leaving Amélioration, Auclert's departure seemed amicable. She later wrote that "the master never lost the occasion to fulminate against his independent pupils." The label "independent," of course, encoded Auclert's discomfort with authority; it meant refractory as well as autonomous. The sharp tone of this later criticism of Richer hints at the hardening of her rebelliousness as she

21. Police reports, 29 October 1876, 11 August 1877, 31 October 1877, and 27 April 1880, Dossier Auclert, APP; Edith Thomas, *Louise Michel, ou la velléda de l'anarchie* (Paris, 1971), pp. 182, 186; Bidelman, *Pariahs Stand Up!*, p. 99.

aged. In 1875 she did not think of Richer as fulminating against her. In fact, he helped her to start her own organization. Richer accepted a position on Auclert's organizing committee and published her manifesto, "Aux femmes!" in *L'Avenir des femmes*. A few months later, he published a supportive article under the name of Jeanne Mercoeur. He told readers that the new group "frankly hoists [the flag of] our program"; he anticipated "a friendly society which will join its efforts with ours." It did not and would not, as Richer soon realized. His name disappeared from the organizing committee, and he never joined the new group; soon, fulmination became a fair description of his censure.[22]

Auclert announced the formation of her society, to be named Droit des femmes, in the fall of 1876. For publicity, she exploited her contacts with the radical and socialist press. Several papers backed her: at first, *Les Droits de l'homme* (the short-lived voice of the ex-communards) and Vacquerie's *Le Rappel*; later, *Le Radical* (a successor to *Les Droits de l'homme*, not the famous paper of that title), *La Lanterne*, and *Le Petit Parisien* (then a newly founded radical paper directed by Louis Andrieux). Late in October, they published Auclert's appeal to the women of France. "We have rights to claim," she wrote; "it is time to leave behind indifference and inertia, in order to advance our claims against the prejudices and the laws which humiliate us." This document rang with the boldness, certainty, righteousness, and aggressive energy that characterized Auclert's prose. The headstrong child and the "crazy" convent student had discovered her *métier*: political propaganda. Auclert concluded her manifesto with a call for anyone who supported her ideas, women or men, to contact her; when enough people had answered, she would call an organizational meeting of Droit des femmes. In the meantime, Auclert outlined the policy of her prospective society, a liberal-republican, moderate feminist program not very different from Richer's.[23]

Auclert's manifesto attracted twenty prospective members within a few days; she proclaimed the existence of Droit des femmes early in November 1876. The ten-person organizing committee, drawn previously from the membership of Amélioration and notably including Antonin Lévrier, a young journalist and Auclert's future husband, arranged the initial meeting and secured prominent speakers. That meeting—closed to the public and open to those with written invitations

22. Auclert, "L'Homme des femmes," *Le Radical*, 13 November 1899 (first quotation); Auclert, "Aux femmes!", *L'Avenir des femmes*, November 1876; ibid., January 1877 (second quotation); Bidelman, *Pariahs Stand Up!*, pp. 89, 109.

23. For the press in this period, see the encyclopedic work by Claude Bellanger, Jacques Godechot, Pierre Guiral, and Fernand Terrou, eds., *Histoire générale de la presse française*, vol. 3, *De 1871 à 1940* (Paris, 1972), 3:219, 225, 231; *Les Droits de l'homme*, 25 and 29 October 1876; *Le Rappel*, 27 October 1876.

only—took place in a rented hall in February 1877. The men who presided over the meeting indicate one of the directions in which Auclert was moving, away from Richer. Armand Duportal, a recently elected deputy from Toulouse, had been a republican-socialist journalist in 1848 and one of those proscribed and transported following the Bonapartist coup of 1851. He brought to Droit des femmes a long leftist biography and greater police attention. Faithful to the utopian socialist traditions of his youth, Duportal proclaimed himself "an absolute partisan of the emancipation of women." He made a political gesture to Richer by asserting that the civil rights of women should probably come first, but added that political rights were "the essential point." Alongside Duportal at the head table sat another deputy of the extreme left, Charles Laisant of Nantes, soon to be the director of *Le Petit Parisien*, who spoke in favor of a radical republic; and Pastor Auguste Dide, later a senator (extreme left, Gard), a republican sufficiently outspoken to have earned his own Bonapartist imprisonment among the arrests following Orsini's attempted assassination of Napoleon III in 1858, and one of many activist Protestants who advocated women's rights.[24]

The radical republicans who collaborated with Auclert in the late 1870s, like Duportal, Laisant, and Dide, were the representatives of a curious moment in French political history. These radicals, sometimes called *intransigents*, briefly constituted the extreme left of the French parliament, until the return of the exiled communards and the subsequent growth of socialist parties. The first proclaimed socialist deputy arrived at the Palais Bourbon in 1879, the same year that the first socialist party, the Parti ouvrier, was founded. The radicals, who generally looked to Georges Clemenceau for leadership, were middle-class reformers with a program of "social justice" aimed at the working class. They considered the republic and most republicans, like Gambetta, too conservative. Their program extended past democratic constitutional revision, laic education, and separation of church and state to a range of ameliorative reforms. "We want," Clemenceau said, "the republic for its consequences: the great and productive reforms which it involves." Their rhetoric continued to stress social justice and the creation of an egalitarian democracy, but they rapidly lost working-class support after 1879. Radicals then constituted the party of the bourgeois left-of-center,

24. Autobiographical fragment, Auclert Papers, 14/58; police reports, 15, 16, 20, and 21 (2) February 1877, Dossier Auclert, APP; *L'Avenir des femmes*, March 1877; "Le DF," *La Citoyenne*, 8 May 1881. For the biographies of Duportal and Laisant, see Adolphe Robert, Edgar Bourloton, and Gaston Cougny, eds., *Dictionnaire des parlementaires français: Comprénant tous le membres . . . (1789–1889)* (Paris, 1891), 2:384–85, 2:508–9, 3:540–41 (hereafter *DdPf*). Ferdinand Buisson was not present, as erroneously reported in some accounts—apparently his name was confused with that of a Parisian municipal councillor present, M. Brisson.

able to cooperate with socialists on some issues but fundamentally separated from them by collectivism.[25]

This radicalism suited Auclert's background and beliefs. She could envision her father alongside Duportal and other purged '48ers. She could recognize her family's Jacobinism in Clemenceau. She could empathize with Dide's passionate calls for the separation of church and state and with the reasoning that led him to leave the pulpit. She could locate her youthful idealism in the talk of republican equality. And she could feel comfortable, as a bourgeois *rentier*, among radicals who did not threaten her income. Hence, Auclert did not trim her founding speech to fit her audience. She simply stressed her republicanism and exhorted the republicans present to fight for the true republic: "The health of the republic depends upon the collaboration of women, disdained until now." Auclert did not hesitate in Richer's presence to insist that this meant the political participation of women, but she gently described Droit des femmes' goals as "the full political and civil rights of women" without stating which should come first. Richer spoke without mentioning women's suffrage; in the spirit of the evening, he attacked overcautious republicans (the "opportunist" circle around Léon Gambetta) and championed the general principle of women's rights. Some of his followers who were choosing to join Auclert also spoke cautiously. Emmanuel Pignon echoed Richer's remarks by emphasizing the need for *recherche paternité;* Victor Savary spoke on Auclert's motto, "No rights without duties, no duties without rights."[26]

One must wonder what thoughts passed through Léon Richer's mind that February evening. Did he receive any intimation that the feminist avant-grade was passing beyond him that night? That despite his signal contributions to French feminism, his leadership would steadily decline? Could he have glimpsed the sad moment two decades in the future when he would call on Auclert in a dispirited mood to ask her what had happened to his position in the women's movement? Probably not. Richer believed that he knew the best route to emancipation. His leadership, sincere and well-intentioned, had become a liberal version of the paternalism of antifeminists. Many emancipation movements have received their stimulus and initial direction exogenously; it is a token of success when the vitality of the movement is endogenous. As Léon

25. For the radicals and the emergence of socialism in the late 1870s, see Samuel Bernstein, *The Beginnings of Marxian Socialism in France* (1933; reprint, New York, 1965), esp. pp. 78–80 and 179–80. For republicanism in this era, see Sanford Elwitt's discussion of the republican revolution in *The Making of the Third Republic: Class and Politics in France, 1868–1884* (Baton Rouge, 1975), chs. 1 and 2.

26. Police report, 21 February 1877, Dossier Auclert, APP; *L'Avenir des femmes*, March 1877.

Richer stepped down from the podium at the Salle Sax in February 1877, a transition from one to the other was beginning in French feminism. He may not have perceived it, but for the next decade vitality would be named Auclert; her bold and stubborn feminism would eclipse his cautiousness in the Parisian press. It is noteworthy that he wrote his account of the meeting under a pseudonym, and he did not mention political rights in it. He never again participated in Auclert's activities, and in March 1877 he began the illegal reconstitution of Amélioration. He would contribute much more to the cause of women's rights, and his contributions would lead Simone de Beauvoir to call him "the true founder of feminism," but Auclert had altered his position in the movement.[27]

Droit des femmes immediately became the subject of feminist controversy. When Auclert announced her intentions in *Les Droits de l'homme*, she had been more cautious than candid. She had published documents that Richer could still sign. Most versions of her program did not stress political rights; some did not mention the issue. Instead, she wrote of Droit des femmes' goal "to give the woman the rights of which she has been arbitrarily deprived." Even her most militant manifesto did not state that the vote was her foremost aim. She emphasized her radical republicanism. She discussed the established feminist goals: *recherche paternité*, the suppression of the *police des moeurs*, equal education, and the opening of all occupations to women. Auclert also restrained her discussion of tactics. "Our means of action will be: private and public meetings . . . courses, lectures . . . petitioning . . . the publication of books and brochures . . . [good] relations with the press . . . the creation of analogous societies." On that basis, approximately thirty founding members joined Droit des femmes.[28]

Controversy arose at the first regular meeting of Droit des femmes in March 1877, when Auclert presented her program for the society (see appendix 2). A preamble promised "the free discussion" of issues, reiterated the motto linking rights and duties, and stated that "the ultimate objective of Droit des femmes is the perfect equality of the two sexes before the law and in morality." Auclert then listed a six-point program, beginning with the blunt statement that the society "*seeks from the beginning and by all means in its power . . .* full civil and political rights." The list ended by calling for "the rigorous application of . . . the

27. Simone de Beauvoir, *The Second Sex* (1949; reprint, New York: Vintage, 1974), p. 137. See the discussion of Richer in Moses, *French Feminism in the Nineteenth Century*, pp. 198–206, esp. p. 205 on his "male perspective."

28. *Le Droit de l'homme*, 25 October 1876 and 29 November 1876; *Le Rappel*, 27 October 1876; "Le Droit des femmes, société en voie de formation," unidentified clipping in Auclert Papers, Carton 1.

economic formula: equal pay for equal work." It did not directly mention *recherche paternité* or the *police des moeurs.*[29]

Auclert's program should not have shocked the people who knew her, but it produced a dispute among her followers. A majority voted to adopt it, but others protested. When she published the new program in *Le Radical,* they parried there. They assailed Auclert as an autocrat who violated Droit des femmes' statutes, who attracted them with one program and then substituted another, who ignored her promise of free discussion. A weeklong squabble ensued in *Le Radical*—the sort of ideological brouhaha common in the political press of the Third Republic. By its end, two members had resigned from Droit des femmes in protest, and the paper had refused more of Auclert's letters because they were "too discourteous."[30] This wrangle accentuated one of the paradoxical aspects of Auclert's career. From childhood, her temperament and her ideology had both contained a rebelliousness against authority. Yet Auclert exhibited an arbitrary style and a need for mastery herself. Her inflexibility as a leader and her intractability as a follower were to increase. Hence, she would be called an autocrat herself, even while championing republican freedom.

Her notoriety taught Auclert a lesson about political combat. Internecine battles with her ideological kin irritated her, but she now presented an inviting target to the right wing, and their treatment horrified her. The conservative press cared little about nuances within the feminist program—they were frankly hostile to the entire doctrine. And they discovered in Auclert someone to ridicule. One right-wing publicist marveled at the idea that women would want to give lectures, much less enter politics: "What more do you want? Aren't you ridiculous enough?" Another suggested that she was a crazy alien and made a pun on her name: *au clair de lune* (Auclert from the moon). Yet another derided her idea of women in parliament with a sexual pun: "I cover with kisses your legislative body" (*corps législatif*).[31]

The abuse from friends on the left and foes on the right hurt Auclert. She protected herself with a self-image, revealed in her intimate diary of later years, that differed from her public persona. Her diary also indi-

29. *Le Radical,* 3 April 1877.
30. See *Le Radical* for 3 April through 8 April 1877, especially the protest of 4 April and Léon David's summary on 8 April. A slightly later program of Droit des femmes (hereafter DF) can be found as appendix C in Bidelman, *Pariahs Stand Up!,* p. 209; it is drawn from Auclert's *Historique de la société le droit des femmes, 1876–1880* (Paris, 1881), a supplement given away with her newspaper of the 1880s, *La Citoyenne.*
31. Illustrations are drawn from the clippings files in the Auclert Papers, Carton 1, and the Dossier Auclert, APP. The worst treatment of Auclert was by the conservative *Le Figaro* and *Le Gaulois;* see Félicien Champsaur, "Hommes-femmes: Les Femmes qui veulent voter," from *Le Gaulois,* copy in both files.

cates her sensitivity to attacks such as she experienced in 1877. Auclert recorded her treatment in tones of self-pity. If one believes her diary, she was a timid and vulnerable creature, a gentle martyr to the good cause. The boldness, aggressiveness, even despotism that made leftists denounce her as an autocrat and rightists lampoon her as a masculinized woman do not appear in this diary. Whether Auclert actually possessed the shyness that she depicted, or believed that she did in self-protection (as seems most likely), or ascribed timidity to herself with a thought for the historical record (one should note that she preserved the diary with the records of her public career, whereas she destroyed her personal letters), or some mixture of the three, this self-portrait suggests the tensions within her.

Auclert publicly reacted to the criticism of her in a predictable way. With the dedication and sacrifice that she had admired in the convent of Montmirail, she compensated by redoubling her work for the cause. Droit des femmes consequently survived and grew. It never became a large organization, however, nor did it introduce mass suffragism into France. Starting with approximately thirty members and ten to fifteen people at a meeting, it reached a nominal membership of more than one hundred fifty with thirty active participants by the early 1880s. It thus encompassed about one-fourth of the people then active in French feminism. Two-thirds of the members were women (68 percent, 1876–1889); the percentage of men declined over the years. Most members were married or widowed (nearly 90 percent of the identifiable cases)—contrary to antifeminist stereotypes about spinster feminists. There was a high turnover of the active members, with most participating for a year or two; the turnover rate was highest among unmarried young women. Widows, on the other hand, were often the most militant members of Droit des femmes. Approximately 10 percent of Droit des femmes consisted of married couples who joined and worked together.

It is difficult to generalize about the background of the members of Droit des femmes; few records survive about most of the women. The men are easier to visualize—they were generally active in other public circles, and the press or the police identified them by their career and politics. Most of them came from the Parisian subculture of journalism, law, and politics; all were radical republicans and socialists. Droit des femmes attracted women from a wider part of the social spectrum, but few came from wealth or high position. Those identifiable by an occupation were chiefly women on the lower fringes of the middle class—teachers, shopkeepers, boardinghouse keepers. When Marie Bashkirtseff, a young woman of elegance and wealth, attended a meeting, she recoiled in horror. Auclert tried to recruit poorer women. The dues of Droit des femmes were minimal, five sous per month. Weekly meetings were held at her apartment, and once a month the group met in a different arrondissement of Paris to ease the difficulties of occasional participation. Its composition made Droit des femmes an unusual group in the feminist movement of the Third Republic. The competing leagues of Richer and Deraismes drew more of their membership from a better-educated, more prosperous level of society. Later, most of Auclert's recruits came from the bourgeoisie too.[32]

The meetings of Droit des femmes followed a fixed format. Auclert governed them strictly. She let other members preside but did not share her authority. The president of the week began each meeting by reading the statutes and program of Droit des femmes—an indication of the high turnover in attendance. Auclert followed with reports on the size and finances of the group. Members then raised questions based on newspaper stories or personal experiences. The remainder of the meeting was devoted to the day's special topic. Auclert, or a guest speaker, would introduce it with a lecture; then she would direct a didactic discussion. Each meeting culminated in the adoption of a resolution of protest or a proclamation which Auclert submitted as a letter to the press.[33]

The format of these weekly meetings, and even the statutes of the group, reiterate Auclert's inconsistency concerning authority. She insisted that the members elect a new president at each meeting, she refused to preside herself, and she wrote statutes (see appendix 2) that stressed participatory democracy: Auclert, the foe of authoritarianism.

32. The collective biography of DF presented here is impressionistic. Membership records, dues rosters, and minutes of DF have not survived for this period, although they have for the years after 1900. Drawing chiefly on press reports, police reports, and the Auclert Papers, I have identified over 150 of Auclert's associates during the period 1876–1885. In most cases this amounts to nothing more than a name. Marital status, for example, has been found in only slightly more than 50 percent of the cases. The data given on percentages of membership are similarly soft, the best approximations after years of study. The generalizations about background are all backed by multiple illustrations, but they represent small percentages of the total membership. A roster of 112 of Auclert's followers, drawn from published sources (chiefly *La Citoyenne*) can be found as appendix F in Bidelman's dissertation (revised and reprinted as *Pariahs Stand Up!*) "The Feminist Movement in France: The Formative Years, 1858–1889," Ph.D. diss., Michigan State University, 1975, pp. 369–71. For further discussion of the social composition of the entire feminist movement, see Steven C. Hause and Anne R. Kenney, "The Limits of Suffragist Behavior: Legalism and Militancy in France, 1876–1922," *AHR* 86 (1981): 781–806; Hause with Kenney, *Women's Suffrage and Social Politics*, pp. 40–45, 114–28; Louise A. Tilly, "Women's Collective Action and Feminism in France, 1870–1914," in *Class Conflict and Collective Action*, ed. Louise A. Tilly and Charles Tilly (Beverly Hills, Calif., 1981). For an unflattering description of Auclert's followers, see Marie Bashkirtseff, *Journal of Marie Bashkirtseff* (Chicago, 1890), p. 522.

33. This description is drawn from the reports of police agents who sometimes attended DF meetings, and from press reports after Auclert became more famous. For more details, see Dossier Auclert, APP; for other accounts, see the clippings in the Auclert Papers, Carton 1, especially from *Le Figaro*.

But the strict control that she exercised over the society in her office of permanent secretary-general, as well as the force of her personality and will, actually gave Auclert personal domination of Droit des femmes. She tolerated no challenge to her supremacy. When members defied her, they provoked a harsh reaction, frequently expulsion. And Auclert held grudges.

Droit des femmes staged no public demonstrations during the late 1870s.[34] Auclert petitioned President MacMahon to resign, but she attempted none of the dramatic gestures that characterized her suffragism in the 1880s. The explanation of this is simple: Droit des femmes was an illegal organization. Auclert had already attracted the attention of the prefecture of police, to which she seemed dangerous as a socialist. At the urging of several members of Droit des femmes, who assumed that the police were watching them, Auclert decided in April 1877 to comply with the Law of Associations by applying to the prefecture for authorization to constitute an association. The police denied permission and ordered the group to disband in July 1877. Three separate police reports expressed concern about the "well-known socialists," such as Lévrier, in Droit des femmes.[35]

Auclert did not disband Droit des femmes. The Law of Associations permitted private meetings of twenty or fewer people, so Auclert simply lied about the size of Droit des femmes, usually claiming seventeen or eighteen members. It was possible to maintain this fiction because fewer than that number attended individual meetings and because not all members of Droit des femmes paid their dues. The police ban, however, meant no demonstrations and meetings generally confined to Auclert's apartment. The police kept their eyes on Auclert. They knew of her activities—much of her recruitment, after all, was done through the radical press—but they did not arrest her. They certainly could have done so: unknown to Auclert, one member of her inner circle was a police informer. The apparent republicanization of the republic, and the formation of a less reactionary cabinet in December 1877, motivated Auclert to reapply for authorization in January 1878. This time the police studied the statutes of Droit des femmes and concluded that the society required authorization at the national level. As the prefecture only dealt with the department of the Seine, they instructed her to apply to the ministry of the interior; politicians could make the decision. She did so, continuing the meetings and expansion of Droit des femmes all

34. In some accounts, Auclert is credited with staging a demonstration on 14 July 1877. She did not. Confusion results from misreading her report (*Le Vote des femmes*, p. 106) of a demonstration on the day of the first "fête nationale"; the correct date is 14 July 1881 (see chapter 4).

35. Police reports, 25 and 29 July 1877, 6 August 1877, Dossier Auclert, APP.

the while. The ministry did nothing. Richer reapplied later and prompt-ly received authorization for Amélioration in August 1878. Finally, in September 1879, after the resignation of President MacMahon and the creation of the republican government of William Waddington, Droit des femmes received authorization.[36]

THE POLITICAL RIGHTS OF FRENCH WOMEN

When the twenty-eight-year-old Hubertine Auclert set out to win women's suffrage in 1876, she could hardly have chosen a more difficult political task. Virtually no one in a nation of forty million supported the idea, except those who acknowledged it as an ideal to be obtained in the distant future. Republicans and monarchists alike opposed enfranchise-ment. Although some women had voted for the Estates General under the ancien régime, the revolutionary constitutions of the 1790s had denied women such rights of citizenship. Restoration or expansion of the right to vote found little support during the nineteenth century. The revolutionary Provisional Government of 1848 summarily rejected a petition for women's suffrage. A leftist deputy, Emile Deschanel, backed the political rights of women in 1849, and a Saint-Simonian deputy, Pierre Leroux, proposed that the Second Republic's Legislative Assembly enfranchise women for local elections in 1851. Republicans laughed at both men and did not even debate the idea. They did, how-ever, briefly discuss one aspect of women's political rights: they consid-ered abolishing the right of women to petition the government.

The record of the right wing was no better. During the Second Empire of the 1850s and 1860s, no assembly even mentioned women's suffrage. The monarchist majority at Versailles during the formative years of the Third Republic did discuss such matters briefly. And they acted just like the republicans of 1848–1851. In late 1872, one monarchist deputy told the National Assembly that he was "profoundly scandalized" that women had signed a feminist petition sent to them, so he suggested outlawing such travesties. (He had not, however, expressed shock when women had signed an earlier petition submitted on behalf of the Cath-olic church.) In the spring of 1874, another monarchist paused in his attack on universal suffrage to joke that there might even be some leftists at Versailles who thought women should vote too. The assembly laughed.[37]

36. Police reports, 22 July 1878 and 27 August 1879, ibid.; Bidelman, *Pariahs Stand Up!*, p. 96; "Le DF," *La Citoyenne*, 8 May 1881.
37. For a more detailed introduction to the political rights of French women before the Third Republic, see Hause with Kenney, *Women's Suffrage and Social Politics*, pp. 2–8.

French republicans and monarchists differed in their shared anti-suffragism. Both groups generally clung to strong beliefs about maintaining the traditional role of women in the family and the home. For conservatives, religion, law, and custom decreed the appropriate sphere for women, and that closed the question; they had not the slightest intention of altering something they held to be divinely ordained and embedded in the biological nature of woman. Republicans were circumspect in advancing arguments based on Christianity or ancient traditions, but many arrived at the same conclusion nonetheless. The principal concern of republican antisuffragists, however, was their fear of how women would vote. They asserted, correctly, that women were the staunchest supporters of the Catholic church in France. Women, they reasoned, would therefore vote as their confessors directed. As the church was closely associated with French monarchism, republicans concluded that enfranchising women would shift the balance of power in France to the right, imperiling the republic. They could admit the justice of women's suffrage, but they could not accept it until women were sufficiently educated not to destroy the regime.[38]

Hubertine Auclert's greatest problem in launching the women's suffrage movement in France, then, was that she had no allies anywhere on the political spectrum, neither inside nor outside parliament, not even the established feminist movement of Léon Richer and Maria Deraismes. Richer was a doctrinaire republican with regard to suffrage; Deraismes, equally republican, was somewhat more interested in political rights but agreed with him on this question. Richer devoted an entire chapter of *La Femme libre* (1877) to explaining why feminists should not seek the vote, stating such conservative arguments as the public's unreadiness for the idea—which could have been turned against his own program—and such republican views as the inadequate education of women. At bottom, he shared the republican fear of the "black peril" of the clergy: "Among nine million women who have attained their majority, only several thousand would vote freely; the rest would take their orders from the confessional." When Auclert unveiled the program of Droit des femmes with political rights as its first point, Richer published an article to remind feminists that women were still "raised to monarchism, imbued with the most false and most retrograde ideas." Deraismes pressed Richer lightly on the subject, but she continued to support his policy.[39]

38. For a more detailed treatment of French antisuffragism, see ibid., esp. pp. 14–18, 237–38, and 248–81.

39. Richer, *La Femme libre*, p. 238. See also the discussion of Richer in Moses and Bidelman; Richer, "La Politique et les femmes," *L'Avenir des femmes*, August 1877. For Deraismes, see Krakovitch's preface to Deraismes, *Ce que veulent les femmes*, pp. 17–20; police reports on Deraismes during the 1870s, Dossier Deraismes, APP.

Auclert initially reasoned that she needed to create allies by converting the republican-feminist movement to suffragism. The stout opposition of Richer and the ridicule of Hardouin notwithstanding, the feminist leagues seemed to be her logical constituency. And Auclert possessed exceptional determination. This trait and the imperious style with which she revealed it partly explain the charge of despotism against her. Supporters called her determination tenacity, even stubbornness. When Auclert contemplated wresting feminist thought away from Richer's antisuffragism, she clung to the self-image of timidity. She often jotted down her thoughts during introspective moods, and many of these *pensées* survive among her papers. Her timidity was a recurring theme: "H. A.—as timid of character as [she is] audacious of thought." She distinguished, however, between her timidity, which she willed herself to overcome, and the docility of most people—particularly women who did not seek emancipation—who were led like sheep. Even in these private reflections, however, Auclert acknowledged that she could not be led, and that the shepherd, Richer, must be shown that.[40]

THE FEMINIST CONGRESS OF 1878

The split between Auclert and Richer became a schism, in Auclert's term, in 1878, when Amélioration sponsored the Congrès international du droit des femmes, the first women's rights congress held in France. Richer began planning the congress after the government announced plans to host an international exhibition in the summer of 1878. The last such exhibition at Paris had attracted nine million visitors; the fair of 1878, which drew sixteen million, seemed an ideal occasion to revive the women's congress originally planned for 1873. The government was eager to encourage participation, and the press was enthusiastic. Richer dreamt of a "dazzling" demonstration of support for feminism that would alter public opinion. Accordingly, he invited Victor Hugo to preside. Auclert, who never forgot the impact of Hugo's words of 1872, enthusiastically endorsed Richer's plan in January 1878.[41]

40. See especially the *pensées* tucked into the folder on the Prix Botha, Auclert Papers, 14/46 (quoted) and her autobiographical fragment, ibid., 14/58. On docility, see Auclert, *Le Vote des femmes*, p. 207; on the duty to act, see Auclert, *Les Femmes au gouvernail*, p. 5. See also her obituary in *Le Figaro*, in which Alfred Capus summarized the two traits discussed here as her "sort of timid energy."

41. For an overview of the French international exhibitions, see Zeldin, *France, 1848–1945*, 2:612–18; for Richer's preparations for the congress of 1878, see his monthly articles in *L'Avenir des femmes*, January through May 1878. For Auclert and the congress, see the police report, 24 January 1878, Dossier Auclert, APP.

Léon Richer persuaded eleven politicians to lend their names to the feminist congress' honorary "commission of initiative." Hugo, already in poor health and committed to presiding over a literary congress at the exhibition, declined the presidency. Senators Victor Schoelcher (republican, life senator) and Eugène Pelletan (republican union, Bouches-du-Rhône), five deputies, three municipal councillors, and one councillor-general accepted invitations. Auclert and Deraismes agreed to serve on both the honorary commission and the organizing committee of feminists that did the actual work of preparation.[42]

These preliminaries encouraged Auclert to believe that she would have an opportunity to convert feminists to suffragism. Schoelcher had been the only member of the National Assembly to defend the political rights of women in 1874 when monarchists were deriding the idea. Among the deputies on the honorary commission were Emile Deschanel and Charles Laisant, both of whom had supported women's suffrage in the past. The organizing committee had twelve members of whom five were founding members of Droit des femmes. And foreigners participating in the congress included representatives from national suffrage societies in Britain and the United States. Seeing allies all around her, Auclert drafted a speech to the congress—an exhortation to feminists to concentrate upon political rights.

The congress of 1878 became the funeral of Auclert's political innocence. She never delivered her suffrage speech to the congress. Richer simply ruled that the subject would not be raised: the congress must show "all the solemnity" possible, and women's suffrage would disturb those whom he courted. His application for the reauthorization of Amélioration was still pending (it was granted a few days after the congress closed), and that undoubtedly affected his decision. But the inescapable fact remained that Richer opposed seeking the vote, and he had the power to enforce his opinion. Maria Deraismes, who provided much of the financing of the congress, chose with some ambivalence to support Richer. So did all the politicians affiliated with the congress.[43]

Auclert had left Amélioration in 1876 in amicable disagreement with

---

42. Dossier Congrès international du droit des femmes, 1878, BMD, containing a complete list of the organizers of the congress. A partial list appears in *L'Avenir des femmes*, April 1878. For the politicians involved, see *DdPF*, 2:350 (Deschanel), 4:572–73 (Pelletan), 3:540–41 (Laisant), 5:287–88 (Schoelcher), 5:420 (Edmont Tiersot, republican union, Ain), 2:146 (Louis Codet, republican, Haute Vienne), 1:414 (Charles Boudeville, republican union, Oise). A list of the participants (official delegates only) appears in *L'Avenir des femmes*, August 1878, and is reprinted as appendix D in Bidelman, "The Feminist Movement in France," pp. 362–67.

43. *L'Avenir des femmes*, May 1878 (quoted); Auclert, *Les Femmes au gouvernail*, p. 8; Krakovitch in Deraismes, *Ce que veulent les femmes*, pp. 24–26; *La Marseillaise*, August 1878.

the policy of her mentors. In 1878 she left in rebellion. She did not boycott the congress, but she resigned from both the commission of initiative and the organizing committee. Four other members of Droit des femmes, including Lévrier and Pignon, followed her. Auclert with-held financial support from the congress, but she did not withhold her opinion of it. She advertised her rebellion by publishing her forbidden speech as a pamphlet entitled "The Political Rights of Women—A Question That is Not Treated at the International Congress of Women." In it, she let Richer, Deraismes, and the world know what she thought of timorous feminists: "I know that the partisans of the emancipation of women find the claim of political rights premature. I have nothing to reply to them, except that woman is a despoiled creature who demands justice, not a beggar who pleads for charity from man. . . . What can the oppressors of women think, if those who desire to liberate women are anxious about not offending their oppressors and timidly ask for a little more education, a bit more bread, slightly less humiliation in marriage."[44]

Over two hundred official delegates participated in the congress of July and August 1878. They discussed a program divided into five sections: history, education, economics, morality, and legislation (devoted to divorce and *recherche paternité*). At some sessions, total attendance surpassed six hundred, forming the largest assembly French feminists had ever achieved. Approximately 20 percent of the delegates either were members of Droit des femmes or later joined the group. Four of them sought to raise the subject of women's suffrage at different sessions; none was permitted to continue speaking, as Richer and Deraismes ruled "this dangerous question" out of order. "They were treated like revolutionaries," Auclert later recalled. Auclert and Lévrier spoke vigorously in other debates, especially on seduction and paternity suits; Auclert used this subject to introduce a successful motion on the right of women to serve on juries. Lévrier contributed a motion for "the absolute equality of the two sexes," which the congress approved in principle. In the midst of one speech, Auclert inserted a reference to political rights, provoking loud applause and the wrath of Léon Richer.[45]

After the closing of the congress, wishing to devote his full time to

44. *L'Avenir des femmes*, December 1878; Auclert to Jeanne Schmahl, June 1895, Auclert Papers, 14/61; autobiographical fragment, ibid., 14/58; Auclert, *Le Droit politique des femmes: Question qui n'est pas traitée au congrès international des femmes* (Paris, 1878), p. 4.

45. *Congrès international du droit des femmes. 25 juillet 1878. Actes et compte rendu des séances plénières* (Paris, 1878); brochure on the congress, Dossier Congrès international du droit des femmes, 1878, BMD; Auclert to Schmahl, June 1895, Auclert Papers, 14/61; autobiographical fragment, ibid., 14/58; unidentified newspaper clippings, ibid., Carton 1; *L'Avenir des femmes*, September 1878.

L'Avenir des femmes (renamed *Le Droit des femmes*), Richer turned the presidency of Amélioration over to Deraismes in the confidence that she would steer his even course. Deraismes, however, was moving closer to calling for political rights. She had frequently spoken on universal suffrage, and her closing speech to the congress had insisted that "women must have the same rights as men. . . . Woman must be the equal of man *in all things.*" Some newspaper accounts of the congress even claimed that Deraismes had applauded when Auclert had mentioned political rights. After the congress, she wrote to Auclert and praised the speech she had helped to censor: "I find it as forcefully thought out as it is well written. Nothing could be more logical and more justly expressed. . . . Continue." At the end of the letter, Deraismes even claimed that she had opposed Richer's decision. "Please believe that if I had presided over the legislative section, your speech on political rights would have been read to the plenary session. Our old master was wrong." Deraismes underscored this attitude by inserting references to women's suffrage in her standard speech on universal suffrage when she delivered it again in September 1878; she now dared to say that the republican suffrage "is incomplete because it has forgotten half of humanity."[46]

Auclert undoubtedly appreciated Deraismes' gesture, but the young rebel was not convinced. She praised Deraismes' "broad-mindedness" and hailed her as the preeminent leader of French feminism; she kept silent about Richer. But Auclert did not forget Deraismes' role at the congress of 1878. She could not abide a slight. In other cases, she bore a grudge for years; sometimes she was nasty about it, sometimes self-pitying. Her anger at Deraismes did not run that deep. But she expressed her private feelings about Deraismes in an eloquent pen stroke without words. Among her private papers there survives a newspaper clipping about the congress in which a reporter asserts that Deraismes "showed a visible sympathy" for Auclert's position. Auclert annotated that article. And she drew a thick black line through the sentence describing her supposed sympathy.[47]

Auclert's reaction to the congress of 1878 can be seen in a small act of daily existence. A few weeks after the congress she vacated her apartment at the rue des Deux Gares, the home of both Richer and Amélioration. This *rite de passage* marked another stage in Auclert's renunciation of authority. She had naively thought that her feminist colleagues

---

46. Deraismes' speech to the congress, 5 August 1878, Dossier Deraismes, BMD; police report, 5 August 1878, Dossier Deraismes, APP (first quotation; italics added); ibid., reports of 15 September 1878 (third quotation) and 16 September 1878; undated letter, Deraismes to Auclert, reprinted in Auclert Papers, Carton 1 (second quotation).

47. Unidentified clipping, Auclert Papers, Carton 1.

would permit her to challenge their ideas at a great public event. The congress of 1878 made Auclert both politically wiser and more refractory. Her remaining obedience to the authority of her mentors passed, like her submission to the authority of the church and her family. At thirty, she had declared herself, and she would remain, utterly independent. Auclert later married, but she never accepted the authority of her husband. She made political alliances, but she never again accepted the domination of a leader.

CHAPTER THREE

Socialist Alliance, 1878–1880

G iven the opposition to women's suffrage expressed by both republicans and feminists, where could Auclert turn for allies? She chose the workers' movement. It has already been seen that she considered a vague form of socialism to have been her maternal legacy, although these youthful sentiments are probably better described as a humanitarian concern for the disadvantaged. Her father's Jacobinism also oriented her toward social republicanism. Auclert's sense of Christian egalitarianism, developed at Montmirail, likewise disposed her to socialism. She became cognizant of socialism in politics during the Paris Commune of 1871; in Allier, she developed idealistic sympathy for the communards. There is no evidence, however, that Auclert arrived in Paris in 1873 with a sophisticated understanding of the workers' movement or of socialist theories.

The friendship of Antonin Lévrier, beginning in 1874 or 1875, was the decisive influence on Auclert's socialist education. Lévrier was then a law student. He had been born in 1849 at Celles-sur-Belle (Deux-sèvres), an ancient Augustinian abbey town a few kilometers east of Niort in western France, and he had come to Paris to study and to make his career. Lévrier scratched out a precarious existence as a journalist, writing for a variety of leftist newspapers and acquiring a police reputation as "a well-known socialist." Auclert and Lévrier met through Amélioration and became close friends. She lent him money so he could complete his legal studies. He moved into an apartment one block away from her. They collaborated in founding Droit des femmes in 1876 and in its early activities, and they worked together at the feminist congress of 1878.[1]

Auclert's affection for Antonin Lévrier became a critical factor in the reciprocal relationship between her public career and her private life. Their close friendship prompted gossip. Police agents called her Lévrier's mistress in several reports, although they habitually speculated that she had sexual relations with other men who supported her. Unaffected by questions of consistency or evidence, they also proclaimed Auclert a puritan and a prude who repulsed all men; their reports thus provide little more than an example of the way others saw Auclert. The press enjoyed the same subject, but the contemporary penchant for litigation and for dueling circumscribed their speculations. The press implied intimacy by calling her Lévrier's fiance despite her repeated denials. Later, Lévrier did indeed propose marriage to Auclert; after years of rejecting this proposal, Auclert married him in 1888. During the late 1870s, these decisions remained to a troubled future. All that can be said with certainty is that they already enjoyed an affectionate and mutually supportive friendship, perhaps love. Their relationship brought happiness to Auclert's private life and increased the self-confidence with which she confronted public issues.[2]

The foremost illustration of the bond between the public and the private can be observed in Auclert's transformation of Lévrier's feminism and in his contribution to her socialism. For several reasons, it is difficult to define the socialism of Auclert and Lévrier or to locate it on the spectrum of the French left of the 1870s and 1880s. First, Lévrier

1. Very little information survives on Lévrier. He later became a *juge de paix*, but his file at the ministry of justice was destroyed. Ministry of justice files at the AN, series BB[8], especially BB[8] 1390 on justices of the peace, and BB[30] ON THE *régime judicaire*, provide little help; neither do the ministry of the interior files on the judiciary, under series F[80]. Lévrier also served in Algeria, but no dossier survives on him in the Archives de France d'outre-mer at Aix-en-Provence. (I thank Charles Uthéza of the Section outre-mer for his efforts to help me track down traces of Lévrier there and through civil and military records.) Some records may survive in Algiers, but the Algerian government denied me permission to search for them. The Prefecture of Police did not consider Lévrier important enough to establish a separate file on him, although much material on him survives in the Auclert dossier. The Auclert Papers also provide much help, but personal correspondence has not survived. It is easiest to trace Lévrier's ideas through his newspaper articles, especially in *La Citoyenne*.

The information presented here is drawn from the Dossiers de la presse parisienne, 1820–1894, F[18] 326/75, AN; and police reports of 3 May 1877, 5 June 1877, 25 and 29 July 1877, 17 February 1878, 19 October 1878, 29 November 1878, and 6 August 1879, Dossier Auclert, APP.

2. Police reports, November 1879, 28 February 1880, 8 April 1880, and 9 December 1880, Dossier Auclert, APP. For newspaper treatment, see the collection of clippings in the Auclert Papers, Carton 1, such as *L'Evénement*, 16 November 1880 and 8 August 1881; *Le Gaulois*, 20 October 1880; *Le Figaro*, January 1881.

never succeeded in politics or became an important thinker; little record of his thought survives. Second, when Auclert split with Richer she ceased to be the follower of anyone, feminist or socialist. Third, socialism was an auxiliary interest for Auclert; she wrote little on socialist theory, leaving only hints from which one can deduce her beliefs. Fourth, Auclert held tenaciously to her secular faith and would not compromise on its tenets. Any socialist group that she joined must accept her republican feminism, including suffragism; although French socialism in those years was highly fragmented, no faction met that standard.

The difficulty of understanding Auclert's socialism is compounded by the transitional and fragmented character of the worker's movement at the end of the 1870s and the beginning of the 1880s. Several forms of socialism inherited from previous generations still survived in discussion, and two of them shaped Auclert's perceptions. First, her reading in the works of utopian socialism of the 1830s and 1840s persuaded her of an affinity between her radical feminism and socialism. Second, the social republican tradition of 1848, especially its emphasis on cooperation in the doctrine of mutualism, coincided with her sense of social justice in "the true republic."[3] The persistence of such doctrines, like the political position of the radical republicans, owed much to the exile of the communards. The amnesty of 1880 and the introduction of Marxian socialism into France, especially by Jules Guesde, rapidly transformed the socialism of the early Third Republic. Mutualism, which Auclert preferred to call "cooperationism," found a last champion in Jean Barberet, but the doctrine soon receded before the growing working-class preference for collectivism. Mutualists advocated associations of workers for mutual aid and the foundation of producers' and consumers' cooperatives. The radical bourgeoisie, like Auclert, could comfortably adapt this doctrine to its republicanism. Collectivists promised a revolution that would abolish private property—a notion

3. For an examination of feminism in the utopian tradition, see Moses, *French Feminism in the Nineteenth Century,* esp. chapter 3; her "Saint-Simonian Men/Saint-Simonian Women: The Transformation of Feminist Thought in 1830s France," *JMH* 54 (1982):240–67; S. Joan Moon, "Feminism and Socialism: The Utopian Synthesis of Flora Tistan," in *Socialist Women,* ed. Boxer and Quataert, pp. 21–50; her "The Saint-Simonian Association of Working-Class Women, 1830–1850," *PWSFH* 5 (1977):274–81; Léon Abensour, *Le Féminisme sous le règne de Louis-Philippe* (Paris, 1918); Marguerite Thibert, "Le Féminisme dans le socialisme français de 1830 à 1850," Ph.D. diss., Paris, 1926. For the persistent traditions of social republicanism within the workers' movement, see Bernard H. Moss, *The Origins of the French Labor Movement, 1830–1914: The Socialism of Skilled Workers* (Berkeley, 1976), esp. ch. 3 and 4, and the analysis in William H. Sewell, *Work and Revolution in France: The Language of Labor from the Old Regime to 1848* (Cambridge, Mass., 1980), esp. chs. 9 and 11. For mutualism, see also Bernstein, *The Beginnings of Marxian Socialism in France.*

with which the radical bourgeoisie, including Auclert, was not wholly comfortable. Thus, Auclert contemplated an alliance with socialism precisely at the moment when it was becoming a doctrine that she did not entirely accept.

Socialist fragmentation offered Auclert many allies. In 1879 collectivists and mutualists together founded the Parti ouvrier, which Guesdist collectivists quickly captured and renamed the Parti ouvrier français. Several variants of collectivism, usually identified by the name of their leaders, emerged before the creation of a unified socialist party, the SFIO, in 1905. The most important development for Auclert and other bourgeois radicals was the appearance in 1882 of "possibilist" socialism, also called "Broussist" after its leader, Paul Brousse.[4] Possibilism accepted

4. All socialist factions that believed in parliamentary politics—that is, all except the anarchists and the syndicalists—joined the Parti ouvrier, except the followers of Auguste Blanqui. In 1880, Barberet and the mutualists left the party, Barberet for republican office and most mutualists for syndicalism. In 1881, the Blanquists (who followed the spirit of his revolutionary insurrectionism rather than the radical republicanism of his last years) founded their own collectivist party, the Comité révolutionnaire central; this faction later adopted the name Parti socialiste révolutionnaire and is also known as the Vaillantists after Edouard Vaillant. In 1882, a split occurred in the Parti ouvrier between the Guesdists and the possibilists, the latter leaving the party to found the Fédération des travailleurs socialistes de France, and the former renaming their party the Parti ouvrier français. The possibilist federation then split between the Broussists, who retained control of it, and the slightly more militant followers of Jean Allemane, who founded the Parti ouvrier socialiste révolutionnaire. Numerous small factions developed, most notably for Auclert the Fédération républicaine socialiste of 1885 (see chapter 6).

This subject has attracted the interest of many scholars. For a more detailed overview of the socialist factions of the 1870s and 1880s, see Maitron's summary in the *DMO*, 10:76–77; Daniel Ligou, *Histoire du socialisme en France, 1871–1961* (Paris, 1962), pp. 7–36; Georges Lefranc, *Le Mouvement socialiste sous la Troisième République, 1875–1940* (Paris, 1963), pp. 11–48. There is a large literature on Blanqui and the Blanquists, the most exhaustive being Maurice Dommanget's multivolume study; for this period, see Maurice Dommanget, *Auguste Blanqui au début de la Troisième République, 1871–1880* (Paris, 1971). The most recent work is Patrick H. Hutton, "The Role of the Blanquist Party in Left-Wing Politics in France, 1879–1890," *JMH* 46 (1974):277–95, idem, *The Cult of Revolutionary Tradition: The Blanquists in French Politics, 1864–1893* (Berkeley, 1981), pp. 59–142. See also Samuel Bernstein, *Auguste Blanqui and the Art of Insurrection* (London, 1971), pp. 335–52; Alan B. Spitzer, *The Revolutionary Theories of Louis Auguste Blanqui* (New York, 1957). For a good introduction to the arguments involved in deciphering Blanquism, see Jolyon M. Howorth, "The Myth of Blanquism Under the Third Republic, 1871–1900," *JMH*, on-demand supplement to no. 48 (1976). Howorth has also produced a thorough treatment of the Vaillantists: *Edouard Vaillant: La Création de l'unité socialiste en France; La Politique de l'action totale* (Paris, 1982). The latter title also includes an "index des organisations," helpful for distinguishing the factions. For the possibilists, see C. Landauer, "The Origin of Socialist Reformism in France," *IRSH* 12 (1967); David Stafford, *From Anarchism to Reformism: A Study of the Political Activities of Paul Brousse . . . 1870–1890* (London, 1971); Michel Winock, "Les Allemanistes," *Bulletin de la Société des études jaurèsiennes* 50 (1973); Sian Reynolds, "La Vie de Jean Allemane, 1843–1935," (Thèse de troisième cycle, Paris, 1981). For the Guesdists, see

the possibility of cooperation with the bourgeois republic and a reformist route to collectivism. It engendered several forms of republican socialism with which Auclert could hope to ally herself. Nonetheless, the socialism of Hubertine Auclert did not precisely fit any of these factions. She was a founding member of the Parti ouvrier for a short time, and she later joined a small republican socialist group, but her total participation in socialist parties amounted to less than two years.

The socialist vision of Lévrier, which first drew Auclert into the movement, was mutualist. His mixture of the traditions of the pre-Marxist left was compatible with Auclert's political thought because its sine qua non was the republic. The clearest exposition of Lévrier's thought appeared in a pamphlet, published through a workers' association in 1879, that reproduced his standard speech to meetings of workers. Lévrier believed that capitalist exploitation could be ameliorated, and gradually ended, through the association and cooperation of workers themselves in a supportive republic. He brought nothing new to the tradition of working-class association, mutual aid, and producers' cooperatives except perhaps a greater stress upon collaboration with the republic—a possibilist version of mutualism. A sad irony awaited Auclert when she espoused Lévrier's cooperationist socialism: mutualists were terrible allies for a suffragist owing to the antifeminism of Proudhon, whose thought greatly influenced the mutualist movement.[5]

Auclert also considered herself a Blanquist—in a special sense of that term. She admired Auguste Blanqui for his republican ardor and radical vision but not for his revolutionary methods; she drew back from the prospect of insurrectionary violence. Auclert later acknowledged Blanqui's impact on her methods of activism—seizing every opportunity for protest, demonstrating in public, speaking vigorously against the authorities, defying attitudes—but she steadfastly rejected violent revolution, cherishing the belief that a true republic would advance without that recourse. Thus Auclert was a Blanquist in the style of his final years when he rallied to the Third Republic and supported women's suffrage

especially Claude Willard, *Le Mouvement socialiste en France, 1893–1905: Les Guesdistes* (Paris, 1965); Michelle Perrot, "Les Guesdistes: Controverse sur l'introduction du Marxisme en France," *Annales* 22 (1967); Bernstein, "Jules Guesde: Pioneer of Marxism in France," *Science and Society* 4 (1940); Leslie Derfler, "Reformism and Jules Guesde," *IRSH* 12 (1967). For the congresses at which many of these schisms occured, see J. A. Clarke, "French Socialist Congresses, 1876–1914," *JMH* 31 (1959). For the relationship between the factions and the women's movements, see Sowerwine, *Sisters or Citizens*, pp. 21–67.

5. Antonin Lévrier, *Discours prononcé par le citoyen Antonin Lévrier à la réunion des travilleurs indépendants* (Paris, 1879); a copy of this pamphlet can be found in the Auclert Papers, Carton 10. For the Proudhonist tradition of antifeminism within mutualism, see Bidelman, *Pariahs Stand Up!*, pp. 41–48; Moses, *French Feminism in the Nineteenth Century*, pp. 152–58.

within it. She was not a Blanquist in the sense intended by some of his followers when they attached his name to a revolutionary collectivist faction in the 1880s. Auclert found collectivists, whatever their appellation, doctrinaire, authoritarian, and insincere in their professed feminism.

The natural allies of Auclert's republican blend of socialism and feminism seem to be the possibilists. They shared an attachment to the republic and a pragmatic, reformist idea of socialism. Lévrier, in fact, was already using the term *le possibilisme* to describe his ideas in the 1870s, years before Paul Brousse formed his own party. Had the Broussists championed women's rights, Auclert would have been won to the party. But another irony intervened: Brousse was a socialist version of Richer. The possibilists whose republicanism appealed to Auclert shared the liberal republican fear of enfranchising women who were dominated by the church: women would turn the republic to the right, destroying the formula of socialist evolution.

Auclert's difficulties in finding compatible socialists must be understood as a function of her personality as well as of their doctrine; neither was flexible. She chose to consider herself a socialist yet remain independent. The psychological importance of independence, and its corollary, not yielding to authority, has been seen developing from her use of the term when her brother returned her to the convent. Auclert's period of active socialism was a stage in which she applied her thirst for independence to ideology as well as to the conditions of daily life. When she explored socialist doctrines in the late 1870s, she had not yet learned the political art of negotiation and compromise while retaining a sense of independence. She learned instead that her combination of suffragism, mutualist support of workers, Blanquist republican activism, and evolutionary socialism was uniquely her own. Thus, had Auclert chosen to devote herself to socialism, she would have filtered it through the alembic of her mind, creating Auclertism.

Auclert began to join socialist activities during the winter of 1875–1876. Her first effort was a campaign supporting a cooperative workshop for Parisian laundrywomen who had appealed for 2,000 to 3,000 francs for this purpose in November 1875. Auclert, not a brilliant fundraiser, began with a small personal contribution and persuaded both Richer and Senator Adolphe Crémieux (republican union, life senator) to make donations. After a few weeks she had raised 128 francs and a painting to be sold. She then hesitated to turn this money over to the laundrywomen because they were not mutualists. Her explanation for this reluctance may have hidden some other argument, for a fight ensued. The workers denounced Auclert for planning a stratagem to keep the funds for herself. Auclert reacted furiously. She terminated her campaign, returned all contributions, and announced that she supported only true cooperationism and worked only with people who made no "wounding insinuations."

What had happened? Was the gulf between a sympathetic bourgeoise and a struggling laundrywoman so large that they could not even communicate? One can understand part of the problem by understanding that Auclert was extremely sensitive to direct criticism of her dedication or sincerity. This vulnerability presumably had its roots in her painful rejection by the Sisters of Charity of St. Vincent de Paul. As an independent adult, she would not tolerate a mother superior questioning her faith or commitment, much less a group of laundrywomen. She reacted impetuously and unforgivingly to such criticism for the remainder of her life. The episode of the laundrywomen—characterized by good intentions, disagreement over cooperationism, and rupture—foreshadowed Auclert's future in French socialism.[6]

Auclert saw the woman question and the class question connected by a shared oppression, a shared exclusion from power. Her first manifesto for Droit des femmes ("To the Women of France!" 1876) discussed this exploitation:

> Despite the benefits of our revolution of 1789, two types of individuals are still enslaved: proletarians and women.
> The proletarian succumbs beneath the burden of labor which, if he lives parsimoniously, procures him a morsel of bread, with no possibility of savings for his old age. . . . He dies, fatally afflicted with poverty.
> The proletarian woman has a fate still more deplorable. To meet the same needs as a man, she is paid half of what he is. . . . To that is added for her as for all other women, vexations and injustices of every sort. We don't have any rights. . . .
> Women of France, we have rights to claim. . . . Let us unite our efforts, let us form associations; the example of the proletarians invites us; let us learn to emancipate ourselves like them.[7]

It is clear from this document that Auclert's foremost interest remained women, not workers. She linked feminism and socialism as kindred movements of the oppressed; together, they could moralize the republic. She envisioned an alliance that would profit the women's move-

6. Auclert, "Les Ouvrières," *L'Avenir des femmes*, February and March 1876.

7. The manifesto "Aux femmes!" appeared in many left-wing newspapers in late October and November 1876. Clippings can be found in the Auclert Papers, Carton 1, and in the Dossier Auclert, APP. It was reprinted in *L'Avenir des femmes*, November 1876; Auclert, *Historique de la société le Droit des femmes*, pp. 8–10; Auclert, *La Citoyenne: Articles de 1881 à 1891*, pp. 19–20.

ment, not a transfer of her attention to the workers' movement, and the laundrywomen of 1876 probably recognized this distinction.

Auclert's orientation attracted both radical republicans and socialists to Droit des femmes. In addition to Lévrier, the active socialists included Emmanuel Pignon, who wrote for *Le Socialisme progressif*, published in Lugano, Switzerland, by the reformist Benoît Malon and other proscribed communards; Lucie Dissat, who founded a seamstresses' cooperative in the working-class suburb of Belleville; Clémence Kéva, an advocate of Proudhonist mutualism; Eugénie Pierre and Léonie Rouzade, who soon became two of the foremost leaders of the socialist women's movement; and Eliska Vincent, a member of Léo's feminist group of 1866 and one of the first women to serve as a delegate to a workers' congress, in Lyons in 1878.[8]

Droit des femmes thus existed on the fringes of both the feminist and the socialist movements of the late 1870s, with a limited role in each. Auclert and her society did not participate in the first two congresses of French workers, although mutualists dominated both assemblies. Police agents, however, found numerous connections between Droit des femmes and the Parisian delegations to those congresses. Auclert's role in the feminist congress of 1878 thus drove her out of the feminist mainstream precisely when an alternative was arising for her. Several members of Droit des femmes, led by Pignon and Lévrier, publicly criticized the feminist congress for inadequate proletarian representation and insufficient attention to working-class interests. A letter from Pignon to Richer, published in November 1878, hinted at the route Droit des femmes would take between the two movements: workers' meetings, he insisted, were more sympathetic to women's rights than Richer's feminist assembly had been to workers' rights. Auclert did not participate in this argument, but her final words on the feminist congress stressed her commitment to the "egalitarian standard of the revolution."[9]

THE WORKERS' CONGRESS OF MARSEILLES, 1879

During the winter of 1878–1879, Auclert focused her campaign for women's rights on the French socialist movement, attending a variety

8. See *L'Avenir des femmes*, October and November 1878, for Pignon; *Le Droit des femmes*, January through March 1879, for Dissat; *DMO*, 10:62–63 for delegates to the workers' congresses; ibid., 12:166–67 (Fauché), 8:111 (Pédoussaut), 7:230–34 (Malon).

9. See police reports of 29 July 1877, 6 August 1877, and 5 September 1878, Dossier Auclert, APP, for connections between DF and the workers' congresses; *L'Avenir des femmes*, October and November 1878, for the acrimonious exchange between Richer and Pignon; Auclert, *Le Droit politique des femmes*, p. 5.

of socialist meetings in and around Paris. The skimpy evidence of these meetings suggests that her sole purpose was to present the woman question to workers and seek recruits for Droit des femmes; she apparently did not become involved in other issues. Auclert also earned some prominence on the Parisian left by organizing a committee to aid the women of the Commune, both those in exile (whose amnesty she sought) and those in straitened circumstances owing to the events of 1871. Auclert demonstrated in these activities the single-mindedness that characterized her career: she analyzed all issues in terms of the political rights of women. Thus, Auclert converted the Commune into an argument for enfranchisement. Just as the tyrannical Versailles government crushed the people of Paris, man crushed woman: "Men are despots and tyrants who only consider women as slaves. . . . They deported (as communards) to New Caledonia those women who took part in politics. Well, for equal repression we must have equal civil rights." Auclert showed in these speeches that she was learning a fiery rhetoric different from the discourse in Richer's circle. "Enough centuries of submission!" she shouted at one meeting. "We must revolt, we must cease to obey!"[10]

Auclert's primary socialist ties in 1879 came from her association with a new socialist newspaper, *Le Prolétaire.* It had begun publication in November 1878, following a resolution at the workers' congress of the same year that called for the establishment of a working-class newspaper to replace the collectivist *L'Egalité,* which had been closed by the government. *Le Prolétaire* initially opened its columns to socialists of all tendencies and published both collectivist and cooperationist articles. Its sympathies in 1879 can be judged from the fact that it was published by a cooperative society, L'Union des travailleurs.[11] Auclert had achieved sufficient stature in cooperationist circles to be elected to

10. Police reports, 22 and 29 July 1879 and 4 October 1879, and unidentified clipping (quoted), 11 February 1880, Dossier Auclert, APP; *La Marseillaise,* 9 and 27 October 1879, Auclert Papers, Carton 1.

11. Disentangling the history of socialist journalism is almost as complicated as distinguishing socialist factions (see note 3 above). *Le Prolétaire* apparently existed as an open forum for socialists, with a slight mutualist orientation, in the period 1878–1879. when Auclert was associated with it. After the congress of Marseilles, it became a collectivist newspaper. In 1882, it changed stance again and became a possibilist, anti-Marxist journal associated with the Broussist tendency; its name was changed to *Le Prolétariat* in 1884. It is sometimes described as an Allemanist-possibilist paper, which is close to the truth for the period 1882–1888, until the Allemanists founded *Le Parti ouvrier* to compete with it. *L'Egalité,* meanwhile, appeared between November 1877 and July 1878 and again between 1880 and 1883. After its disappearance, collectivists increasingly turned their attention to *Le Cri du peuple,* the newspaper of Jules Vallès and Séverine, initially open to all tendencies but essentially Guesdist between 1884 and 1887, after which it quickly passed through possibilist and Blanquist periods. Throughout the 1870s

the commission that founded *Le Prolétaire* and wrote its statutes. The paper briefly supported women's rights in December 1878, inserted items about Auclert's activities, and supported her petition campaign of February 1879.[12]

Through *Le Prolétaire* Auclert became involved in the preparations for the third congress of the French workers' movement, to be held at Marseilles late in October 1879. This led to ambitious dreams. If she could persuade a socialist newspaper to accept women's rights, why not ask the workers' congress to do the same? If Richer thought her too revolutionary, perhaps the revolutionaries would think that she made sense. Her chances of success, however, did not seem great. Despite long-standing connections between socialism and feminism, the workers' congresses of 1876 and 1878 had opposed women's rights and adopted resolutions endorsing the traditional role of women in the family. Even Richer had lambasted the Lyons congress of 1878 for arguing that "the organization of society must allow the labor of the man to suffice for the existence of the family, the woman having the duty to raise and oversee the education of the family." Consistent with that opinion, it had been difficult for women even to participate in the congresses—a total of nine delegates to the first two assemblies were female.[13]

Two groups nominated Auclert for the Parisian delegation to Marseilles, Droit des femmes and Lucie Dissat's cooperative, the Travailleuses de Belleville. The organizing committee for Paris invited Auclert to present her ideas to it at a private meeting in late September 1879. She told it bluntly that she would go to Marseilles to demand the political and civil equality of women and that her foremost economic concern was to obtain equal pay for equal work. The committee knew what it would be choosing if it elected Auclert. Or did it? According to a police report, Auclert told the committee that she was a collectivist, supported the abolition of private property, and favored the collective appropriation of capital. Yet Auclert never made such statements in writing or in public speech. It is improbable that she said these things to the committee, even as a cynical tactic to win election—after all, the

and 1880s, Auclert was more sympathetic to *Le Prolétaire/Le Prolétariat* and had several disputes with the collectivists of *L'Egalité* and *Le Cri du peuple.*

See Michelle Perrot, "Le Premier journal marxiste français: *L'Egalité* de Jules Guesde, 1877–1883," *L'Actualité de l'histoire* 28 (1959); Bellanger et al., *Histoire générale de la presse française,* 3:231, 234, 371–72. For another view of *Le Prolétaire,* see Stafford, *From Anarchism to Reformism,* esp. pp. 154–55.

12. Police reports, 12 August 1879 and 8 October 1879, Dossier Auclert, APP; clippings files, ibid., and Auclert Papers, Carton 1.

13. Sowerwine, *Sisters or Citizens,* pp. 24–25; Albistur and Armogathe, eds., *Le Grief des femmes,* 2:68; *L'Avenir des femmes,* March 1878 (quoted); *DMO,* 10:62–63.

men who were voting knew her mutualist sympathies and had before them her nomination by a cooperative society. Auclert was not an anticollectivist in the sense of opposing a society based on collective ownership, but she frequently clashed with collectivists, usually over the woman question, and she opposed elements of collectivist thought such as class war and violent revolution. One must assume that the police erred in their description of her statement, perhaps because they assumed that all socialists were collectivists. Whatever happened, two things are clear: the committee elected Auclert as a delegate to Marseilles, and Droit des femmes defended the mutualist position in socialist battles.[14]

Hubertine Auclert became a socialist celebrity on the second day of the Marseilles congress. She had been named to a special commission to consider the equality of women and was permitted to address the congress for an hour (some five thousand words) on the subject. Her speech left no doubt that Auclert had come to Marseilles as a feminist, as "the slave delegate of nine million slaves." She was there as a woman, not as a worker; she was an outsider among the proletarians, an outsider who came to propose a "defensive and offensive alliance against our common oppressors." She did not hesitate to attack the attitudes of socialists and workers. As sincere advocates of human equality, they must learn that this meant more than the equality of all men. Women were "under the yoke," she told them, just as workers were; women were subjected to the will of men, including proletarian men, just as workers were subjected to the will of the bourgeoisie: "You must understand, Citizens, that to claim your accession to freedom, you can only rely upon the equality of all beings. If you do not base your claims upon justice and natural law, if you, proletarians, wish to protect privileges, the privileges of sex, I ask you what authority you have to protest against the privileges of class?" The poor could exploit women just as thoroughly as the rich. Could not the proletarians recognize that they had "companions in misfortune"? That to be free themselves, they must cease to be unjust themselves?

Auclert avoided issues of socialist doctrine in phrasing her friendly attack. She scarcely mentioned economics. She acknowledged the ideological division of the assembly and noted that the different factions were "far from unanimous in recognizing our equality." Auclert realized the irony of her being a mutualist and admitted that women could count on the backing only of collectivists. Nonetheless, she assailed collectivists for giving support without succor: women would be equals only in the future society created by the workers' revolution. She used

14. Police reports, 30 September 1879, 7 and 20 October 1879, Dossier Auclert, APP; *DMO*, 10:165 (Auclert).

terms like "authoritarians" (an epithet of utter condemnation in her mind) and "pretended socialists" to criticize those who postponed emancipation. Auclert insisted that she did not "doubt the good faith of the collectivists who spoke of making no distinction between the woman and the man," but she told them that future liberation was not good enough:

> "In the future society, these pretended socialists continue, women will have their rights. In this they imitate the priests who promise to the disinherited of the earth the joys of heaven. Neither the disinherited of wealth nor the disinherited of rights, neither the poor nor women can always content themselves with holy promises. . . . Women of France, I tell you from the height of this podium: those who deny our equality in the present will deny it in the future. . . . For too many centuries we have been the victims of bad faith to forget ourselves and believe that in working for the common good we will have our share of the common good."

Auclert's challenge to the congress could hardly have been stated more directly. Would socialists of all factions, especially the mutualists, admit the oppression of women and call for equality? Would they, especially the collectivists, seek it now?[15]

It was a rousing speech—closing with the slogan "Equality among all men! Equality between men and women!"—and it enjoyed an immediate success. Thunderous applause broke out (according to the press), repeated in a "triple salvo" (according to the minutes of the congress). Auclert won yet more applause when a delegate moved that the congress vote her its thanks; more again when she responded, "I have only come to defend my rights; why vote me thanks?"[16]

The congress voted Auclert more than thanks. It unanimously named her to chair a subsequent session and to preside over the commission charged with examining the woman question. This did not pass without protests, and one delegate even tried to read an antifeminist

15. *Séances du congrès ouvrier de France . . . 1879.* The session on women (pp. 145–223) met on 22 October 1879; Auclert's speech is on pp. 148–58. Auclert also published the speech as a pamphlet, *Egalité sociale et politique de la femme et de l'homme: Discours prononcé au Congrès ouvrier de Marseille* (Marseille, 1879). A long excerpt is reprinted in Albistur and Armogathe, eds., *Le Grief des femmes,* 2:107–10, and in Madeleine Rebérioux, Christiane Dufrancatel, and Béatrice Slama, "Hubertine Auclert et la question des femmes à 'l'immortel congrès' (1879)," *Romantisme* 13–14 (1976): 123–42. See also Auclert, *Le Vote des femmes,* pp. 105–06; Chaumont's treatment of it in "Hubertine Auclert," p. 9; Sowerwine's analysis in *Sisters or Citizens,* pp. 25–26.

16. *Séances du congrès ouvrier de France . . . 1879,* p. 158; *La République française,* 26 October 1879; *Le Citoyen de Marseille,* 23 October 1879.

report into the record. Auclert delivered her commission's report on the last day of the congress. The commission contained a sympathetic majority, including two other women, but the rhetoric of the report left no doubt about its principal author. Woman was "a slave, a humiliated being, a martyr." The report proclaimed that "the absolute equality of the two sexes" was a basic principle of socialism. Upon that principle, the commission accepted "for women the same social and political rights as for men." Auclert, who could hardly have missed the difference between the workers' congress of 1879 and the feminist congress of 1878, was ecstatic. Unlike the bourgeoisie, she said, "workers have extended their hands to the woman, with the justice that characterizes them. . . . This will be their claim to glory in the eyes of posterity." This was not far from the mark. The congress adopted her report, after several arguments and procedural votes, as the official policy of the movement. This resolution in favor of the political rights of French women was the first such declaration by any major political faction in French history. No republican party matched it for half a century, during which time socialists themselves often seemed to have forgotten the resolution of 1879.[17]

How did Auclert achieve this dramatic success at Marseilles, reversing the explicit resolutions of previous workers' congresses and making socialists seem more feminist than the feminists? In part, it was the personal triumph of a true believer whose passion and conviction moved others. Her words resonated with a great truth about human justice, shaming professed egalitarians into voting for equality. She also employed good political judgment in avoiding issues that might have alienated delegates. But no individual succeeds in turning the tide unless the moon is in the appropriate part of the heavens. Politicians may be more open to moral suasion than the tides, but they too respond better to widespread developments than to a single voice. French socialism in 1879 was changing and Hubertine Auclert was the right person in the right place to point toward a major change. It is no small irony that the change that permitted her success was the steady conquest of mutualist socialism by collectivist socialism. Collectivists generally supported sexual equality even if their perspective differed from that of feminists; most mutualists did not. Had Auclert addressed a congress that shared her mutualist ideas, the fate of her resolution might have been different. It must be added, however, that it would also have been different had she returned to collectivist congresses during the 1880s, when socialists again became reluctant to support feminism.

Auclert had some difficult moments at Marseilles which underscore

17. The text of the Marseilles resolution can be found in the minutes of the congress and in Guibert, *Les Femmes et l'organisation syndicale*, pp. 156–57.

the persistence of socialist antifeminism even in 1879. Adverse remarks about her public speaking, which she explained with another reference to her natural "timidity," led to problems. This stereotype of the weak woman became troublesome when Auclert presided over one session in which she experienced difficulty in maintaining order between quarreling factions; opponents argued that even Auclert showed the unalterable differences between men and women. She also suffered personal attacks. One delegate, Hippolyte Pédoussaut, insisted that Auclert was an agent provocateur sent to distract socialists. Another, Charles Cival, answered Auclert's speech with Proudhonist misogyny to defend his rights as a husband. So indignant was Cival at feminist usurpation that he tried to organize a walkout and finally left the congress himself. One Marseilles newspaper was even more frightened by equality: it claimed to have exposed Auclert as a Russian nihilist come to undo the French family. Auclert's worst moment at Marseilles resulted from the behavior of Gustave Fauché, a Parisian Guesdist. He had gone to the congress committed to supporting equal rights, but he had spoken against her. Auclert detested duplicity, and nothing angered her more than betrayal. She bitterly denounced Fauché and never forgave him.[18]

These experiences at Marseilles—passionate speech, political triumph, acrimonious counterattack—provide another opportunity to examine the relationship between the individual and the event. The act of going to Marseilles and speaking against the masculine orientation and goals of the workers' movement typified Auclert's temperamental strengths of defiance, challenge, and assertiveness. The wording of her speech, like that of the manifesto of 1876, vividly revealed her boldness and confidence. In fact, her speech is difficult to quote because virtually every line burns with her passion, her aggressiveness, her defiance of the leaders of French socialism. Winning the ensuing vote, arguably the greatest political victory of her life, made the notoriety, acrimony, and ridicule bearable. Indeed, Auclert found the experience of the Marseilles congress so exhilarating that in later years she recalled it as one of the happiest moments of her life.[19] Her success, and her continuing pride in it, had lasting effects on her character, encouraging her to maintain the style of frontal assault upon opponents, discouraging her from acquiring the irenic skills of modulation and compromise.

In exploring such developments in Auclert's character, it is important to note that even in her moment of triumph she denied that the

18. For press accounts of Auclert at Marseilles, see the clippings in Carton 1 of her papers and in her police dossier, especially those from *La Marseillaise.* These include several accounts of the disputes with Cival, Pédoussaut, and Fauché. See also police reports of 13 November 1879 (on Fauché) and 3 November 1879 (on Pédoussaut), in Dossier Auclert, APP; Dossier Congrès ouvrier socialiste de Marseille, 1879, Bª 37, APP; *DMO,* 10:166 (Auclert).

19. Auclert's recollections in *La Libre parole,* 2 June 1894.

forceful, self-confident orator of Marseilles was truly she. Faced with criticism of her public speaking and her direction of a meeting, Auclert took refuge in the image of herself as a timid person obliged to force herself to speak—a defense perilously close to the accusation of her critics that even strong-willed women were weak compared to men. Timidity was precisely the same defense that Auclert had used when the foundation of Droit des femmes in 1877 had provoked hostility and ridicule. She later painted this self-portrait in her diary and obviously cherished this view of herself. Yet it absolutely contradicts the evidence of her behavior and her ideas. No trace of timidity can be found in her words, no implication of shyness in the act of delivering them. If Hubertine Auclert at Marseilles was timid, the entire world would recoil when a forceful person entered it. Why, then, did she project this misleading image? One may assume that Auclert had a few habits, memories, or feelings that she could cite to herself as evidence of her purported timidity—discomfort with men, and with herself, as sexual beings seems one possibility. But she definitely was not a timid political leader. Thus, it seems likely that Auclert kept this deceiving self-image to satisfy other internal needs, such as denying that she was belligerent or explaining her defeats.

THE SOCIALIST ALLIANCE, 1879–1880

Auclert returned to Paris in November 1879 with enthusiasm for her alliance with the Parti ouvrier. She expanded the meetings of Droit des femmes in working-class districts to encourage attendance by "our brothers the workers." She participated in other socialist meetings around Paris. She resumed her collaboration with *Le Prolétaire*, although it increasingly turned toward collectivism. She repeated her Marseilles speech in a working-class suburb to enable women of the proletariat to hear it; the committee that had sent her adopted a resolution stating that she had "fulfilled quite well" her mandate. Auclert expressed her personal satisfaction in the socialist press. She praised the party for admitting women to participation and for its feminist resolutions, which "have gone out as messengers of good news, even to the small hamlets, to shine a ray of hope on those to whom until now one has preached resignation and submission to their conditions." This overstatement was rhetoric, not an indication of naïveté; when she reported to Droit des femmes she criticized socialists who thought that women's rights must be delayed, and she excoriated Fauché.[20]

20. *Le Temps,* 17 May 1880; *Le Figaro,* 9 November 1879 (first quotation); *Le Réveil social,* 8 February 1880; *La Fédération,* 16 January 1880; (third quotation); police reports, (second quotation) 2 and 18 November 1879, 28 December 1879, and 29 January 1880, Dossier Auclert, APP.

The foundation of a socialist women's group early in 1880 clarified Auclert's position in French socialism. The Union des femmes (sometimes the Union des femmes socialistes) was the first such group in France. It was the accomplishment of Léonie Rouzade, a friend of Auclert who shared a similar political history: a republican family background (including a representative of 1789), an awakening through Richer's *Amélioration*, a founding membership in Droit des femmes, participation in the feminist congress of 1878, and attraction to socialism through *Le Prolétaire* and the Marseilles congress (although Rouzade was not a delegate). Unlike Auclert, however, Rouzade supported Guesdist collectivism.

The Union des femmes socialistes attracted most of the socialist-feminists of Paris, including Eugénie Pierre and Auclert, whose Droit des femmes banner proclaiming "No Duties Without Rights" was hung at the union's 1880 meetings. But the union attracted fewer feminists than socialists, who were perhaps drawn by Guesde's speech to the founding meeting in April 1880. By late 1880, after the amnesty of the communards, it also drew revolutionary women who had been in exile, including both Paule Mink and Louise Michel. Auclert found herself on the right wing of the group, isolated among Guesdists and women who put their socialism ahead of their feminism—an indication of her future within the Parti ouvrier.[21]

Auclert also collaborated with Auguste Blanqui during 1880. At the beginning of the year, she decided to capitalize on her success at Marseilles by launching a major campaign for women's suffrage. She organized a public meeting in March to announce her plans, and she sought a prominent political figure to preside over the meeting. A few months earlier, Auclert would have chosen Victor Hugo; in the spirit of her new alliance, she asked Blanqui. The seventy-five-year-old revolutionary agreed to participate in a way that surprised and pleased Auclert. When the meeting elected him to preside, he declined to accept the chair and gave a feminist speech arguing that it was important for a woman to have the experience of presiding. He also repeated his support for women's suffrage. After that beginning, Auclert and Blanqui cooperated

21. For Rouzade and the Union des femmes, see Sowerwine, *Sisters or Citizens*, pp. 29–42, and his "The Organization of French Socialist Women, 1880–1914," pp. 3–24. Rouzade published the group's program as a pamphlet, *Développement du programme de la société l'union des femmes par la citoyenne Rouzade* (Paris, n.d. [1880]). See also her occasional items in *Le Prolétaire* and *L'Egalité,* and her other writings: *Petit catéchisme de morale laïque et socialiste* (Meudon, 1895); *Les Classes dirigeantes et les travailleurs jugés par une femme* (Nancy, n.d.). There is a vicious sketch of Rouzade in Jehan Des Etrivières (pseud. of Marie-Rose Astié de Valsayre), *Les Amazons du siècle* (Paris, 1882). Little survives on Auclert's role in the group; see police reports of 2 October 1880, Dossier Paule Mink, Bᵃ 1178, APP, and 12 March 1880, Dossier Auclert, APP.

in other activities, such as the founding of a socialist free thought society. She accompanied him on his lecture tour of the provinces during the fall of 1880, preceding his addresses with a call for women's rights. In November 1880, for example, Auclert and Blanqui spoke before a crowd of five to six thousand in Lille. Blanqui died a few weeks later, and Auclert soon parted from his followers. But she always remembered him as "a martyr . . . a gentle and generous battler . . . a revolutionary saint."[22]

In the months after Marseilles, Auclert also developed her contacts with former communards—a group of socialists that she considered, correctly, to have been more influenced by Proudhonian mutualism than by Marxist collectivism. She began in December 1879 by participating in one of the political rituals of the cult of 1871, the burial of a communard amidst the verbal incense of leftist eulogy. A few days later, she attended a fundraising soirée to aid orphans of the Commune. By March 1880 Auclert had emerged as one of the leading activists in defense of the Commune. She named Louise Michel, who had not yet returned from exile, the honorary president of Droit des femmes and sang her praises in a lecture on the women of the Commune. Auclert updated Virgil to *Arma feminamque cano:* the women warriors of 1871 had proven the political capacity of women with bullets rather than with ballots, but would it not be better to let Michel run for president?

"The immortal, the sublime" Michel, "the heroic woman" of the barricades, remained Droit des femmes' honorary president until she and Auclert met for the first time in the fall of 1880—when they discovered that they disagreed utterly. Meanwhile, Auclert was her staunchest defender. She headed a committee in favor of a full amnesty and began a petition campaign to that end. She joined in ceremonies to honor Gustave Flourens ("the dashing knight-errant" of the Commune), led Droit des femmes in raising funds for the families of communards, and participated in the great demonstration of May 1880, all with the igneous ardor that characterized her politics.[23]

Auclert's manifold activities with Rouzade, Blanqui, and the com-

---

22. Auclert's reminiscences on Blanqui, "Un miracle socialiste," Auclert Papers, 6/168; police reports, 12 and 15 March 1880, 12 May 1880 (2), Dossier Auclert, APP; *XIXe Siècle,* 13 March 1880; *Gil Blas,* 12 March 1880; *Le Petit nord,* 23 December 1880; Maurice Dommanget, *Auguste Blanqui au début de la Troisième République: Dernière prison et ultimes combats* (Paris, 1971), p. 137.

23. For Auclert and the Commune, see police reports, 27 November 1879, 22 January 1880, 11 March 1880 (2), 4, 16, and 27 April 1880, 2, 16, and 25 May 1880, Dossier Auclert, APP; *Gil Blas,* 12 March 1880; *XIXe Siècle,* 13 March 1880; *Pays,* 20 May 1880; *Le Prolétaire,* 3 and 10 April 1880; *DMO,* 6:55–56 (Flourens); Jean T. Joughin, *The Paris Commune in French Politics, 1871–1880: The History of the Amnesty of 1880* (Baltimore, 1955), 2:377–78.

munards gave her a recognized position among Parisian socialists in 1880. She became "a Sarah Bernhardt of socialism" to the conservative press and "the Jeanne d'Arc of the feminine proletariat" to the liberal. Some socialists considered her too bourgeois and others thought her feminism wrong, but she had become an important figure in their movement. Auclert thus became one of the founding members, and Droit des femmes one of the founding organizations, of the section of the Parti ouvrier for the Paris region, the Union fédérative du Centre. Auclert labored to organize this section, from a committee meeting in January 1880 through the founding regional congress in July. In recognition of this effort, the congress selected Clémence Kéva of Droit des femmes to be the first treasurer of the regional socialist party. But all was not well with Auclert's alliance. The unshriven Gustave Fauché had been chosen first secretary of the section; in April 1880, he had led its Guesdist majority in rejecting a party program that included the civil and political rights of women. Feminism was set aside as reformism; the emancipation of women was set aside until after the revolution. Little wonder that Kéva was elected instead of Auclert.[24]

Auclert, Kéva, and Droit des femmes nonetheless played an important role in the preparations for the fourth workers' congress (the first of the Parti ouvrier), scheduled for November 1880 in Le Havre. After Fauché's reversal of the Marseilles program in the Parisian federation, Auclert told a meeting of Droit des femmes that she would not participate in the discussions at Havre; she had made her point at Marseilles. Droit des femmes would be represented, however, and its goal for the congress would be to see that "the woman question be inscribed at the head of the program" once again. Given Kéva's position in the party, she was the natural choice to be Droit des femmes' delegate.[25]

The Havre congress of 1880 marked a turning point in the history of the French socialist party and a catastrophe for Auclert's socialist-feminist alliance. The Marseilles congress is remembered, in Guesde's words, as "the immortal congress" because it led to the creation of the first workers' party (and because collectivists dominated after two congresses led by the mutualists). The assembly at Havre should therefore be called "the mortal congress" because collectivists and mutualists immediately fell into internecine battle, resulting in the division of both the congress and the Parti ouvrier. Jean Barberet, founder of a Parisian bakers' cooperative, author of a column on workers' associa-

24. *Le Temps*, 17 May 1880 (first quote); unidentified clipping in the Auclert Papers, Carton 1 (second quote); police reports, 14 Janaury 1880, 8 and 16 May 1880, 21 and 25 July 1880, Dossier Auclert, APP; Sowerwine, *Sisters or Citizens*, p. 26; Stafford, *From Anarchism to Reformism*, p. 158.

25. Police report, March 26, 1880, Dossier Auclert, APP.

tions for *Le Rappel*, and leader of the mutualists at the congresses of 1876 and 1878, challenged Guesde for control of the party, although neither he nor Guesde was an official delegate. The elected delegates supported Barberet, 71–51, largely because he controlled the organizing committee which ruled on the validity of voting credentials. When his committee announced its decisions invalidating many collectivist delegates, the collectivists withdrew from the congress and organized their own in another part of town. With them went Paule Mink, Léonie Rouzade, and the future of the socialist women's movement. Among those who stayed with Barberet was Clémence Kéva—not a surprising decision, as Kéva was a lacemaker who belonged to Lucie Dissat's cooperative.[26]

When Droit des femmes' delegate stayed with the mutualists in November 1880, Auclert's "pact of alliance" came to an end. The mutualists neither sustained an independent socialist party nor supported women's rights through their syndicalist remnants. Indeed, their rump congress of 1880, their last national congress, voted to return to the policy of 1876–1878, maintaining that women belonged in the home; it is doubtful that Auclert's oratory could have altered that vote. So rapidly did mutualist strength dissolve after the Havre meeting that Barberet gave up the struggle and accepted an appointment in the ministry of the interior, where his reformist approach to human rights shaped the landmark legislation on public meetings (1881), trade unions (1884), and the right of association (1901). Collectivists, who retained control of both the regional federations and the Parti ouvrier, quickly purged the party of his followers. Fauché wasted no time in expunging troublemakers from the Parisian federation. Auclert and seventeen members of Droit des femmes who had joined the party with her were among the first to be thrown out.[27]

The women of the Union des femmes socialistes supported the Parti ouvrier's expulsion of Auclert. Leading moderates such as Rouzade and Pierre kept up amicable relations with Auclert, but the revolutionaries such as Mink and Michel completely rejected her. The union still advocated the emancipation of women, and both Mink and Michel spoke on the subject, but this emancipation was to come through the workers' revolution, not through the reform of the bourgeois republic. Nothing spoke more eloquently of Auclert's rejection than the behavior of Louise Michel. Auclert had virtually canonized Michel during 1880

26. Ligou, *Histoire du socialisme en France*, p. 43; DMO, 10:77; Bellanger et al., *Histoire générale de la presse française*, 3:225; Sowerwine, *Sisters or Citizens*, p. 27; Bidelman, *Pariahs Stand Up!*, p. 135; *Le Figaro*, 5 January 1881.

27. DMO, 10:198–99 (Barberet); Sowerwine, *Sisters or Citizens*, pp. 27–35; Bidelman, *Pariahs Stand Up!*, p. 135; unidentified clippings in the Auclert Papers, Carton 1 (includes quoted clipping of Kéva's report to DF).

and worked hard for her return to France, although she opposed Michel's anarchism and revolutionary violence. Auclert had been at the front of the enthusiastic crowd that welcomed Michel back from exile in November 1880. After the congress of Havre, Michel delivered a speech on the woman question to the Union des femmes. Emancipation could come only with the revolution, Michel said. She attacked Auclert's ideas, especially her emphasis on political rights: parliament was a bourgeois institution not worth changing, and concentration on it was a snare that took energy from true change. Paule Mink did not go that far, but she attacked women's suffrage because it would turn the republic over to clericals and reactionaries. Mink even took the socialist anti-suffrage argument directly to a meeting of Auclert's society, and she later accepted an explicit socialist charge to rebut Auclert's ideas. Together, Michel and Mink dislodged Auclert from the Blanquist inner circle. Auclert reacted typically. At the personal level, she took this as an "attack" by "enemies." She never forgot, nor forgave, the behavior of Michel and Mink. At the political level, she rejected her rejectors, dismissing them and their insistence upon the primacy of socialism. Michel and Mink had provided another opportunity to demonstrate her independence.[28]

Might Auclert have saved the socialist alliance after November 1880? It seems unlikely. She had mercurial fires in her personality; her disputes ended in rupture, not reconciliation. Consider the quarrels of her brief career: in 1876 she abruptly ended her campaign to support a laundrywomen's cooperative; in 1877 some of the founders of Droit des femmes denounced her leadership and two resigned; in 1878 she split with Richer over women's suffrage and resigned from the organizing committee of his congress; in 1879 she denounced Gustave Fauché for betraying women, thereby alienating one of the most powerful socialists in Paris; and in 1880 she resigned in anger from both the Free Thought society and the committee to aid communards within weeks of founding them. Even in her moment of triumph at Marseilles she chastised collectivists. Can one imagine her now going before Fauché and the federation of the center as a supplicant, begging to remain in the Parti ouvrier?

There was actually no longer an alliance to be saved. From the point of view of the party, Auclert was a bourgeois reformer whose socialist

28. Police reports, 2 (2), 3, and 29 October 1880, 12 November 1880, and 7 December 1880, Dossier Mink, APP; Mink to Michel, 3 October 1880, ibid.; Paule Mink, *Communarde et féministe (1839–1901): Les Mouches et les araignées, Le Travail des femmes, et autres textes*, ed. Alain Dalotel (Paris, 1981), pp. 23–26; Thomas, *Louise Michel*, pp. 185–86, 194–96; Paule Lejeune, *Louise Michel l'indomptable* (Paris, 1978), pp. 287–88; Bidelman, *Pariahs Stand Up!*, p. 280; Dommanget, *Blanqui au début de la Troisième République*, pp. 137–39.

sympathies belonged to a repudiated faction and who subordinated her meager socialism to her feminism. Droit des femmes was a tiny organization of negligible influence, more bourgeois than proletarian, whose raison d'être was an agenda utterly different from the party's. A revolutionary elite had no need for such people. Even the more feminist members of the Parti ouvrier saw little need for such an alliance after Rouzade created her Union des femmes socialistes—Rouzade was a collectivist (albeit a moderate) without Auclert's contentiousness. What profit would there be to the party from an alliance with Droit des femmes?

From Auclert's point of view, the benefits of the socialist alliance were paltry after November 1879. What had the party done to advance the cause of women's rights, and political rights in particular, after the historic resolution at Marseilles? Auclert had contributed a year of labor for socialism—over two dozen meetings, lectures, committees, demonstrations; where were the two dozen socialist activities for women's rights? Far from offering support, the Parti ouvrier had repudiated the alliance in April 1880 by the vote of the Parisian federation; that vote may have been a truer indication of socialist attitudes than the resolution of 1879. Why should Droit des femmes follow Guesde at Havre when the Guesdists had already relegated the woman question to a secondary position, where women must wait for the prior emancipation of labor? This was precisely the socialist reasoning that Auclert had denounced at Marseilles; why ally with it now? Or with its hurtful advocates, like Fauché, Michel, and Mink, who attacked her and her ideas?

No, Hubertine Auclert did not weep and rend her garments at her socialist excommunication. She never considered humbling herself at some Guesdist Canossa. She answered instead with a typical rejection of authority; she would not accept "feudal subservience to any system." Auclert insisted on remaining independent from the dictates of others; no alliance seemed worth the loss of freedom. Indeed, *alliance* is a misnomer for the briefly perceived community of interests which both partners accepted in opportunism and for which neither partner would compromise doctrine by a jot. Predictably, when Droit des femmes discussed the Havre congress and their expulsion from the Parti ouvrier, the members agreed. The group voted "to keep its autonomy."[29]

29. Auclert, *Le Vote des femmes*, p. 105.

CHAPTER FOUR

The First French Campaign
for Women's Suffrage,
1880–1881

H ubertine Auclert's role at the Marseilles congress of 1879 established her as the most militant feminist in France. She soon
became the most notorious woman of her generation, as Louise
Michel had been before her and George Sand before Michel. Auclert was
not a flower born to blush unseen. During the next two years she
launched the first French campaign for women's suffrage. It did not
come close to winning the vote, but it established the question of the
political rights of women so thoroughly in French discourse that the
debate did not cease until women had won. It is no exaggeration to say
that Auclert achieved this through indefatigable dedication. In 1880–
1881, she led a campaign to register women to vote, stated a tax protest,
fought two court cases, pressed women into running for office, founded
a suffragist newspaper, produced dozens of speeches and articles, organized a strike against the national census, led two public demonstrations, and directed six petition campaigns—all in addition to her manifold socialist activities of 1880.

VOTER REGISTRATION AND TAX BOYCOTT, 1880–1881

Auclert's crusade began in February 1880 when she attempted to
register to vote. The republic revised electoral lists at the beginning of
each year. An announcement appeared in the *Journal officiel,* in the
press, and on placards outside the town hall (*mairie*) of every arrondisse-

ment, advising citizens that "All persons (*Toute personne*) omitted from the list can claim their inscriptions" by presenting the mayor with proofs of identity, age, and six months' residency in that arrondissement. Auclert, reasoning that the term *toute personne* included her, examined the constitutional laws of 1875, which formed the Third Republic. The language of these electoral laws, which let stand those of the Second Republic, was equally comprehensive. Auclert concluded that the terms *l'universalité des citoyens français* and *tous les Français, universel* and *imprescriptable,* used in these laws likewise included her, and so she decided to register.[1]

The members of Droit des femmes adopted Auclert's reasoning at their January 1880 meeting, and on February 2 they set out to visit the *mairies* in a dozen different arrondissements, there to do their civic duty. Those joining Auclert included Eugénie Pierre, representatives from the Travailleuses de Belleville, and several of Auclert's more daring young followers, such as Mlle LeLoup. They got no farther than Julie Daubié in September 1870. In the Tenth Arrondissement, Auclert's home, functionaries turned the matter over to the mayor. He ruled that he did not have the power (*non possumus*) to issue an electoral card to a woman; despite Auclert's constitutional citations, only the Chamber of Deputies could permit her to register. Two days later, he sent her formal notification of her rejection: "Considering that, from 1789 until today, all successive electoral laws, without any exception, have been interpreted and applied in this sense, that they have conferred and do confer rights only on men and not on women . . . we have decided that in the present state of legislation, the request of Mlle Hubertine Auclert is declared inadmissible."

Auclert immediately took her outraged constitutionalism to the court of public opinion, submitting a letter of protest to the republican press. Born of French parents, fulfilling all the duties and obligations prescribed by the law, she wrote, "we appeal to opinion [to redress] the injustice perpetuated by the republic." So long as the public jury remained deaf, "women will not cease to protest." A few days later, Auclert restated her case in a public lecture. "Are we in France or in Turkey?" she asked a republican crowd assembled by Sigismond Lacroix, the radical journalist who had founded *Le Radical, Les Droits de l'homme,* and *La République française.* She told it where her reasoning

1. Article One stated, "Sovereignty resides in the entirety of French citizens. It is inalienable and uninfringeable." Article Twenty-four stated that the suffrage was universal; Article Twenty-five defined electors as "all of the French people [*tous les Français*] twenty-one years old and enjoying their civil and political rights." See the discussion of French constitutional law in Hause with Kenney, *Women's Suffrage and Social Politics,* pp. 10–12; Auclert's ideas in "La Révision des listes électorales," *La Citoyenne,* 23 January 1882.

led: if the term *tous le Français* did not include her in electoral legislation, neither could it in tax law. This logic impressed many editors, but their response was succinctly expressed by Emile Girardin's liberal *La Liberté:* "Dura lex, sed lex" (a harsh law, but the law). Auclert announced in another lecture shortly thereafter that she was preparing to fight the ruling by legal appeals and other forms of protest.[2]

Auclert capitalized on the favorable impression that her reasoning produced by persuading the radical press (including republican journals in the provinces, such as *La Victoire* of Bordeaux) to reprint a petition to the Chamber of Deputies which she had drafted, with instructions for signing it. This petition asked simply that the term *les Français* mean the same thing in all legislation. Auclert might have judged the efficacy of the petition by noting the reaction of other women to it. Sarah Monod's *La Femme,* the organ of the largely Protestant philanthropic-reformist women's movement, which was not feminist in 1880, refused even to publish the petition. "We differ totally with her on this question," *La Femme* announced, adding that *La Femme* wished to avoid politics, that Auclert's claim was "inopportune," and that women's suffrage "would introduce vexatious discussions into families." The Chamber of Deputies was no more antisuffragist than that in declining the petition.[3]

Her letters, speeches, and petitions having changed little, Auclert turned to militant protest. Shortly after receiving the mayor's letter refusing her registration, she addressed a republican fundraising meeting. In describing her attempt to register, Auclert suggested that women should refuse to pay personal property taxes (*contribution mobilière*) until they received the right to vote.[4] That idea, and perhaps the audience's reaction to it, captured her imagination. She drafted a letter of

2. Mayor of Tenth Arrondissement to Auclert, 4 February 1880, Auclert Papers, 10/6 (first quotation); folder, "Suffrage des femmes," ibid., 12/21; manuscript on political rights, ibid., 6/311; untitled speech, ibid., 10/107; Auclert, *Le Vote des femmes,* pp. 125–26; Auclert, *Les Femmes au gouvernail,* p. 10; Auclert, "Les Femmes électeurs," *La Citoyenne,* 13 February 1881; Auclert, "Le Vote des femmes," *La Fronde,* 13 December 1897; *Le Journal des débats,* 9 February 1880; *La Liberté,* 16 February 1880, *Le XIXe siècle,* 13 March 1880; *Le Pays,* 11 February 1880 (speech quoted), *Le Courrier,* 11 February 1880; *L'Union,* 11 February 1880 (letter of protest).

3. *Le Rappel,* 30 April 1880; *La Victoire,* May 1880; *La Femme,* May 1880.

4. French tax laws of the early Third Republic provided for four chief direct taxes, which constituted about 15 percent of the national budget: a land tax, which Auclert no longer owed, having sold her property in Allier; a business tax (trades' licenses), which did not apply to her; the *contribution mobilière,* which she refused to pay; and a door-and-window tax, which fell due later. The personal property tax was a capitation tax levied on everybody who was not a pauper (that is, who paid over four hundred francs per annum in rent), at rates ranging from 1.50 francs to 4.50 francs. For Auclert's minimal property, this produced a bill of 30.85 francs.

refusal to be sent to the prefect of the Seine and took it to the March 1880 meeting of Droit des femmes. The group voted to support her, and seven other women, including Dissat and two of Auclert's older militants, Madame Bonnair and the widow Leprou, agreed to cosign the letter. Their message was blunt—if men wanted to control money, they could provide it as well:

> I leave to men, who arrogate to themselves the privileges of governing, of making the rules, of allocating the budget—I leave to men the privilege of paying the taxes that they adopt and portion out according to their pleasure.
>
> As long as I do not have the right to control the use of my money, I no longer wish to give it.
>
> I do not want to be an accomplice, through my complacency, in the vast exploitation that the masculine autocracy considers that it has the right to impose upon women. I have no rights, therefore, I have no taxes; I do not vote, I do not pay.[5]

Auclert, of course, did not send this letter to the prefect alone. She blanketed the republican press with it, receiving especial support from Vacquerie in *Le Rappel*. The government, however, did not have to wait to read the letter or the newspaper reprints of it; a police agent participating in the Droit des femmes discussions had reported on them days earlier.[6]

Having seized the initiative, Auclert did not wait quietly for the government to respond. She recruited nineteen other resisters as well as a group of women in Lyons prepared to join the tax boycott. She drafted another petition in April 1880, circulated by *Le Rappel*, calling on the Chamber of Deputies to declare that the term *Français* had a consistent legal meaning. She demanded the right to go before the council of the prefecture for the department, with an attorney, to substantiate her

5. Untitled manuscript, Auclert Papers, 10/13; police reports, 8 February 1880 and 26 March 1880, Dossier Auclert, APP; Auclert, *Le Vote des femmes*, pp. 136–38; *Le Rappel*, 8 and 11 April 1880; *L'Estafette*, 8 April 1880; *Le XIXe siècle*, 9 April 1880; *Le Mot d'ordre*, 7 April 1880. There are several drafts and paraphrases of this letter; the quotation used is from the manuscript in the Auclert Papers and is closest to the version published in *L'Estafette*.

6. I have been unable to identify which of the members of DF was the police agent. Police reports on Auclert for the period up to 1884, when the police began to use code numbers, bear nineteen different names. Five agents filed almost all reports during 1880: (M.M.?) Brissaud, Girard, Martin, Athanase, and "A.P."; the reports clearly originating in Auclert's inner circle, not in public meetings, especially the reports of 12 and 15 March 1880, were filed by "A.P." Those initials correspond to none of her known associates. It is possible that the agent was one of the women active in the feminist movement. It has been possible to identify the person who reported Auclert's plans for demonstration in 1904, and she was a member of the LFDF (see ch. 10).

argument. And she avidly worked on public opinion from April through June with a series of lectures around Paris. Her notoriety drew large crowds—six hundred to a thousand at three separate lectures—from which she collected more signatures for her petition. Over one thousand people packed the Théatre Oberkampf on June 7, 1880 (according to the estimate of the *Journal à un sou,* where Lévrier was an editor), to hear Auclert argue against taxation without political participation. She invoked the revolutionary tradition and denounced the insincerity of republicans a century after the Revolution: "You, men, you made the Revolution in order to be able to vote the taxes that you pay and to oversee their distribution; we, women, we want like you to pay only what we have voted."[7]

Auclert's argument won favorable comment, both in the lecture halls and in the press. *Le Petit Parisien* devoted the entire top half of page 1 to Auclert's protest. Even the right-wing *Le Gaulois* admitted that she had "one of those rare grievances having logic, a shadow of common sense."[8] Many republicans shared her criticism of the caution of Léon Gambetta and the opportunist cabinets of 1880–1881. Others admired the clarity of her assault upon the legal double meanings of *Français* and *citoyen,* even if they were unenthusiastic about women's suffrage. Some responded to her republican appeal to justice. Auclert recognized the opportunity that sympathetic opinion presented and pressed her analysis harder. The effect of women's having no voice in the disbursement of their taxes, she pointed out, could be seen in the national budget. One of the hottest political debates of the moment was the republicanization of the schools. In the ministry of education budget, Auclert showed the result of taxation without participation: over two-thirds of the budget went to the education of men.

The government responded to Auclert's tax boycott in July 1880. After issuing the standard requests, warnings, and threats, the mayor of the Tenth Arrondissement notified Auclert of the seizure of her personal property, which was to be sold to pay her bill of 30.85 francs. A bailiff was dispatched to put seals on the furnishings of her apartment, which were left in her care. Auclert sat down at the government's table, formerly hers, and described the seizure for the press. "I who am nothing," she wrote, "I declare that in this struggle of all against one, I am not capitulating."[9]

7. Manuscript on the tax case, Auclert Papers, 10/15; file on the tax case, ibid., 12/31; Auclert, *Le Vote des femmes,* pp. 136–43; police reports, 16 May 1880 (2), 7 and 8 June 1880, Dossier Auclert, APP; *Le Temps,* 13 April 1880; *Le Pays,* 20 May 1880; *Le Rappel,* 11 April 1880; *Le Journal à un sou,* 8 June 1880 (quoted).

8. *Le Petit Parisien,* 27 July 1880; *Le Gaulois,* 11 August 1880.

9. Auclert, *Les Femmes au gouvernail,* pp. 10–11; *Le Figaro,* 25 July 1880; *Le Rappel,* 26 July 1880 (quoted).

The Council of the Prefecture of the Seine heard Auclert's case in August 1880. Auclert chose to be represented by Lévrier, now licensed to practice law, who was aided in preparing the brief by another of her strong supporters in Droit des femmes, Léon Giraud, also a lawyer. The proceedings followed a predictable, legalistic course. The councillors asked Auclert why she refused to pay. She answered by linking taxation with the right to vote. The councillors responded that the issue was the law, not rights. And the law was precise: Article Twelve of the Personal Property Tax Law of 1832 stated that "every inhabitant of both sexes, whether French or foreign, even financially independent minors," except for the indigent, owed the *contribution mobilière*. A foreigner or a child who wished to vote before paying the tax would be told the same thing. If Auclert wished to discuss rights and legislation, she must address herself to the Chamber of Deputies. So clear did the law seem that the council rejected Auclert's appeal without further deliberation. Shortly thereafter, Bonnair and Leprou lost in similar cases.[10]

The French legal system includes a separate jurisdiction for administrative justice in which individuals may press claims concerning the services of the state. After appealing to her mayor and to the council of the prefecture, Auclert had almost reached the pinnacle of this jurisdiction. The Third Republic had reestablished the Council of State (*Conseil d'état*) as the final appellate court in administrative matters. Auclert filed an appeal with the Council of State in September 1880. The simple act of filing that appeal produced the most infuriating moment of her tax rebellion and a vivid illustration of how inferior French women were before the law. Women, as minors, were excluded from being witnesses. This provision had a frustrating effect on the daily lives of women as well as important implications for courtroom testimony. Women could not cosign as witnesses the myriad documents that intruded into daily life: birth and death records, marriage registries, business contracts, and public documents requiring witnesses to identify an applicant.

Auclert encountered this aspect of her subjection when she sought to file her appeal with Council of State. She went to the correct office, presented the appropriate documents, and provided the required identification. That was insufficient, of course. A functionary explained that she must bring two witnesses to identify her, and both must be men. Auclert answered that she knew several women, but no men, who

10. Conseil de préfecture de la Seine to Auclert, 6 August 1880, Auclert Papers, 10/12; manuscript of Auclert's speech to the council, ibid., 10/22; police reports, 11 August 1880 (2), Dossier Auclert, APP; Auclert, *Le Vote des femmes*, pp. 144–47; *Le Rappel*, 13 August 1880; *Le Soleil*, 12 August 1880; *Le Mot d'ordre*, 10 and 13 August 1880; *La France*, 12 August 1880; *Le XIXe siècle*, 13 August 1880; *Le Journal à un sou*, 13 August 1880.

lived in that quarter. Her documents were returned to her unfiled and the next applicant summoned. It was a moment of modern life recognized by all who have encountered bureaucracies. French law simply redoubled the frustration for women. Auclert swallowed her rage and the indigestible irony of the rejection, and she searched for strangers who would identify her. She asked a policeman at the *mairie;* the law forbade him to witness. She stopped passersby on the street and offered to pay them for witnessing a document. They cheerfully asked details about the birth of the child; being told that the document was an administrative appeal, they hastened to escape involvement. For an hour she stopped pedestrians to ask for help; they evaded her, made crude remarks, insulted her. At length she found two unemployed day laborers happy to be paid to identify an unknown woman. When the irritating chore was completed, Auclert publicized the episode in another letter to the press: "So I lost a lot of time, submitted to insults, spent my money—all in order to satisfy the hypocrisy of the law which prefers the lying testimony of the unknown, of passersby who have never seen one—given that they be men—to the valid testimony of women who know one."[11]

While awaiting the action of the Council of State, Auclert kept her tax protest before the public with lectures and letters to the press. Her arguments did not change: neither a true republic nor universal suffrage existed. Insincere republicans in the Chamber of Deputies ("our lords and masters") appropriated the wealth of women without consulting them, keeping the largest share for the use of men and leaving to women's interests only an "indispensable and completely insufficient" amount. Denied their rights, women still had the right to say no.[12]

Auclert's publicity campaign attracted the support of Clovis Hugues, a young politician who was to provide some of her most valuable backing in the 1880s. Hugues was a seminarian turned poet. He had participated in the commune of Marseilles as an eighteen-year-old socialist journalist, for which he was imprisoned until 1875. In 1878 he became a councillor of the Bouches-du-Rhône; in 1879 he met Auclert at the congress of Marseilles and applauded her militant feminism; in 1880 he began a career in Parisian journalism, editing *Le Mot d'ordre,* where he gave Auclert's tax case good coverage. Shortly thereafter the voters of Marseilles sent Hugues to the Chamber of Deputies, where he sat on the extreme left and spoke as one of the few strong feminists in

11. Auclert to Vacquerie, *Le Rappel,* 30 September 1880. See also Auclert, "Les Monopoleurs du témoignage," *La Citoyenne,* 12 March 1882.

12. Police report, 17 October 1880, Dossier Auclert, APP; *Le Mot d'ordre,* 19 October 1880; *La Vérité,* October 1880.

that body. Hugues joined Droit des femmes the same year and gave the group occasional financial support; Auclert, in turn, frequently asked him to preside at meetings. During Auclert's fall 1880 lecture series, Hugues responded in the Chamber of Deputies with a strong defense of her and of the emancipation of women.[13]

Publicity and support notwithstanding, Auclert's hearing before the Council of State proved unsuccessful. She rebutted the arguments of the Council of the Prefecture, still talking of logic, of justice, and of rights. She argued, for example, that the exclusion of male minors and foreigners from political rights was not analogous to the disenfranchisement of women because their condition was temporary—boys would become men, foreigners could return to the land of which they were citizens. Neither time nor travel brought rights to women. The Council of State took six months to hand down a decree in Auclert's case. It ruled against her in March 1881, adding nothing to the interpretation of the tax law of 1832. In April 1881, the prefecture of the Seine notified Auclert that she had lost all appeals and must pay or see her possessions sold. Auclert raged against the slowness of French justice, dreamt of a national tax boycott, and dispatched another petition to the Chamber of Deputies. But she paid, saying that she did not concede, she merely yielded to the power of the state.[14]

What did Hubertine Auclert achieve with her tax protest of 1880–1881? She made women's suffrage a national issue for all who were politically engaged. For over a year, the press constantly treated the subject. Even the police reports on Auclert agreed that she produced an immense reaction. Whether the press found her courageous or ridiculous, brilliant or naive, they wrote about her and her ideas. Not only small left-wing newspapers like Lévrier's *Journal à un sou*, Hugues' *Mot d'ordre*, or even Vacquerie's *Le Rappel* followed the case; *Le Petit Parisien*, now one of the most widely circulated newspapers in Paris, devoted great attention to her. Richer and Deraismes never did that for French feminism, much less for the issue of women's suffrage. Auclert also won support from the famous. She took especial pride in the encouragement of Alexandre Dumas, who wrote several articles about her and lauded her tax rebellion in *Les Femmes qui tuent et les femmes qui votent* (1880). More important, Auclert won women to feminism. Jeanne Oddo-Deflou, a leading turn-of-the-century French

13. Ibid.; *DdPF*, 3:370–71.

14. Manuscript of Auclert's appeal to the Conseil d'état, Auclert Papers, 10/25; decree of the Conseil d'état, 31 March 1881, ibid., 10/7; Prefecture of the Seine to Auclert, 8 June 1881, ibid., 10/10; Auclert, *Le Vote des femmes*, pp. 148–57; Auclert, "Que fait le Conseil d'état," *La Citoyenne*, 22 May 1881; *Le Rappel*, 20 June 1881; Auclert, "L'Arrêt du Conseil d'état," *La Citoyenne*, 19 June 1881.

feminist, recalled her conversion to feminism: it happened the day that her father read her a newspaper account of Auclert's tax protest. "I had found my road to Damascus," Oddo-Deflou wrote; "who will count them, the conversions determined by that energetic act? Who knows how many uncertain vocations this new courage determined?"[15]

THE DEMONSTRATIONS OF 1880–1881

Given the list of Auclert's socialist activities during 1880 and her energetic tax protest of 1880–1881, one may wonder how she had the time and energy for other feminist activities. Auclert was young (thirty-two in 1880) and buoyed by faith in her secular religion; the feminist cause virtually became her life. No other concern intruded into her tightly regulated existence. One searches in vain through the cartons of her personal papers, the reams of her writings, and the pages of her intimate diary for traces of leisure activities or nonpolitical interests. The rich cultural life of Paris, its art, music, and theatre, does not appear. Nor does the relaxed pace of café afternoons, nor the so-ciability of the drawing room, nor the lure of elegant restaurants, nor the appeal of railway excursions. No hobby or avocation diverted her, no interest in the accumulation of possessions, no musical instru-ment; not even a domestic pet appears to distract her from the hours of reading and writing. Doubtless, some extraneous interests were part of Hubertine Auclert's diurnal routine, but none left its imprint on the thousands of pages of evidence about her life. Whatever her small and private joys, leisure and entertainment clearly had no significant place in her regimen. While her optimism and energy remained high, Auclert did not look into the face of her loneliness.[16]

An indication of Auclert's dedication can be seen in her private

15. Police report, 17 April 1880, Dossier Auclert, APP; *Le Petit Parisien,* 27 July 1880; Alexandre Dumas *fils, Les Femmes qui tuent et les femmes qui votent* (Paris, 1880), esp. pp. 180–81, 187–89; Jeanne Deflou, "Instantané: Madame Hubertine Auclert," *L'Entente,* December 1905.

16. Auclert on one occasion substituted for the cultural columnist of *La Citoyenne* and reviewed a concert under one of her pseudonyms ("Jeanne Voitout"), but even this may have been an act of duty to complete the paper (see *La Citoyenne,* May 1883). Her writings mentioned rail travel on several occasions, although it was virtually always for some feminist purpose; in one case she noted with apparent surprise how pleasant first-class coaches could be (diary, 11 August 1883, Auclert Papers). When Levrier later left Paris, Auclert went to meet him a few times; she marveled at how much fun a vacation could be (ibid.). At some unknown date, her sister Marie moved to Paris and became her closest friend, but no trace of their activities survives. When Auclert later moved to Algeria, she had a pet which she adored, but this came at a time when feminism consumed much less of her time (see ch. 7).

relations with other people. She had virtually no intimate friends and limited contact with her family. By her own testimony, she drew close to only two people during fifteen years in Paris (1873–1888), Antonin Lévrier and her younger sister, Marie Chaumont. In 1880, Marie and her pharmacist husband, Lucien, had not yet arrived in Paris. The other Auclert children were scattered around France and took no direct interest in their famous sister's political activity. None of them contributed a sou to financing Droit des femmes, none appear in any of Auclert's attendance or membership rosters, none cosigned her manifestos or petitions. Until the Chaumonts arrived in Paris, Auclert's family's only appearance in her papers was in the business record of Théophile's payments for the land that she had inherited.

The absence of family and close friendships from Auclert's life increases the importance of understanding her relationship with Lévrier. By 1880–1881, their constant companionship had convinced most observers that they were lovers. That possibility certainly exists, but it is more probable that their intimacy remained platonic, and that Auclert was a virgin when she married several years later. Hints of this survive in both her public and private writings. She felt the power of love ("Love transforms even the freest woman") and of sexuality ("No revolution will hinder sexual attraction at all"), but in her diary she bemoaned the absence of such love in her life. In public, Auclert stoutly defended traditional conceptions of virtue. She demanded the end of the sexual double standard, of course, championing "one single and same morality" for men and women. But she hastened to add that she did not wish women to follow masculine licentiousness. Auclert reasoned from feminism more than from prudery: "For some women who would benefit from the dissolution of morality, the greater number would suffer from it." Her analysis of the socioeconomic position of women concluded that sexual emancipation would leave many women alone with children that they could not support. Auclert feared that many such women would be driven to prostitution as their only economic recourse (there were approximately twenty thousand prostitutes in Paris in the late nineteenth century). Hence, sexual emancipation held unacceptable consequences, and feminists must oppose it. Considering the tenacity with which Auclert defended her principles, her lifelong sense of ascetic sacrifice for the cause, her admiration of clerical chastity, her burning desire for consistency in her life, and her comments in her diary, Auclert and Lévrier probably did not become lovers.[17]

17. *Pensées*, Auclert Papers, 13/123, 13/134 (first quotation), and 13/126 (second quotation); notes, ibid., 13/65 and the same text in Auclert, *Les Femmes au gouvernail*, pp. 55 (quoted).

Lévrier responded to this situation by proposing marriage to Auclert, first sometime in 1880–1881, then "several times" in the early 1880s. Auclert declined. She loved Lévrier, but he was summer to her heart, not the four seasons. It was feminism that filled her calendar. She wanted Lévrier to accompany her in the great battle. For several years he accepted this arrangement, but he continued to press his affections on her. After Lévrier's death, Auclert recalled that "Monsieur Lévrier solicited my hand several times. I refused, not out of antipathy, but because I wanted to devote myself entirely to my work."[18]

Auclert publicly revealed her feelings about marriage by her feminist demonstrations during the spring of 1880. Civil weddings at the *mairies* of Paris occurred on Saturdays, and Auclert attended them to protest against the conditions of marriage as defined in Article 213 of the Civil Code. She spent her Saturday afternoons during March and April 1880 visiting randomly chosen civil weddings; after the completion of the ceremony and the departure of the officiating magistrate, Auclert stood up and denounced the subservience of women within marriage. This idea had occurred to her during a brief membership in a free thought society, where several discussions focused on the residual influence of the Catholic church upon secular life.

Auclert's wedding-day protests appeared exceptionally militant in the context of French feminism in 1880. The members of Amélioration, for example, deplored any action taken in public. To them, Auclert seemed dangerously aggressive, thoroughly undignified, and wantonly undisciplined. Even the free thought society disavowed her. Such criticism did not daunt Auclert, however. She grabbed her copy of "this hideous code" and went to weddings to rebut the magristrate's words. She read "to the young woman the litany of the numerous duties upon which her free will foundered." After the text came the sermon: "No Madame! You do not owe *obedience* and *submission* to your husband. . . . You are his equal in everything. . . . Live at his side and not in his shadow . . . lift up your head . . . be his friend, his wife, his companion, and not his slave, his servant."[19]

These *salle de mariage* demonstrations provoked shock and anger. The press considered them ill-mannered harangues. The free thought society was so furious that it declared that only men could speak for it. Police witnesses reported that Auclert seemed "struck by madness or hysteria"—a common late nineteenth-century diagnosis of vigorous action by women. The government simply forbade such outbursts. The

18. Auclert's recollections in *La Libre parole*, 2 June 1894.

19. *La Libre parole*, 2 June 1894 (quoted; italics in original); Auclert, *Le Vote des femmes*, p. 59; *La Liberté*, 3 May 1880; police report, 6 April 1880, Dossier Auclert, APP; Auclert to Lepelletier, 6 September 1882, Auclert Papers, 2/4.

prefect of the Seine sent a circular to the mayors of every arrondissement in late April, stating that respect for the law and the dignity of the
ceremony demanded the prohibition of "such intolerable acts." He
lumped Auclert together with priests who periodically attended civil
marriages and sought to give religious blessings to the newly wed, and
he excluded all uninvited guests from the civil ceremony. Auclert had
made her point and did not test the ruling. Of course, she submitted a
letter of protest to the press. She explained that she never interrupted
marriage ceremonies and always spoke respectfully to the couple; she
asserted that the prefect had no right to restrict the use of the *mairie,*
"the common home," which belonged to the people.[20]

Auclert believed in seizing every such opportunity to educate the
nation about the condition of women. Her mind drew connections from
both the small and large events of daily existence to the lives of women;
her personality gave her the will to act, to teach others about those
connections. "One must act," she jotted down among her *pensées,* "as if
one can do everything."[21] Hence, adverse comments on her marriage
demonstrations did not deter her from other public protests.

Her next step was into the streets. The majority of the French feminists deemed this unacceptable, and public opinion labeled it unseemly.
Respectable women did not march in the streets. The government of the
republic did not react kindly when they did. Owing to the narrow
margin by which the Third Republic had been established in the 1870s
and to the unequivocal antirepublicanism of monarchists, Bonapartists,
socialists, and anarchists, public protest was strictly regulated. A riot
act (*Loi sur les attroupements*) dating from June 1848 remained in force,
complemented by a law of December 1875 intended to repress public
attacks on the constitution or the "rights and powers of the government." This legislation seemed inadequate to republicans, so they
added a law in June 1881 forbidding meetings in the streets. Even this
did not make the majority in the Chamber of Deputies feel that the
republic was secure; throughout the early 1880s a committee of the
chamber considered further regulation of dissent. In the words of the
reporter for that committee, "if our democracy has the passion for
liberty, she has a reflective love of order."[22]

Facing such combined opposition to feminist demonstrations in the
streets, Auclert eagerly seized the opportunity for a lawful protest

20. Auclert, *Le Vote des femmes,* pp. 60–62; police report, 29 April 1880, Dossier
Auclert, APP; *Le Temps,* 28 April 1880; Prefect to mayors of Paris, 21 April 1880, printed in
La Citoyenne, 9 January 1882; Auclert to prefect, published in *Le Rappel,* 3 May 1880.

21. *Pensée,* Auclert Papers, 8/145.

22. See the ministry of justice files, AN, especially BB[30] 1457/dossier 1, Manifestations
sur la voie publique. The quotation is from Alcide Dusolier's report of 5 November 1883,
also found in *JO,* Chambre des députés, documents, 5 November 1883, no. 2327.

march in July 1881. The government had announced plans for the first official celebration of Bastille Day as a national holiday with a parade to the place where the prison had stood. Auclert decided that Droit des femmes would also march to the Place de la Bastille. They would go to "assault one of the modern Bastilles—prejudice" (see illustration 3). They would go to mourn what "masculine tyrants" had done to reward the women who fought in the revolution with them—"replace a fortress of stone . . . [with] a fortress of injustice: the Code."

On the morning of the *fête nationale,* three dozen members of Droit des femmes assembled at Auclert's apartment on the rue Cail, near the Gare du Nord. They draped the society's blue banner, proclaiming women's rights, with black crepe to signify their grief: the republican revolution had betrayed its principles with the subjection of women. Then they marched in a column to the arterial ring of boulevards and thence to the Place de la Bastille. There, Auclert and Laura Marcel hoisted the banner and attached it to the monument. Auclert read a speech on the emancipation of women. The entire demonstration attracted both applause and criticism, not least from moderate feminists who deplored Auclert's activism. Auclert answered that women dared not entrust their rights to those who "were paralyzed by the fear of ridicule."[23]

Another of Auclert's protests in 1881 underscores her ability to seize every opportunity to publicize the feminist cause. The government conducted a census in the first and sixth years of each decade. Auclert proposed another boycott: as women counted for nothing, they should not be counted. Recent electoral reforms had established multimember constituencies (*scrutin de liste*) in which the number of deputies in a district were determined by its population. An effective census boycott would thus reduce the size of the Chamber of Deputies and thereby the number of men feeding at the trough of women's taxes. The system employed to count the population required residents at every address to fill out census reports. Auclert urged people to return the forms with only male names; women who lived without men should record a zero under the count for their address.

Few people participated in the census boycott. Bonnair and Leprou again joined Auclert, as did Libussa Slavenko, a financial backer of Auclert's activities, and Maria Martin, an English-born feminist who became one of the leaders of French feminism. A total of thirty members

23. Speech, "Le 14 juillet et les femmes," Auclert Papers, 6/1; manuscript, "Les manifestations féministes," ibid., 6/124 (first quotation); police report, 14 July 1881, Dossier Auclert, APP; Auclert, "La Bastille des femmes," *La Citoyenne,* 10 July 1881; Auclert, "La Manifestation de la Société le DF," ibid., 17 July 1881; Auclert, "DF," ibid., 26 June 1881; Auclert, *Le Vote des femmes,* p. 106 (second quotation).

of Droit des femmes joined the boycott. It had no significant impact on the census, and Auclert probably never expected otherwise. Even the government ignored the action. But Auclert's connection of women's rights and current events earned her more press attention. Once again, Paris read and discussed an appeal to the women of France, penned in Auclert's vigorous style: "Women of France, let us have the energy and the dignity to rise up proud beneath the scissors that shear us. Horses and cattle passively let themselves be counted by the proprietors who calculate their fortune; but women cannot debase themselves to the level of animals, to let themselves be counted in order that men may compute, according to their number, masculine honorific and pecuniary advantages. . . . Resist the census."[24]

THE ELECTIONS OF 1881

Auclert's suffrage campaign of 1880–1881 coincided with two general elections in Paris, a parliamentary renewal during August 1881 and elections to the Municipal Council of Paris in December 1881. As early as April 1880, at the beginning of her tax boycott, Auclert had considered presenting herself as an illegal candidate at the elections in which she had been denied the right to vote. The first woman to stand for office, Jeanne Deroin, had sought election to the Second Republic's Legislative Assembly in 1849, after failing to persuade George Sand to run, and was sent to prison for plotting against the state. Had elections been scheduled for 1880, Auclert might have followed Deroin's lead. Neither her writings nor her private papers fully explain why she did not run in 1881. Auclert took part in both elections that year, and she urged other women to be candidates. In later elections, especially in 1885, she expressly refused to run, wishing to avoid the accusation that her campaign for political rights constituted self-aggrandizement; she would have been delighted to secure the election of another woman first.

Droit des femmes opened the electoral campaign of 1881 with a second effort to register women to vote. Auclert and a dozen followers, including the secretary of Droit des femmes, Louise Lasserre, sought to register in February 1881. Their rejection was the utterly predictable outcome of an action taken for its propaganda value; they did not press the matter, and Auclert was not discouraged. Quite the opposite. While she attempted to register, five women received votes as candidates for local councils in the provincial elections of February 1881. A landed proprietress in the village of Vornay, near Bourges, in Cher, actually won

24. Auclert, "Les Femmes et recensement," *La Citoyenne,* 12, 19, and 26 December 1881.

election, immediately nullified, to her municipal council. In the small town of Thorey (today Thorey-Lyautey) in eastern France, a few kilometers south of Nancy in Meurthe-et-Moselle, three women each received a few votes. Further north, in the town of Grandpré, halfway between Reims and Verdun, a local businesswoman, Madame Jules Lefebvre, also received several votes for the municipal council. Auclert interpreted this as an indication of progress, and she claimed credit for producing it.[25]

These small successes moved Auclert to consider a woman's candidacy for the upcoming parliamentary elections in Paris. She concluded that the strongest candidate would be Maria Deraismes, who was famous, thoroughly respectable, an outstanding orator, wealthy enough to finance a campaign, and the senior stateswoman of the feminist movement. The masculine political establishment also regarded her highly. Indeed, during March 1881, Deraismes hosted strategy meetings of sixty prominent radical republicans to plan a republican victory in August. Auclert had not forgotten Deraismes' letter, written after the confrontation at Richer's congress in 1878, claiming that she supported Auclert's position. In May 1881, Auclert sought to manipulate Deraismes into running. Deraismes played a leading role in an anticlerical congress held in Paris that month, where she persuaded delegates to adopt a resolution endorsing women's rights. Immediately afterward, Auclert's lieutenant of the moment, Louise Lasserre, published an article on the congress criticizing Deraismes for not fighting for the rights she espoused. Auclert gave Deraismes a few days to absorb this rebuke, then invited her to accept the honor of representing the women of France as a candidate in the parliamentary elections. Deraismes declined, citing the danger to the republic from enfranchising women controlled by the clergy.[26]

The republican press lauded Deraismes for having "spoken the language of reason and of patriotism" and chided Auclert for being "seduced by the mirages of a too-ardent imagination." Auclert rarely let such matters pass in silence. Droit des femmes adopted a resolution at its June 1881 meeting, regretting Deraismes' decision and criticizing her reasoning. A letter from the society detailing this action immediately went to the radical press. Deraismes responded with letters to Auclert and to the same newspapers. She reproached Auclert for lacking the political sense to link women's rights to the progress of the republic.

25. Manuscript on women candidates, Auclert Papers, 6/109; Auclert, *Le Vote des femmes*, pp. 16–17; *La Citoyenne*, 20 February 1881 and 17 April 1881. Louise Lasserre was the pseudonym of Mlle Drouin.

26. Police report, 29 March 1881, Dosier Deraismes, APP; Deraismes, *Ce que veulent les femmes*, p. 29.

Auclert hindered the republic and her own cause with her embarrassing "sterile agitations." Deraismes bluntly told Auclert that her actions retarded rather than hastened the day of victory. In her letter to the press, Deraismes rejected Auclert's plan more gently, stating "I am too much a republican, too much a patriot, to add to the difficulties."[27]

After this contretemps, Auclert dropped the idea of a woman's candidacy and sought other ways to profit from the elections. Her first step involved polling the 526 members of the Chamber of Deputies, of whom 318 were republicans and 208 conservatives, to identify those incumbents willing to endorse women's suffrage. Only two deputies, Alfred Talandier (Seine) and Joseph de Gasté (Finistère), gave her their written support. Talandier was a republican lawyer; proscribed after the Bonapartist coup of 1851, he had taught English at the Lycée Henri IV until he became a socialist-radical deputy in 1876. He supported Auclert in the early 1880s, until ill health forced his retirement from politics. De Gasté was an engineer, the son of wealthy landed proprietors in the Orne, who had undertaken several unsuccessful electoral campaigns as an opponent of the Second Empire before entering the chamber as a center-leftist in 1876. Throughout the 1880s he was by far Auclert's greatest financial backer and one of the very few deputies who would actually speak in favor of women's suffrage on the floor of the chamber. Other deputies gave Auclert mixed indications of support in 1881; her highest estimate claimed that 1 percent of parliament agreed with her.[28]

Auclert had slightly more success obtaining professions of support from candidates for the Chamber of Deputies in 1881. Eight major candidates, in addition to the incumbents, endorsed some form of women's suffrage: Clovis Hugues (socialist, Bouches-du-Rhône), Tony Révillon (radical, Seine), Camille Pelletan (radical, Bouches-du-Rhône), Severiano de Hérédia (republican, Seine), Jean de Lanessan (radical, Seine), Emile Digeon (socialist, Aude), Ferdinand Gambon (democratic socialist, Nièvre), and Henry Maret (radical, Seine). Hugues, Maret (who later founded and directed the influential *Le Radical*), and Révillon all supported Auclert in Parisian radical journalism. Several candidates knew and respected Auclert from her work defending the communards: Digeon had been the leader of the Commune of Narbonne, Gambon the representative on the Paris Commune from Auclert's Tenth Arrondissement, and Hugues a communard at Marseilles. De Hérédia, who had

27. Deraismes to Auclert, June 1881, and Deraismes to *Le Rappel*, in Deraismes, *Ce que veulent les femmes*, pp. 125–29; clipping from *Le Progrès* in Auclert Papers, Carton 1 (first quotation); *Le Rappel*, 9 June 1881 (second quotation); *La Citoyenne*, 12 June 1881; *Le Mot d'ordre*, 15 June 1881; Bidelman, *Pariahs Stand Up!*, pp. 130–31.

28. *DdPF*, 3:127–28, 5:355; *Le Mot d'ordre*, 15 June 1881; Auclert, "Réponse d'un député," *La Citoyenne*, 12 June 1881; ibid., 19 June 1881 and 3 July 1881.

served on Richer's commission for the congress of 1878, de Lanessan, Maret, and Révillon were friends of Lévrier from the time of his membership in a group of Parisian municipal politicians called *l'autonomie communale*. Lévrier was also a member of Pelletan's electoral committee in his race in the Tenth Arrondissement.[29]

Auclert's efforts during the elections of 1881 did not end there. After seeking to vote herself, to persuade Deraismes to run, to identify suffragists in the chamber, and to win commitments from candidates, she tried to help defeat antifeminists in the chamber. She had harsh words for almost every deputy in the legislature of 1877–1881, including such friends of Richer as Naquet and Simon, both of whom she deemed too tepid in their support. She was especially hostile to Gambetta ("the Jupiter of the Palais Bourbon") and to moderate-opportunist republicans, whom she considered insufficiently republican. Auclert focused her efforts to defeat antifeminists on Henri Brisson, a radical who represented her own district in the Tenth Arrondissement. She blamed Brisson for the defeat of divorce legislation during the previous legislature. Where, she wrote, was the candidate to stand up to "the pale imitator of Robespierre" who had condemned French women "to the perpetual prison of marriage?"[30]

The search for a candidate to defeat Brisson caused Auclert and Droit des femmes major problems. Two male members of Droit des femmes, Lévrier and Célestin Epailly, both wanted to run. Epailly would not back down, so Lévrier did. After an acrimonious feud, which was continued in the press, of course, the members of Droit des femmes voted overwhelmingly to expel Epailly and his strongest supporter, Louise Lasserre, and to elect Lévrier to replace Lasserre as the society's secretary. Auclert and Lévrier then found themselves named in three separate lawsuits, including one for defamation of character (Lévrier had called Epailly a pimp) and another to recover contributions totaling ten francs made to Droit des femmes. Other members of Droit des femmes also were sued for their statements at Droit des femmes meetings or in the press. Long before the melee was resolved in the courts, Brisson had garnered 88 percent of the votes cast.[31]

The elections of August 1881 produced a landslide victory for republicans, who took 445 of 541 seats. Despite the easy victory of Brisson, Auclert had reason to be pleased with the balloting; three of her four supporters in the previous legislature were reelected (de Gasté was

29. *DdPF*, 3:100–101, 3:312–13, 3:370–71, 3:574, 4:265–66, 4:573–74, 5:125; *DMO*, 12:54–55; *La Citoyenne*, 7, 14, and 28 August 1881.

30. Auclert, "L'Education des souverains" (first quotation) and "Les Elections prochaines," *La Citoyenne*, 7 August 1881; ibid., 28 August 1881 (other quotations).

31. *La Citoyenne*, 10 and 31 October 1881; Bidelman, *Pariahs Stand Up!*, p. 128.

beaten and remained out of office until 1889), and six of the eight candidates who endorsed women's suffrage—all save Digeon and Gambon—won seats (Gambon entered the chamber in a by-election a few months later). At 2 percent of the deputation, Auclert's backers were scarcely a formidable bloc, and some of them soon moderated their views. Nonetheless, she had put women's suffrage on some programs and in the press while doubling the number of her friends in parliament, where their support was worth more than their numbers suggest for the purposes of depositing her petitions and rebutting her foes. Auclert was far from satisfied, however. Her essay on the new chamber put her feelings succinctly: "Ah! Republic! you will perish from your injustice towards women."[32]

Municipal elections followed the legislative elections in December 1881. Again Auclert chose not to run. Instead—doubtless still angry over the race against Brisson—she encouraged Lévrier to stand. He entered the race in the Sixth Arrondissement and won the endorsements of the influential *l'autonomie communale* group (which included the backing of many sitting municipal councillors) and the committee of radical republicans in that quartier (thanks to the support of two new radical deputies, Revillon and de Lanessan). Many republicans, both in office and in the press, were aghast at his candidacy. Many opportunists, who blamed him for attacks upon Gambetta, and not a few radicals worked hard for his defeat. As one radical newspaper put it, "Anyone rather than Lévrier." The sole issue of the campaign was apparently his ardent feminism, which the opportunists made the subject of numerous posters, suggesting that women would soon be in the municipal council and Auclert would have great influence there. Lévrier himself stressed his feminism; Auclert wrote soon after his defeat, "He is a man of integrity [*un pur*] who has always sacrificed his interests to his beliefs."[33] Auclert did not yet realize it, but Lévrier's defeat portended difficulties for their relationship. Lévrier expected to establish a career of his own, and he would not spend his life as Auclert's factotum. Thwarted in his attempt to establish a political career, Lévrier faced difficult choices of employment. His best prospect, in the French judiciary, was likely to take him from Paris. Difficult moments for the platonic couple lay ahead.

The electoral period did not end without another small feminist victory. Léonie Rouzade stood for the municipal council in the Twelfth Arrondissement as the official candidate of the Parti ouvrier français,

32. Auclert, "La Nouvelle chambre," *La Citoyenne*, 7 November 1881.

33. Lévrier, "L'Election du VIe arrondissement," *La Citoyenne*, 28 November 1881; ibid., 5, 12, and 19 (quoted) December 1881; manuscript on municipal elections, Auclert Papers, 7/20; note, Auclert Papers, 14/45.

despite the opposition of Guesdists who considered her race "an encumbrance"—an argument that contributed to the Guesdist-Broussist split at the socialist congress of 1882. Rouzade, with the best wishes of Auclert, continued her race nonetheless and won fifty-seven votes. The socialist rupture notwithstanding, this was more votes than the previous socialist candidate had won in that constituency. It was a happy conclusion to Auclert's two years of tireless efforts to begin a women's suffrage campaign in France. She could with justification reflect in January 1882 that she had achieved "a real step along the route of our emancipation."[34]

34. *La Citoyenne,* 12 and 19 December 1881, 2 January 1881 (Auclert quotation); Stafford, *From Anarchism to Reformism,* p. 324; Boxer, "Socialism Faces Feminism," pp. 79–80 (Guesde quotation).

CHAPTER FIVE

The Effort to Construct
a National Suffrage Movement,
1880–1885

Neither Hubertine Auclert herself nor any other French feminist ever matched Auclert's prodigious work for women's suffrage in 1880–1881. For all her efforts, however, the results seemed few in number. Droit des femmes grew no larger, although it certainly became better known in Parisian politics. Most feminists and most republicans, as well as the government, refused to support the enfranchisement of women. Auclert could take pride in the theoretical support of socialists, the existence of women candidates, the demonstrations she had staged, and the backing of ten deputies. This left her a long way from the ballot box.

Auclert's campaign of 1880–1881 must nonetheless be considered a success. Almost alone, she brought the political rights of French women into political discourse. She articulated and forced the political subculture to consider an idea that had no other advocates. When political history is examined over the *longue durée*, Auclert's accomplishment assumes a larger importance than many of the ephemeral parliamentary battles by which contemporaries defined political success. In this perspective, it is less important that relatively few converts came to suffragism in 1881 than that Auclert's idea, though opposed, could not be dismissed. The campaign for women's suffrage waned and waxed in the sixty-four years before women finally voted in 1945, three decades after Auclert's death. But she had achieved the essential first step by forcing discussion of that right, opening a debate that would not cease.

This was the accomplishment of Auclert's life, one she reinforced for thirty years as a publicist, an agitator, a propagandist. Auclert's skills were, however, better suited to the opening of a debate than its resolution. The next stage—constructing a political movement that attracted thousands of converts, forging instruments for reshaping national opinion, and winning the support of a parliamentary majority—required different abilities, different personalities. Auclert certainly tried to build a national movement in France, but administration and diplomacy were not her forte. She founded a weekly newspaper (*La Citoyenne*) to spread her ideas, made Droit des femmes a national organization, and pressed the Palais Bourbon in every way she could imagine. But she never found the route to mass appeal. She did not yet realize it, but her career reached its perihelion in the early 1880s, taking her as close to the sun of public attention as she would ever go. When that discouraging thought began to enter her mind, a painful personal crisis awaited her.

LA CITOYENNE

Auclert made her greatest effort to expand the suffrage movement by creating her own weekly newspaper. *La Citoyenne* first appeared in February 1881 and survived as a monthly until 1891. This was no small accomplishment, despite the apparent ease of publication suggested by the existence of over one hundred daily and weekly newspapers in Paris in 1880. Since the promulgation of the constitutional charter of 1815, every French citizen (*tout citoyen*) had had the legal right to publish his or her opinions in this way, but a variety of authoritarian legislation restricted this freedom. In Auclert's case, the foremost legal obstacle was a familiar one: the law held, until the press law of July 1881, that a woman was not a citizen in this sense. Auclert could not be the proprietor of her newspaper. When she decided in 1880 to publish a feminist newspaper, Lévrier had to accept official responsibility. Auclert financed *La Citoyenne* by redeeming some of the bonds upon whose income she lived. In the leader for the first issue, she denounced "the absurd law" regulating the press.[1]

1. Police reports, 5 and 30 January 1881, Dossier Auclert, APP; Dossier *La Citoyenne*, in Dossiers de la presse parisienne, 1820–1894, Ministry of the Interior files, F18 326/75, AN. For the constitutional treatment of freedom of the press, see the Constitutional Charter of 1815, Article 64 (quoted) and the Constitution of 1848, Article 8. For press legislation and its application, see Irene Collins, *The Government and the Newspaper Press in France, 1814–1881* (Oxford, 1959). "La Citoyenne," a translation of Auclert's first leader, is included in Erna O. Hellerstein, Leslie P. Hume, and Karen M. Offen, eds., *Victorian Women: A Documentary Account of Women's Lives in Nineteenth-Century England, France, and the United States* (Stanford, 1981), pp. 445–46. For *La Citoyenne* in the context of feminist journalism, see Li Dzeh-Djen, *La Presse féministe en France de 1869 à 1914* (Paris, 1934).

Auclert chose the newspaper's name—"The Citizeness"—thoughtfully. It was a weekly reminder that women were not citizens under French law, and summarized her aspiration to make women equal citizens of the republic. *Citoyen/citoyenne* was also redolent of revolution; it had been the favored appellation of the 1790s and remained so among French socialists. Auclert thus stated her feminism, republicanism, and radicalism in a single word. She also acknowledged Hugo's words of 1872 that had summoned her to Paris: "In today's civilization . . . there are citizens, there are no citizenesses. This is a violent fact; it must cease." Someday soon, she was answering him, there will be citizenesses, for today there is *La Citoyenne.*[2]

To found *La Citoyenne,* Auclert needed the help of three men: Lévrier, Giraud, and Dr. Verrier. Giraud (better known to the Parisian public by the anagram "Draigu") had collaborated with Auclert since the early days of Droit des femmes. He established his feminist reputation in 1880 with *Le Roman de la femme chrétienne,* to which Auclert contributed a preface. He gave Auclert legal advice, and he gave *La Citoyenne* so much of its initial financing that one hostile feminist described him as a modern Croesus with wealth to throw away. Verrier, a physician, briefly handled the business affairs of *La Citoyenne,* especially the advertising.[3]

La Citoyenne began as a four-page paper in a full-sized folio format. It had no paid staff and informed all authors that they were contributing their work to the cause. Auclert wrote a signed leader for every issue and contributed many other articles (see appendix 1); to fill some issues she wrote articles under the characteristic pseudonyms of Liberta and Jeanne Voitout ("all-seeing"). Lévrier was her most frequent contributor, producing several series of articles—on the conditions of working women in various occupations, on the defenders of women's rights, and (with hidden personal significance) on marriage. Giraud wrote a long series on the Civil Code; Verrier wrote on public health and hygiene. Auclert also received work from her friends in politics and often published Clovis Hugues' poetry. Among prominent feminists, Eugénie

2. For Hugo's letter, see ch. 1; for Littré, see Auclert's *Vote des femmes,* pp. 108–10, and her "Dernier grimace du singe Littré," *La Citoyenne,* 12 June 1881. For Auclert's definition of the *citoyenne,* see the masthead of *La Citoyenne* and *Les Femmes au gouvernail,* p. 34.

3. See the masthead and legal notices on p. 4 of *La Citoyenne* for the changing roles of these men in compliance with French law. For Auclert's acknowledgement of their contribution, see *Le Vote des femmes,* p. 108; autobiographical fragment, Auclert Papers, 14/58. The scathing attack on Auclert, Giraud, and others is in Des Etrivières, *Les Amazons du siècle,* pp. 14–15, which used a double entendre—calling Giraud Auclert's *bailleur des fonds*—to imply that Auclert was sleeping with him in return for his financial backing. Auclert almost certainly never learned that Astié de Valsayre had written this vicious book; they collaborated a few years later.

Pierre was her most frequent contributor. Members of Droit des femmes, chiefly Louise Lasserre in the early years and Maria Martin after Lasserre's expulsion, occasionally submitted articles.

The contents of *La Citoyenne* were determined by Auclert's resolve to win political rights. Most of her leading articles touched on the subject. In addition, she published the documents concerning her campaigns, her petitions, correspondence on women's suffrage, reports of Droit des femmes meetings and activities, and surveys of suffragism in other countries. Auclert made this focus explicit in 1882 by adding to the masthead the subtitle: "Journal to Claim Women's Suffrage." Beneath that proclamation, Auclert regularly published a drawing that bore the heading "universal suffrage" and depicted a man and a woman casting ballots simultaneously (see illustration 4).

Auclert's concentration on political rights did not submerge other feminist concerns. In the first issue she stated the policy that everything affecting women would be treated, and she opened *La Citoyenne*'s columns to anyone desiring to point out a new issue. "I intend," Auclert insisted in that issue, "the abrogation of every one of these laws of exception that release men from responsibilities and weigh down women with the heaviest burdens." But all issues led her back to women's suffrage. "Who can abolish the iniquitous laws that oppress women in civil life? . . . The voters and the legislators." To be freed from "masculine tyranny" women must have "the possession of their share of sovereignty; they need the title of *citoyenne française;* they need the ballot."[4]

Auclert's noteworthy accomplishments in *La Citoyenne* include one of the earliest efforts, perhaps the first, to popularize the term *féministe*. Fourier is considered to have coined *féminisme* in the 1830s, although this remains unverified. The women's rights movement in France did not adopt the word, nor did its derivatives appear in other languages. Instead, terms such as "women's rights" and "the emancipation of women" characterized the debate. The word *féministe* had appeared in French by 1872, when Dumas *fils* used it as a term of disparagement. As late as the 1880s, however, no French organization or periodical yet used *feminisme* or *feministe* in its title. Auclert later claimed, in *Le Vote des femmes* (1908), that she had popularized both terms beginning in 1882; she asserted that they "have been used since then." Only part of that claim withstands investigation. *Féministe* did appear in *La Citoyenne* as early as 1882; *féminisme*

---

4. Auclert, "La Citoyenne," as translated in Hellerstein et al., *Victorian Women*, pp. 445–46. For Auclert's treatment of working women, see Guibert, *Les Femmes et l'organisation syndicale*, pp. 246–50.

did not. Auclert also used the expression *le mouvement féministe* in print on other occasions in the mid-1880s (see appendix 1). The French women's rights movement still did not accord the term general usage—perhaps because Auclert gave it an unwanted breadth and militancy—until the 1890s, when several periodicals and organizations, such as *La Revue féministe* (1895) and the Groupe féministe socialiste (1899), adopted it. It is unclear whether Hubertine Auclert was the first advocate of women's rights to call herself a feminist. At the least, she deserves credit for her role in establishing *féministe* in the French lexicon, and, by extension, in international usage.[5]

Sustaining the weekly publication of *La Citoyenne* placed a heavy burden on Auclert. Typically for the feminist press in the Third Republic, she fought a ceaseless battle for higher circulation and greater revenue. She reduced prices, gave premiums to subscribers, included a subscription to *La Citoyenne* in the cost of dues in Droit des femmes. She pressed subscriptions on the audiences at her lectures. She went into the streets to find unemployed workers to distribute each issue. She financed the paper as well as she could, then pleaded for the support of her associates. All was inadequate. Through tireless work, she achieved a circulation of a thousand copies. Many political newspapers printed fewer than ten thousand copies in 1880; only a labor of love could survive on a thousand. After one year, Auclert announced a plan to make *La Citoyenne* "the collective property" of those who produced it, by incorporating and offering shares for sale. She sought to raise 24,000 francs by selling 240 shares in the *société anonyme* at 100 francs each; Auclert would retain 260 shares at the same value for her investment. She devoted page 4 to this plan for several weeks, then abandoned it without filing for incorporation. Auclert could not find 240 feminists with 100 francs to spare; it is unlikely that she found twenty-four.[6]

The financial burden left Auclert at the mercy of individual donations. She asked for contributions, just as she had proposed in her first

5. The attribution of *féminisme* to Fourier is found in several sources, but none of them cite its source. See, for example, Zeldin, *France, 1848–1945*, 1:345. Dumas *fils* used *féministe* in *L'Homme-femme* (Paris, 1872). *Le Vote des femmes* reprints Auclert's letter of 4 November 1882 to the Prefect of the Seine, using both words (p. 63), and her claim that she established (not coined) both words (p. 64). The original letter, containing only *féministe*, appeared in *La Citoyenne*, 4 September 1882. Two days later, Auclert used the word again in a personal letter to Lepelletier, 6 September 1882, Auclert Papers, 2/4. I am indebted to Karen Offen, who has long been interested in this question, for prompting me to pursue it and for sharing her own findings with me in an unpublished manuscript entitled "Toward an Historical Definition of Feminism: the Contribution of France."

6. For circulation data on the Parisian press in 1880, see Bellanger et al., *Histoire générale de la presse française*, 3:234. *La Citoyenne*, 19 February 1882.

publication, in 1874, that women finance the work of Richer. Starting in 1882, she published in every issue a notice of the aid recieved. From April 1882 to March 1883, forty-eight individuals and two organizations supported *La Citoyenne* with a total supplemental revenue of 1,529.65 francs—slightly more than 6 percent of the capital Auclert thought necessary to guarantee publication. Two contributors gave most of this aid. Libussa Slavenko, a member of Droit des femmes, gave 455 francs; Joseph de Gasté gave larger donations every month, totaling 350 francs for the year. For the rest of the decade, de Gasté kept *La Citoyenne* alive with a subvention of several thousand francs. His gifts and the small contributions collected at the meetings of Droit des femmes and at public lectures were each carefully acknowledged, down to the 1.25 francs that Dissat's cooperative could afford. All the donations together could not support a weekly newspaper. *La Citoyenne* became a monthly in the spring of 1882, and adopted a smaller format in January 1884, but it survived.

The unwillingness of French women to give financial support to the feminist movement was one of Auclert's worst disillusionments. As a neophyte in Amélioration, she had thought that women would naturally support their emancipation. She soon learned that French women had no tradition of funding political movements, certainly not in the style of American feminists. It shocked her to review the list of her financial backers: the foremost contributor was a man, de Gasté; the only other major contributors were foreign women residing in Paris, Libussa Slavenko and Marie de Kapcevitch; of the other regular contributors, Virginie Griess-Traut was foreign, Maria Martin was foreign-born, and several of the rest were men. Of the French women who contributed, an alarming percentage insisted that the gift be kept anonymous.

Auclert addressed this problem in an editorial in *La Citoyenne* entitled "The Greed of Women." She traced the problem to the domestic frugality celebrated as a virtue (or necessity) of French housewives. Auclert shared this trait and admired it; she believed that it was one of the characteristics that women must bring to government, curbing the excesses of men. However, French women must recognize that they practiced "a parsimony that borders upon greed." Their "excessive economy" denied them the principal element of their emancipation— the money needed for propaganda. She illustrated the problem with the story of one of her subscribers, "an arch-millionaire" so committed to the cause that she insisted upon signing a petition on her deathbed, yet she left no legacy to the cause in her will. So Auclert pleaded with prosperous women to finance feminism. How well did it work? In the next quarter she received six contributions totaling 228 francs; 152

francs came from two men, 50 francs came anonymously, 25 francs came from a foreigner, and exactly one franc came from a French woman.[7]

Auclert produced her newspaper almost singlehandedly. Her diary includes several moving entries on this work. She invited readers to join her in the labor of emancipation at the office of the newspaper (her apartment) on Tuesday and Saturday afternoons. Few ever came. So Auclert wrote and edited alone. "Life would be good," she wrote in her diary, "if I were not alone. But I am alone everywhere, alone in public life as in private life! Alone at home, alone at the suffrage society, alone at the newspaper, always alone, everywhere alone." But she continued to do it alone, including the hated task of finding vendors to sell *La Citoyenne*. Her diary graphically records the emotional burden this added to the physical and financial weight of publishing—how she approached workers to distribute her newspaper; how they abused and insulted her; how she forced herself to continue dealing with men she found repulsive, intimidating, drunken; how they stole her profits; how they disappeared with her newspapers and never returned; how they appeared at her apartment at irregular hours to demand more money. "So much time, so much pain, so much suffering uselessly wasted," Auclert wrote. But *La Citoyenne* continued to appear.[8]

The picture of excruciating loneliness in Auclert's diary included difficulties in her private life. In 1882 Antonin Lévrier broke off the platonic relationship that she had insisted on. Auclert had become firmer in her moral convictions. In her private papers from this period she repeatedly compared herself to the Chevalier Bayard, a national hero of the Renaissance whom Auclert admired because her behavior, like his, was "beyond reproach." She wrote vehemently against unmarried cohaitation (*l'union libre*), an arrangement so common in the 1880s that it had acquired the name "Parisian marriage." "We say it publicly, once and for all," she wrote in *La Citoyenne*, "we are declared enemies of these clandestine unions." She did not condemn the unmarried mothers in such relationships but saw them as victims of society—a sensitivity that she had learned from her mother. Her public stand (and presumably her private answer to Lévrier) became so clear that feminists spoke of her "very dignified private life." She excoriated colleagues who lived differently, especially Marguerite Durand in later years, as "demi-mondaine feminists." Her sexual conser-

---

7. Auclert, "L'Avarice des femmes," *La Citoyenne*, April 1884, and monthly subscription reports, ibid.

8. Diary, 2 March 1884 and 6 March 1885, Auclert Papers. The diary entries appear after Lévrier's departure from Paris.

vatism became so well-known that it later served as the subject of one of the speeches at her burial.[9]

Lévrier still pressed Auclert to marry him. Auclert still refused. Her essays for *La Citoyenne* had refined her thinking about marriage, and they leave no doubt about her conclusions. Those articles, in fact, show a fascinating confluence of her public and private lives. During 1881 and 1882, Auclert and Lévrier conducted a disguised and perfectly discreet courtship in the columns of *La Citoyenne* by exchanging a total of eight articles. The casual reader finds feminist essays on dowries, marriage contracts, adultery, divorce, the division of marital property (*séparation des biens*), and other aspects of marriage in the Civil Code. The informed reader recognizes Lévrier exalting the feminist position while saying, "Yes—but," and Auclert responding with a clear rejection of marriage. William Butler Yeats described Auclert's dilemma in *The Choice*: "The intellect of man is forced to choose/ Perfection of the life, or of the work." Auclert chose her work. She admired marriage in the abstract, if it were reformed: "The marriage dreamt of is an association, in a communion of ideas and feelings, of two beings who possess the same moral and material prerogatives." But she found marriage as then constituted in France intolerable; it "requires the annihilation of the personality and the will." Auclert would not surrender her will, would not marry Lévrier.[10]

The question of their relationship assumed particular importance in 1882 because of developments in Lévrier's career. Following his electoral defeat in December 1881, his friends in politics offered to find him a judicial or administrative appointment in the French bureaucracy. Their patronage resulted in Lévrier's nomination as a justice of the peace, the bottom rung of the French magistracy. The post, however, required relocation to Niort. The discussion of marriage thus held poignant and painful choices for both Auclert and Lévrier. Lévrier might have declined this appointment—although it represented the first major opportunity of his legal career, coming at the age of thirty-three—in favor of marriage to Auclert in Paris. But he lacked her established career and her financial security, and he would not sacrifice the job if she would not marry him. She, on the other hand, had already reached an unalterable conclusion about love and marriage, and she

9. Auclert, "L'Union libre," *La Citoyenne*, 26 December 1881; note on "mariages Parisiens," Auclert Papers, 13/108; folder on "Police des moeurs," ibid., Carton 13, esp. 13/37 and 13/54; Arria Ly, "Hubertine Auclert," *Le Combat féministe*, July 1914.

10. Pensées, Auclert Papers, 13/126; notes, ibid., 8/143; folder entitled "Le Mariage," ibid., Carton 13, esp. 13/77; manuscript entitled "Mariage," ibid., 6/2; *La Citoyenne*, February 1884 and February 1887. See *La Citoyenne* of 1881–1882 for the articles on marriage, beginning with Lévrier's article of 13 February 1881; Lévrier, *Histoire des Deux-Sèvres* (Niort, 1886); *La Citoyenne*, February 1886.

would not sell her beliefs to save the hour. Auclert also recognized a classic woman's dilemma, being forced to choose between the man she loved and the career she cherished. She remained firm. He left for Niort.

Auclert began her diary during the rupture of her relationship with Lévrier. Her *cri de coeur,* "I am everywhere alone," reveals much about her. Obviously, loneliness describes her political isolation and her difficulties in recruiting followers; the same loneliness appears in her personal life, without friends, without lover. It is important to realize that this loneliness also constituted an essential part of her self-image. Her suffering was real, but Auclert intentionally chose her isolation in several ways and catalogued it in exquisitely punishing detail. To read her diary is to watch her build her image of being "all alone, utterly alone always." Auclert needed to suffer loneliness. Why? She perceived herself as a "wretched pariah," a *déclassé,* a "martyr." Loneliness was the hair shirt of her martyrdom. It proved her dedication, showed her sacrifice. The more she adopted this pose, the more it affected her decisions and became a self-fulfilling prophecy. And the more she suffered from genuine loneliness.

Auclert's diary gives other indications of her sense of martyrdom. She practiced literary self-flagellation. She revealed genuine insecurities, but exaggerated her inadequacy. For example, she described her lecture trip to Nîmes in 1883 in remarkable terms: "What am I saying to them? Nothing! Some commonplaces, some wind! How unhappy I feel, therefore, to be so little up to the eminence of my mission. The terrain is prepared, there is much to do, and I . . . cannot do it. I am profoundly incompetent." She administered these blows regularly: "I am a failure." "I feel humiliated." "My life is a continuity of wasted efforts."

While this tormented self-portrait must be understood as a chosen image, it must also be seen in relationship to Auclert's experiences. This document represents her response to events, many of which were nasty. She faced a good deal of public ridicule, such as the witticisms about her mental health and sex appeal. Auclert learned not to be surprised at such treatment, but she never ceased to be sensitive to it. She hid her pain, however, in the belief that the fear of ridicule kept some women from feminism; as a role model, she dared not succumb to malicious treatment. Thus, Auclert absorbed the demeaning jokes, but they shaped her sense of being an outcast, and probably a failure as well.

Two examples, one private and one public, show the ridicule that Auclert endured. She kept some of the hate mail that she received. One such letter contained an anonymous cartoon (see illustration 5) portraying her as ugly and ready for the lunatic asylum. Auclert already worried that she was too ugly for a happy love life; as she kept this crude joke for the rest of her life, it must have had a strong impact on her. An example of public ridicule, not to mention defamation and libel, can be seen in the pages of *L'Escrime*, a magazine devoted to fencing. The author, Maurice Dancourt, proposed a series of regulations to govern "The Duels of the Future." One of his rules prohibited married duelists from sending their wives to fight in their place; "an exception will always be made in favor of Mlle Hubertine Auclert, whose sex is not yet clearly defined." Another stipulated that the penalty for improper behavior would be marriage to "the previously mentioned, so-called demoiselle Hubertine Auclert."[11] Little wonder that Auclert needed a diary to cope with her feelings.

SUFFRAGE DES FEMMES

Hubertine Auclert's second major effort to expand French suffragism in the 1880s was the transformation of Droit des femmes into a new organization, the Société pour le suffrage des femmes (hereafter Suffrage des femmes), sometimes wishfully called the National Society for Women's Suffrage. Auclert wished to tighten the focus of her organization, to create a national suffrage league on the model of English and American groups, and to reemphasize the difference between herself and the feminist mainstream. Auclert achieved the sharp focus and the distinction from moderates without difficulty. She never built the national league she dreamt of; Suffrage des femmes never surpassed the size and activity of Droit des femmes.

There were two important stimuli for the creation of Suffrage des femmes, one coming from Parisian feminists, the other from American feminists. In 1882 Léon Richer announced that he also planned to found a new league to establish feminism as a mass movement. Its name, almost identical to Droit des femmes', would be the Ligue française pour le droit des femmes (hereafter the LFDF). Richer had left Amélioration to Deraismes in 1878 to concentrate on writing and lobbying for laic education and the restitution of divorce. Deraismes' periodic flirtation with suffragism troubled him, however. In October 1882 she delivered a speech sufficiently suffragist to win Auclert's praise in *La Citoyenne*. Thus, Richer also created the LFDF to guarantee the proper evolution of French feminism. He hoped to emulate the extraparliamentary pressure groups begun by his friends Jean Macé, who founded a league for educational reform, and Léo Taxil, who founded an anticleri-

11. Maurice Dancourt, "Les Duels de l'avenir," *L'Escrime* 8(1881): 95–96. I thank Robert A. Nye and Karen Offen for providing me with a copy of this article.

cal league. Deraismes was then shifting her energies from directing Amélioration to editing a radical weekly, *Le Républicain de Seine-et-Oise*, which she had taken advantage of the press law of 1881 to purchase. Deraismes was also deeply involved in the politics of Freemasonry in 1882, when, sponsored by Richer, she became the first woman admitted to a masonic lodge in France (the lodge was soon closed). She encouraged him to create the LFDF and she accepted its honorary vicepresidency. By early 1883, Richer had 142 founding members; by the end of the year, nearly 200.[12]

The American stimulus to Auclert came with the visit to Europe of Susan B. Anthony in 1883. Auclert had admired Anthony for years and had exchanged a few letters with her. Anthony, twenty-eight years older, seemed to be the role model Auclert had never found in France. Her determination to win the vote, her travels for the cause, her uncompromising leadership even at the price of schism, her financial struggle to publish a suffragist newspaper (*Revolution*), and her membership in the Working Women's Association all indicated to Auclert a kindred spirit. Anthony, however, presided over a large, national suffrage league, the National Woman Suffrage Association, and had already seen women receive the vote in some western territories of the United States. Auclert wrote to Anthony to say that she gave inspiration to French women, and to ask, in her vivid style, for help: "In our impatience to throw off the despotic yoke of men, we stretch our slaves' arms towards you, to sisters almost freed. We call you to our aid, as a century ago your compatriots called France to their aid to deliver America from the English yoke. Will you come to our aid as Lafayette and his legion flew to yours? . . . The role of liberators is extended to you." Auclert suggested that Anthony organize an international congress for women's suffrage, to be held in Paris ("the capital of the world"); with the help of Anthony's congress, Auclert could launch a national campaign in France.[13]

Susan B. Anthony cherished for many years the idea of organizing international suffragism. Her dream led ultimately to the creation of the International Woman Suffrage Alliance (hereafter the IWSA) in Berlin in 1904, with Anthony, then eighty-four, as honorary president. Such a

12. For a detailed description of the activities of Léon Richer during the 1880s, see Bidelman, *Pariahs Stand Up!*, pp. 155–83, and Bidelman, "The Politics of French Feminism: Léon Richer and the Ligue française pour le droit des femmes, 1882–1891," *HR/RH* 3(1976):93–120. For Deraismes, see Krakovitch's preface to Deraismes, *Ce que veulent les femmes*, pp. 31–32.

13. Auclert to Anthony, undated draft letter (early 1880s), in Auclert's address book, Auclert Papers, Carton 5; Alma Lutz, "Susan B. Anthony," in Edward P. James, ed., *Notable American Women, 1607–1950: A Biographical Dictionary* (Cambridge, Mass., 1971), 1:51–57.

congress did not seem possible in the early 1880s, owing to pressing activities in America and the comparative weakness of continental suffragism; Anthony could only encourage Auclert in her ambition. Then, in late 1882, as Richer was founding the LFDF, Anthony informed Auclert that she had planned a European vacation for early 1883; she wanted to observe the strength of the international movement for women's rights. Anthony would be traveling with Theodore Stanton, the son of her close ally Elizabeth Cady Stanton; Stanton and Auclert were already corresponding about his preparation of a book, *The Woman Question in Europe*, to which Auclert contributed. Thus, Auclert eagerly invited Anthony and Stanton to participate in a meeting of her society.[14]

In response to Richer's new organization and to Anthony's visit, Auclert announced the foundation of Suffrage des femmes in February 1883. She devoted most of page 1 of *La Citoyenne* to explaining the transformation of Droit des femmes. Auclert realized that she had already sown the seed of women's suffrage in French politics. Having nurtured it during "its period of incubation," she must now, she said (in the sort of mixed metaphor that never bothered her), "make it germinate, bloom." For this, she proposed a propaganda campaign, "heating up public opinion until it's white hot." That called for a national organization, "modeled upon the powerful English and American associations which have already obtained fruitful results for women." She reminded French feminists that Anglo-American suffragists had already won the municipal franchise in England (1869) and full political rights in two territories of the United States (Wyoming, 1869; Utah, 1870), and added that Suffrage des femmes "will have even more success than the foreign associations."[15]

The triumph of Suffrage des femmes would come through persuasion, not force. Persuasion would begin with feminists themselves. All men and women in the movement must rally to the cause of political rights, abandoning their timidity and their antisuffrage rationalizations: "At the present, French feminism splits itself into two camps: the old school which desires for women rights with restrictions, subdivided rights, and which awaits civil rights at the covenience of the deputies;

14. Theodore Stanton to Auclert, 3 March 1882; *La Citoyenne*, 12 March 1882; Theodore Stanton, *The Woman Question in Europe: A Series of Original Essays* (New York, 1884); Auclert to Theodore Stanton, undated draft letter (1883), Auclert Papers, Carton 6.

15. For a comparative study of the women's movement in this period, see Richard J. Evans, *The Feminists: Women's Emancipation Movements in Europe, America, and Australasia, 1840–1920* (London, 1977). For an analysis of French suffragism in a comparative context, see Hause with Kenney, *Women's Suffrage and Social Politics*, pp. 18–22, 114–24, and 253–61.

and the young school which, affirming the principle of equality without restriction, wants for women rights without restriction, integral and immediate rights." The difference between the two schools of French feminism, Auclert claimed, was the difference between a creditor demanding her due and a beggar holding out a hand for alms. Richer's begging might produce some reforms, such as divorce, but that, Auclert correctly predicted, would not give feminists the complete rights of divorce that they wanted. Only by coming to Suffrage des femmes, by bringing their parents and their friends, only by making the society truly national could feminists gain the emancipation they desired.[16]

Auclert assembled an organizing committee of eighteen members for Suffrage des femmes. Unlike her earlier committees, these members came almost exclusively from the world of politics, the liberal professions, and the middle class. There were three deputies (Hugues, Talandier, and Maret), two men who would soon sit in the chamber (de Gasté, presently an engineer, and Yves Guyot, a future minister), and two sitting members of the Municipal Council of Paris (Guyot and Auguste Desmoulins, a contributor to *La Citoyenne* and the son-in-law of Pierre Leroux); two lawyers (Giraud and Lévrier), two physicians, a journalist, a professor, an artist, and an author; and three women of independent means (Auclert, Kapcevitch, and Madame Salès-Saxton, who agreed to serve as treasurer). This list included several socialists, but Suffrage des femmes was unmistakably a bourgeois organization tinted with republican socialism. Auclert insisted that expansion dictated a liberal openness, "beyond any political or religious opinion."

Auclert broidered the tapestry of Suffrage des femmes with dreams. She wrote statutes that spoke of the need to limit the leadership to a committee of twelve until the size of the society dictated expansion to twenty-four; of honorary memberships for the famous figures who would endorse their efforts; of the annual congress to report to the membership, following monthly reports issued by the committee; of the work of the provincial members and the relationship of their local chapters to the national committee; of the three separate treasuries that Suffrage des femmes would maintain, for the regular expenses of the society, for its projected publications, and for its lecture series and travels. One can visualize Auclert, sitting alone in her austere apartment contemplating these annual congresses, provincial chapters, and multiple treasuries. But she did not have them in 1883, and they never came to be. She understood the structure of a national suffrage union, and her dream was a prescient description of the Union française pour le suffrage des femmes (hereafter the UFSF) founded by others in 1909, a few

16. Auclert, "Le Suffrage des femmes," *La Citoyenne*, 5 February 1883; police report, 22 March 1883, Dossier Auclert, APP.

years before her death. And she had created the tightly focused suffrage league that she wanted. The "unique goal" of Suffrage des femmes was, by statute, the political rights of women: "All questions other than the question of obtaining for women the vote and eligibility for office are rigorously banned from the discussions and publications of the society."[17]

By the time Anthony and Stanton arrived in Paris in May 1883, it was clear that Richer's LFDF was going to be a larger league than Auclert's Suffrage des femmes but that neither would become the mass movement that the founders desired. (The LFDF, six times the size of Suffrage des femmes in 1883, reached a peak in 1883–1884 of approximately two hundred members.) The distinguished visitors attended a meeting of Suffrage des femmes, but Auclert and Anthony had no important discussions because neither spoke the other's language. If we read between the lines of Theodore Stanton's letter to his mother, their foremost impression seems to have been how tiny the French suffrage movement was. Stanton made a small donation to Auclert and praised her as "brave, far-seeing"; Anthony was apparently more moved by the annual commemoration of the Commune at Père Lachaise cemetery and more concerned with Richer's antisuffragism. No more was heard of the plan for an international suffrage congress at Paris or of an international suffrage alliance. Auclert agreed to keep the connection with American suffragists by accepting a position as "foreign corresponding secretary" in the National Woman Suffrage Association, whose convention of 1884 ratified the appointment. Her enthusiasm for collaboration with American suffragists ebbed, however, and she declined an invitation to attend an international congress a few years later. When she resumed relations with American suffragists at the turn of the century, she found herself in bitter disagreement with Anthony's successor, Carrie Chapman Catt.[18]

The cool reception that Suffrage des femmes received did not immediately discourage Auclert. She called on the readers of *La Citoyenne* to join Suffrage des femmes to "demasculinize the country," and she used her old tactic of letters to the press to gain further publicity. Maret's *Le Radical*, for which Auclert became a columnist in 1896, supported her. So did the conservative *L'Univers;* Auclert pragmatically accepted this support, despite the vigorous criticism of friends who argued that their

17. Statutes and organizing committee of SF, *La Citoyenne,* 5 February 1883 and following weeks.

18. *La Citoyenne,* 2 July 1882; Theodore Stanton to Elizabeth Cady Stanton, quoted in Elizabeth Cady Stanton, *Eighty Years and More: Reminiscences, 1815–1897* (1898); reprint, New York: Schocken, 1971), p. 177 (quoted); Susan B. Anthony and Ida H. Harper, *The History of Woman Suffrage* (Rochester, 1881–1922), 4:27; Anthony to Mrs. Spofford, 20 May 1883, in Ida H. Harper, *The Life and Work of Susan B. Anthony* (Indianapolis, 1898), 2:562.

republicanism must come before their feminism. Auclert did not flinch. She preferred the support of radical republicans and socialists, with whom she agreed on most issues, but she would accept women's suffrage from the hands of the extreme right if they could offer it—an attitude she later showed by collaborating with Edouard Drumont in 1894. Her pragmatic acceptance of right-wing friends, her denunciation of "the old school" in French feminism, and her open competition with the LFDF for members ultimately forced some feminists to choose sides. Auclert lost several influential supporters in this way. Most politicians, including Emile Deschanel, de Hérédia, Laisant, Naquet, Revillon, and Schoelcher, chose Richer's group; others, including Hugues and Guyot, tried to maintain dual memberships in Suffrage des femmes and the LFDF. Similar losses of support occurred in the radical press; Auguste Vacquerie became an honorary vice-president of the LFDF and adopted Richer's antisuffrage stance, although he still kept *Le Rappel* open to Auclert.[19]

More frustration awaited Auclert when she sought to make honorary members of the famous, who would publicize Suffrage des femmes with their names. She offered the honorary presidency to Hugo, who refused. Shortly thereafter he accepted a similar position with an antivivisection society. Auclert worked out her feelings in her diary: "Why this difference? Because those who asked him to join the suffrage society of progress were poor . . . even the genius Hugo prefers to be reactionary and feted with the rich." Worse yet, Hugo turned around and accepted the honorary presidency of the LFDF, owing to his long-standing friendship with Richer. It is difficult to judge whether this rejection by one of her few heroes hurt Auclert more than the answer by Dumas *fils* did. He declined the honorary presidency of Suffrage des femmes in a letter asserting that he could help her more by remaining independent, adding the bald insult that no one would listen to him on women's rights at the academy if they knew that he was affiliated with Auclert. Thereupon Auclert stopped courting celebrities and bestowed the honorary presidency on de Gasté, who accepted.[20]

Her efforts to expand Suffrage des femmes reveal a maturing of Auclert's political style. They also highlight another of the apparent inconsistencies in her career: why did some people find her stubborn and dogmatic, while others thought her pragmatic and opportunistic? In

19. *La Citoyenne*, 4 June 1883 and 6 August 1883; *Le Radical*, 24 October 1883; Auclert, "Emile Deschanel," ibid., 9 February 1904; *L'Univers*, 5 February 1884; Bidelman, *Pariahs Stand Up!*, pp. 158–59. For a list of the founding members of the LFDF, see Bidelman, "The Feminist Movement in France," appendix H, pp. 374–78.

20. Diary, 7 February 1884, Auclert Papers; Auclert, *Le Vote des femmes*, p. 107; *La Citoyenne*, July 1884; Auclert, "Victor Hugo, féministe," *Le Radical*, 7 March 1902; Bidelman, *Pariahs Stand Up!*, pp. 149, 159–60.

fact, she possessed all of these characteristics. Her strong will and her uncompromising faith had produced inflexible politics; one truth existed, and throughout her life she acted in the certainty that she possessed it. But her tactics began to change in the early 1880s. She realized that she and a few like-minded colleagues alone could not alter the world. Yet her experience with her natural allies discouraged her. Auclert's conflicts with liberal feminists like Richer and Deraismes, her disappointments with socialists, and her disillusionment at seeing republicans in power taught her that dealing solely with the people nearest to her ideologically might not win the vote. Thus, she became increasingly flexible in her tactics precisely because she remained inflexible in devotion to her goal. Accepting the support of *L'Univers,* to the horror of some republicans, merely illustrated this increasing flexibility. Auclert's behavior only appeared to be inconsistent; she was being pragmatic in pursuit of an ideal.

Her efforts to found a national suffrage society had deeper effects. Sometime during 1883–1884, Auclert's tremendous confidence and energy began to dim: "I have lost courage and faith," she wrote in her diary. A registration campaign in the press in November 1883 netted exactly one subscriber to *La Citoyenne,* one new member of Suffrage des femmes, and one curious journalist. Another effort, in February 1884, signed up no one. "Wasted pains!" she wrote. Hurt, then despair, appeared in her private reflections. The painful realization of her human limits and the limited prospects of success began to dawn on her, compounding the loneliness she had begun to feel in 1882. These experiences and feelings were the first stages of a personal crisis that would take Auclert years to resolve. They provide another illustration of the reciprocal relationship between her public career and private life. The departure of Lévrier in 1882 left Auclert with no intimate companion at precisely the moment when she most needed emotional support. The separation from Lévrier might have had less impact on Auclert if it had come in her years of burgeoning optimism. Because it preceded a period of doubt and anxiety, it contributed to her depression about the suffrage campaign; this depression, in turn, deepened her sense of loss.[21]

Initially, Auclert had the greatest difficulty with her public problems, with accepting that Suffrage des femmes would not become a great national league. She quietly dropped the word *national* from its name and the dreams from its statutes. She admitted that she could attract only a handful of activists, and she reduced the scope of Suffrage des femmes until it was little more than a discussion circle. In her diary she bitterly lamented how little help "these worthy simpletons" (*ces braves*

21. Diary, 25 September 27 and 28 October 1883, 21 February and 2 March 1884, Auclert Papers.

imbéciles) were: "Jesus in the Garden of Olives had faithful apostles; as for me, I feel that I really have no one with me; the end of each meeting, seeing that it has been useless, is my Calvary. . . . After every Wednesday's meeting I am more weary than if I had labored in the fields. Every meeting I must start all over again. . . . I am always at the same point, as little listened to as a puddle of water by these worthy simpletons whom I incubate to help me."[22]

This passage reveals the extent to which Auclert's sense of martyrdom had developed. Her personal mythology—the combination of reality and fantasy that people project for themselves—did not stop with the comparison of herself to Jesus. Admiration of other martyrs, both religious and political, now filled her private papers and spilled over into her feminist essays. She alluded to the suffering of the early Christian martyrs. She adopted Jeanne d'Arc as "the personification of feminism"; Jeanne represented the strong and independent woman who suffers and dies for her cause. It is not coincidental that Auclert chose "Jeanne" as a pseudonym. The American radical abolitionist John Brown also appears frequently in Auclert's notes as a model of the person who fights injustice with religious fervor—and who dies for the cause. "Every effort for liberation costs," Auclert wrote in one discussion of John Brown. She concluded that the least that feminists could do would be to endure ridicule, rejection, and ostracism. Auclert, of course, would endure more; she even described herself as "dead for her cause."[23]

Auclert recorded her martyrdom in detail. Her diary is a catalog of daily tribulations—ugly arguments with rental agents for lecture halls; funds so limited that she had to lecture by candlelight; timid supporters who worried about police observation and canceled participation at the last moment; a treasurer who refused to give an accounting or to return the society's books; audiences whose heckling drowned out the applause; arguments with newspaper editors for the right to rebut demeaning articles; being spit upon by total strangers. These moving vignettes stand in jarring contrast to Auclert's impassioned and enthusiastic public rhetoric about justice. The contrast is especially vivid, and her loss of confidence clear, in her summary of 1884: "My life is a continuity of wasted [*inutiles*] efforts."[24]

Another diary entry powerfully illustrates the degree to which Auclert embraced her martyrdom and consciously contributed to her joyless loneliness: "I do not light up my home, I do not decorate it, my

22. Diary, 25 September 1883, 21 February 1884, and 24 April 1885, Auclert Papers; *La Citoyenne*, March 1884.

23. For her comparisons to religious martyrs, see Auclert's diary; for Jeanne d'Arc, see ch. 10; for John Brown, see her notes, Auclert Papers, 11/128 and 11/344, and her reference in Jeanne Voitout (Auclert), "Séverine," *La Citoyenne*, January 1886.

24. Diary, 1884 passim; quotation from entry for 14 June 1884, Auclert Papers.

three large windows are black. One must be very logical. Being subjected by my sex, I must separate myself from joy just as I am separated from rights." This passage confirms the impression noted above that Auclert's daily life contained few pleasant diversions. Martyrs were not permitted to play the flute or dine elegantly. On the contrary, the only specific reference to food in Auclert's diary shows how martyrs behave. One night, while working on an article, she cooked herself a cutlet. After several distractions, she had a burnt cutlet and great hunger. Her reaction was to go to bed hungry after recording the sacrifices she had made for the cause.[25]

Reviewing Auclert's attempt in 1883–1884 to establish a French national suffrage campaign raises interlocking questions about her political and personal difficulties. The political question is easy to answer: given her great expectations of February 1883, when she brashly predicted that French suffragism would overshadow the movement in England and America, why did Auclert attract so little support? The personal question is harder: given the depressing descriptions in her diary, how did Auclert persist in her efforts and actually launch new works in 1885?

The political answer has little to do with Auclert. It rests on the simple fact that French opinion was not prepared to support a radical feminist movement. In contrast to her success at Marseilles in 1879, no eloquence could have made the tides of opinion turn. The problem was not just women's suffrage, or her militancy, or the stridency in her personality. Richer and Deraismes had friends in influential places, greater resources, moderate ambitions, and respectable behavior. Yet they could attract only a few hundred people to the LFDF and Amélioration combined. Even if Auclert's attack on "the old school" had somehow persuaded other feminists to desert Richer, Suffrage des femmes would not have become the national league dreamt of in Auclert's statutes. Centuries of Roman Catholic belief and the Roman-Napoleonic legal system, reiterated even in the revolutionary tradition, could not be quickly overcome. No matter how well Auclert had embedded women's suffrage in Parisian political discourse, raising up legions of followers was a far different matter.

The answer to the personal question about Auclert's ability to persist must begin with her character. It has been seen repeatedly, in the testimony of those who knew her and in her behavior, that Auclert had an exceptionally strong will and a religious sense of determination. Balancing these characteristics against her private descriptions of vulnerability and suffering enriches our perception of her. We thus obtain a reminder that since she did continue, she possessed remarkable

25. Diary, 2 March 1884 and 24 April 1885, Auclert Papers.

strength and faith; a portrait of a person with doubts and insecurities, rather than a stereotyped image of stubborn, inhuman strength; a sense of the exceptional price—emotional, psychological, and physical—that Auclert paid to sustain her unpopular crusade; a glimpse of the common human weakness, which she shared in difficult moments, of succumbing to self-pity; and an inner view of the evidence that Auclert used to form her self-image as a lonely martyr. After making these adjustments to our picture of Auclert, what remains amid the inconsistencies is a better sense of the will that enabled her to persist. As she wrote in a less tormented moment, "However dispiriting the struggle may be, I have an unquenchable faith." Similarly, her sister Marie remembered her saying, "As dispiriting as the battle and the isolation are, I have an extraordinary faith, one of those Christian faiths at the stake and in the lion's den [*aux bûchers et aux bêtes*]."[26] It is instructive that Auclert found the imagery for both her martyrdom and her faith in the vocabulary of her lost Christianity.

In explaining her persistence, it is also important to note an experience in her private life that fortified Auclert. Her relationship with Antonin Lévrier had improved. They had remained in contact during 1882, although their relationship was awkward; Auclert encouraged Lévrier to write a social history of his home department, the Deux-Sèvres, and gave the book a glowing review in *La Citoyenne*. Auclert visited him once in Niort in 1882, but that reunion was unsatisfactory, and presumably contributed to Auclert's low spirits in the following months. Then, in August 1883, they met again. No entry in Auclert's diary describes a time of greater happiness—a word she almost never used—than their vacation together, chaperoned by Marie and Lucien Chaumont, at the Atlantic resort town of Royan. She felt "joy to see him again," although he had gained so much weight that she scarcely recognized him, and she felt nervous around him at first. A long dinner together restored their intimacy, and the vacation became a success. They found that they loved to play in the ocean, and they swam twice daily. Suddenly, Auclert found life "delightful." The reunion at Royan did not end their separation or change their minds about careers and marriage. It did, however, reinvigorate the relationship and give Auclert a sense of happiness and hope, renewing her strength to face the frustrations in Paris.[27]

The trip to Royan buttressed Auclert's will to continue by producing anger as well as happiness. She traveled alone by train, spending a night in Rochefort en route. Every major hotel in Rochefort refused to rent her

26. Ibid., June 1883; Chaumont, "Hubertine Auclert," p. 13.

27. Lévrier, *Histoire des Deux-Sevres; La Citoyenne*, February 1886; Diary, 11 August 1883, Auclert Papers.

a room on the grounds that "respectable [*honnêtes*] women do not travel alone." Auclert returned to Paris infuriated at this treatment. She wrote a blistering editorial for *La Citoyenne*, naming the hotels that had acted as if she were *une horizontale*. This incident not only reminded her of the importance of her work, but galvanized her with such rage that twenty-six years later she still wrote on the subject with anger.[28] Thus, Auclert's persistence in 1883–1884 was due to a mixture of refueled anger, rediscovered happiness, and the strength of her determination.

LETTERS AND PETITIONS AS A POLITICAL TACTIC

Faced with the difficulties of producing *La Citoyenne* and the disappointment of Suffrage des femmes, Auclert concentrated on a strategy of presenting women's suffrage to parliament singlehandedly. She adopted two easy tactics: letters to politicians and petitions to political bodies. She initially attempted a third tactic—going to electoral meetings and questioning the candidates—until she provoked a ruling that such meetings could be closed to women. Her labors did not significantly expand the suffrage movement, but they perpetuated women's suffrage as an issue in French politics.

The letter-writing campaign required more imagination than effort. Auclert realized that a letter simply asking for enfranchisement, or repeating old arguments, would hardly be noticed. She sought attention by drawing connections between women's rights and current issues. When Gambetta announced plans to create two new ministries, for agriculture and for fine arts, Auclert implored him to name women to a few prominent posts. This act would be possible without dislodging present male bureaucrats, would support the gradual acceptance of women in government without threatening the republic, and would demonstrate the administrative capacity of women. She made similar arguments to the ministry of commerce upon the announcement of plans to organize a centennial exposition in Paris in 1889. When colonial wars filled the news, Auclert wrote to the minister of war urging him to accept women volunteers for ancillary humanitarian services; this would free soldiers for other duties and rebut the antisuffragist argument that women should not vote because they did not serve in the military. When republican dissatisfaction with monarchical aspects of the constitutional laws of 1875 led to plans for a constitutional congress, Auclert rained letters on politicians pointing out their oppor-

28. Diary, 11 August 1883, Auclert Papers; Auclert, "La Femme en voyage," *La Citoyenne*, 3 September 1883; Auclert to Arria Ly, 3 September 1909, Arria Ly Papers, Bougle Collection, BHVP.

TABLE **5.1.** Auclert's Petitions, 1877–1887

Date	Recipient	Subject
1877	President MacMahon	Call for his resignation
1879	Chamber of Deputies	Right to file paternity suits
1880	Chamber of Deputies	Amnesty for communards
1880	Chamber of Deputies	Suffrage (interpretation of *Français*)
1881	Chamber of Deputies	Suffrage (interpretation of *Français*)
1881	Chamber and Senate	Suffrage (linked to absentee ballots)
1881	Chamber and Senate	Suffrage (linked to taxes)
1881	Chamber of Deputies	Population base of parliamentary constituencies
1882	Chamber of Deputies	Suffrage
1883	Chamber of Deputies	Women in the constitutional assembly
1883	Chamber of Deputies	Suffrage (linked to domestic servants)
1884	Chamber of Deputies	Suffrage (linked to taxes)
1884	Chamber of Deputies	Women in the constitutional assembly
1884	National Assembly	Addition of equal rights to the constitution
1884	Chamber of Deputies	Suffrage (for unmarried women only)
1885	Municipal Council (Paris)	Endorsement of suffrage
1885	Council General (Seine)	Endorsement of suffrage
1885	Chamber of Deputies	Suffrage
1885	Chamber and Senate	Population base of parliamentary constituencies
1885	Chamber and Senate	Right of women to attend electoral meetings
1886	Chamber and Senate	Suffrage (for unmarried women only)
1886	Chamber of Deputies	Women on Board of Labor Arbitrators
1886	Council General (Seine)	Endorsement of suffrage
1887	Chamber of Deputies	Suffrage (municipal suffrage only)

tunity to republicanize the women of France. When the ministry of the interior ordered a campaign against prostitutes soliciting on the streets, Auclert wrote the minister to explain how a more sensitive treatment of women could result in their serving the nation, rather than the needs of men. Such letters produced almost no changes. They won Auclert a few interviews with ministers—the army was most interested in her ideas—and continued publicity.[29]

Auclert's petition campaigns required more work, but they forced the Chamber of Deputies to discuss women's suffrage. It is doubtful that any individual in French history submitted more petitions to the government than she (see tables 5.1, 7.1, and 9.2). Petitioning, after all, was virtually the only way in which French women could directly participate in the political process.[30]

29. *La Citoyenne,* 17 October 1881, 21 November 1881, 12 December 1881, 6 May 1882, December 1884; letters in Auclert Papers, Cartons 5 and 9; Auclert, *Les Femmes au gouvernail,* pp. 30–32; *Le Français,* 21 November 1881.

30. The right to petition may have been an accident of constitutional phraseology. It did not appear in the Declaration of the Rights of Man (1789) or the Constitution of 1791. Article Thirty-two of the Constitution of the Year I (1793) established it as a republican

Auclert acquired the habit of petitioning during her apprenticeship in Amélioration in the mid-1870s. Richer approved of this tactic and used it to call for the abolition of regulated prostitution. Records survive for at least sixteen separate petitions by Auclert between 1881 and 1885. As she explained a few years later, "When one petition was rejected, another was signed and deposited, to be rejected in its turn." That was an understatement; she often had multiple petitions awaiting a hearing. The law obliged parliament to send all petitions to a committee (usually the Commission of Petitions, but sometimes the appropriate standing committee, such as the Commission of Universal Suffrage), whose reporter then had to deliver a written report, however cursory it might be, for debate. Most petitions were abruptly dismissed by a procedural vote to pass to the next item on the order of the day. Nonetheless, this process permitted Auclert to force a few sentences about women's suffrage on parliament every few months, obliged the government to print numerous reports on the subject, required committees to discuss it regularly, and provided an opportunity for her parliamentary sympathizers to speak about it. This tactic won no victories in the 1880s, but it kept her unpopular idea alive in a truculent legislature.[31]

Persistent petitioning suited someone with few supporters. The mechanics of parliamentary examination were the same no matter how many signatures a petition bore. Auclert alone could obligate a parliamentary commission. This was fortunate because she could not hope to produce the immense petitions typical of the feminist campaigns in other countries. Fragmentary records suggest that only three of Auclert's petitions between 1881 and 1885 held 1,000 or more signatures, the largest bearing 2,000. These figures might be compared to the first British petition for women's suffrage (1866), bearing 1,499 names, or to an Icelandic petition for women's rights (1895), with 2,200. But the former was a generation earlier than Auclert and the latter represented

principle. The wording there did not include any of the terms (*homme, citoyen, français,* or "in full possession of civil rights") by which the courts had excluded women from other constitutional rights: "The right to present petitions to depositories of the public authority cannot, in any case, be forbidden, suspended, or limited." The Constitution of the Year VIII (1799) reiterated the right to petition in Article Eighty-three, again without using language that could be employed to exclude women: "Everybody has the right to address petitions." The Constitution of 1848 introduced the first qualification of this right by limiting it to citizens; it was treated, however, in the same passage as the rights of association and assembly. The courts could not exclude women from one right without excluding them from the others. That would have challenged the existence of any association of women, whether religious, charitable, or educational; even antifeminists were unwilling to go that far, so the right to petition survived in spite of irritating a few politicians.

31. *L'Avenir des femmes,* January 1873 and April 1877; Auclert, "Le Vote des femmes," *La Fronde,* 13 December 1897 (quoted).

approximately 4.5 percent of Iceland's total population (equivalent to 1.7 million signatures in France). The Women's Christian Temperance Union in Australia obtained 30,000 signatures for suffrage in Victoria alone; Susan B. Anthony obtained 6,000 in New York as early as 1853 and 400,000 in the Woman's National Loyal League's suffrage petition of 1864–1865. Auclert could not hope for such results working alone. Anthony's petition of 1853 was the work of 60 local "captains" who each obtained an average of 100 signatures, one-tenth of Auclert's better work. Furthermore, women in other countries had significant experience with great petition campaigns, such as the Chartist petitions of 1839 and 1842 in Britain and the antislavery petitions of the 1830s and 1840s in the United States, in which Anthony learned the art. Auclert, however, could exploit French parliamentary procedure by submitting a petition bearing only the names of the three tax protesters of 1880, herself, Bonnair, and Leprou.[32]

Auclert often associated the text of her petitions with her well-publicized activities. Her tax case of 1880–1881, for example, provided the basis for four petitions. In 1880 and 1881 she asked for legislation proclaiming that the legal term *français* included women; in 1881 and 1884 she asked parliament to declare that the franchise and taxation were interdependent, so that women either should vote or should not pay. Similarly, her census boycott of 1881 led to two petitions in 1881 and 1885 asking that the distribution of seats in parliament be based only on a census of electors, which would cut the size of the Chamber of Deputies by half. Other petitions followed the method of connecting women's suffrage with current political debates. The republican plan for a constitutional congress produced three petitions in 1883 and 1884 to include women in the congress and their rights in the revised constitution. In the same way, Auclert capitalized on debates concerning absentee ballots for traveling businessmen, in 1881, and the rights of domestic servants, in 1883, to ask for women's rights.[33]

Auclert's torrent of petitions produced two important ideas for the future of French suffragism. The first was partial political rights for women as a first step; the second was an appeal to local political bodies to join her in applying pressure on the Chamber of Deputies. The former illustrates Auclert's increasing pragmatism in tactics—she would use

32. For petitions in other countries, see Evans, *The Feminists,* pp. 60, 65, and 89 for the cases cited; for American illustrations, see Anthony and Harper, *History of Woman Suffrage,* 1:604–5, 2:78–80.

33. The text of several petitions and reports on their progress can be found in *La Citoyenne,* although this provides only a partial record. See, for example, 22 May 1881 and March 1884 (tax petition); 13 February 1881 and 13 March 1881 ("français" petition); 24 October 1881 (absentee ballots); 6 August 1883 (servants). Several petitions, again forming an incomplete record, can be found in the Auclert Papers, Cartons 10 and 11.

the thin edge of any wedge. Her conclusion typified suffragism around the world; legislators often considered the enfranchisement of women in local elections while withholding it for national races. By the early 1880s, women had already won the municipal vote in more than a dozen places, including both England and Russia, but nowhere could they vote for parliament. Auclert did not use this approach until 1887. Instead, she developed a version of partial enfranchisement that she deemed more suited to French *mentalités*. Reasoning that antisuffragism derived in part from attitudes concerning marriage, Auclert proposed the enfranchisement of unmarried women, including widows and divorcées, in petitions of 1884 and 1886. This circumvented the conservative argument that women's rights threatened the family. If need be, the government could enfranchise unmarried women only for local elections, quelling republican anxieties about religious women threatening the republic.[34]

The second innovation in Auclert's petition campaign was her attention to local governments. The municipal councils for French cities and communes and the general councils for the departments of France had no power to grant women's suffrage—only the Chamber of Deputies and the Senate could do that. Nonetheless, Auclert reasoned, women could use their local influence to persuade their councils to adopt motions in favor of women's suffrage; such resolutions were automatically forwarded to parliament, much like a petition from within the government. Auclert adopted this tactic in petitions to both the Municipal Council of Paris in 1885 and the General Council of the Seine in 1885 and 1886. These petitions won no resolutions, but once again Auclert saw a generation ahead of political realities in France. Twenty-seven years later, the UFSF adopted her tactic and won prosuffrage resolutions from fifty-one local governments on the eve of World War I.[35]

The parliamentary reaction to Auclert's petitions was minimal. Hugues, de Gasté, Talandier, Revillon, and a few other deputies supported her by depositing them; they occasionally said a few words on her behalf, although they never made an issue of women's suffrage. The parliamentary reports on Auclert's petitions rarely added anything new to the debate. Some hid behind condescending gallantry, as Frédéric Thomas (opportunist republican, Tarn) did in 1881: "Let us regard it [the

34. For Auclert's thinking on this subject, see her manuscript entitled "Pétition pour le vote des célibataires," Auclert Papers, 6/79.

35. The petition to the general council of the Seine (1885) is the best known of these efforts because it led to a serious debate. See *La Citoyenne*, August 1885; Auclert, *Le Vote des femmes*, pp. 171–75; Auclert, "Voeu à émettre," *Le Radical*, 9 July 1906; Conseil général du département de la Seine, *Procès-verbaux des séances*, 2 December 1885, AD-Seine. For the UFSF campaign for local resolutions in 1912–1914, see Hause with Kenney, *Women's Suffrage and Social Politics*, pp. 144–46.

petition] as the illusion of a sensitive and adventurous heart . . . treating it softly and courteously in moving to the order of the day." Several pronounced traditional attitudes about the position of women, as the Vicomte Lévis-Mirepoix (monarchist, Orne) did in rejecting a public role for them: "We believe that woman has her place marked out in the bosom of the household . . . her principal role consists precisely in the practice of private virtues." Occasionally, however, deputies delivered reports sympathetic to feminism; none of these endorsed women's suffrage, but some suggested that it would be a logical development in the future. Frédéric Escanyé (republican, Pyrénées-Orientales) delivered a report in 1885 citing the ideas of John Stuart Mill but urging the policy of Richer: civil rights first. The largest report of this sort was produced by Godefroy Cavaignac (republican union, Sarthe), the son of the republican general who suppressed the revolt of June 1848. He too held out the hope of civil rights and eventual enfranchisement, but he told Auclert what she already knew: her supporters were too few in number. Until that changed, he concluded, the reform "is not ripened."[36]

36. The parliamentary reaction can be traced by reviewing the reports printed in *JO*, Chamber of Deputies, Documents. The dates for the reports cited are: Thomas Report, 23 May 1882 (quoted); Cavaignac Report, 20 June 1882; Escanyé Report, 12 March 1885; Lévis-Mirepoix Report, 26 October 1886 (quoted). Many reports are preserved in the Auclert Papers, 9/9–18; several are discussed by Auclert in *Le Vote des femmes*, pp. 156–78. See also the long discussion of the Cavaignac Report in *La Citoyenne*, 2 July 1882.

1. Auclert in the early 1870s

2. Antonin Lévrier, circa 1880

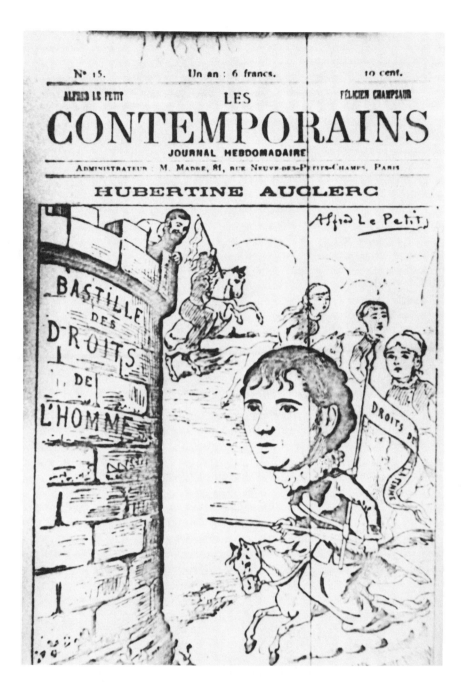

3. A cartoon of 1881 depicting Auclert leading the assault on the fortress of masculine privilege.

4. *La Citoyenne,* with Auclert's cartoon depicting men voting for war while women vote for peace.

5. An anonymous cartoon sent to Auclert. She is shown going to the lunatic asylum at Charenton, saying, "I am neither beautiful . . . nor a maiden." She is answered, "We know it, madam. Come in; your place is reserved."

6. Auclert's propaganda stamp of 1901.

7. Auclert (third from the right) and members of Suffrage des femmes, circa 1905. Gabrielle Chapuis is on Auclert's right.

8. Auclert, holding a folded copy of Suffrage des femmes' 1906 election poster.

Le Petit Journal

Le Petit Journal   5 centimes   SUPPLÉMENT ILLUSTRÉ   5 centimes   ABONNEMENTS

CHAQUE JOUR — 6 PAGES — 5 CENTIMES

Le Petit Journal agricole, 5 cent. — La Mode du Petit Journal 10 cent.

Administration : 61, rue Lafayette   Le Petit Journal illustré de la jeunesse, 10 cent.

Les manuscrits ne sont pas rendus   On s'abonne sans frais dans tous les bureaux de poste

DIX-HUITIÈME ANNÉE   DIMANCHE 17 MAI 1908   Numéro 913

L'ACTION FÉMINISTE

Les « suffragettes » envahissent une section de vote et s'emparent de l'urne électorale

9. A fanciful depiction of Auclert's demonstration of May 3, 1908. It contains many errors of fact, such as its casting of Madeleine Pelletier (center), instead of Auclert (arm raised), as the person who knocked over the ballot box.

10. Auclert at her desk, 1908

11. Auclert striking a candidate's pose, 1910

LE SUFFRAGE DES FEMMES
151, Rue de la Roquette

PROGRAMME

Les Hommes et les Femmes, pareillement justiciables et contribuables, sont égaux devant la Loi et jouissent de leurs droits civils et politiques.

Le suffrage restreint aux Hommes, devient réellement universel en s'universalisant aux Femmes.

La Nation, formée d'Hommes et de Femmes, est intégralement représentée dans les Assemblées administratives et législatives. Les Françaises comme les Français — en attendant qu'ils gèrent directement la Commune et l'Etat — chargent des Mandataires de défendre leurs intérêts au Parlement et à l'Hôtel de Ville.

Les seuls électeurs sont comptés pour établir les circonscriptions électorales. Si les Femmes qui ne sont pas représentées ne contribuaient point à créer des sièges législatifs, il y aurait 310 députés de moins, près de cinq millions d'épargnés.

Les Hommes et les Femmes reçoivent le même développement physique, moral, intellectuel, professionnel.

Toutes les carrières, les emplois, les fonctions publiques sont accessibles aux Femmes comme aux Hommes.

A production égale, salaire égal pour les deux sexes.

L'Etat oppresseur qui nous prend notre argent et qui restreint notre liberté, est remplacé par l'Etat libérateur qui diminue les charges, assure le travail aux Français valides, l'assistance aux malades et infirmes.

Les ménagères, qui font gratuitement à la maison le travail d'homme de peine, de cuisinier, de blanchisseur, ont comme les salariés, droit à la retraite ouvrière.

Chacun touche la totalité du prix de son labeur. Les syndicats responsables, remplaçant les entrepreneurs, sont seuls aptes à recevoir des patrons le travail et à le répartir aux travailleurs.

L'Homme et la Femme sont dans le mariage, des associés égaux qui restent maîtres de leur personne et de leur avoir.

La maternité est la première des fonctions sociales. Les mères dépourvues de moyens d'existence, pendant qu'elles perpétuent la Nation, sont comme les soldats pendant qu'ils défendent le territoire, nourries, logées, vêtues par la société.

Toutes les denrées alimentaires de première nécessité, sont exemptées d'impôts.

La justice est gratuite. Les tribunaux et les jurys sont composés d'hommes et de femmes.

Les électeurs délèguent leurs pouvoirs pour un an, jusqu'à ce qu'ils gardent en permanence leur souveraineté en exerçant directement le gouvernement.

Les candidates :

HUBERTINE AUCLERT, GABRIELLE CHAPUIS, RENÉE MORTIER

ELECTEURS, votez pour ces candidates.

Imposez l'entrée des femmes dans le droit commun, elles vous aideront à pénétrer le mécanisme de la politique et bientôt, vos serez à même de rester vos maîtres.

La Société le SUFFRAGE des FEMMES, 151, rue de la Roquette.

imp. LOMBARDIN, b° Voltaire, 148. Paris.

12. Auclert's program during her candidacy for the Chamber of Deputies in 1910. She made a handwritten change on many copies of this poster so that the call for state aid for mothers read, "Mothers, married or unmarried . . . "

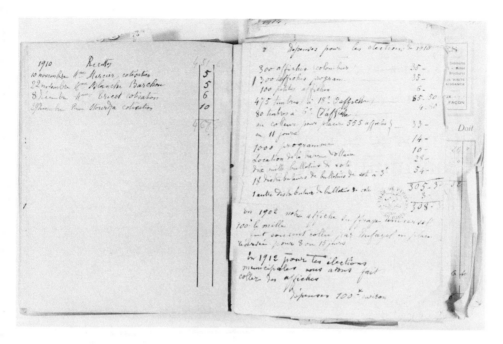

13. Auclert's financial records for Suffrage des femmes, showing her expenses for the parliamentary elections of 1910. Notes pinned to the foot of the page reveal the sharp increase in costs since 1902 and the subsequent reduction of her activity in 1912.

❧

CHAPTER SIX

Renewed Socialism and Continuing Loneliness, 1885–1888

W hen Hubertine Auclert reconsidered the question of where to turn for support in the mid-1880s, she turned again to socialism. After her expulsion from the Parti ouvrier in 1880, Auclert had paid little attention to the party. Her articles about it were mostly critical, her private feelings angry. Five years of exhausting work to win the vote did not increase her sympathy for the Guesdist policy of postponing women's rights; her political instinct told her that those who did not support women in the present would betray them in the future, as the men of 1789 and 1848 had done. She denounced "the ridiculous class war" and scorned the women of "ridiculous abnegation" who preferred socialism to feminism. She exposed the antifeminism of workers and the insincerity of their leaders: "Shame on the cowards of the far left who have promised women so much." She blasted individual socialists whom she found retrograde. Jules Vallès, a communard who wrote for several leftist newspapers before founding the socialist daily *Le Cri du peuple* in 1883, invited her wrath with an article in 1881 suggesting that feminists were producing a generation of lesbians and bearded women.[1]

1. See *La Citoyenne*, 24 and 31 July 1881, 31 October 1881, 28 November 1881, 1 October 1882 (first two quotations), and January 1884 (third quotation) for Auclert's criticism of socialist attitudes on the woman question. For a good illustration of her perception of working-class antifeminism, see 3 December 1883; see 26 December 1881 for her response to Vallès. Auclert's rage at Vallès never abated, and as late as December 1910 she was denouncing his memory at a meeting of sf. See minutes of sf meeting, 8 December 1910, Auclert Papers, 4/21; see also an untitled manuscript, ibid., 6/237.

Auclert nonetheless considered herself a socialist. She continued to support mutualism, especially cooperatives of women workers, to write fondly of Blanqui, to admire the reformist socialism of her parliamentary allies, such as Hugues, and to publish occasional reports on the socialist congresses. These congresses gave Auclert hope that a feminist, republican socialism could emerge in France. The sixth socialist congress, held at Saint Etienne in September 1882, ended in another splintering of the movement. The majority of the delegates, including Hugues and Mink, followed Paul Brousse in creating a possibilist party; a minority left for Roanne with Guesde, to regroup as the Parti ouvrier français. Could this split lead to a sympathetic socialism led by Hugues? Auclert still had good relations with Hugues and with Pierre, who both continued to contribute to *La Citoyenne*. She also maintained cordial relations with Benoît Malon, a possibilist, and Eugène Fournière, who defended women's rights in *Le Progrès social* and produced the possibilist *La Revue socialiste* from 1885. The possibilists disappointed Auclert, however, and she never joined their federation. They were sufficiently republican, and she accepted their socialism, but, aside from a few individuals, she found them unsympathetic to suffragism. Indeed, Auclert blamed the possibilists for encouraging Mink to denounce feminist priorities. This dispute worsened in 1884 when Mink publicly criticized Auclert several times. Despite her criticism of socialists, however, Auclert was even more disillusioned with "the little Robespierres" of the republican left, and she kept looking for that socialist home.[2]

THE FEDERATION REPUBLICAINE SOCIALISTE, 1884–1885

Auclert believed that she had found her niche in French socialism during the winter of 1884–1885, when she joined a socialist party for the second time. In the fall of 1884, she had participated in a free thought congress at Paris. Republican socialists there carried a motion in favor of the political rights of women. Auclert thereupon joined discussions about forming a federation of dissatisfied republican socialists, in anticipation of the parliamentary elections of October 1885. These talks led, in December 1884, to the assembly of 150 moderate socialists in the basement meeting hall of a Montmartre café, where Auclert and Giraud represented Suffrage des femmes. They agreed to found a Fédération républicaine socialiste in the Paris region and to accept women as

2. *DMO*, 10:76, 78; Dalotel preface to Mink, *Communarde et féministe*, p. 26; police report, 20 April 1884, Dossier Auclert, APP; *La Citoyenne*, 16 January 1882, 4 September 1882, 15 November 1883, 3 December 1883, January 1884 (quoted), and February 1885; diary, 19 April 1884, Auclert Papers.

members. Auclert obtained membership card number sixteen (bright red and embellished with both the revolutionary *bonnet rouge* and masonic emblems) and election to the five-person organizing committee.[3]

Auclert fought tenaciously to make the federation adopt her ideas from the beginning. With the approval of the organizing committee, she put the equality of women, including political equality, on the agenda for the founding meeting. Following a vigorous two-day debate, this program won the divided endorsement of the 150 men and 2 women who were founders. She described the victory in her diary: "I am returning from the Republican Federation. It is almost two o'clock in the morning. After two days of discussions, we succeeded in putting political equality in the program. But how it has been necessary to fight. I was as happy as possible. But in coming home I felt sad. Isolated. I was hurt to see that I had so many enemies and no friends." How important was this victory, and the apparent discovery of an ideological home, to Auclert? In the thousands of pages of her private papers and published writings there are not five other instances of her saying that she was happy.[4]

Auclert's success transformed the Fédération républicaine socialiste, but it also led indirectly to its death. Some militant feminists enrolled; their truculent opponents departed. Among the newcomers were two rivals of Auclert, Jules Allix and Louise Barberouse, both former members of Suffrage des femmes, who destroyed the federation that she envisioned. Barberouse, forty-eight years old, was an *institutrice* who ran a small school for girls in Paris. Allix, sixty-six, was an impoverished lawyer, supported by his sisters who also aided Barberouse in the operation of her school. He was also one of the most eccentric figures of the French left, with the remarkable record of having been arrested by the Second Republic, for involvement in the radical plans of June 1849; three times by the Second Empire, including a long exile after a conviction in 1853; by the Commune, despite being an elected member of it; and by the Third Republic, for being a communard. Along the way, Allix had been twice confined in the asylum of Charenton for being mentally infirm, a judgment shared by the governments that imprisoned him and by many colleagues on the left. His eccentricities included the belief that he was a supernatural being, the refusal of medical treatment because physicians were possessed by the devil, and a series of lectures

3. Police reports, 26 September 1884, 17 and 24 (2) December 1884, Dossier Auclert, APP; *La Citoyenne,* October 1884; note on the FRS, Auclert Papers, 7/1; Auclert's membership card, ibid., 10/31.

4. Diary, 19 December 1884, Auclert Papers; police report, 19 December 1884, Dossier Auclert, APP.

TABLE 6.1. **Parisian Feminist Leagues in the 1880s**

Name	Founded	Leader(s)	Publication	Program	Membership
Amélioration	1870	Deraismes	none	moderate	c. 150
Droit des femmes; later, Suffrage des femmes	1876	Auclert	*La Citoyenne*	militant	c. 100
Union des femmes	1880	Rouzade	none	socialist	
LFDF	1882	Richer	*Le Droit des femmes*	moderate	c. 200
Ligue de la protec- tion des femmes	1884	Barberouse, Allix	none	militant	c. 100
Egalité	1888	Vincent	none	militant	

Note: Little evidence exists about other, ephemeral organizations. Among the figures mentioned, Allix also led a "women's committee" in 1880; Astié de Valsayre led a short-lived "Groupe des femmes indépendentes" in 1889; Potonié-Pierre attempted to found a "Ligue socialiste des femmes" the same year.

in 1870 to explain how women could wear acid-filled devices to prevent being raped by the Prussians.[5]

In 1884 Allix and Barberouse were members of the eight-person committee that directed Suffrage des femmes. Perhaps this suggests how much Auclert needed dedicated followers; perhaps it indicates that they were not quite the odd pair that contemporaries depicted. Both had the feminist credentials of membership in Amélioration; both later served as officers of that moderate league, after a period of interest in anarchism. They also shared Auclert's advocacy of mutualism. Their role in Suffrage des femmes was short-lived, and they departed after an unexplained argument with Auclert in 1884; Auclert merely recorded in her diary that Barberouse had insulted her. Allix and Barberouse then founded their own militant feminist society, usually called the Ligue de la protection des femmes (the name varies). As Rouzade's Union des femmes had collapsed following the socialist schism of 1882, the creation of this league brought the number of feminist societies in Paris back to four (see table 6.1).[6]

The Ligue de la protection des femmes dogged Auclert's footsteps in the winter of 1884–1885, emulating many of her actions, past and present. The federation spent January 1885 studying the electoral program (*profession de foi*) of every incumbent deputy in the Paris region as

5. See Allix's biography in *DMO*, 4:107–10, which leaves no doubt that he "had a deficient mental state." See also the report on him in the Ministry of Interior files, F[18] 369.

6. *La Citoyenne*, July 1884; diary, 31 December 1884, Auclert Papers. For the fate of Rouzade's group, see Sowerwine, *Sisters or Citizens*, pp. 41–47.

well as the manifesto of every socialist or radical republican faction preparing for the elections of October. Auclert sought a policy of supporting candidates who endorsed the federation's program of December 1884 (which would include some possibilists, such as Hugues) or who included certain key points in their *profession de foi*. In the midst of delicate negotiations with the antisuffragists who had lost the vote in December, Allix and Barberouse joined the federation and replaced diplomacy with warfare. In February 1885 the schism in the Fédération républicaine socialiste was complete; all remaining antisuffrage feminists left for the radical-socialist parliamentary faction (the Union socialiste) of George Clemenceau, Charles Floquet, and Camille Pelletan.

The rupture of the Fédération républicaine socialiste left Auclert in an ironic position. Her suffragist career had been characterized by uncompromising militancy, but she felt her isolation and her need for allies. If she wanted to expand her activity beyond the small nucleus of Suffrage des femmes, if she wanted a republican-socialist base from which to participate in French politics, she must learn to be more conciliatory. For nearly two months she had courted the federation with patience and tact. Suddenly, the federation had been shattered by the uncompromising militancy of others. After the schism, the federation ceased to be a socialist party; it was another feminist group in the guise of a political party. Auclert, of course, had no true choice in the schism. Allix and Barberouse had practiced Auclertism. Clemenceau, an undisguised antisuffragist, would not have accepted Auclert, even if she had wished to follow her recent rivals. So she stayed with the federation, and she even briefly held its presidency in March 1885. She continued, as her diary shows, to give herself passionately to the federation. But she had lost her opportunity to rejoin the socialist movement, and she knew it.[7]

THE ELECTIONS OF 1885

Feminists anticipated the parliamentary elections of 1885 by remembering the municipal elections of 1881 and 1884. They considered that the striking feature of both elections had been women candidates. Several provincial candidacies in 1884 had followed Rouzade's campaign of 1881 with encouraging results. The mayor of a commune in Landes permitted two women to vote, for which he was fined two hundred francs. In communes in Cher, Lot-et-Cher, and Seine-inférieure, women won election to municipal councils; although invali-

7. Police reports, 11, 14, 28, 29 and 31 January 1885, 3, 5, 11, 12, and 18 February 1885, and 11 March 1885; diary, 6 March 1885, Auclert Papers.

dated, these events were widely noted. Even the resolutely antifeminist *Le Figaro*, which had recently been taunting Auclert with the notion that she would next want votes for cattle, noted that "there is, in these still isolated facts, a beginning."[8]

Suffragists concluded that it was time to organize a major feminist candidacy in Paris. There is little evidence of Auclert's thoughts on this subject during the winter of 1884–1885, but her papers contain three separate sets of notes on the 1884 results, so it was clearly on her mind. The January meeting of Suffrage des femmes discussed women's candidacies and reached two conclusions: Maria Deraismes was the best possible candidate and Louise Michel was completely unacceptable. This presumably means that Auclert did not wish to run. She certainly intended the Fédération républicaine socialiste to be the focus of her electoral activities; she participated in three to five meetings every week during January to prepare electoral strategy. Aside from her work in the federation, she exhorted women to register to vote. In January *La Citoyenne* published this appeal and Auclert and a few members of Suffrage des femmes sought to register. They received a polite denial and had their requests forwarded to the electoral commission; formal rejections arrived on schedule early in February. Auclert did not appeal, as she had in 1881, because she had other uses for her time.[9]

Louise Barberouse and a few members of her league chose to contest the denial of registration. The Ligue de la protection des femmes had sponsored a registration campaign in the First Arrondissement, where Barberouse was denied a voter's card. She and one supporter, retracing Auclert's four-year-old footsteps, appealed to a *juge de paix* in that quartier, then turned to the court of appeals. Léon Giraud and Jules Allix represented Barberouse with a brief almost precisely the same as Auclert's had been: that the term *Français* included women. This produced a long decree that examined the law in detail and concluded that women were indeed excluded from voting. Barberouse thus joined the Fédération républicaine socialiste in February 1885 in a belligerent mood, comparable to Auclert's when she began her tax rebellion.[10]

Auclert initially reacted to Barberouse's militancy by attempting to save the federation as a political party. She was perturbed that the press

8. Note on 1884 elections, Auclert Papers, Carton 1; manuscript on women in politics in the 1880s, ibid., 6/311; Auclert, *Le Vote des femmes*, p. 131; Auclert, "Parias françaises," *Le Radical*, 2 May 1908; Auclert, "Les Conseillères municipales," *La Citoyenne*, June 1884; *Le Figaro*, 7 June 1884.

9. Mayor of Tenth Arrondissement to Auclert, 10 February 1885, Auclert Papers, 10/3; *La Citoyenne*, January, February, and March 1885; Auclert, *Le Vote des femmes*, p. 127; *La Tribune*, 26 January 1885.

10. M. Dalloz et al., eds., *Recueil périodique et critique de jurisprudence, de législation et de doctrine* . . . (Paris, 1885), pp. 105–8; *Le National*, 10 February 1885.

described Barberouse as the leading suffrage activist and Auclert as her follower. Barberouse angered her further by insisting upon actions that divided the federation. The press spoke of "a women's war," but for once Auclert chose not to fight her rival. She persuaded the rump federation to act as if it were a political party by seeking electoral alliances. Such arrangements were traditional in French politics, the product of a multi-party system and a two-stage system of voting. Auclert perceived plausible alliances with groups ranging from the possibilists to the Union socialiste. The federation appointed a five-person committee, led by Auclert, to attend the electoral meetings of other factions and propose collaboration.

The search for allies exacerbated Auclert's frustration. Most parties cited the court ruling of 1883, which Auclert herself had provoked, permitting electoral meetings to be closed to women. They refused to admit her, much less to hear her. Only twice did she get inside the doors. A small group of Blanquist socialist revolutionaries allowed her to join them but answered her proposal with the old argument that the emancipation of women must await the liberation of the working class. Auclert attended the second meeting illicitly. At the invitation of Adolphe Maujan, editor of the socialist *La France libre* and later a radical-socialist deputy, Auclert went to several meetings of the Union socialiste. Each time, the doorkeeper denied her entry, although he offered to admit her male companions. Then, at a meeting in the Fourth Arrondissement, she sneaked into the hall. Her presence among the Clemencists, Auclert recalled with a nice play on words, produced "a great agitation among the men who discovered a 'citizeness' there, [and] they said, in the tone in which one would have remarked the presence of a tiger, 'women don't have the right to come in here.'" Several apoplectic citizens demanded Auclert's removal. After being shouted down when she spoke of the principles of 1789, she left. She entered no other electoral meetings in 1885.[11]

Auclert aired her anger in the May 1885 issue of *La Citoyenne*. She published a petition calling on the Chamber of Deputies to amend the Law of Public Meetings of 1881 to permit women to attend electoral meetings. In two separate articles, she raged at socialists and republicans alike. The first of these, a leader entitled "Class Struggle, Struggle of the Sexes," illustrates some of the tensions between bourgeois feminism and socialism, and partly substantiates the assertion that Auclert was not a socialist. Auclert was indeed not a socialist in 1885 if the term is defined as a revolutionary collectivist. She, however, believed herself

11. Jeanne Voitout (Auclert), "Le Péril," *La Citoyenne*, May 1885 (quoted); police reports, 18 March 1885, 15 and 23 April 1885, Dossier Auclert, APP; note on the FRS, Auclert Papers, 7/1.

to be a socialist and used the term. Her essay echoed the ideas that she held at Marseilles in 1879. In fact, it is difficult to distinguish her thoughts on the two occasions. Was it the socialist heroine of 1879 or the socialist outcast of 1885 who pled for full social justice:

> While one works to put an end to the inequalities between the rich and the poor, without working at the same time to put an end to the inequalities between women and men, one does the work less of lovers of justice than of the ambitious, impatient to leave their ranks. . . .
>
> Those who set off for war against the monopolists of capital do not bear in mind that men are like the rich, the monopolists in society.
>
> Is the rich woman freer in marriage than the poor woman? Can the one better dispose of her dowry than the other of her salary?
>
> Does the rich woman have more right than the poor woman to participate in the government of her country?"[12]

In both 1879 and 1885, Auclert left no doubt that she would attack any doctrine that delayed women's rights.

The same issue of *La Citoyenne* included Auclert's excoriation of French republicans. She had not lost her faith in republicanism any more than she had in egalitarianism. But the behavior of republicans seemed to menace France. "Where is the peril?" she asked. "The peril comes from the side of the republicans who refuse to put into practice the principles that they pronounce. . . . These men [are] more arrogant with women than the nobles before 1789 were with other men." Directing her words to Clemenceau and the radical republicans, she concluded that "the *word* Republic is sufficient for them, and they do not intend to organize the *thing.*"[13]

When it became clear that the Fédération républicaine socialiste would not become a parliamentary party, Auclert agreed to exploit it as a feminist party. She returned to the idea of an electoral campaign by Deraismes, whom *La Citoyenne* dubbed "a future deputy." Barberouse and Allix again seized the initiative, asking the federation to announce a full slate of feminist candidates. Their list included Deraismes, Auclert, Barberouse, Mink, Michel, Séverine (a socialist who directed Vallés' *Cri du peuple*), Rouzade, Potonié-Pierre, and Juliette Adam (the editor of *La Nouvelle revue*, whose feminist credentials dated to a book rebutting

---

12. Auclert, "Lutte de classes, lutte de sexes," May 1885. This essay is reprinted in Taïeb's edition of articles from *La Citoyenne*, pp. 99–101, and in Albistur and Armogathe, *Le Grief des femmes*, 2:110–11.

13. Jeanne Voitout (Auclert), "Le Péril," *La Citoyenne*, May 1885.

Proudhon's antifeminism in 1861). It ended with a group of celebrities: Sarah Bernhardt, Madeleine Godard (a noted violinist), and Madame Clovis Hugues (notorious for murdering a detective who erroneously reported that she was the "other woman" in an adultery case, for which *crime passionel* she was acquitted).

This plan irritated Auclert, who felt that better publicity could be generated by concentrating on a single candidate who had some hope of success. She considered the inclusion of celebrities a demeaning gimmick, and strongly opposed the invitations to those women with whom she had strained relations, namely, Mink, Michel, and Séverine, whom she considered tarred with the brush of the despised Vallès). To her dismay, the federation, including many present and former members of Suffrage des femmes, supported Barberouse. In August 1885, all the women on her list were invited to be candidates for the Chamber of Deputies.[14]

Virtually all the women asked to run refused, beginning with Auclert. She wrote a letter to the federation, and sent copies of it to the press, stating that it was inappropriate for her to run because people might conclude that she had labored for the political rights of women in order to aggrandize herself. She would feel more comfortable working for the principle, not for personal success. A wave of refusals followed. Mme Hugues declined because "I have never accomplished any political act capable of attracting the attention of my fellow citizens." Mink gave the collectivist answer: "I do not believe that it will be by the conquest of their political rights that women will have their situation ameliorated." Michel added an anarchist perspective: "You know quite well that I am not in favor of candidates. . . . Each of us fights with the weapon that she believes the best, but the ballot is less than ever mine." Juliette Adam asserted that French women were not ready for such emancipation. Séverine said she had no taste for martyrdom. Pierre, who still wrote for *La Citoyenne*, cited Auclert's original answer: "I do not see any chance of success in multiple candidacies." Auclert presumably took an impolite pleasure in devoting several columns of *La Citoyenne* to these letters.[15]

Three of the invited feminists ran for parliament in 1885: Barberouse, Rouzade, and, to the surprise of many, Deraismes. The pendulum of Deraismes' thinking about political rights had swung toward support in

14. *La Citoyenne*, May 1885 (quoted); *Paris-Journal*, 19 June 1910; *Paris*, 20 August 1885.

15. Auclert to FRS, 18 August 1885, printed in many newspapers, such as *Le Cri du peuple* and *La Liberté* of 19 August 1885); in Taïeb's edition of articles from *La Citoyenne*, pp. 39–40; and with all of the other rejections in *La Citoyenne*, September 1885 (quoted). Police reports, 18 and 26 August 1885, Dossier Auclert, APP.

the spring of 1885. In an article entitled "Women in Politics," she explained that she had known that politics concerned her directly since the day in 1870 when three thousand Prussians had occupied her country estate. That experience had led to her active role in the republican politics of the 1870s, at the same risk of proscription as her male colleagues. She now concluded that "the civil and political equality of the two sexes is near, it is a necessity of historical evolution." Her answer to Barberouse, however, was still ambivalent. Because men would determine women's rights, she would let them decide on the appropriateness of her candidacy; she would allow her name to be put before them, but she would do nothing to seek their votes. "I do not refuse," she put it, "but I do not propose [to act]."[16]

The Fédération républicaine socialiste's slate did not remain small. When the prominent feminists repulsed her offer, Barberouse, now fully in control of the federation, extended the opportunity to any member willing to run. This produced a list of more than two dozen candidates even before Deraismes accepted. None were known outside feminist circles, except Céleste Hardouin, Eliska Vincent, and Lara Marcel. Fully half the slate consisted of followers of Auclert who defected to join Barberouse.[17]

This was the final straw for Auclert. There had been an unresolved tension in her relationship with Barberouse since she and Allix had left Suffrage des femmes. Auclert blamed her for the destruction of the original Fédération républicaine socialiste, for ruining the electoral strategy of a single feminist candidate, for a variety of personal insults, and quite possibly for usurping her spot in the public's attention. Until now she had stopped short of attacking a fellow militant. But Barberouse's siphoning off a dozen members from Suffrage des femmes' tiny cadre changed that. In interviews and lectures during August 1885 (before Deraismes' acceptance), Auclert branded the federation a group of "blustering nonentities" (*nullités tapageuses*) who possessed ambition but neither merit nor intelligence. Barberouse's followers might number more than one hundred, but they "did not include one serious woman." Auclert later denied using the precise words attributed to her, and calmed down enough to write a leader for *La Citoyenne* urging men to vote for the women candidates, whose number dropped to six by election day. She even printed a biographical sketch describing Barberouse as intelligent—adding that she was "a bit difficult" (*un peu*

16. Deraismes, "Les Femmes et la politique," *Le Républicain de Seine-et-Oise*, 18 April 1885; Deraismes to Barberouse, as published in *Le Rappel*, 3 September 1885; police reports, 15 and 21 September 1885, Dossier Deraismes, APP.

17. The full list is given in a clipping of August 1885 in the Auclert Papers, Carton 1; a shorter list is in *La Citoyenne*, September 1885.

forte), that "she knows how to assimilate ideas," and that she lacked "personal originality." Whatever the true extent of Auclert's anger, neither the entry of Deraismes nor the passage of time mollified her. More than twenty years later she still wrote scornfully of the elections.[18]

Auclert dropped out of the Fédération républicaine socialiste in mid-1885, but she did not cease her own activity. In a single week at the end of May, she organized the two largest feminist marches yet seen in the streets of Paris. In the first, over two hundred participants assembled to honor Jeanne d'Arc on the anniversary of her execution. Auclert had been thinking for months that a patriotic celebration of Jeanne d'Arc was more appropriate for women than Bastille Day, which was a glorious anniversary of freedom for men only. Jeanne d'Arc (who became a right-wing symbol only during the campaign for her sainthood in the early twentieth century) remained Auclert's "personification of feminism," a woman who continued her battle "despite sarcasm and abuse." Auclert organized the march to lay a wreath at the gilded statue of Jeanne d'Arc on the Place des Pyramides. The second march, the very next day later, was part of a vast public demonstration, the funeral cortege for Victor Hugo. Auclert still admired Hugo, despite his rejection of the presidency of Suffrage des femmes. His funeral procession marched from the Arc de Triomphe to the Pantheon, where he was interred. Auclert secured a position for Suffrage des femmes with other political groups at the end of the procession. So enormous was the tribute to Hugo—an estimated two million attended—that the members of Suffrage des femmes, assembled in line at 9:00 A.M., entered the Panthéon at 6:00 P.M., spending nine hours on their feet the day after they had marched several miles. Auclert found the crowds along the streets, especially in the Quartier Latin, "truly sympathetic" at the sight of Suffrage des femmes' banner which, with typical frugality, she had sewn on the back of the Droit des femmes banner used in the march to the Bastille in 1881.[19]

Auclert took only a small role in the actual election campaigns. She agreed to give a public lecture on behalf of the candidates in September

18. See especially the accounts in *Le National*, 27 August 1885, and *Le Figaro*, 23 and 27 August 1885; police report, 12 September 1885, Dossier Auclert, APP; Auclert, *Le Vote des femmes*, p. 111.

19. Diary, 22 May and 1 June 1885, Auclert Papers; *La Citoyenne*, 20 February 1881, 6 March 1881, July 1884, and June 1885; Auclert, *Le Vote des femmes*, p. 107; manuscript on public demonstrations, Auclert Papers, 6/124; Auclert, *Les Femmes au gouvernail*, pp. 60–64 (quoted); police report, 29 May 1885, Dossier Auclert, APP. See also the description of Hugo's funeral in his biographies, such as André Maurois' *Olympio: The Life of Victor Hugo* (New York, 1956), pp. 442–45, an in contemporary accounts, such as Maurice Barrès, *Les Déracinés*, 2 vols (Paris, 1961).

1885, despite her grudge against Barberouse. According to her diary, she was again feeling insecure, lonely, and inadequate. She hated being "forced to mount the rostrum." In a pained entry afterwards she pronounced herself "so ineloquent." After the lecture that entry described, Auclert began to withdraw. She confined her activity to *La Citoyenne*, where she could "defend the principle" without being involved in Barberouse's campaign. She composed a feminist electoral program and urged the candidates to adopt it (see appendix 2). This program suggested that her thinking had turned toward radical republicanism again—her social policy sounded more like radical solidarism than socialism. But she made no effort at a new rapprochement with republicans; instead, she ignored the elections and concentrated on a petition to the council of the Seine.[20]

No record of the success of feminist candidates in the balloting of October 1885 exists because the government refused to count their votes. The six women who remained in the race, including Barberouse, Rouzade, and Deraismes, undoubtedly received few "stolen votes" (Auclert's term); even in the twentieth century, with suffragism well established, women candidates fared better in municipal elections than in parliamentary elections. Auclert could not resist suggesting in *La Citoyenne* that it was Barberouse's fault that the votes remained uncounted: "If there had been, as we asked, only one or two candidates, certain farcical scenes would not have taken place and the votes could have been counted."[21]

The events of 1885 constituted an important feminist accomplishment, although less important than Auclert's voter registration and tax boycott campaign of 1880–1881. Auclert had begun suffragist activity in France, generated a great deal of publicity, and placed the issue on the national agenda. The demonstration of 1885 extended Auclert's work.[22] It represented an increase in the scale of feminist activity—perhaps two hundred people participated—and was sustained over several months. Before 1885, antisuffragists might have claimed that only one woman crusaded for political rights. After 1885 they could consider the movement small, or internally divided, but they could not deny its growth or its permanence on the political landscape. That someone else had generated the electoral demonstration also was an accomplishment for

20. Diary, 12 September 1885, Auclert Papers (quoted); Auclert, "Programme électoral des femmes," *La Citoyenne*, August and September 1885.

21. Voitout (Auclert), "Voix volées," *La Citoyenne*, October 1885.

22. See Bidelman, *Pariahs Stand Up!*, p. 137, for the argument that the feminist "shadow campaign" represented "the single most important women's suffrage demonstration during the feminist movement's formative years." Bidelman stresses that the multiple races were an effective tactic because they required few women and offered numerous stages of activity.

Auclert. She felt weary and frustrated in 1885, but her energy and determination had maintained the suffrage campaign until other women took the initiative. She would never again dominate center stage as she had from 1881 through 1884. But she could draw comfort from the knowledge that her cause would outlive her.

The year 1885 had begun with enthusiasm. A new republican-socialist party welcomed Auclert, put women's rights in its program, and envisioned representation in parliament. Within a few months, the Fédération républicaine socialiste was moribund. The established parties scorned Auclert as much as ever, and she wound up in angry fights with both socialists and republicans. In the process, she alienated political friends and got involved in another battle with Richer, who accused her in *Le Droit des femmes* of damaging republican electoral prospects. Auclert next lost control of the federation to a group of her former followers. When she challenged Barberouse over multiple candidates, she watched in pain as her supporters defected. Throughout it all she saw the cold face of journalism, as articles discussed her loss of leadership and her hypocrisy in not running herself. Hubertine Auclert did not feel victorious in 1885; she again felt alone. Her diary provides sad evidence of her growing depression. In March 1885: "It would be good to live if I were not alone." April: "All alone, without friends, without advice." May: "Victor Hugo is dead. . . . Oh, why, stupid death, did you not take me, the lonely, the sad, the hopeless, in place of this god of the earth, so loved and adored?"[23]

Auclert's invocation of death suggests how vulnerable and dispirited she had become, even if those lines were written in a fit of self-pity or with a diarist's self-dramatization. A diary is difficult to interpret; entries cannot be taken as pure facts. But people do not contemplate their own death in this way, even melodramatically, unless they have experienced significant pain. Auclert lacked intimate friends with whom to discuss her problems. She wanted to believe herself a calmer and gentler person than her career had demanded and the press had depicted. She needed to assimilate her identity as a leader, a female in a traditional male role. She had denied herself the domestic and maternal feminine role, and she feared that she had thereby lost joy and love. Her diary emerged from these difficulties. It could replace the friends she had sacrificed for her career. In her diary she could be timid and insecure—traits she never showed in public, partly because she had to act with presumed masculine strength to compete in a masculine world,

---

23. See Bidelman, *Pariahs Stand Up!*, pp. 167–72, for arguments between Auclert and Richer during this period. Diary, 6 March 1885, 24 April 1885, and 22 May 1885, Auclert Papers.

partly because her character was not, in fact, very timid. In her diary she could admit to feeling lonely or hurt by the ridicule she faced. In her diary she could acknowledge how much she wanted love and how she suffered from the loss of Lévrier, while knowing that she still must refuse him. When Auclert felt the weight of these choices, she explained them to herself with the image of the martyr, an image, chosen from the vocation from which she had been rejected, that strengthened and clarified her role in the career she built. When that self-image did not satisfy the needs that made her a diarist, she extended it to its logical conclusion, death. She did not fundamentally desire death (although she risked creating another self-fulfilling image), but death suited martyr-dom and was the ultimate resolution of the conflicts that produced her diary.

Auclert had begun building this bridge of words between her public persona and her private existence when the question of marrying Lévrier drove her to introspection. The diary ended on the same question. Lévrier had remained a theme in its pages. Auclert did not dwell on her anxieties concerning him, but they emerged regularly: "No news from Antonin." "I think that Antonin will not return to Paris." Even during the struggles over the Fédération républicaine socialiste, he occupied the center of her thoughts: "How my character has changed! Now I feel the anxiety of love more than anyone else." She had not reached her emotional nadir. The promotion that might have returned Lévrier to Paris came in early 1886. But he was posted to Tahiti. Auclert recorded her feelings:

> I sensed a feeling of well-being, I was happy for a few days. Then this morning I received a letter from Antonin that turned my joy to tears; it announced that he was about to be sent to Tahiti to replace the imperial procurator. . . . I cried, cried, cried, rum-maged through an atlas. Marie tried to comfort me, but every-thing has become bleak for me. This will pass, and if I went with Antonin to the end of the world, I would never forgive myself for having sacrificed Marie, my library, the cause, my quasi well-being to a man who has always brought me more pain than joy. Love was always thus, so fragile, so easily broken! How much I have sacrificed as I have loved, to be loved so little. Beautiful women have the joys and triumphs of love. Ugly me has had only its sorrows and sacrifices. Is nature so cruel as to put into the bodies least made for love the hearts most avid for love?"

Auclert pleaded with Lévrier to stay in France, but she still would not marry him. Neither would abandon their careers. Within three weeks, it was over: "Despite my prayers and supplications, Antonin is leaving.

He told me coldly, without hesitation: 'I have no choice but to stab you to the heart.' " These were the last words that Auclert recorded in her diary.[24]

LA CITOYENNE, 1886–1888

The intersection of her political and personal crises in 1885 and 1886 deeply affected Hubertine Auclert, and she sharply curtailed her feminist activity. She continued to write for *La Citoyenne*, but she no longer worked at the hectic pace of 1880–1885. By 1888, she even lost interest in her paper and let its circulation tumble. She staged no more public demonstrations. She attempted no new overtures to political parties. She still submitted petitions, but without apparent enthusiasm; her correspondence with politicians and newspapers virtually ceased.

Because writing had become the sole expression of her feminism, it is important to examine Auclert's essays in *La Citoyenne* to understand the person and her politics. Auclert published 258 signed articles there between 1881 and 1891 (see appendix 2) under her own name and those of "H.A.," "Liberta," and "Jeanne Voitout." She produced hundreds of other articles to fill the paper, but these were primarily simple reports of meetings, reproduced documents, announcements, and the like.

Auclert's essays display an educated, if not a polished or literary, style. Her provincial youth shows in her penchant for rural metaphors. For example, she derided French electors for their docile acceptance of any regime by calling them "well-trained sheep" (August 1881). Her convent education shaped her style even more. Christian imagery, Biblical allusions, and the vocabulary of the church abound. Women, for example, were "excommunicated from public life" (March 1881). She liberally sprinkled her articles with her conventual Latin. The Third Republic could not represent *res publicum*, only "res hominum" (July 1882). She demonstrated familiarity with French history and frequently drew historical parallels in her analyses. Her knowledge extended, for example, to the texts of the debates at the Estates General of 1614, which provided her with a comparison between republican antisuffragism and the speeches of the Marquis de Sennecy, who spoke against accepting members of the Third Estate as equals because they were different (August 1881). For an essay on the dowry, Auclert explored the roots of the institution in the laws of Numa Pompilius, the Justinian Code, and the decrees of the Council of Arles in 524 A.D. (December

24. Diary, 6 March and 24 April 1885, 12 March 1886 (translated by Bidelman, *Pariahs Stand Up!*, p. 150), Auclert Papers; Lévrier to de Gasté, 26 October 1891, ibid., 13/23; police report, 1 December 1893, Dossier Auclert, APP.

1881). Auclert must have acquired much of her historical education through her own reading. She regularly demonstrated an interest in the French Revolution of 1789; she delighted, for example, in quoting or paraphrasing revolutionary rhetoric to show that it should apply to women but actually exposed male hypocrisy. In one clever article, she mimicked the Abbe Sièyes' *What is the Third Estate?* with the refrain "What are women?" (July 1881).

The distinctive and revealing aspect of Auclert's rhetoric is the passion with which she approached her subjects. One can see the aggressive and bold individual, feel the strong will and stubborn character, and recognize the dedication in her fiery prose. Auclert might call herself timid in her diary, but her essays bespeak no timidity. Instead, her words are frontal assaults upon "Masculinism"—the male "tyranny" or "despotism" that "annihilates" women or reduces them to "slavery." Her obituary for Gambetta, for example, lambasted him as a "masculinist to the bitter end" (January 1883). Such rhetorical vehemence separated Auclert from the caution of Richer and Deraismes as much as did their disputes about tactics. She frequently showed her candor in her disagreements with them. Even when she wrote to praise Richer for his *La Femme libre* and to claim the Botha Prize for him, she could not resist adding, "To be sure, M. Richer's book is far from living up to its title" (June 1881).

Auclert used language that suited her and her policies: the language of activism, the exhortative style of street demonstrations, rather than the discretion of the salon and drawing room. This does not mean that she wrote without wit. She relished the sarcastic needle as well as the ideological sword. To an argument that superior education made men the electors, she responded that only "pants make an elector" (February 1881). Fulminating against the exclusion of women from a state banquet, she inquired if republicans thought that "women lacked the discernment to eat too" (July 1882). Criticizing Camille Sée for aspects of shortsighted inequality in his education bill, she proposed "a subscription campaign to buy him some binoculars" (July 1881). On the whole, however, Auclert preferred to use a verbal broadsword to slash monarchist "clods" (October 1882) and senatorial "criminals" (March 1883). And she could wield her sword with ferocity; the deathbed conversion to Catholicism of a foe, the positivist lexicographer Emile Littré, earned the headline, "The Last Grimace of the Monkey Littré" (June 1881).

As her aggressive style implies, Auclert aimed *La Citoyenne* chiefly at an audience of Parisian feminists and the urban women whom she hoped to convert. Although she realized that Parisian journalists read her essays, she directed her articles to women, whom she often addressed directly as *vous*, telling them that her campaigns were to win "your rights" (for example, May 1884). Her paraphrase of Sièyes suggests the politically conscious woman whom she sought to reach: "What are *you*, women?" On the other hand, *La Citoyenne* depicted men as the "kings" of marriage who acted with "egoism," "rapacity," "brutality," and "despotism." She assumed that her readers understood her hostility toward "our little masters." Auclert occasionally reassured the male readers who produced "an avalanche of maledictions," explaining that women only wanted to "share" with them, but an equal share (July 1881). She reiterated her concomitant sense of duty and recognition of the roles of women as wife and mother (for example, January 1882). Periodically, she inserted a motto linking rights and duties on the masthead of *La Citoyenne*. But her focus remained on women who wanted "to demasculinize" France.

What ideas did Auclert's essays offer these readers? She did not intellectualize her feminism to elaborate a system of analysis or abstract argument; she did not aspire to be a theorist remembered for contributions to feminist thought. Auclert was a great propagandist, agitator, and activist. Her impressive body of articles is an encyclopedia of the militant feminism of her generation. She wrote on a wide range of questions, without developing overarching theories, because she believed herself to be (in a term from her later writings) an "integral feminist": *all* aspects of the woman question concerned her and she excluded none from her columns. It was self-evident to her that men controlled France and constructed the laws to their own advantage. Women must realize this, must demand the demasculinization of France, and must obtain an equal share of all rights. In return, they would accept an equal share of all duties and bring their feminine virtues, such as thrift, to all occupations and roles in life. Auclert's essays thus presented a weekly lesson and an exhortation to demasculinization.

Nonetheless, it would be unjust to Auclert to dismiss her essays as a mere inventory of grievances without intellectual structure simply because she presented them as a propagandist rather than a theorist. Her unifying conception was political: the republic. Auclert had had since her youth an idealistic certitude that the wellsprings of republican justice were bottomless, combining admiration for her father's Jacobin republicanism, contemporary enthusiasm for republican opposition to the Second Empire, and excitement over 1870–1871. She believed that France—indeed, the Western world—had entered "the republican era" and must create an ideal republic, "the true republic" (August 1881). Her republic would be an egalitarian society founded on complete democracy. Republicans who stopped short of the latter or resisted the former were "insincere republicans" (October 1881). They had not abandoned monarchical *mentalités;* they had projected themselves as a new aristocracy (November 1883). Thus, the Third Republic was hardly a true republic, but merely a beginning. Until the aristocrats of the new regime accepted the equality of her republican socialism and shared all of its rights through republican feminism, she would not hesitate to denounce republicans or to accept the aid of antirepublicans. The republic, after all, only provided the best means to reach the goal of a just society (August 1881).

Auclert's republican feminism began with the *sine qua non* of women's suffrage. There could be no democracy, no universal suffrage, while the republic excluded women. Enfranchising women would, in her view, inevitably lead to the victory of integral feminism; simultaneously, it would convert the Third Republic into the true republic. Her diagnosis and her prognosis both rested on idealistic confidence in democracy. The ballot represented "a part of national power" (February 1881) that could be used by the oppressed as a "great machine for progress" (September 1881). Any republican or socialist politician who opposed full citizenship for women or any other oppressed group showed himself to be a hypocrite whose behavior put him "in flagrant contradiction of egalitarian theories" (March 1881). His republic was a "fraud" (May 1881).

Contradictions remained in Auclert's own republicanism, of course. In common with politicians of the Third Republic, she had difficulty balancing her proclaimed *liberté* and *égalité.* By stressing individual rights for women, she stood squarely in the camp of classical liberalism. By cherishing egalitarianism, she repeatedly turned to social doctrines that placed the collective interest above the individual; both her early Catholicism and her periodic socialism expressed this sentiment. Naturally, her inflexible insistence upon winning the vote resolved this conflict in favor of individual liberties—a choice Auclert unconsciously admitted by adopting the pseudonym "Liberta," not "Aequalita."

Auclert concentrated her energies on women's suffrage for the general good both of women and of the republic. Not surprisingly, suffragism dominated her writings. She rebutted the standard arguments against enfranchising women—women were insufficiently educated (April 1881), women were controlled by the clergy (April 1881), men earned the vote with their military service (March 1881), women were not interested in politics (July 1881) or had no aptitude for it (May 1881), women would neglect their other duties (March 1881). Similarly, she produced a series of articles to show the benefits of women's suffrage— for example, women would vote for peace (see illustration 4). Auclert's persistent hammering on the theme of republican feminism made her imaginative in linking women's suffrage with any subject. This was simple for her program of integral feminism; if the subject were divorce, for example, she merely argued that the legislation would be rapidly enacted if deputies knew that they had to answer to women electors. But she also found ways to introduce suffragism into articles about scandals and corruption (there would be less when women were citizens) or the falling stock market (women would manage the economy better).

As the dates of the articles cited here suggest, Auclert developed her ideas and her style in the early 1880s, adding little of substance after 1885. She still wrote three articles for each issue of *La Citoyenne* in 1886, but her enthusiasm had diminished. Others did more of the work. Maria Martin (who had become treasurer of Suffrage des femmes), Eugénie Potonié-Pierre (who had hyphenated her name after marrying Edmond Potonié-Pierre, a pacifist, utopian socialist, and occasional contributor to *La Citoyenne*), and Marie-Rose Astié de Valsayre helped produce the paper; de Gasté continued to provide over 90 percent of its supplementary financing. In early 1887, Auclert began merely to initial her articles rather than sign them. In November, someone else (Astié) wrote the leader for the first time; Martin soon assumed the task of writing them. In the spring of 1888, *La Citoyenne* began appearing without any articles by Auclert.

During this period the circulation of *La Citoyenne* declined sharply, leading to the inference that Auclert no longer exhausted herself for greater readership as she had in the early 1880s. No precise figures survive for these years, but it is possible to estimate them accurately by interpolation. It has been seen that the circulation of *La Citoyenne* peaked at a thousand copies in the early 1880s. Other evidence reveals that a significant *increase* in sales in 1889, achieved under the direction of Maria Martin, produced a circulation far below a thousand. One must conclude that the total had tumbled in 1886–1888 to the vicinity of five hundred—perhaps fewer—copies.

Given the severe contraction of *La Citoyenne*'s circulation and the cessation of Auclert's writing and other activities, it was not wholly shocking when a brief note appeared in her newspaper stating without explanation that Auclert had left Paris. In July 1888, Martin's name appeared on the masthead as directrice, beneath Auclert's as the founder. For several months, there was no word of Auclert. Then in September 1888, a single sentence, in large bold type, announced that she had gone to Algeria and married Lévrier.

What had happened? The answer again demonstrates the reciprocal relationship between Auclert's public and private lives. Isolation and loneliness still dominated her self-perception. Her political exhaustion and frustration in 1885, combined with her sadness at the departure of Lévrier for Tahiti, induced withdrawal from her myriad activities. Fortunately, Marie and Lucien Chaumont had moved to Paris upon Chaumont's retirement. Auclert turned to her sister for emotional support. This placed Auclert in the situation of depending upon, and probably envying, Marie's happy marriage. Lévrier certainly remained on her mind. She used her political connections to seek his transfer back to France. In a touching letter to one deputy, Auclert told how she missed "the true friend whom I have the great remorse of having sacrificed to my love of an idea." Ironically, this was one of Auclert's few appeals that produced results. In early 1888, Lévrier received a post as *juge de paix* in Frenda (Oran), Algeria. Efforts by both Auclert and Lévrier to secure him an appointment in Paris failed. Lévrier then learned that he was critically ill. His affliction is unknown, but his physician said the North African climate would be beneficial; tuberculosis seems the most likely diagnosis. Auclert decided that she would turn aside no more to brood upon love's bitter mystery; she would go to Algeria and marry Lévrier. Having discussed such matters for a decade, they had no difficulty in preparing a premarital contract, although its terms remain unknown. Auclert left Paris in the summer of 1888; early in July, she married Lévrier in Algiers.[25]

25. Draft letter, Auclert to unspecified deputy, 8 November 1887, CP 4247, BHVP. (This file is not part of the Auclert Papers contained in the Bouglé Collection at the BHVP.) Lévrier to Lucien Chaumont, 4 November 1888, Auclert Papers, 2/10; wedding announcement, ibid., 2/11; Auclert's recollections in *La Libre parole*, 2 June 1894.

CHAPTER SEVEN

Algerian Interlude, 1888–1892

Hubertine Auclert went to Algeria in the summer of 1888 hoping that she would soon return to live in Paris.[1] If Lévrier's health improved, their combined political influence might secure him a position there. Neither his career nor his health flourished in North Africa, however. When Auclert returned to Paris late in 1892, it was as the widow of a former magistrate.

North Africa made a deep and favorable impression on Auclert. At first she considered it "this terrestrial paradise." She soon developed a political critique of life there, but Algeria retained its appeal for her. After returning to Paris, she recalled "what a beautiful land, what a delightful climate, what a fascinating people" she had lived among.[2]

After their marriage in Algiers, Lévrier's initial appointment took them to Frenda, in the department of Oran—a small town on the high plateau between the Atlas Mountains and the rich coastal plain. A transfer in 1889 relocated Lévrier and Auclert at Laghouat, an oasis town on the southern side of the Atlas range. This life in the Algerian hinterland awakened Auclert's rural instincts. She became, in Lévrier's punning words, "the leader of twenty-six *pensionnaire* hens"—incubating eggs, settling disputes between her chicks and ducklings, scrambling through the underbrush to keep her followers together. So different was Auclert's life in 1888 and 1889 that she found time for three

1. Chaumont, "Hubertine Auclert," p. 43.
2. Auclert, *Les Femmes arabes en Algérie* (Paris, 1900), p. 1 (first quotation); *La Libre parole*, 2 June 1894 (second quotation).

domestic pets, especially a gazelle named Yzette. "This little jewel of the desert" became the object of great affection. Auclert later wrote a prizewinning essay about Yzette and included a touching chapter about her in a book on Algeria (1900). After her return to Paris, Auclert often dreamt about the tranquility she had found during these days with her gazelles in Africa.[3]

This does not mean that Auclert quietly rusticated as the wife of a minor magistrate in a small Algerian town. Neither her temperament and political passion nor Lévrier's health and career permitted this. After a few months at Frenda, she told Lévrier, "I am too bored. I cannot rest any more." She tried to maintain her connections with the Parisian feminist movement and to begin a study of the condition of Arab women in Algeria.[4]

Auclert's life in Algeria changed dramatically late in 1889, when Lévrier lost his position as a *juge de paix*. Precisely what happened is unclear because the ministry of justice destroyed all personnel files from the late 1880s. According to a police report of 1893, Lévrier's superiors replaced him because of his debts, complaints against him, and "his professional ignorance." One must wonder about the reliability of this document, however; it also reported that Lévrier's superiors had forced him to "regularize his situation" by marrying Auclert after she came to Algeria as his mistress. It is possible, therefore, that Lévrier left the judiciary for some other reason, such as his failing health. Removal for incompetence is, nonetheless, a plausible explanation. Other fragmentary evidence suggests that he made enemies in the Algerian administration, as he had in his brief political career in Paris, perhaps as a result of his outspokenness and his left-wing opinions. Shortly after his death Auclert wrote to a friend that Lévrier had been ill-used and had died "a dupe and a victim."[5]

Whatever the explanation for the end of Lévrier's judicial career, it did not involve total disgrace. His health still requiring the climate of North Africa, he and Auclert moved to Algiers, where he took an editorial position on the staff of *Le Radical algérien*. The circle of their friends included leading political figures, among them the prominent

3. Lévrier to Lucien Chaumont, 4 November 1888, Auclert Papers, 2/10 (first quotation); "Ma Gazelle Yzette," in *Les Femmes arabes en Algérie*, pp. 204–14 (second quotation, p. 206). The original version of this essay appeared in *La Citoyenne* in October and December 1890.

4. Lévrier to Lucien Chaumont, 4 November 1888, Auclert Papers, 2/10.

5. Ibid.; police report, 1 December 1893, Dossier Auclert, APP; Auclert to (name illegible), 10 October 1893, Auclert Papers, 14/14. For the fate of the personnel dossiers at the ministry of justice, see R. Anchel, "Répertoire de BB[8] 1 à 2188. Juges de paix, an IX-1925," revised by M. Ally, typescript in the AN Salle des inventaires, p. 49 n. 1. The Algerian government denied me permission to search in the ministry of justice files in Algiers.

radical deputy, Eugène Etienne. Their alleged indebtedness did not prevent them from obtaining a residence in Algiers with sufficient grounds to maintain Auclert's gazelles. In any case, Lévrier's health soon prevented all work, judicial or journalistic; he died in May 1892.

CONTACT WITH THE PARISIAN FEMINIST MOVEMENT

When Auclert left Paris in 1888, Suffrage des femmes collapsed for want of a leader. Auclert took pains, however, to guarantee the survival of *La Citoyenne*, her link to the feminist movement. The subvention by Joseph de Gasté provided enough money for a dedicated editor to keep up monthly publication without great personal expense. Gasté was reelected to the Chamber of Deputies in 1889 at the age of seventy-eight after campaigning for the full civil and political equality of women, and he had written a bequest to the newspaper into his will, so his backing seemed assured.[6]

Auclert entrusted the direction of *La Citoyenne* to Maria Martin, who had participated in Suffrage des femmes and contributed to the newspaper for several years. Martin was English-born and, as she told an interviewer in 1899, "never dreamed of the existence of a women's question" until she married a Frenchman, Jules Martin, and moved to Paris in 1872. Concern about the status of women in France and interest in the welfare of children led her to the women's rights movement. Martin joined Droit des femmes during Auclert's campaign of 1880–1881 and supported her publicly in the dispute with Epailly and Lasserre. She was one of the few women who remained active in Droit des femmes and Suffrage des femmes for the rest of the decade. In 1882 she began to make small financial contributions to *La Citoyenne* and to write occasional articles on women's suffrage. In 1884 she became a member of the committee that directed Suffrage des femmes, and, a year later, the group's treasurer. Martin took an active role in Auclert's 1885 campaign and thereafter contributed regularly to *La Citoyenne*. Thus her enthusiasm peaked just as Auclert entered her period of depression in the late 1880s. This made Martin the obvious choice to edit *La Citoyenne*. She had distinguished herself by years of dedication, she had given uncompromising support to women's suffrage, and she seemed utterly reliable. Martin hesitated to accept the responsibility and urged Auclert to choose another collaborator, such as Blanche Mon, who had worked on *La Citoyenne* since its beginning. Auclert insisted that no

6. Jean Jolly, ed., *Dictionnaire des parlementaires françaises: Notices biographiques sur les ministres, députés, et sénateurs français de 1889 à 1940* (Paris, 1960–1977), 5:1789; Auclert, *Le Vote des femmes*, p. 111.

one else would do and that Martin must accept the directorship as a feminist duty. Martin began writing the leaders for *La Citoyenne* in March 1888, with Auclert and several other militants, notably Eugénie Potonié-Pierre, Libussa Slavenko, and Marie-Rose Astié de Valsayre, contributing articles. Auclert ceased writing before leaving for Algeria.[7]

When Auclert found herself bored without feminist politics, she returned to the pages of *La Citoyenne*. Her first article appeared in December 1888, and she contributed regularly thereafter, usually an article on page 1 following Martin's leader. Her style was more vigorous than it had been in years. Women were still "slaves" who must become *citoyennes*. (When a deputy spoke of the dangers of a new form of French slavery in Guadeloupe, Auclert answered, "As if slavery had ever ceased to exist in France!") She still demanded "a true republic" and denounced republican politicians as "Orleanist republicans." "If the republicans do not cease to contradict their principles," she wrote, "they will push towards insurgency the disinherited of the Republic—women." To these basic themes, Auclert added new emphasis on equality within marriage, which she had happily found for herself, and greater national- ism, consistent with both the mood of Boulangism in Paris and her Jacobin memories. ("Oh, my *patrie!*" Auclert once wrote privately. "You must be incomparable since I prefer to live as a slave with you than to be free elsewhere.") Auclert also wrote increasingly about Algeria because she concluded that "the masculine incapacity to govern" be- came "even more visible in the colonies than in France."[8]

According to later interviews, Auclert began to work "more than ever for the cause" in Algeria.[9] She exaggerated, of course. No absentee leader could match her herculean labors between 1876 and 1885. Yet the claim expresses an important psychological truth; Auclert needed to feel active in Parisian events. In addition to her articles for *La Cit- oyenne*, she corresponded with leading feminists, chiefly Eugénie Pot- onié-Pierre.

The marginality of Auclert's feminist position became clear during 1889, when two women's congresses met in Paris in conjunction with the international exhibition celebrating the centennial of the French

---

7. For more information on Martin, see Hause with Kenney, *Women's Suffrage and Social Politics*, pp. 50–51. For Martin's role at *La Citoyenne* during the 1880s, see her articles there, esp. in August 1881, April and May 1882, July 1884, June 1885, April– November 1886. For the terms of her acceptance of the directorship of *La Citoyenne*, see Martin to Auclert, 25 January 1891, Auclert Papers, 13/33.

8. See *La Citoyenne*, December 1888–November 1891 (articles listed in appendix 2); for quotations, see "Sensiblerie masculine," September 1890; "Les Déshéritées de la République," October 1889; "Voile et viol," January 1889. Diary, undated entry (summer 1883), Auclert Papers.

9. *La Libre parole*, 2 June 1894.

Revolution. As early as 1884 Auclert had contemplated the propaganda opportunity that 1889 would present. She repeatedly urged the government to include women in the plans for the exhibition; early in 1886, for example, she asked Edouard Lockroy, the radical minister of commerce and industry, to name women to his planning committee. She similarly exhorted feminists to prepare a great demonstration. Neither appeal received much attention. And when feminists organized their congresses in 1889, they rejected her ideas.[10]

The women's congresses of 1889 reprised Richer's congress of 1878. Both adopted moderate programs and rejected women's suffrage; both led to schism on the feminist left.[11] The Congrès français et international du droit des femmes of June 1889 was organized by Richer and Deraismes in reaction to the plans for the second congress, the Congrès international des oeuvres et institutions féminines, to be held in July. Richer and Deraismes had initially cooperated in planning the officially sanctioned second congress. That congress had the republican prestige of Jules Simon's presidency as well as the middle-class respectability of philanthropic societies such as the Libérées de Saint-Lazare, an organization devoted to aiding women (chiefly prostitutes) released from Saint-Lazare prison. Richer and Deraismes had ties both to Simon and to the philanthropic movement, so they comfortably joined in preparations for congress. Simon's emphasis on Christianity, however, collided with the anticlericalism of Richer and Deraismes. Furthermore, moderate women like Mme de Morsier and Isabelle Bogelot of Libérées and Sarah Monod of *La Femme* balked at the radicalism of claiming full civil equality. Hence, Deraismes' Amélioration and Richer's LFDF organized their own congress under Deraismes' presidency.[12]

Auclert occupied an ironic position on the outskirts of these proceedings. She and the Simonian moderates had long since rejected each other. She and the philanthropic women likewise had little patience with each other, as Monod's opposition to Auclert in 1881 had shown. There was no question of her participating in the Second congress, nor

10. Auclert to Lockroy, March 1886, Auclert Papers, 13/49; *La Citoyenne*, March and April 1886; *La France libre*, 4 December 1884; *L'Univers*, 2 March 1886.

11. There were, of course, some important differences between the congresses of 1878 and 1889. It is important to note, as both Bidelman and Evans have stressed, that the congresses of 1889 represent a turning point in the evolution of French feminism because participation was overwhelmingly by women. See Bidelman, *Pariahs Stand Up!*, p. 175, and Evans, *The Feminists*, p. 130.

12. For the congresses of 1889, see, in addition to Bidelman and Evans, Sowerwine, *Sisters or Citizens*, p. 67; Albistur and Armogathe, *Histoire du féminisme français*, 2:524–29; Krakovitch, preface to Deraismes, *Ce que veulent les femmes*, p. 27. For police reports on the congresses of 1889, see Dossier B^a 30, APP. Martin gave the congresses extensive coverage in *La Citoyenne*, producing three issues in July 1889 (nos. 146–48), two of which reprinted speeches.

was she surpised when Simon categorically ruled out women's suffrage at that assembly ("having other things to do, we shall do other things"). Instead, Auclert had the amusement and satisfaction of seeing Richer and Deraismes split from a congress that they considered too conservative. This gave her hope that their congress would attract disproportionate participation by militants who would adopt a suffragist program at last. Auclert savored the prospect of a victory she had expected eleven years earlier. After all, Deraismes was presiding at this congress, not Richer, and Deraismes had increasingly accepted the necessity of political rights, even running for office herself in 1885. In addition, Maria Martin would be sitting as the secretary of the congress.

Deraismes and Auclert corresponded about the projected congress during the spring of 1889. Portions of this correspondence are missing, but it appears that Deraismes insisted that Auclert attend, Auclert that Deraismes endorse political rights. Neither happened. Deraismes suggested that Auclert's presence was needed to combat the argument that she had deserted the cause: "You are too valiant for that." The crisis in Lévrier's career, and perhaps the unsatisfactory negotiations with Deraismes, prevented Auclert from going to Paris. Instead, she wrote a report on women's suffrage to be read to the congress.[13]

Despite these preparations, a shock awaited Auclert. For the second time, Léon Richer ordered a feminist congress to ignore suffragism. Auclert's report was declared out of order and never read, like its predecessor in 1878. Deraismes defended Auclert's report in private discussions with Richer, but she would not defy him. Her own speech to the congress touched lightly on political rights, but Deraismes refrained from making an issue of them. She did secure the publication of Auclert's report, along with a hundred others, in the official record of the congress. But she obeyed Richer's order, closing debate whenever Auclert's former collaborators, especially Jules Allix and Léon Giraud, raised the forbidden subject. When Allix persisted, Deraismes censured him and ordered his words purged from the transcript of the congress.[14]

This new rejection stunned Auclert. It reawakened her sense of martyrdom, which she revealed in an unpublished manuscript entitled "The Worst Enemies of Women are Women": "At the time of the congress of 1889, one beseeched me to attend. I did not go, but I sent a speech. The good ladies found a way to dismiss it by sleight of hand [*escamoter*]. It happened to be mislaid and was not read to the session. . . . It seems that although I am no longer present, these women

13. Deraismes to Auclert, 12 May 1889, Auclert Papers, 2/13 (quoted); note on the congress of 1889, ibid., 11/330.
14. Bidelman, *Pariahs Stand Up!*, pp. 152, 175–76, 181; Evans, *The Feminists*, p. 130; text of Deraismes' speech, Dossier Deraismes, BMD.

have not disarmed and they are tearing me apart because I stick to my tenacity despite everything inflicted on me."[15] The sense of persecution shown here and its vivid description had previously been a leitmotif in Auclert's diary. Between 1883 and 1885, she had written, "For me, nothing! . . . except . . . suspicion, envy, ridicule, hate!" Later, "more abuse, always abuse without reason." Then, "Wretched being that I am, tracked down like an animal, reviled, humiliated" And, in the closest parallel, "I daily allow myself to be drawn and quartered in spirit. And yet women hate me!" At the time of these diary entries, however, Auclert's feeling of feminist martyrdom had been inextricable from her lamentations about the emptiness of her private life, her desire for "the supreme relaxation: affection! love!" Having found contentment in her marriage to Lévrier at the price of leaving Paris, her sense of persecution worsened rather than improved. Her feeling of fighting alone, *contra mundum*, increased.[16]

Auclert was not the only feminist dismayed by Richer and Deraismes, however. Immediately after the congress, several militants decided to fill the vacuum created by the disappearance of Suffrage des femmes and the Union des femmes. Potonié-Pierre and Astié de Valsayre announced the creation of a Ligue des femmes (sometimes Ligue socialiste des femmes). That league never emerged from the planning stage, apparently because of the emotional instability of Astié, who was still unsuspected of being the author of *Les Amazons du siecle* (1882), which had viciously attacked Auclert, Potonié-Pierre, and Rouzade. Potonié-Pierre did not give up her effort to unify the left and created Solidarité des femmes (hereafter Solidarité) in 1891. Solidarité attracted both suffragists, including Maria Martin, and socialists, including the communard Nathalie Lemel. Potonié-Pierre corresponded with Auclert during this period; Auclert gave her blessing and her charter member's dues to the group. Thus, while Auclert remained on the fringe of French feminism *La Citoyenne* and Solidarité were her fingerholds on the movement. If troubles arose there, her sense of persecution would be immense.[17]

ALGERIA AND ARAB WOMEN

Auclert went to Algeria intending to study Arab women and their condition. She would have preferred to give her time to Parisian femi-

15. Manuscript, "Les Plus grands ennemis des femmes sont les femmes," Auclert Papers, 11/330.

16. Diary, June 1883, 21 February, 1 April, and 18 April 1884, Auclert Papers.

17. For the founding of the Ligue des femmes and Solidarité, see Sowerwine, *Sisters or*

nism, but her physical isolation dictated attention to North Africa. She arrived in Algiers as ignorant of colonialism as she had been of feminism upon her arrival in Paris in 1873. During four years of residence in Algeria, she hardly became an expert in Muslim history or Islamic law, but she seriously studied the condition of Arab women from the resolute cultural perspective of the republican feminism of Paris.[18]

Predictably, Auclert was shocked. Her notion of a "terrestrial paradise" dimmed when she observed a group of women going through the streets with bundles of dirty laundry on their heads. They looked to Auclert like the living dead, "ageless and sexless creatures." She saw the imprint of slavery upon their faces, "turned to parchment, cracked, furrowed, hewn." She saw not human beings but "statues of suffering, personifying a race tortured by hunger."[19]

Auclert sought to meet Arab women and to learn about Algerian marital customs, polygamy, divorce, and prostitution. She was aghast at their stories. She had heard marriage called a prison before, but the stone walls and iron bars the Arab women described defied any creature to soar above them. Auclert responded with a series of articles for *La Citoyenne* and a book entitled *Les Femmes arabes en Algérie* (1900). There she denounced the practice of buying wives, who were often prepubescent girls: "Arab marriage is child rape." French tribunals in Algeria shocked her by enforcing the law of the Koran rather than the French codes in such cases. To illustrate, Auclert related the experience of a young Arab woman she had met. The woman had reached her majority and wished to marry. Her father sold her into another marriage, and French courts enforced the sale. In another case, Auclert described a nine-year-old girl, sold into marriage, whose husband overcame her unwillingness to have sexual relations by chaining her down; French courts would not convict him of rape.[20]

Auclert also condemned the Algerian practice of polygamy. It was "anti-natural" to her, "contrary to human dignity." It led to a high incidence of murder among a wealthy man's wives; it caused the wifeless poor man to turn to homosexuality or bestiality. It contributed to the acceptance of prostitution as "pious work" performed by a "priesthood" of temporary wives, whose decision Auclert understood when a

---

Citizens, pp. 67–68; Bidelman, *Pariahs Stand Up!,* p. 182; Krakovitch, preface to Deraismes, *Ce que veulent les femmes,* p. 27; *La Citoyenne* for 1891; the obituary of Martin in *Le Journal des femmes,* January 1911. For Auclert and Potonié-Pierre, see Auclert to Potonié-Pierre, undated (November 1891), Auclert Papers, 13/5; Potonié-Pierre to Auclert, 21 May 1892, ibid., 2/26.

18. See Auclert's note on her study of Algeria, Auclert Papers, 13/108.

19. Auclert, *Les Femmes arabes en Algérie,* pp. 1–2.

20. See "Le Mariage Arabe est un viol d'enfant," in *Les Femmes arabes en Algérie,* pp. 42–57.

prostitute explained that they found greater freedom in the brief rental of their bodies than in their absolute sale into undesired marriages. Algerian sexual and marital practices so appalled Auclert that she concluded they caused the deterioration of the race: "Polygamy not only hastens physical decrepitude, it leads to intellectual degeneracy. In concentrating all of the cerebral activity of the Arabs on the animal instinct, it annihilates their intelligence and atrophies their brains." Polygamy and its hypersexual culture even caused early death among the Arabs. Auclert's abhorrence of alien sexual and marital practices that debased and abused women had led her into polemic exaggeration; this evoked the derisory suggestion that she correlate atrophied brains and the sexual practices of the French academy, the Chamber of Deputies, and the women's movement. Parisian journalists proposed to test her theories by permitting polygamy in France. Auclert's horror only worsened as she understood other Algerian customs, such as Islamic divorce by repudiation, which was permitted to men but not to women.[21]

Auclert soon realized that improving the lot of Arab women could not be separated from the question of French attitudes toward Algeria. She found French policy to be racist (*préjugé de race*). "There is only a very small elite of the French," she noted, "who classify the Arab race as human." French Algerians gave Arab Algerians "less consideration than sheep"; they acted as if the Arabs were "created in order to be crushed." The French, she concluded, "are accustomed to living on the backs of these poor Arabs." Algeria had become "a vast prison where the mistreated Arab often does not even have the morsel of bread due to prisoners."[22]

Auclert's analysis of the Arab mistreatment of women and the French mistreatment of Arabs led her back to her republicanism. As her vision of the true republic had evoked republican feminism and republican socialism, she now advocated republican colonialism, although without using that term. The rectified republic she envisioned would bring tremendous benefits to Arab Algerians, in a feminist version of the imperialist theory of the civilizing mission: enlightened rule would abolish polygamy and associated evils. This does not mean that she ceased criticizing the French administration of Algeria, or prejudice

21. See "La Polygamy," ibid., pp. 57–71 (quotations, pp. 63, 65); "Où la prostitution est un sacerdoce," ibid., pp. 111–17 (quotation, p. 111); "La Répudiation—Le Divorce," ibid., pp. 77–80. See also her articles in *La Citoyenne* during 1890–1891, esp. "La Polygamie en France," April 1891.

22. Auclert, *Les Femmes arabes en Algérie*, pp. 3 (first three quotations), 32 (fifth quotation); note on Algeria, Auclert Papers, 14/58 (fourth quotation). See also Auclert's "Préjugé de race et de sexe," ibid., 12/14.

with which it operated; she did, however, accept the principle of French administration of Algeria.

This reasoning induced Auclert to embrace the colonial theory of assimilation. Algerian Arabs should be assimilated to French citizenship, sharing in the language, education, institutions, laws, and rights of the republic. Consequently, she denounced the republic for excluding Arabs from the government of Algeria, although they numbered 3.75 million in a population of 4 million. They elected representatives to municipal councils, but their representation could not exceed one-fourth of the French membership. Arabs had one delegate to the general council, named by the governor-general. Auclert concluded that colonial administrators who opposed political assimilation alienated the Arabs. Politicians who claimed that Arabs did not want assimilation talked only with leaders who profited from the French reinforcement of their position. Those who opposed even the minimal assimilation of teaching the French language to the Arabs did not recognize the dangers of their policy.[23]

Auclert's prescription for improving conditions in Algeria thus duplicated her prescription for metropolitan France: start by extending the franchise. She understood the oppression of race and the oppression of gender as parallel manifestations of an unjust regime; assimilation and suffragism were parallel remedies. Women's suffrage remained her essential cure, however, the *sine qua non* of the true republic. French women, once enfranchised, would not tolerate the perpetuation of racism: "If women shared power in France, the would not permit the existence, in any land made French, of laws accepting the rape of children. Men tolerate this crime because there is a solidarity among those who profit from it."[24] French women would alter the administration of Algeria because they recognized that "Europeans have the same prejudices towards Arabs that men have towards women." Women understood what it meant to have their opinions dismissed with a haughty "It is only an Arab."[25]

It should be noted that Auclert recognized problems within the

23. For a general discussion of assimilation, see Raymond F. Betts, *Assimilation and Association in French Colonial Theory, 1890–1914* (New York, 1961); Hubert Deschamps, *Méthodes et doctrines coloniales de la France* (Paris, 1953). For specific attention to Algeria, see Vincent Confer, *France and Algeria: The Problem of Civil and Military Reform, 1870–1920* (Syracuse, 1966); Charles-Robert Ageron, *Les Algériens musulmans et la France, 1871–1919* (Paris, 1968). For Auclert's ideas; see *Les Femmes arabes en Algérie*, pp. 9–17, 20–26, 30–36; her articles in *La Citoyenne*, esp. "Francisons l'Algérie," 15 April 1891; folder, "Affaires Algériennes," Auclert Papers, Carton 12, esp. 12/7.

24. Auclert, *Les Femmes arabes en Algérie*, pp. 16–17.

25. Ibid., p. 49 (first quotation); Auclert, "Préjugé de race et de sexe," Auclert Papers, 12/14 (second quotation).

doctrine of assimilation. She did not doubt the importance of applying the Napoleonic Code (revised, of course) in Algeria, but she worried about the implications of such changes. Assimilation, she stated, must be modified, so that it would not mean the destruction of a distinctive Arab culture and life. She offered no plans for preserving some traditions while demanding the extirpation of others, and her ideas may have struck no deeper than a desire to preserve a quaint distinctiveness in mores, such as Arab clothing. But she did insist that assimilationists face this issue.[26]

Having located her understanding of Algeria within her republicanism, Auclert found her response in her previous political behavior. She publicized her opinions in the Algerian press (especially in *Le Radical algérien* after Lévrier became an editor there), in her articles for *La Citoyenne* (by 1891 Algeria had become her chief theme), and in her book on Arab women. Auclert also returned to her favorite political tactic, the petition. In 1891 alone she dispatched four petitions to Paris (see table 7.1), one calling for a policy of assimilation, one demanding the protection of Arab women, one to outlaw polygamy, and one asking for the establishment of a French primary school for Arab girls. She had no more success with her Algerian petitions than she had had with her suffragist efforts. Neither the Chamber of Deputies nor the Senate responded to the claim that Arab women were "barbarously treated, with the tolerance of France," or to her plea "to substitute, in our African territory, the state of civilization for the state of barbarism."[27]

Auclert pragmatically concentrated her efforts on the school for Arab girls. The objective was precise, relatively inexpensive, and easily defensible. Educational reforms of the Second Republic had created two French primary schools for Arab girls in 1850, which attracted several hundred pupils before they were suppressed by the general council of Algiers in 1861. Thereafter, only exceptional circumstances allowed the education of an Arab Algerian in schools for French Algerian girls. Auclert argued that the republic violated the Algerian Treaty of 1830 and French educational law by perpetuating the Bonapartist decision of 1861. She petitioned the government, she wrote to ministers and under-secretaries, she courted the press in Paris and Algiers, and she enlisted the support of friends like de Gasté. This effort forced the government to consider Auclert's proposal, but it won no victories. The *rapporteur* for the Algerian budget in the Chamber of Deputies decried the cost of such schools and asserted that they would only create a group of *déclasée* women who had no place in either French or Muslim culture. In Algiers,

26. Auclert, *Les Femmes arabes en Algérie*, pp. 39–42.
27. Some of Auclert's petitions can be found in ibid. (quotation, pp. 69–70), and in *La Citoyenne* for 1891, such as 1 March 1891.

TABLE **7.1.** **Auclert's Algerian Petitions, 1891–1893**

Date	Recipient	Subject
1891	Chamber of Deputies	Assimilation
1891	Chamber of Deputies	Legal situation of Arab women
1891	Chamber and Senate	Polygamy in Algeria
1891	Ministry of the Interior	School for Arab girls
1892	Senate	School for Arab girls
1893	Chamber of Deputies	School for Arab girls

the determined conservatism of Araba politicians, in alliance with French "arabophobe" opinion, blocked change.[28]

Having failed to obtain a primary school for Arab girls, Auclert left Algeria in 1892 without any tangible accomplishment. She had contributed her skills as a publicist to the education of French opinion about Algeria, much as she had done for the woman question in the previous decade. She had written with her old passion, "I cry out: Some schools!"[29] And once again she wound up as a lonely pioneer. She never forgot the situation of Arab women in Algeria, however, and submitted petitions on their behalf for the rest of her life.

THE FIGHT OVER *LA CITOYENNE*, 1891–1892

Auclert's last months in Algeria were marked by bitter arguments with Maria Martin that resulted in the death of *La Citoyenne*. The newspaper symbolized the efforts of her youth. It was her most enduring creation, the vehicle for her essays, and the home to which she expected to return. Hence, its loss had a tremendous psychological impact.

Martin had maintained La Citoyenne as one of the most important bases of the women's movement. The newspaper had not flourished, if one measures by dramatic increases in circulation or revenue. But it had survived, had retained its influence among militants, and had prospered enough to expand to fortnightly publication. Martin earned this success through dedication: "I am before all and above all a feminist." She combined hard work, although less dogged than Auclert's, with social skills, notably more diplomacy than Auclert had shown, to expand the range of *La Citoyenne*. She had, in the words of one obituary, "infinite tolerance for the beliefs of others." Thus she was able to build links between militants and moderate women. Martin, for example, dealt

28. See esp. the Auclert Papers, 9/141 and Carton 12, folder "Affaires algériennes," for her ideas on the schools question; Auclert, *Les Femmes arabes en Algérie,* pp. 138–44.

29. Ibid., p. 143, quoting her petition of 1891.

successfully with women of the Congrès international des oeuvres et institutions féminines, such as Bogelot and Monod. She remained a militant feminist, a strong advocate of women's suffrage, and an ally of moderate socialist causes. She did not press such themes with Auclert's uncompromising insistence, however, nor did she dramatize them with demonstrations.[30]

The business relationship between Auclert and Martin succeeded as an amicable partnership if not an intimate friendship. (After ten years of collaboration and three years of correspondence, they still addressed each other as "Chère Madame.") They did not establish a formal partnership with rights and responsibilities stipulated in a written contract, relying on an informal agreement between colleagues. This arrangement contained the potential for an emotional dispute. Who owned *La Citoyenne*, its files, its subscriber list, its few contracts with advertisers?

By early 1891, the relationship between Auclert and Martin had become strained. Martin informed Auclert about the operations of *La Citoyenne* in a monthly letter. Late in 1890, she reported "a pleasant surprise": her efforts at the congress of 1889 had expanded the subscriber list enough to finance fortnightly publication. Auclert responded with a terse note criticizing Martin for not keeping her informed, for acting as if she, Auclert, were dead. This brusque response to good news hurt Martin, who answered that she did not understand Auclert's feelings. She thought it unreasonable that Auclert should expect prior consultation about changes in *La Citoyenne*; the responsibility, the pains, and the financial loss belonged to Martin. "You well know, from your own experience," Martin added, "that this responsibility brings only fatigue, enemies, raillery, and criticism." Nonetheless, Martin tried to mollify Auclert, offering to return the directorship of *La Citoyenne* (significantly, "the newspaper that you founded," not "your newspaper"). Martin also provided a financial accounting; the cost of two issues averaged 155 to 160 francs per month. De Gasté's subvention reduced this by 100 francs. After income from subscriptions, other contributions, and advertising, Martin still had to absorb losses.[31] One can deduce from these figures that Martin sold fewer than a thousand copies of each issue; circulation must have been very low indeed in 1886–1888.

---

30. *Le Journal des femmes*, January 1911 (first quotation). See also the small collection of Martin's correspondence, 091 MAR, BMD (second quotation from unidentified letter). There is an undated clipping from *Le Soleil* in the Dossier Auclert, APP, which reports an interview with Martin and describes her editorship of *La Citoyenne*.

31. There is a large folder of Auclert-Martin correspondence, labeled "Affaire *La Citoyenne*," in the Auclert Papers, Carton 13; see esp. Auclert to Martin, 25 January 1891 (quoted). See also police report, 8 March 1889, Dossier Auclert, APP.

Subsequent letters prevented a rupture but distrust grew. Auclert reassured Martin of her pleasure at the expansion of *La Citoyenne;* she only wanted more consultation, as a mother is interested in her child. She stressed, however, that *La Citoyenne* had not become Martin's "personal property"; it remained a "collective" enterprise. "You cannot suppose, madame, that because I am momentarily far from Paris, I have abandoned the cause, or that because I have entrusted the direction of *La Citoyenne* to you I have surrendered all claims to look after it." A coolness characterized their correspondence thereafter, and Martin no longer hesitated to criticize Auclert's articles, especially for their nationalism.[32]

The fight that led to the death of *La Citoyenne* began late in the autumn of 1891. In mid-October, Martin wrote about "a serious proposition—too serious to permit me to respond without having consulted you." Léon Richer, now sixty-seven and suffering from declining health and finances, had decided to cease publishing *Le Droit des femmes,* the only other feminist periodical at the time. He proposed to Martin that they merge their publications; she would become editor-in-chief, and he would serve on a directing committee without interfering with the publication. He asked only that the new periodical adopt a new name and format. Martin favored this merger. She believed that her editorship and Richer's promise would mean the perpetuation of *La Citoyenne's* suffragist program, that the combination would promote feminist unity, that a single newspaper would be comfortably solvent, and that weekly publication could soon be achieved. Martin had consulted de Gasté about the merger and found him mildly opposed to it. He advised Martin to continue directing *La Citoyenne* and to exploit the opportunity to increase its circulation at the expense of *Le Droit des femmes,* but he pledged support for whatever she chose.[33]

Auclert unequivocally rejected the merger of *La Citoyenne* and *Le Droit des femmes:* "It is from the moral and the material point of view impossible." Her moral opposition was simple: the merger would diminish *La Citoyenne's* singular insistence on the political rights of women. Furthermore, Richer had opposed her for twenty years. His policy had driven Auclert out of Amélioration and prevented her from speaking to the congress of 1878. He had excoriated her for the suffragist campaign of 1885. He had excluded her report from the congress of 1889. How could she now abandon *La Citoyenne* to please him? The material argument also was forceful. Auclert stated that her 1882 campaign to incorporate *La Citoyenne* had resulted in investment by "a crowd of

32. Folder, "Affaire *La Citoyenne,*" Auclert Papers, Carton 13, esp. Auclert to Martin, 31 January 1891 (quoted).

33. Martin to Auclert, October 1891, ibid., 13/27.

shareholders." Neither Martin nor Auclert had the right to close *La Citoyenne* and surrender its independence to a new group of directors. Put bluntly, Martin did not own *La Citoyenne*. "You must not dream of doing it, you do not have any right to do it." Auclert told Martin that she was free to accept the editorship of *Le Droit des femmes* if she wished, but *"La Citoyenne* must remain *La Citoyenne* and not fall into the opportunist trap." The newspaper must survive for her to resume its direction when she returned to Paris.[34]

Auclert also tried to outflank Martin. She and Lévrier wrote to de Gasté warning him of Martin's "opportunist enterprise." They urged him to stand "with the radicals of the feminist movement" against the diminution of *La Citoyenne*'s suffragism. Accepting a merger with "less advanced" feminists would "deliver us, tied hand and foot, to our jealous adversaries."[35]

This dispute requires a delicate assessment because it had important implications for Auclert's future in the feminist movement. One can sense Martin's enthusiasm for what she considered an exciting opportunity to expand feminist publication and enlarge her own role in it; one can feel her genuine shock at the sharpness of Auclert's response. Martin did not distinguish herself by her abundant sensitivity to Auclert's feelings, but she seems to have acted with sincerity rather than duplicity. Auclert, however, had reasons to be wary of Richer's role in this enterprise, as well as understandable personal interest in opposing the disappearance of *La Citoyenne*. Her blunt and emphatic answer to Martin was typical of Auclert's assertive personality. There was a shade of disingenuousness in her talk of "a crowd of shareholders"; her assertion that Martin did "not have any right to do it" was dubious. At the very least, it must be noted that Auclert did not act with a realistic recognition of her dependence upon Martin, nor did she demonstrate any recent acquisition of tact or diplomacy in dealing with colleagues. At worst, Auclert behaved as if her closest collaborator were another persecutor. When she denounced Martin to de Gasté, employing the overstated language she favored ("tied hand and foot"), she increased the risk of precisely what she feared—Martin turning against her and destroying *La Citoyenne*.

The correspondence between Auclert and Martin rapidly became acrimonious. Martin challenged Auclert's ownership of *La Citoyenne*. Auclert threatened to name a new director. Martin announced that she would treat Auclert's subsequent manuscripts as unsolicited submissions. Auclert insisted that *La Citoyenne* remained collective property which Martin was trying to appropriate illegally. Martin responded that

34. Auclert to Martin, 26 October 1891, ibid., 13/25.
35. Lévrier to de Gasté, 26 October 1891, ibid., 13/23.

Auclert had never completed the legal process for incorporation as a *société anonyme*. Auclert resigned from Solidarité because Martin was one of its leaders. This duel ended in December 1891 when Martin broke off relations with Auclert. She blamed Auclert for the entire affair, claiming that Auclert's behavior—her bickering, her tactlessness, her violent reactions—had converted a courteous inquiry into a rupture. "My devotion to the cause remains forever," Martin concluded; "my devotion to you is forever ended. Friendship between us being henceforth impossible, we can no longer work together."[36]

Martin ceased publishing *La Citoyenne* in November 1891 and immediately founded her own newspaper, *Le Journal des femmes*, which remained the organ of French militants until she died in 1910. She informed Auclert that her lawyers believed that *La Citoyenne* had become her literary property, but she would leave the title to Auclert. De Gasté, disgusted by the proceedings, withdrew his subvention and struck the bequest from his will. Without his backing, Martin reduced *Le Journal des femmes* to monthly publication. Richer retired in 1892 and turned *Le Droit des femmes* and the presidency of the LFDF over to Maria Pognon, who had joined the league at the congress of 1889. Pognon preserved the LFDF but could not keep *Le Droit des femmes* afloat. It ceased publication in the 1890s, leaving Martin's newspaper the sole voice of French feminism for a short period.[37]

The fight with Martin and the loss of *La Citoyenne* devastated Auclert. It caused her "very violent pain" to see her bridges to Parisian feminism in ashes. Solidarité, the LFDF, and *Le Journal des femmes* were all closed to her; Suffrage des femmes and *La Citoyenne* no longer existed; de Gasté was exasperated. Only Amélioration remained, and Auclert could hardly submit herself to the woman who had denied her and her ideas on so many occasions. At first, Auclert contemplated suing Martin for appropriating *La Citoyenne* by changing its name and keeping its resources. Lévrier's friends in the judiciary advised Auclert to take legal action at once. The public prosecutor of Algiers advised a suit for breach of trust.[38]

In the midst of this crisis, Antonin Lévrier's health turned much worse, and he died early in 1892. Grief immobilized Auclert. The loss of both *La Citoyenne* and Lévrier drove her to despair. She dropped all plans for a lawsuit. Auclert later explained that "denouncing a coreli-

36. Folder, "Affaire *La Citoyenne*," Auclert Papers, Carton 13; quotation from Martin to Auclert, 10 December 1891, ibid., 13/16.

37. Ibid.; Auclert, *Le Vote des femmes*, p. 111; Paul Richer, manuscript on his father, Dossier Léon Richer, Dossier 624, Bouglé Collection, BHVP. For more on Pognon, see Hause with Kenney, *Women's Suffrage and Social Politics*, pp. 52–54.

38. Chaumont, "Hubertine Auclert," p. 43 (quoted); Auclert to (name illegible), 20 December 1892, Auclert Papers, 14/15; autobiographical fragment, ibid., 14/58.

gionist" would damage the cause that they both loved. This undoubtedly entered her thinking, but her notes show that her depression was more important.[39]

Auclert never forgave Maria Martin for the death of *La Citoyenne.* For the rest of her life she had difficulty even saying Martin's name, substituting "that woman," "Madame X," "the foreigner," or "the pickpocket." Martin became the personification of her ostracism. In a manuscript from this period, Auclert brooded on her treatment by other feminists. Her sense of persecution increased. "One knows what feminine hatred I have attracted," she wrote. Other feminists were jealous of her, abhorred her, calumniated her; "they applaud when something terrible happens." Auclert felt that the end of *La Citoyenne* proved this: "All of the feminist phalanx applauds. This time H.A. was really dead, she would no longer eclipse them."[40] Lévrier's death meant that Auclert would soon return to Paris. But in what state of mind? To what feminist reception?

39. Chaumont, "Hubertine Auclert," pp. 43–44; autobiographical fragment, Auclert Papers, 14/58 (quoted).

40. Interview in *La Libre parole,* 2 June 1894; Auclert to Marie Duclos, undated, Auclert Papers, 5/5; Auclert to Schmahl, June 1895, ibid., 14/61; Auclert to (unidentified), 26 May 1904, ibid., 2/372; manuscript, "Les Plus grands ennemis des femmes sont les femmes," ibid., 11/330 (quoted); Auclert, *Le Vote des femmes,* p. 111.

CHAPTER EIGHT

Solitude and Return to Feminism, 1892–1900

Hubertine Auclert did not linger in Algeria after the death of her husband. Within a few months she had found the small apartment in the Eleventh Arrondissement of Paris where she resided for the remaining twenty-two years of her life. Auclert's physical return to Paris was easier than the return to mental and emotional activity. The experiences of 1891 and 1892 had left her despondent. Auclert wore the widow's weeds of black thereafter and with them, the cloak of sorrow. During the 1890s, she struggled with her despair and played only a marginal role in the women's movement. The determination and the faith that had served her in previous trials seemed lost. Instead, she succumbed to the self-pity that had hindered her before and to an increasing sense of persecution. Auclert ultimately fought off these potent toxins. But for years she lived her self-image as the pariah, the martyr. Before she could overcome the dark temptation to martyrdom, Auclert had to battle the strongest poison that her mind had yet distilled, the idea that death suited martyrs.

Auclert's first concern upon returning to Paris was to arrange for the transfer of Lévrier's remains. She wanted to see him buried in the famous cemetery of eastern Paris known as Père Lachaise. This bourgeois necropolis, filled with phalanxes of guardhouse tombs watching over the real estate of death, offers dramatic evidence of middle-class *mentalités* in nineteenth-century France. One of the century's most famous novels about social status, *Père Goriot*, appropriately concluded there. So did the social rebellion that Auclert had defended, the Commune of Paris; the execution of the last resisting communards took place against the walls of the cemetery. By the 1890s, Père Lachaise had become the Elysium of the famous and the prosperous. One could seek eternity alongside Napoleonic marshals or republican radicals.[1]

Auclert wrote to the prefect of the Seine and to influential friends for help in arranging reinterment of Lévrier. "Overwhelmed by misery," she wrote, she had simply buried her husband in the first available location. Now she wanted "to be less isolated, less far from my dear dead one." She had chosen her apartment, on the rue de la Roquette, in order to live only a few hundred feet from the entry to Père Lachaise. Her mournful appeals succeeded. In October 1892, Lévrier's remains were transferred to a central plot at Père Lachaise, in the company of Balzac, Delacroix, Delescluze, and the Duc de Morny. Few events of the decade caused Auclert such pleasure. "For my dear Antonin and for me, this is truly good fortune. . . . I cannot tell you how happy I am." Visits to Lévrier's tomb became a part of Auclert's daily routine; she continued them with such frequency that the police noted her devotion a decade later.[2]

Auclert's grief at the loss of Lévrier remained strong for years. She showed it not only in the black clothes of mourning but in the name that she wore. After years of insisting that women keep the name of their birth, she started to use a hyphenated name. Throughout the 1890s, on calling cards, letters, and manuscripts, she referred to herself as Hubertine Auclert-Lévrier. Simultaneously, she wrote to friends to obtain copies of old photographs of Lévrier. She told interviewers of "the most exquisite" years of her life, in Algeria, with Lévrier and her gazelles. And she reflected, "That which is good is, alas, of short duration. . . . One only recognizes that one has been happy when one no longer is."[3]

This period of grief became abnormally protracted. The woman who once showed extraordinary energy now withdrew from the world. She stayed in her "modest apartment," finding comfort in solitude. She became more reserved. She avoided talking to the concierge or her neighbors. She told people that she could not have a pet because it would

1. For the cemetery, see Frederick Brown, *Père Lachaise: Elysium as Real Estate* (New York, 1973) and Philippe Ariès, *The Hour of Our Death* (New York, 1981), esp. pp. 531–36.

2. Unidentified draft letters by Auclert, October 1892, Auclert Papers, 14/12 and 14/14 (all quotations); Auclert to the prefect of the Seine, 6 September 1892, ibid., 14/13; police reports, 1 December 1893 and 21 December 1901, Dossier Auclert, APP. See also Senator Jouffrande to Auclert, 11 November 1892, Auclert Papers, 2/24. Auclert, Marie Chaumont, and Lucien Chaumont were also buried at the same site. Today the tomb bears an effigy of Auclert holding an SF banner. It is concession 90,590 and is located on the Chemin Casimir Delavigne, in the 49th Division of Père Lachaise.

3. For Auclert's use of "Auclert-Lévrier," see the correspondence in the Auclert Papers, Carton 12. For the comments on Africa, see *La Libre parole*, 2 June 1894 (first quotation); Auclert, *Les Femmes arabes en Algérie*, p. 211 (second quotation); *Pensées*, Auclert Papers, 8/134 (third quotation).

remind her of the happy days in Algeria. She said that the grimness of her neighborhood, dominated by a cemetery and the prison of La Roquette, suited her life; she favored "so sad a quartier . . . [because] this sadness corresponds to the state of my soul." The words *despair* and *loneliness* recurred in her notes: "To be alone, to live alone is to live unhappy. . . . In loneliness the body and the soul wither, like a flower without sun." "A sullen despair invades the soul." "A flood of sobbing rises from the heart to the throat . . . I [am] so alone!"[4]

These laments reveal her contradictory understanding of her loneliness. On the one hand, she consciously chose solitude; she immured herself in lonely isolation because she believed it appropriate to both her personal bereavement and her political martyrdom. On the other hand, she keenly felt the pain of solitude and ached when she looked into the merciless face of loneliness. As long as she chose that life, she would hear a fugue of pain.

Auclert pressed the logic of her loneliness toward the conclusion of death, and she considered committing suicide. Auclert's diary has shown her susceptibility to severe depression and her thoughts of death. Her remark after Hugo's funeral that "stupid death" should have taken the "lonely, sad, hopeless" Auclert is only one example of her morbid gloom. Other entries show that *thanatos* held a seductive power: "What is the best thing in life? It is death!" "How much death seems a good and sweet refuge." Auclert left no diary for the 1890s, but there is abundant evidence that she again saw pale death beckoning. Her crisis, after all, derived from the deaths in quick succession of her newspaper and her husband. Auclert turned fifty in 1898, and it could not have escaped her attention that her mother had died at age fifty-one, her father at fifty-seven. She reacted by living adjacent to a cemetery, visiting it often, and talking of "being with" her beloved. She called herself withered in body and soul, and "quite dead."[5]

Still, why suicide? It should be clear that suicide was—in general terms—consistent with Auclert's ideas and behavior. The disapproval of her contemporaries, or of institutions such as the church and the law, did not inhibit her. She revered her independence and could reason that suicide constituted an act of independence, an act of liberation. Indeed, it offered "the best thing in life." Auclert left many direct hints that she thought about suicide. She suddenly began to use the word *suicide*,

4. Marguerite Durand's speech on Auclert, at the installation of her memorial tablet, 28 December 1924, Dossier Auclert, BMD (first quotation); police report, 21 December 1901, Dossier Auclert, APP; *La Libre parole*, 2 June 1894; Chaumont, "Hubertine Auclert," pp. 44–45 (second quotation); autobiographical fragment, Auclert Papers, 14/58; undated note (1890s), ibid., 14/33 (last quotations).

5. Diary, 21 February, 18 April, 14 June, and 31 December 1884, Auclert Papers; manuscript, "Les Plus grands ennemis des femmes sont les femmes," ibid., 11/330.

which she had never done before. In November 1893, for example, she wrote to the Municipal Council of Paris about the problem of suicide among poor and lonely women; she criticized the government for not studying the subject. She began a study of the frequency of suicide among women. In 1894, she founded an organization, Les Tuteurs des pauvres, to combat suicide among lonely and unhappy women. According to the group's statutes, "It has for a goal to assist morally the desperate and to take them away from suicide." This society met only in her mind. Auclert had projected an institution to address a general problem as a means of resolving it in her own life. She based it on erroneous data on suicide, exaggerating its frequency among women in her situation. These misperceptions did not result from flawed research; she did none. They represented an extrapolation of her personal thoughts. Les Tuteurs des pauvres provided a means of externalizing and controlling those thoughts.[6]

Auclert's condition had improved by 1895, although it can hardly be described as cheerful. Talk of suicide disappeared, and with it went the phantom Les Tuteurs des pauvres. Neither the word nor the organization appear in her writings for the next twenty years. Still she had not recovered sufficiently to redirect herself to suffragism. Instead, she created another society, Le Secrétariat des femmes, in another attempt to resolve her feelings. Auclert described the secretariat, which also had more statutes than meetings, as a support group for lonely women facing adversity. "They are legion," these women of "anguished spirit," she explained. The secretariat would "help them to recover hope and courage." How revealing that Auclert now invented an organization to discuss recovery instead of suicide! It would be the end of the decade before this recovery had rekindled the embers of her will and faith.[7]

THE FEMINIST MOVEMENT OF THE 1890s

The decade of the 1890s marked a transitional period in the history of the Parisian women's rights movement. The dominant figures from the founding of the movement in the 1870s and 1880s—Richer, Deraismes, and Auclert—were no longer preeminent. When *Le Figaro* in 1894 and *L'Eclair* in 1895 published surveys of French feminism, all three founders were missing from their stories; when a short-lived feminist federa-

6. Auclert to the Municipal Council of Paris, 16 November 1893, Auclert Papers, 12/7; manuscript, "Assistance publique," ibid., 12/8; manuscript, "Les Tuteurs des pauvres," ibid., 12/1; brochure, "Les Tuteurs des pauvres," ibid., 10/104 (quoted); Emile Durkheim, *Suicide: A Study in Sociology* (1897; reprint, New York, 1951), esp. appendix 6, p. 397.

7. Brochure and statutes of Le Secrétariat des femmes, Auclert Papers, 10/25bis; note secrétariat, ibid., 10/105bis.

tion appeared, none of them participated. Richer remained in retirement until his death in 1911. Deraismes died in 1894—from emphysema according to some reports, from breast cancer according to others. Auclert remained isolated, a secondary figure.[8]

Richer's LFDF continued to be the largest feminist society in France, with 95 members in 1892 and approximately 150 by 1900. Under the leadership of Maria Pognon and Marie Bonnevial, it became more militant. Amélioration remained the best-financed group, with 15,000 francs in investments and 1,400 francs in working capital; it slowly grew to 124 members by 1900. Under the direction of Deraismes' older sister, Anna Feresse-Deraismes, it became even more cautious after Deraismes' death. Solidarité, directed by Potonié-Pierre and several of Auclert's former associates, occupied Suffrage des femmes' position at the militant end of the feminist spectrum; it had better relations with socialist women than Auclert had managed and put less emphasis on the primacy of women's suffrage. Alongside these established organizations there stood several new groups indicative of the growth of the movement. Eliska Vincent founded L'Egalité in 1888 to help fill the suffragist and activist void left by Auclert. Jeanne Deflou, who began her career in Solidarité, created another small society, the Groupe français d'études féministes (hereafter Etudes), to concentrate on winning civil rights. Jeanne Schmahl, another English-born feminist, admired Auclert but preferred caution. She concentrated upon acquiring the economic rights of married women through her league, L'Avant-Courrière, founded in 1893. By the end of the 1890s, similar groups began to appear among socialist women, social reform-oriented Protestants, and even Catholic feminists, but the total membership in women's rights organizations did not surpass two thousand in 1900.[9]

Despite her sense of persecution, Auclert had the sympathies of several feminist leaders. Vincent, Schmahl, Deflou, Feresse-Deraismes, Potonié-Pierre, Rouzade, and Astié all invited her to their activities. But they also liked Maria Martin and felt that she had treated Auclert fairly during her four-year administration of *La Citoyenne*. Martin had become a leader of the movement, active in Solidarité, Amélioration, and the lodge of "mixed" Freemasonry, Le Droit humain, which included many prominent feminists. *Le Journal des femmes* served as the voice of French feminism in the early 1890s and the organ of militants after the

8. *Le Figaro*, 9 November 1894; *L'Eclair*, 12 February 1895.

9. Evans, *The Feminists*, p. 130 (LFDF data); Amélioration, *Bulletin*, August 1900 (membership lists); Dossier Amélioration, BMD (statutes); Amélioration, *Assemblée générale du samedi 26 avril 1890* (Paris, 1890), p. 14 (financial data). For a more detailed overview of the feminist movement at the end of the nineteenth century, see Hause with Kenney, *Women's Suffrage and Social Politics*, pp. 28–71; for socialist women, see Sowerwine, *Sisters or Citizens*, pp. 67–107.

appearance of Clotilde Dissard's *La Revue féministe* (1895) and Durand's *La Fronde* (1897). Martin's version of the events of 1891—that she simply stopped doing Auclert's work and founded her own newspaper—became the accepted feminist history. Thus, as Auclert recovered her enthusiasm, she saw few chances to rejoin the movement. She would not join groups in which Martin was a leader or nonsuffrage societies. Furthermore, Auclert's pride made her reluctant to accept a secondary position.

Both Astié and Eugénie Potonié-Pierre tried to involve Auclert in the elections of 1893 but found her unready for such activity. They each planned to run a slate of women candidates for the Chamber of Deputies, as the Fédération républicaine socialiste had done in 1885. Potonié-Pierre envisioned her own candidacy as well as races by Deraismes, Rouzade, Séverine, Clemence Royer (the French translator of Darwin), Vincent, Martin, Auclert, and even Mink, who was still hostile to seeking enfranchisement. Astié, who had founded a short-lived group named the Ligue (sometimes the Ligue socialiste révolutionnaire) pour l'affranchissement des femmes, proposed a longer list that included the unlikely combination of Auclert and three of her former rivals, Mink, Céleste Hardouin, and Louise Barberouse.[10]

The result of these invitations must have surprised everyone. The only woman to conduct an earnest campaign in 1893 was Paule Mink. This did not betoken a new era in socialist-feminist relations. Mink ran as a socialist, "a disciplined soldier of the Worker-Party," not as a feminist. She continued to derogate the idea that the emancipation of women could be achieved without a socialist revolution first. Nonetheless, both the Allemanist and the Guesdist socialists refused to support her candidacy.[11]

Auclert's role in these events is unclear. Some newspapers reported her candidacy, but no trace of it survives in her personal papers, in the police reports on her, or in the electoral records of the departmental archives. When *L'Eclair* surveyed the candidates, Auclert did not respond. Several newspapers published an unaltered copy of the Suffrage des femmes document of 1885 as her program. She apparently had

10. For the efforts to prepare a slate of women candidates in 1893, see Sowerwine, *Sisters or Citizens,* pp. 70–72; Boxer, "Socialism Faces Feminism," pp. 85–86; Krakovitch, preface to Deraismes, *Ce que veulent les femmes,* pp. 30–31; *L'Evénement,* 10 August 1892 (Astié's list and Auclert's program); *L'Eclair,* 30 October 1892 (the survey) and 17 August 1893 (Auclert); *Le Matin,* 18 December 1892 (invitations and refusals); *Le Journal,* 9 January 1893 (Séverine); *Le Journal des femmes,* June 1910 (Potonié-Pierre).

11. For Mink's race and the socialist-feminist question, see n. 10 above and: Mink's explanation, "Pourquoi j'ai posé ma candiature," *L'Eclair,* 1 May 1893; ibid., 7 April 1893; *La Petite république,* 19 August 1893; Dossier Mink, Bª 1178, APP; Dalotel, preface to Mink, *Communarde et féministe,* pp. 30–34.

submitted it to support the principle of the political rights of women, but she certainly did not participate as she had in the elections of 1881 and 1885.[12]

A clearer indication of Auclert's marginal position in the feminist movement of the 1890s came at the feminist congress of 1896, organized by the LFDF. There had been a small congress in 1892, organized by the federation of feminist groups, before Auclert had returned to Paris. The congress of 1896 was larger and more significant. In the words of a moderate, "all of the left wing of feminism" took part—except Auclert. Unlike Richer's carefully orchestrated congresses of 1878 and 1889, militants dominated the leadership, and they intended to discuss women's suffrage. Surely the moment had come for the founder of French suffragism to deliver the great speech forbidden in 1878 and again in 1889. But the organizers of the congress of 1896 did not summon Auclert—not as an officer, not for the organizing committee, not as a speaker. Auclert was ready to rejoin the battle in 1896. Her papers contain notes on the congress revealing her wish to participate and her anguish at being ignored. She stood in the crowd for the first two days of the congress and concluded that newcomers acted as if they had invented the movement. On the third day, when the congress debated political rights, Auclert endured complete rejection. She arrived late and found the doors to the session closed, so she waited until someone she recognized came out. Several feminists saw Auclert; none invited her inside to hear the suffrage debates.[13]

The great suffragist was shattered, again convinced she was persecuted. She stumbled home and vented her feelings in a sad note. Why, she asked, did all her suffering for the cause not count? Would time utterly efface all memory of her efforts? Why did new recruits triumph while she received no credit for creating their program? "Why does my brain burst, to the point that I'm not able to walk a straight line?"[14]

Perhaps the answer was the years of uncompromising combativeness that had alienated many people. Perhaps it was her contumacious personality, as she realized in the same note, that did not mix well with her colleagues. Perhaps it was her withdrawal since 1885. Perhaps it was simply the fact that Martin served as the administrative head of the

12. In addition to the sources in notes (10 and 11,) see: Dossier Auclert, APP and the electoral files at AD-Seine, D2 M²/30 and D3 M²/7. For Auclert's petition of 1893, see Auclert Papers, 6/189, 6/193, and 6/195.

13. See Wyona H. Wilkins, "The Paris International Feminist Congress of 1896 and Its French Antecedents," *North Dakota Quarterly* 43 (1975): 16–27; Avril de Sainte-Croix, *Le Féminisme* (Paris, 1907), pp. 138–39 (quoted); Dossier "Congrès (documents)," Carton 1, Bouglé Collection, BHVP.

14. Notes, "9 avril au congrès" and "11 avril 1896," Auclert Papers, 11/339 and 11/346 (quoted).

congress, whose offices were in her apartment. From some mixture of these facts arose a scene appropriate to Greek tragedy: Hubertine Auclert standing in the hallway while a feminist congress finally debated women's suffrage.

LA LIBRE PAROLE AND LE RADICAL

Auclert returned to prominence through journalism. After the loss of *La Citoyenne*, she contributed articles to several newspapers, notably *Le Radical algérien*. She missed *La Citoyenne* more than Suffrage des femmes because she wanted a forum for her ideas more than a base for further activism. She felt more comfortable writing articles alone in her apartment. An autobiographical note from this period reveals her ambition. Recreating *La Citoyenne* was beyond her resources, physical, emotional, and financial. The death of Joseph de Gasté in 1893, the expected bequest stricken from his will, drove the final nail into the coffin of her career as a publisher. Auclert aspired to a position on the staff of a major newspaper, where she could write a column on feminist questions. Still an ardent republican, Auclert first approached the great radical newspapers. Several republican editors, however, "refused their hospitality."[15]

Denied a place in radical journalism, Auclert sought any opportunity. The tactical pragmatism that she had learned in the 1880s led to her appointment to a remarkably inappropriate newspaper, Edouard Drumont's *La Libre parole*, one of the most influential voices of the extreme right wing in French politics. Drumont had acquired a large following through the invective of racist nationalism, of which the foremost element was obsessive anti-Semitism. Beginning with his notorious and popular *La France juive* in 1886, Drumont published five books denouncing the political and economic influence of Jews in France before founding *La Libre parole* in April 1892. This newspaper, subtitled "France for the French," soon circulated one hundred thousand copies, largely owing to the Panama scandal of 1892–1893. Drumont exulted in the exposure of corrupt officials and their connections with Jewish bankers involved in the French attempt to build a canal through the Isthmus of Panama. He combined anti-Semitism with a general xenophobia to restate several themes of right-wing thought: revenge upon Germany for the war of 1870–1871, French national unity, defense of traditional institutions. Drumont thus became one of the most impor-

15. Autobiographical fragment, ibid., 14/58; Auclert to Séverine, 27 January 1895, ibid., 2/33 (quoted); Auclert to the director of *Le Radical algérien*, 14 November 1893, ibid., 12/6; Chaumont, "Hubertine Auclert," p. 46.

tant figures in the transformation of French nationalism from a left-wing doctrine in the tradition of the Jacobins, Gambetta in 1870, and Clemenceau in the 1880s to a right-wing doctrine.[16]

The popularity of Edouard Drumont was more complex than it seems at first glance. He did not appeal solely to conservative constituencies, nor was he universally rejected by the French left. Recent controversial scholarship has shown how Drumont attracted some workers and socialists. Popular nationalism ("plebian nationalism" in the words of one Drumont scholar) survived despite socialism's theoretical internationalism. Xenophobia was not difficult to popularize among workers, especially in those frontier regions that experienced competition from foreign migrant laborers. Drumont's attack upon the bourgeois republic, upon bourgeois liberalism, and upon capitalism, which he considered a Jewish phenomenon, attracted some socialists, especially followers of less well defined doctrines. Even his anti-Semitism attracted a number of former Proudhonists, Blanquists, and communards. Drumont's occasional support of strikers increased his success with workers.[17]

Whatever the complexities of Drumont's position in French politics, *La Libre parole* seems an extraordinary place to find a woman who had devoted her life to the defense of human rights and had unceasingly championed the republic. Curiously, at the moment that she joined *La Libre parole*, Auclert had been rethinking her opposition to anarchism. She had consistently opposed it and had spurned Louise Michel for her violent beliefs. She reconsidered after witnessing the execution of Auguste Vaillant, the anarchist who hurled a bomb in the Chamber of Deputies in 1893. It is difficult to imagine Drumont describing the scene with Auclert's empathy; she, however, recognized Vaillant as a fellow martyr:

> The Place de la Roquette is full of wild animals. The hyenas and jackals are assembled there tonight to bleed a lamb.
> It is a question of bread that led to this conflict. The lamb wished for his brothers and for himself to graze in the prairies of

16. For Drumont and *La Libre parole,* see *DPF,* 4:1497–98; Bellanger et al., *Histoire générale de la presse française,* 3:343–45; E. Beau de Loménie, *Edouard Drumont, ou l'anticapitalisme national* (Paris, 1968), which reprints many columns from *La Libre parole;* Michel Winock, *Edouard Drumont et Cie: Antisémitisme et fascisme en France* (Paris, 1982); Zeev Sternhell, *La Droite révolutionnaire, 1885–1914: Les Origines françaises du fascisme* (Paris, 1978); Robert F. Byrnes, *Antisemitism in Modern France,* vol. 1, *The Prologue to the Dreyfus Affair* (New Brunswick, N.J., 1950); Michael R. Marrus, *The Politics of Assimilation* (Oxford, 1971).

17. For Drumont's success with workers and socialists, see esp. Sternhell, *La Droite révolutionnaire,* pp. 177–214 ("L'Antisémitisme de gauche") and Winock, *Edouard Drumont et Cie,* pp. 80–114 ("La Gauche et les juifs").

the Republic by the width of a tongue. So the wild beasts rushed for him and are going to cut his throat, to make him pay for his whimsical desire to eat.

When I saw Vaillant walking boldly to the guillotine, his head held high and his face transfigured, I understood that this was a martyr, a victim dying for an ideal. . . .

Yesterday, I execrated anarchy. The execution of Vaillant has almost made me adopt it. In any case, I want to study the doctrine seriously.[18]

It is also remarkable that Auclert chose to collaborate with such a virulent racist. Auclert's record as an opponent of racism rests on her Algerian writings of 1889–1901. There she stoutly defended a policy of assimilation. Drumont wanted precisely the opposite. He considered true assimilation impossible and held attempts at it responsible for French ills. There is no evidence of anti-Semitism in Auclert's writings or in her private papers. She wrote little about the Dreyfus affair, except for attempts to exploit the controversy to the advantage of women's rights. Her papers do include some grumbling about the prominence of foreign women in the French feminist movement, so it might be argued that she was not without a trace of xenophobia. This, however, never appeared in her political theories; it probably had more to do with Maria Martin than with prejudice. Auclert's position at *La Libre parole* surprises most because Drumont had derided women's rights; he held women's suffrage to be "absurd."[19]

Auclert collaborated with *La Libre parole* for six months during 1894. This can be explained partly by her willingness to use any forum to advocate her cause, partly by the fact that republican editors had rejected her. Surely another part of the explanation must have been Auclert's sense of persecution. One must add, however, that Auclert was comfortable with some aspects of Drumont's thought. She had been a Jacobin nationalist since her youth. She believed, despite her ill-defined pacifism, that France must be prepared to defend herself against Germany. After the Schnaebelé affair of 1887, she expected war at any time. Auclert's nationalism led her to respect Paul Déroulède for "total love of *la patrie*," to find the Boulangist nationalism of 1886–1889 attractive, and to applaud the Franco-Russian alliance of 1891–1894. Juliette Adam became her heroine for her ardent patriotism. Thus,

18. Manuscript, "Lundi gras. 5 février 1894," Auclert Papers, 6/169.

19. For Auclert's silence on the Dreyfus affair, see appendix 2 for the subjects that she chose to write about during the crisis; for her use of the crisis, see her "Nouveau complot," *L'Echo d'Oran*, 17 October 1899, where she argues that those concerned with conspiracies should look into the masculine conspiracy to deny women republican rights. For Drumont's "absurd," see *L'Entente*, April 1906.

unresolved contradictions in her Jacobinism probably permitted Auclert to accept Drumont as a nationalist. She somehow ignored his
racism in order to advance her suffragism through his widely read
newspaper. His defense of workers may provide the key: Auclert
thought that Drumont's articles on strikers proved that he would "defend all of the weak and the oppressed of the present system." Do these
mental gymnastics suggest that she sought some rationalization for her
collaboration with a notorious racist? Or that she sincerely admired
him? Whatever the explanation, others made the same strange alliance
before 1898, when the Dreyfus affair made it impossible. Séverine, a
passionate defender of Dreyfus in *La Fronde* in 1898 and 1899, wrote for
La Libre parole, not for six months, but for four years (1893–1896).[20]

   Auclert's connection with *La Libre parole* began in May 1893 when
she wrote to Drumont about Algeria. He had published an article that
she deemed sympathetic to Arabs, so she wrote to him about creating a
school for Arab girls. This led to a meeting in early 1894 at which
Auclert suggested that she submit an article on women's suffrage.
Drumont gave her a "cold greeting, hesitant" but agreed to consider a
"very short" unpaid piece. He suggested that she survey foreign suffragism. According to her account, Auclert insisted that "we French women, we want our rights," so she would write about France. Drumont
considered Auclert "a gentle creature . . . [with] a force of invincible
tenacity." Her forcefulness, Drumont wrote, induced him to answer,
"Go ahead and explain your ideas! I lost eight hundred subscribers at a
stroke for supporting the strikers at Carmaux. . . . I don't see how this
can turn out more disastrously." He suggested that she "say that you
want the rights that women possessed before the revolution." Auclert
then asked bluntly to write regularly on women's rights for *La Libre
parole*. Drumont capitulated, adding, "but I cannot be occupied with
women's rights all the time."[21]

   The strange collaboration of Auclert and Drumont included his long
interview with her, published in June 1894. She spoke candidly about
her youth, her feminist career, her experiences with socialism, Algeria,
her "affectionate and tender" relationship with Lévrier, "Madame X"
who had stolen *La Citoyenne*, and the current "sadness" in her soul.

20. Undated notes, Auclert Papers, 8/157, 10/46, and 10/52; unidentified Drumont
article, "Les Droits de la femme," ibid., Carton 1 (quoted); Chaumont, "Hubertine
Auclert," pp. 86–87. For Séverine at *La Libre parole*, see Lecache, *Séverine*, pp. 134–61; Le
Garrec, *Séverine*, pp. 130–44.

   21. Auclert to Drumont, 31 May 1893, Auclert Papers, 14/30; note, 12 March 1894,
ibid., 14/28 (first quotation); unidentified Drumont article, "Les Droits de la femme,"
ibid., Carton 1 (second and third quotations); note, 16 March 1894, ibid., 14/29 (fourth
quotation); Auclert to Drumont, 23 March 1894, ibid., 14/27; note, "2 avril 1894 à *La
Libre parole*," ibid., 14/26 (fifth quotation).

Drumont concluded, in print, that "she is neither a fanatic nor a mad woman, much less an ogre," but a proud woman animated by "the love of liberty for all." And he praised her journalistic abilities, especially an essay on her gazelle published in 1894, which he supported for a literary prize. (It won the medal awarded by the Society for the Protection of Animals in 1895.) With that support, Auclert placed twelve articles, all under the heading of "Women's Rights," in *La Libre parole* between March and September 1894 (see appendix 2).[22]

It was Drumont's decision, not Auclert's, that her column would not become a lasting feature in *La Libre parole.* She continued for several months to submit articles that he never printed, even contributing one as late as 1896. A note in Auclert's papers suggests that Drumont lost patience with her when she repeatedly refused to follow his advice. Auclert, still sensing the hatred of other women, believed that her opportunity had been lost through the jealousy of Séverine and told her so. She never treated Drumont so curtly. Years later, she still praised him for giving her a chance to state feminist aspirations. He, in return, later published prosuffrage articles, albeit sometimes with a sarcastic tone.[23]

Auclert's attempts to talk her way onto the staff of a major newspaper produced lasting results in 1896, when she joined the paper closest to her natural home in Parisian journalism, *Le Radical.* This paper, the third of that name since 1871, never reached the circulation of *La Libre parole,* but it exercised great influence among radical republicans, whose party organ it later became. Henry Maret directed *Le Radical* from its founding in 1881 until 1904. He had been an associate of Henri Rochefort during the Commune, for which he had served five years in prison. Elected to the Paris municipal council in 1878, he joined the *autonomie communale* faction in which Lévrier participated. In 1881 he entered the Chamber of Deputies from Paris as a candidate of the "extreme (republican) left" and remained for twenty-five years. Maret won feminist praise as a neophyte deputy in 1882 for his amendments to the divorce bill. He supported Auclert as early as 1880, endorsed women's suffrage while a candidate in 1881, served on the committee of initiative that founded Suffrage des femmes in 1883, and made small contributions to the society in the 1880s. Maret's support had declined

22. *La Libre parole,* 2 June 1894 (quoted); "Ma Gazette Yzette," reprinted from *L'Intransigeant illustré* in Auclert, *Les Femmes arabes en Algérie,* pp. 204–13; certificate of Société protectrice des animaux, 3 June 1895, Auclert Papers, Carton 14, folder "Divers."

23. Note, 25 July 1896, Auclert Papers, 14/25; Auclert to Séverine, 27 January 1895, ibid., 2/33; minutes of SF meeting, January 1904, ibid., Carton 4; *La Libre parole,* 28 July 1897, 9 June 1906, and 18 April 1910.

by the 1890s, although he sometimes used his column in *Le Radical,* "Carnet d'un sauvage," to back women's rights.[24]

Auclert persuaded Maret to give her a weekly column, to be entitled "Le Féminisme," late in 1896. No correspondence about this decision survives, but Maret explained to his readers in October 1896 that it was appropriate for a newspaper that wished to remain in the vanguard of "advanced opinion and free thought." Auclert, he added, was the best-qualified person in France to write such a column. For the next thirteen years, *Le Radical* was the forum Auclert had sought. She produced over four hundred articles (see appendix 1), expanding the integral feminism that she had developed in *La Citoyenne.* Her constant theme was the political rights of women, but scarcely a feminist issue escaped her attention. Auclert's column, of course, contrasted sharply with the rest of *Le Radical;* she had to endure the irony of writing for a newspaper that opposed women's suffrage and a political faction that repeatedly blocked the subject in parliament.[25]

Her essays in *Le Radical* show that Auclert's thinking had remained essentially unchanged, with one major exception, since the early 1880s. She had found new issues to add to her lexicon of feminist *revindications,* especially a strong interest in the subordination of women through language; this resulted in frequent articles about a single appellation for all women (*madame,* not *mademoiselle*), about the importance of the name of the married woman, and about the need to "feminize" the language. She also showed a greater interest in children— defending, for example, the rights of illegitimate children, and seeking state aid for motherhood, in anticipation of the Law of Large Families of July 1913. Her integral feminism, however, was largely the same comprehensive concern for all social, economic, and legal interests of women; her attitudes, such as favoring easier divorce and opposing *libre union,* had not significantly altered. In the large number of articles that she wrote for *Le Radical* she had an opportunity to reflect on the history of French feminism, especially the role of people she had known, from Richer and Deraismes to Hugo, Macé, and Emile Deschanel. She assumed the role that Lévrier had performed in the early years of *La Citoyenne,* surveying the conditions of women in many different occupations, from dentists and midwives to saleswomen and factory workers. She fixed her analysis in the same matrix of republicanism that had always characterized her thought, now underscored by her collab-

24. Bellanger et al., *Histoire générale de la presse française,* 3:230, 365–66; DdPF, 4:265–66; *DPF,* 7:2366–67; *La Citoyenne,* 11 September 1881; police reports, 14 January 1880 and 22 March 1883, Dossier Auclert, APP; unidentified clipping of "Carnet d'un sauvage," Auclert Papers, Carton 1.

25. *Le Radical,* 3 October 1896.

oration with the organ of the radical republican parliamentary faction. The foremost development of her republicanism, stimulated by her years in Algeria, was a greater interest in questions of colonial and foreign policy. This revealed an increase in her Jacobin nationalism, consistent with the thought of other republicans in the early twentieth century, at the expense of her pacifism. Throughout these articles, Auclert still demonstrated her vigorous rhetoric of assault. Women were still "slaves," treated like "the negroes of France." As befitted a columnist for a radical newspaper during the Dreyfus affair and the conflict over the separation of church and state, Auclert also denounced the oppression of women by the church: women were "victims of theology."

This description of Auclert's articles for *Le Radical* would be incomplete if it failed to note signs of an important change, the harbinger of her twentieth-century notoriety as "the French suffragette." Her frustration with the slowness of reform and the timidity of the new generation of feminists, combined with her emotional acceptance of the role of martyr, led her to think about greater militancy. She had been the most radical Parisian feminist in the 1880s because she had led demonstrations in the streets. She now began to ask if violence would also be necessary.

THE FEMINIST CONGRESSES OF 1900

One of the most important factors in the expansion of the women's rights movement in France was a series of three congresses held in conjunction with the Paris exposition of 1900. Each congress assembled separate parts of the women's movement. A congress of Catholic women, the Congrès catholique des oeuvres de femmes, foreshadowed the day when Catholics would become more active in feminism, including suffragism. A congress of moderates, the Congrès des oeuvres et institutions féminines, was the successor to the congress of the same name held in 1889. Its participants now endorsed more of the feminist agenda, especially the civil rights of women, but they still opposed the vote.[26]

The third congress of 1900, the Congrès international de la condition et des droits des femmes, was the successor to the series of congresses that Léon Richer had started in 1878 and that included the assemblies of 1889, 1892, and 1896. The LFDF organized this assembly of over five hundred delegates; it included representatives of all feminist leagues.

26. For more detail on the congresses of 1900 as part of a turning point for French feminism, see Hause with Kenney, *Women's Suffrage and Social Politics*, pp. 28–40.

They debated the most comprehensive feminist program yet considered in France, and they endorsed seventy-three reforms, including women's suffrage. The actions of the congress received extensive press coverage because Marguerite Durand served as its secretary-general.[27]

The women's rights congress also accomplished the return of Hubertine Auclert to energetic participation in feminist activities. Her column in *Le Radical* had made her a prominent figure in the movement again, but her role had essentially been limited to writing. Auclert had shown signs of activity during the parliamentary elections of 1898, but she had not participated in the work of other groups. Her official role in the congress was to be a member of the organizing committee, at the invitation of the LFDF. As the congress had fourteen officers and a committee of thirty-four, any other decision by Durand and Pognon, the president of the congress, would have been an insult. After all, of the committee members, only Vincent had been active in French feminism as long as Auclert; none had attended the first congress in 1878, of which Auclert had been on the organizing committee; several had entered the movement through Droit des femmes or Suffrage des femmes. Nonetheless, the appointment must have required some diplomacy. Martin was an officer of the congress and Auclert was listed on the program as the founder of *La Citoyenne*; this was the first time in a decade that they had shared any activity. Once there, Auclert participated vigorously. In addition to championing women's suffrage, in a resolution based on a petition that she circulated at the exposition, she introduced a torrent of other motions. Many of them seem timely decades later, particularly the concerns about language that she had expressed in *Le Radical*. She called for all women, married or not, to use the title *madame*, just as all men used *monsieur*. She asked the Académie française to undertake the feminization of the language—creating, for example, *avocate* for female lawyers to accompany *avocat*, or *electrice* for a female elector. She urged women to keep the surname of their birth, rather than adopting the name of their husbands. This last motion provides an interesting indication that Auclert had dealt with her personal crisis of the early 1890s;

27. Ibid. For more on the militant congress, see the extensive daily coverage in *La Fronde* and the dossiers on the congress and on the LFDF, BMD, and the congress in the Bouglé Collection, BHVP; for the published debates, see Marguerite Durand, ed., *Congrès international de la condition et des droits des femmes* (Paris, 1901); for the list of motions voted on, see Comtesse Pierre Lecointre, *Etat de la question féministe en France en 1907* (Paris, 1907), pp. 20–24. For the socialist role in the congress, see Marie Bonnevial's reports in *Le Mouvement socialiste*, 15 October and 1 November 1900; Sowerwine, *Sisters or Citizens*, pp. 76–79; Boxer, "Feminism Faces Socialism," pp. 95–96. For Durand's role, see Sue H. Goliber, "The Life and Times of Marguerite Durand: A Study in French Feminism," Ph.D. diss., Kent State University, 1975, pp. 53–59.

she submitted the motion with the signature that she had been using, Hubertine Auclert-Lévrier, with the Lévrier crossed out.[28]

What accounts for Auclert's return to activism in 1900? No convenient explanation survives in her personal papers. The best answer seems to be the obvious one. Time had passed, time in which she adjusted her feelings about loneliness, time over which the bitterness of her relations with other feminists lessened, time during which her desire increased to return to the great passion of her life. The intimate notes that Auclert left from this period reveal only one direct stimulus. In October 1899 she received a sad, unexpected visit from Richer, then seventy-five years old. He told Auclert that he wanted to see her one last time before he died and to apologize to her for fighting her program. Then Richer exposed his own loneliness to her: "No one comes to see me. Yet I've helped so many people. I've done more [for feminism] than Maria Deraismes, and I was a man." Did Auclert glimpse in the lonely Richer a vision of her own life, her isolation stretching into an old age in which young feminists would forget her pioneering suffragism? She accepted the committee appointment a few days after Richer's visit.[29]

28. Auclert, "Le Vote des femmes," *La Fronde*, 13 December 1897. For her electoral activity in 1898, see her letters to candidates for the Chamber of Deputies, Auclert Papers, Carton 12; her electoral program, ibid., 10/45; and clippings in Dossier Auclert, BMD. For her role in congress, see the program and motions of the congress, Dossier Congrès (divers), Carton 1, Bouglé Collection, BHVP; Auclert's suffrage motions, Auclert Papers, 6/116 and 6/1; Auclert's feminism motions, ibid., 6/115, 6/117, and in the Auclert correspondence, 091 AUC, BMD; Auclert, "Les Femmes à l'exposition," *Le Radical*, 19 June 1900; Amélioration, *Bulletin*, January 1900; *La Fronde*, 8 August and 10 September 1900; *Le Soir*, 31 August 1900; *L'Eclair*, 11 November 1901; *Le Journal*, 23 April 1906. For the development of Auclert's ideas on feminizing names and the language, see Auclert, "Féminisez la langue," *Le Radical*, 12 August 1900; "'Madame,'" ibid., 20 November 1901; "Gardez votre nom," ibid., 21 November 1901; Auclert, *Le Nom de la femme* (Paris, n.d. [1905]); Jeanne Voitout (Auclert), "Le Nom," *La Citoyenne*, December 1884; Suzanne Dudit, "Le Nom de la femme mariée," *Minerva*, 10 April 1932.

29. Note, 25 October 1899, Auclert Papers, 13/7.

CHAPTER NINE

Beginning a Second Suffrage Career, 1900–1904

The feminist movement that assembled in 1900 was larger and more diverse than the movement of 1885, when Auclert had last been a dominant figure. Excluding the provincial groups and the Catholic organizations that had emerged between those years, and three moderate leagues founded following the congresses, there were now seven important feminist organizations in France (see table 9.1), compared to four in 1885. The combined membership had also doubled. Feminist periodicals and pamphlet series had proliferated. And the growth of the movement was just beginning. With the creation of the Conseil national des femmes françaises (hereafter CNFF) in 1901, feminists claimed an active membership of twenty to twenty-five thousand; in the next decade it surpassed one hundred thousand.

Hubertine Auclert had better relations with the seven organizations of 1900 than she had had with her three rival leagues in 1885. Nothing separated her from Amélioration and the LFDF except bad memories and the belief that they were still too moderate. Vincent and Egalité shared Auclert's militant suffragism. Potonié-Pierre had died in 1898, but Solidarité survived; its new leader, Caroline Kauffmann, admired Auclert and corresponded with her. Jeanne Deflou, now Oddo-Deflou, respected Auclert so much that she published an article lauding Auclert for converting her to feminism. Schmahl publicly concentrated on the economic rights of married women but privately supported Auclert's suffragism. Even one of the founders of the Groupe féministe socialiste, Elisabeth Renaud, shared this respect for Auclert.[1]

1. For a more detailed survey of the feminist movement at the turn of the century, see

TABLE **9.1.** **Parisian Militant Feminist Leagues in 1900**

Name	Founded	Leader(s)	Publication	Membership
Amélioration	1870	Feresse-Deraismes	*Bulletin*	100–150
LFDF	1882	Pognon, Bonnevial	none	under 200
Egalité	1888	Vincent	pamphlet series	under 100
Solidarité	1891	Kauffmann	none	under 100
Avant-Courrière	1893	Schmahl	pamphlet series	c. 200
Etudes	1898	Oddo-Deflou	*Bulletin*	c. 100
Groupe féministe socialiste	1899	Renaud, Saumoneau	*La Femme socialiste*	under 100

Note: Table excludes the moderate Catholic, Protestant, and provincial feminist groups, and all societies founded after the congresses of 1900. See Hause with Kenney, *Women's Suffrage and Social Politics*, pp. 41–42.

This is not to say that everyone suddenly feted Auclert as the senior stateswoman of the cause. But her old rivals, except Martin, had passed from the scene. More of the movement now accepted suffragism. Thus, as Auclert resumed activity between 1896 and 1900, she heard supportive voices urging her to reestablish Suffrage des femmes.

REBUILDING SUFFRAGE DES FEMMES

Why did Auclert decide to rebuild Suffrage des femmes? One likely answer must come from the interplay of the personal and the political in her career. "What cannot be cured," wrote Rabelais, "must be endured." Auclert could not cure herself of her instinctive reactions nor completely conquer the mental habits that conceived the self-portrait of loneliness and persecution. It is another testimony to the strength of her will and the depth of her faith that she again learned to endure. Few people could have recovered and resumed as she did. Given the nature of her personality, she had paid a frightful price for rejecting traditional women's roles to compete in the male world of politics. But she endured. The stubborn defiance in her character reasserted itself and prompted renewed political involvement.

In addition to Auclert's remarkable endurance and the stimulus of feminist expansion, the decisive factor appears to have been the positive

---

Hause with Kenney, *Women's Suffrage and Social Politics*, pp. 28–70; for the Groupe féministe socialiste, see Sowerwine, *Sister or Citizens*, pp. 81–107; "Le Groupe féministe socialiste," pp. 87–120.

reinforcement from her colleagues. The women of Solidarité invited her to address them several times. The Protestant reformers of the Congrès des oeuvres et institutions féminines even asked her to join in founding the CNFF. Oddo-Deflou strongly urged the recreation of Suffrage des femmes. If that were too arduous a task, Auclert should participate in Etudes, where she would be received "with great pleasure." Oddo-Deflou also pressed Auclert to join her in the CNFF: "It seems to me that no one has an older or better title than you." And she discreetly offered the necessary financial assistance. Similar encouragement came from Pognon, Schmahl, Vincent, and Rouzade. For a person who had felt so persecuted, such encouragement must have been invigorating.[2]

Auclert never considered alternatives to Suffrage des femmes. Her personality was not suited to a secondary role in another woman's organization, however amicable the invitation might be. The new national council did not interest her; she considered its leaders, the women of Protestant philanthropy, "chilling women" of patronizing arrogance. They had also made Martin an officer of the CNFF, and Auclert told friends that she could not join a group "which includes at its heart dishonest women."[3]

In recreating Suffrage des femmes she followed her old organizational tactics, with one imaginative addition. She announced in her column in *Le Radical* that Suffrage des femmes would begin meetings at the end of 1900 and that she would be at home every Tuesday afternoon to discuss the society with anyone interested. Whenever she left her apartment, Marie stayed there in case someone called. Articles for the feminist press and some republican newspapers followed, discussing the need for women's suffrage. She underscored her message with huge green posters displayed around Paris, and she distributed four thousand handbills on the streets. Auclert did not organize public lectures, as she had when creating Droit des femmes, but she spoke to other feminist groups and she undertook an energetic correspondence to circulate the news.

Auclert's innovative idea was a propaganda stamp, to be affixed to envelopes beside the legal postage stamp. Her design (see illustration 6) portrayed a woman and a man voting together before the rising sun of universal suffrage. The stamp alluded to two postage stamps of the era, one celebrating the Declaration of the Rights of Man, the other, known as *la semeuse* (the sower), depicting Marianne spreading the seeds of

2. Oddo-Deflou to Auclert, 25 December 1901, CP 4248, BHVP; police report, 12 August 1902, Dossier "Le Mouvement féministe," Bª 1651, APP; minutes of SF meeting, 12 June 1903, Auclert Papers, Carton 4; Kauffmann to Auclert, undated, ibid., 3/662; handbills for Solidarité meetings, Dossier Auclert, BMD.

3. Notes on the congresses of 1900, Auclert Papers, 6/9 (first quotation); police report, 15 February 1902, Dossier Auclert, APP (second quotation).

republican France. The idea of such propaganda stamps did not originate with Auclert—the Radical party used similar stamps for fundraising— but her version attracted considerable publicity. Newspapers and phi- latelists admired it, and virtually all women's groups bought sheets of it to attach to their correspondence. The idea was so successful that the initial run of one hundred thousand soon sold out. Auclert reprinted the stamp several times and added a feminist postcard with the same il- lustration.[4]

Auclert received considerable support in launching Suffrage des femmes. The mayor of the Eleventh Arrondissement permitted her to use a meeting room on the third floor of the *mairie,* on the rue de la Roquette a few blocks from her apartment. Three political friends from the 1880s who were still active in 1900—Hugues, Maret, and Guyot— lent their backing and joined Suffrage des femmes. Jeanne Schmahl gave Auclert a large donation to help start the society—one hundred francs, or almost half of Suffrage des femmes' average annual budget for the next few years. She told Auclert that the years of struggle for an earnings law had taught her that "those who called for women's suffrage were right." Léonie Rouzade and her husband also contributed money for publicity. Along with Schmahl and Rouzade, several prominent femi- nists joined Suffrage des femmes as dues-paying members: Vincent, her sister Florestine Moriceau, Oddo-Deflou, Kauffman, and Feresse-De- raismes. Others supported Suffrage des femmes with purchases of Auclert's propaganda stamp, namely, Bonnevial, Marguerite Belmant ("Marbel," who founded the Union fraternelle des femmes, or UFF, in 1901), Odette Laguerre (the leader of the feminist movement in Lyons), Durand, Astié, and the Bélilon sisters. After Auclert personally trans- ferred 190 francs to the society, Suffrage des femmes had raised 631.30 francs for 1901.[5]

---

4. For Auclert's efforts to reestablish SF, see her articles in *Le Radical,* 25 December 1900 and 1 January 1901; her correspondence at the BMD, 091 AUC, esp. her requests to Durand to insert notices of SF in *La Fronde;* the new statutes of SF, which include a brief history, in the Dossier SF, BMD; the initial financial accounts of SF, Auclert Papers, 10/53; recruitment poster headed "Suffrage réellement universel," ibid., Carton 1; police report, 21 December 1901, Dossier Auclert, APP. For examples of her press campaign, see *L'Abeille,* 20 January 1901; *La Petite république,* 27 May 1901. For the suffrage stamp, see Auclert, *Le Vote des femmes,* p. 120; Chaumont, "Hubertine Auclert," p. 71; Auclert to Jules Clarétie, 17 January 1906, Auclert Papers, 5/6; undated speech, ibid., 6/110; the regular discussion in the minutes of SF for 1901, ibid., Carton 4; interview with Auclert in *La Patrie,* 5 January 1902; *La Presse,* 19 October 1901; *L'Eclair,* 17 October 1901; Auclert to Durand, 2 January 1904, Auclert Correspondence, 091 AUC, BMD.

5. For Auclert's use of the *mairie* of the Eleventh Arrondissement, see her speeches on the subject, Auclert Papers, 6/88 and 6/110. For the financial support of SF, see Auclert's meticulous financial records, ibid., Carton 4; illustration 13, above; minutes of SF meet- ing, 8 March 1901, ibid., Carton 4 (quoted).

Such support was a well-deserved tribute to Auclert's work a generation earlier and a boost to her labors in 1900 and 1901. By late 1901, police agents reported that Auclert was receiving several visitors and approximately thirty pieces of mail every day. One hundred people attended some of Suffrage des femmes' first meetings; fifty-three became dues-paying members. In addition to the well-known feminists who joined Suffrage des femmes, Auclert recruited two of her sisters, Marie, who remained her amanuensis for the rest of her life, and Delphine Paradis, who had moved to Paris upon the retirement of her husband. The balance of the membership, as it had been twenty years earlier, was chiefly composed of married women of the middle class, few of whom were wealthy. A few men participated, mostly husbands of members, such as Auguste Rouzade. The recruiting efforts of the society concentrated on the young women employed by the government as teachers and postal clerks, but they yielded no great numbers.[6]

Despite this auspicious beginning, which soundly reestablished the group, Suffrage des femmes did not become a major feminist league in size or wealth. Other leagues grew into hundreds and even thousands of members. Auclert settled for being the militant conscience of the movement, the ceaseless advocate of converting all feminists to suffragism, the gadfly advocating more assertive action, the daring individual who risked ridicule in public demonstrations. As she and Suffrage des femmes embraced this role, membership stabilized between fifty and one hundred, of whom fifteen to thirty paid the three francs of dues in any year; the same number might attend any single meeting. The police, as well as some feminists, disparaged Suffrage des femmes for its small size, but Auclert was still the only person in Paris who put feminist marchers in the streets until Madeleine Pelletier introduced Solidarité to the same tactics. The members of Suffrage des femmes gave no sign of discouragement over their numbers. As Rouzade insisted at a 1901 meeting, "a small nucleus of militants can defeat general indifference."[7]

Suffrage des femmes operated on a precarious financial basis. Helpful contributions came from Schmahl, and occasionally from Vincent, who

6. See the police reports in Bª 885 (esp. 21 November 1901) and Bª 1651 (esp. 12 July 1902), APP. For SF recruiting discussions, see the minutes of meetings on 26 April 1901 and 27 November 1903, Auclert Papers, Carton 4. For the middle-class composition of SF, see Auclert's undated note, ibid., 12/56. The number of active male members can be deduced from the minutes; 10 to 20 percent of those present were men. See especially the discussion of male members at the meeting of 22 March 1901.

7. Membership in SF can be followed precisely in Auclert's financial records, ibid., Carton 4; participation in SF meetings is periodically reported in the minutes of SF meetings, ibid., and in the police reports in the Dossier Auclert, APP. Minutes of SF meeting of 26 April 1901, Auclert Papers, Carton 4 (quoted).

had inherited over one hundred thousand francs on the death of her husband, but no donor approached the support that de Gasté had given in the 1880s. Auclert hoped that one of her wealthy supporters would bequeath the society a legacy sufficient for greater activities, but none did, although one left fifty thousand francs to a group of utopian socialists and another bequeathed one hundred thousand francs to aid the glass workers of Carmaux. Auclert again lamented "the propensity of women towards a parsimony bordering on greed" and made do with an average annual budget of 234 francs for the years 1901–1904. Her meticulous financial records survive for the early twentieth century (see illustration 13). They reveal how much she accomplished on her scant income: 16 francs for four thousand circulars to be distributed in the streets; 15 francs for one thousand large posters to blanket Paris with during an election; 54.60 francs to hire ten men to march in suffragist sandwich boards. As these examples suggest, printing was Suffrage des femmes' largest expense, postage and tax stamps a distant second.[8]

The society's importance resulted from the same militancy that kept it small. Auclert wrote that militancy into the statutes; Article Four described their "incessant propaganda . . . in public and private places, *even in the street.*" When asked to explain the meaning of this passage, she said, according to the police, that Suffrage des femmes would claim women's rights "by all the means in its power." The prefecture of police concluded that the group held revolutionary opinions. The police exaggerated, but they concluded correctly that Suffrage des femmes was unusually militant. The minutes kept by Suffrage des femmes reveal this more clearly. One sees Auclert chastising her followers because "we lack boldness"; one sees her lieutenants exhorting the group to be daring; one sees a long debate over "agitation" and how bold to be in launching it. These debates foreshadowed Auclert's militant campaign of 1904–1908, when police worries about her seemed almost justified.[9]

THE GAUTRET BILL

During the first years of the century, Auclert and Suffrage des femmes followed the route that she had marked out during her first suffragist career. Every year, she and a few followers tried to register to vote. Every

8. Financial accounts, Auclert Papers, Carton 4. For her reflections on the support of French women, see Auclert, *Les Femmes au gouvernail*, pp. 203–5 (quoted). For Vincent's wealth, see the collection of her letters, 091 VIN, BMD.

9. Statutes of SF, Dossier Suffrage des femmes, BMD (first quotation); police reports, 2 July 1904 (second quotation) and 22 July 1904, Dossier "Le Mouvement féministe," APP; minutes of SF meeting, 22 May 1903 (third quotation), 22 January 1904, and 22 April 1904 (fourth quotation), Auclert Papers, Carton 4.

year, they were refused; one of the seasonal verities had returned to French politics. The only change was a bureaucratic refinement. Functionaries no longer argued with applicants and denied their request. They recorded the application and gave a receipt marked "does not necessarily imply inscription"; rejections arrived punctually by mail. Auclert did not push further than that; the court rulings of 1881, 1885, and 1893 seemed sufficiently clear. She similarly concluded that there was no point in presenting a woman candidate during the municipal elections of 1900 and 1904 or the parliamentary elections of 1902. Younger members of Suffrage des femmes disagreed, but Auclert convinced them that they were not yet strong enough to succeed, citing letters from prominent feminists who feared the ridicule such races would draw. Instead, Suffrage des femmes used electoral periods for intensive propaganda—covering Paris with the society's electoral posters, passing out handbills, asking questions at electoral meetings.[10]

Auclert's foremost goal was the introduction of a women's suffrage bill in the Chamber of Deputies. De Gasté had introduced the first such bill in 1890, but it had died quietly in the Commission of Universal Suffrage without obtaining a report or stimulating a feminist campaign. Auclert began her campaign for a second bill with a petition to the Chamber of Deputies, for which she labored with a singular devotion. Day after day, she went to the Paris World's Fair and sought signatures from the crowd. Then she spent weeks going to Les Halles, the central food distribution markets for Paris, to seek the support of working women. During the afternoons, she went from table to table in Parisian cafes. In the evenings, she stood outside political meetings that she could not enter. Her notes reveal the dedication with which she approached this task—a fifty-two-year-old woman, usually alone, walking mile upon mile seven days a week, determined to persist even if she got more harassment than signatures. There was a happy evening when a single political meeting produced eighty signatures, but there were many depressing days when hours on the pavement yielded less than

10. For Auclert's registration efforts, 1901–1904, see folder, "Inscriptions électorales," ibid., Carton 10 (receipt quoted); minutes of SF meetings, 22 January 1904 and 12 February 1904, ibid., Carton 4; Auclert, "L'Actualité: La Revision des listes électorales et l'inscription des femmes," *L'Abeille*, 1 February 1901; Auclert, "L'Inscription électorale des femmes," *Le Radical*, 29 January 1901. For her other electoral activities, see minutes of SF meetings, 22 January 1904, 25 March 1904, and 8 and 22 April 1904, Auclert Papers, Carton 4; notes, May 1900, ibid., 6/76 and 6/79; unidentified clipping, ibid., Carton 1, and in Dossier Vote des femmes, 1900–1908, BMD; Auclert, "Les Féministes et les élections," *Le Radical*, 3 January 1902; Auclert, "L'Affiche des femmes," ibid., 15 April 1902; Auclert, *Le Vote des femmes*, pp. 45, 178; police report, 15 February 1902, Dossier Auclert, APP; *L'Aurore*, 21 June 1904; Suzanne Grinberg, *Historique du mouvement suffragiste depuis 1848* (Paris, 1926), p. 103.

one-tenth that amount.[11] Her feelings about this work can be judged by the fact that she submitted twenty-six more petitions in the next twelve years (see table 9.2).

Auclert based the text of her petition on her longstanding belief that suffragists must realistically begin with a request for partial enfranchisement. She asked, as she had in petitions of 1885 and 1886, for political rights for *célibataires*—unmarried women, including widows and divorcées. Her petition stated that such independent women were "mistresses of their persons, of their wealth, of their own success," but that they needed the vote "to protect their interests, in the city and in the state, which are currently abandoned." She thus circumvented the argument that women's suffrage threatened the family; her solution, however, would enfranchise only 45 percent of adult women, or 6.5 million women.[12]

When the petition had 3,000 signatures, in the middle of the year, Clovis Hugues deposited it at the Palais Bourbon. A few weeks later, he deposited another 1,080 signatures. By early 1901 the total exceeded 6,000—few in some international comparisions, but a daunting labor if one contemplates gathering them alone in a hostile environment. Auclert chose not to strain for higher numbers, however. Instead, she sought to capitalize on the petition through secondary petitions, in her name alone, to the Municipal Council of Paris, the Council General of the Seine, and the Radical Party, seeking their endorsement of her suffrage petition; through newspaper publicity; and through letters to prominent politicians asking for their support. The results proved frustrating. None of her secondary petitions succeeded. The municipal council, for example, chiefly expressed anger at Auclert's calling the mayors' banquet "this fine masculine party, paid for by all inhabitants of France." Those few political celebrities who responded to her letter gave little encouragement. Alfred Naquet answered that "there are contingencies" (the clerical peril) that would not permit him to vote for the petition if he were in the Chamber of Deputies. Auclert was especially disappointed by the response of Paul Deschanel, the president of the chamber and the son of one of her earliest supporters, who declined to comment owing to the political neutrality of his office.[13]

11. Grinberg, *Historique du mouvement suffragiste*, p. 103; Auclert, *Le Vote des femmes*, pp. 45, 178; notes, May 1900, Auclert Papers, 6/76 and 6/79.

12. Copies of the petition can be found in the Dossier Auclert, BMD, and in many daily newspapers of March 1900 (see the Auclert Papers, Carton 1). For her earlier advocacy of the same idea, see *La Citoyenne*, December 1885. See also Hause with Kenney, *Women's Suffrage and Social Politics*, p. 72.

13. Folder, "Le Vote des célibataires," Auclert Papers, Carton 6; petition to the municipal council, ibid., Carton 1; protest against the mayor's banquet, ibid. (first quota-

TABLE 9.2. Auclert's Petitions, 1898–1912

Date	Recipient	Subject
1898	Chamber and Senate	Seats for women working in shops
1900	Chamber and Senate	School for Arab girls
1900	Municipal Council	Careers open to women
1900	Chamber of Deputies	Civil incapacity of women
1900	Municipal Council	Support for suffrage petition
1900	Council General	Support for suffrage petition
1901	Chamber of Deputies	Suffrage (for unmarried women only)
1901	Radical Party Congress	Support for suffrage
1903	Chamber of Deputies	*Séparation des biens* in marriage
1903	Chamber of Deputies	Suffrage (for unmarried women only)
1903	Chamber and Senate	Economic rights of married women
1904	Chamber of Deputies	Equality of the sexes
1904	Chamber of Deputies	Suffrage (for unmarried women only)
1904	Chamber and Senate	*Séparation des biens* in marriage
1905	Chamber of Deputies	Retirement insurance for mothers
1906	Chamber of Deputies	Suffrage (linked to salaries)
1906	Council General	Support for suffrage
1907	Chamber and Senate	Action on the Council General motion
1907	Radical Party Congress	Suffrage on party program
1908	Radical Party Congress	Suffrage on party program
1908	Chamber of Deputies	Suffrage (linked to capital punishment)
1908	Commission of Universal Suffrage	Report on the suffrage bill
1909	Chamber of Deputies	Suffrage (for all women)
1910	Commission of Universal Suffrage	Suffrage on the order of the day
1911	Commission of Universal Suffrage	Suffrage (linked to salaries)
1911	Chamber and Senate	Condition of Algerian women
1911	Municipal Council	Support for suffrage
1912	Municipal Council	Suffrage (linked to Queen Wilhelmina)
1912	Council General	Suffrage (linked to Queen Wilhelmina)

Auclert's efforts to locate political support produced only one notable success, but she only needed one to advance her suffrage bill. Jean Gautret, a new deputy (independent republican, Vendée) elected in 1898, signed her petition, and she immediately began a correspondence to cultivate his support. Gautret had previously aided Auclert by introducing a bill based on her 1898 petition, which asked that department stores provide seats for the saleswomen who were on their feet all day long. He now wrote Auclert a long letter expressing several concerns but

tion) draft letter to "célébrités politiques," ibid., 12/30; Deschanel's secretary to Auclert, 24 February 1900, ibid., 2/44; minutes of SF meetings, 14 and 28 June 1901, 12 February 1904, ibid., Carton 4; *Bulletin municipal officiel*, 5 July 1900; police report, 14 December 1901, Dossier Auclert, APP; Auclert, *Le Vote des femmes*, p. 178; Auclert, "Le Suffrage des célibataires," *Le Radical*, 7 March 1900 (second quotation); Auclert, "Emile Deschanel féministe," ibid., 9 March 1904.

gladly offering his help. Auclert's request was simple: that he deposit her petition as his own bill for women's suffrage.[14]

The Gautret Bill of July 1901 was a simple one-article adaptation of Auclert's idea: "The right to vote in legislative, cantonal, and municipal elections is accorded to adult women, *célibataires* or divorced. Voting conditions imposed on male votes are equally applicable for women to vote." Gautret added several pages of explanation, covering traditional suffrage arguments and culminating with Auclert's critique of republican hypocrisy: "We have written at the head of our constitution the words Universal Suffrage . . . but we have only so-called universal suffrage." Gautret apologized for altering Auclert's wording, but she was extremely pleased with "our bill" and immediately sent letters to all deputies asking them to consider the rights of women who were "on their own in life." Rouzade led Suffrage des femmes in a motion declaring that Gautret "has well served our cause."[15]

The Gautret Bill faced many difficulties, the most obvious of which was a complete absence of support in parliament. Auclert had estimated that five deputies backed her in the legislature of 1876–1881, ten in the legislature of 1881–1885; perhaps her support had again doubled, reaching 5 percent of the legislature of 1898–1901. At that rate of progress, her suffrage bills would languish long in the Commission of Universal Suffrage, just as her petitions did down the hall in the Commission of Petitions. In fact, the Gautret Bill was buried by a hostile committee which never discussed it, much less delivered a report on it.[16]

Auclert also faced a battle over the Gautret Bill within the women's movement. Some members of Suffrage des femmes questioned the focus on unmarried women before agreeing to accept the tactic. Other femi-

14. Auclert, *Le Vote des femmes*, pp. 45, 178; Auclert, "Le Vote des célibataires," *Le Radical*, 16 January 1900; Auclert, "Le Suffrage des célibataires," ibid, 7 March 1900; Auclert, "Notre projet de loi," ibid., 9 July 1901; Gautret to Auclert, 19 February 1900, Auclert Papers, 2/46 (quoted).

15. *JO*, Chambre des députés, débats, 1 July 1901; ibid., documents, no. 2529, 1 July 1901 (first and second quotations). The original, with Gautret's handwritten notes, is in the Chamber of Deputies papers, C 5659/1736, AN. See Auclert's notes on the bill, Auclert Papers, 6/79 and 6/85; Auclert to all deputies, ibid., 12/39; minutes of SF meeting, 12 July 1901, ibid., Carton 4 (third quotation); Auclert, "Notre projet de loi," *Le Radical*, 9 July 1901. Gautret's arguments are reproduced in André Leclère, *Le Vote des femmes en France: Les Causes de l'attitude particulière de notre pays* (Paris, 1929), pp. 99–107; see the analysis of them in Ferdinand Buisson, *Le Vote des femmes* (Paris, 1911), pp. 326–27; clippings about them in the Dossier vote des femmes, 1900–1908, BMD; Grinberg, *Historique du mouvement suffragiste*, p. 103; Auclert, *Le Vote des femmes*, p. 45; Hause with Kenney, *Women's Suffrage and Social Politics*, pp. 72–73.

16. See the analysis of the parliamentary prospects of women' suffrage in Hause with Kenney, *Women's Suffrage and Social Politics*, pp. 12–14, 73, 94–100. For Auclert's feelings about these prospects, see her notes, Auclert Papers, 6/85, and Auclert, *Le Vote des femmes*, p. 178.

nists were harsher. "So you think that marriage is a moral disqualifica-
tion?" one wrote her. Another accused her of "the glorification of
celibacy." Martin praised the bill in the *Journal des femmes* as a step
forward, but she blasted its division of women: "Why separate French
women into two categories, electresses and non-electresses, and base
this distinction not upon intelligence, abilities, or moral value, but
upon the fact—scarcely criminal, it seems to us—of being married?" *La
Fronde* refused to print Auclert's petition to enfranchise *célibataires*.
On the feminist right, there was no support for suffragism of any kind;
on the feminist left, Auclert received a blistering attack from Louise
Saumoneau of the Groupe féministe socialiste for her "individualist and
egoist bourgeois interests."[17]

Auclert could rebut feminist opposition with simple pragmatism
when it stemmed from ideological differences, but she also faced an
awkward personal conflict involving Marguerite Durand. Durand believed that the time was not right for women's suffrage; she accepted the
idea at the congress of 1900, however, when it came from an intimate
ally, René Viviani (republican socialist, Seine). Viviani had been active
in the LFDF for a decade and had accepted (or acquiesced in) Richer's
antisuffragism. Then, in September 1900, he told the LFDF congress that
"all laws that we can propose will be in vain if women are not armed
with the ballot to expand and to defend them. . . . Legislators make the
laws for those who make the legislators." He persuaded the congress to
adopt women's suffrage and promised to introduce a bill in the chamber.
After the congress, Viviani published suffragist articles in *La Lanterne*
and *La Grand revue*, specifying his plans for municipal suffrage only, for
married women only.[18]

This prospective Viviani Bill caused Auclert several problems. She
had announced her plans first and had worked for months to achieve
them. Durand had declined to help her; the LFDF offered neither advice
nor help. Viviani's speech and influence were certainly welcome to
Auclert, but without consulting her he had proposed a suffrage plan that
utterly contradicted hers—municipal suffrage instead of complete suf-

17. Minutes of SF meeting, 8 March 1901, Auclert Papers, Carton 4; Auclert, *Le Vote
des femmes*, pp. 45–46 (first quotation); Clotilde Dissard, "Le Vote des femmes," *La
Fronde*, 30 January 1900 (second quotation); Martin, "Le Suffrage des femmes devant la
chambre," *Le Journal des femmes*, August 1901 (third quotation); Auclert to Durand, 9
October 1901, Auclert Correspondence, 091 AUC, BMD; Louise Saumoneau, "Les Droits
politique des femmes et le projet de loi Gautret," *La Femme socialiste*, August 1901
(fourth quotation).

18. For more on Viviani's speech, see Durand, ed., *Congrès international de la condition et des droits des femmes*, pp. 195–205 (quoted); *La Fronde*, 10 September 1900;
Viviani, "Le Féminisme," *La Lanterne*, 7 September 1900; Viviani, "La Femme dans
l'état," ibid., 11 September 1900; Viviani, "La Femme," *La Grande revue*, 1 February
1901; Hause with Kenney, *Women's Suffrage and Social Politics*, pp. 32 and 36; notes,
Auclert Papers, 6/177.

frage, married women instead of *célibataires*. Worse yet, Viviani published an article criticizing Auclert's ideas, asserting that she asked for too little. In one sense that was accurate, for Viviani's plan would enfranchise 7.9 million women instead of 6.5 million. Auclert's voters, however, would participate in elections at three levels rather than in municipal elections only. Viviani also contended that unmarried women already had more civil rights and were "the least sensitive to our [republican] propaganda." Married women, on the other hand, suffered more injustice.[19]

Such disagreements might not have been an obstacle to compromise—giving all women the vote in municipal elections, for example—if the two sides had tried. But when Durand and Viviani ignored Auclert, then attacked her, there was no question that she would counterattack. Auclert already disapproved of their sexual relationship, sarcastically referring to them as "the Chevalier Viviani" and "his lady." Privately, she questioned his sincerity in calling for women's suffrage; he was "a bourgeois opportunist" who acted with the "Italian duplicity" that he had shown in his socialist career, in which "the proletariat has been only a stepping stone." Publicly, she restricted herself to criticizing his articles and proposed bill. The introduction of the Gautret Bill marked her victory over Viviani, who never submitted his own bill. It was a Pyrrhic victory, however, because Viviani never supported Gautret's bill, and he remained inactive in French suffragism for a decade.[20]

Auclert's feud with Durand and Viviani never caused a complete rupture as her quarrel with Martin had. Indeed, years later Durand delivered Auclert's eulogy at the installation of her memorial plaque on the rue de la Roquette. Auclert never completely trusted Durand, but having experienced similar spats for thirty years, she adjusted to another. This adjustment is probably the most revealing aspect of the disagreement about the Gautret Bill, for it shows Auclert's emotional strength in 1901. This time she wrote no brooding *pensées*, denouncing those who persecuted her. She shrugged off the clash and went on.

INTERNATIONAL SUFFRAGISM AND THE BERLIN CONGRESS OF 1904

After Auclert's contact with Susan B. Anthony in 1883–1884, French feminists played a small role in the evolution of international feminist

19. Viviani, "La Femme dans l'état," *La Lanterne,* 7 September 1900.

20. Note, Auclert Papers, 6/17 (first quotation); note on the Gautret Bill, ibid., 6/79 (second quotation); Auclert, "La Femme majeure," *Le Radical,* 18 March 1901. For the relationship between Durand and Viviani, see Hause with Kenney, *Women's Suffrage and Social Politics,* pp. 289–90 n. 20; for the fate of the Gautret Bill, ibid., p. 73; for Viviani's later suffragism, ibid., pp. 225, 229, 241, 244, 246, 248.

connections, but not in the international suffragist movement. Isabelle Bogelot, a leader of the Protestant women's philanthropic movement, had ties to her counterparts in America, especially May Wright Sewall. Bogelot, who was financially independent, attended several international women's congresses in the late 1880s, including the meeting in Washington, D.C., in 1888 at which Sewall and Frances Willard formed the National Council of Women. She was with them in Chicago in 1893 when they made it an International Council of Women, and she was elected one of the five members of the international council's permanent committee, although France did not have a member society until the creation of the CNFF in 1901. When the International Council of Women met at London in 1899, a large French delegation was participating that included such diverse members as Martin as the secretary of the congress, a large Protestant deputation from the Conference de Versailles, Kauffmann, and even Paule Mink.[21]

Auclert was unimpressed by the feminism of the international council, sharing the judgment that the French participants were "a representation from a big charity bazaar." But she retained her interest in creating an international suffragist organization. In 1901, Carrie Chapman Catt revived Anthony's idea for such an organization and proposed to create it at the quinquennial meeting of the International Council of Women, scheduled for Berlin in 1904. Catt's opinion of French suffragism was comparable to Auclert's opinion of the international council. She felt that national suffrage organizations existed in only five countries, the United States, Britain, Norway, Sweden, and Holland; that "well-defined movements" toward creating them could be found in three other countries, Australia, New Zealand, and Canada; and that "sympathetic interest" in founding them was apparent in six more, Germany, Denmark, Austria-Hungary, Russia, and Finland. It did not bode well for the relationship between Catt and Auclert that the American suffragist did not consider that Auclert's lifetime of work constituted "a well-defined movement" or even "sympathetic interest." Nonetheless, because Auclert's name remained in Anthony's records, Catt invited her (to the consternation of other French feminists) to attend a meeting in Washington in 1902 to organize the Berlin delegation.[22]

21. For the French role in the International Council of Women, see International Council of Women, *Histories of the Affiliated Councils, 1888–1938* (Brussels, 1938), p. 121; Hause with Kenney, *Women's Suffrage and Social Politics*, pp. 37–38; papers on the London conference, Charlotte Perkins Gilman Manuscripts, Box 1/Folder 6, Schlesinger Library, Cambridge, Mass. Dossiers Sarah Monod and Julies Siegfried, BMD; Dossier Bogelot, Bouglé Collection, BHVP; Deraismes' report to the Chicago congress of 1893, Dossier Deraismes, BMD; Deraismes, *Ce que veulent les femmes*, pp. 114–20; Caroline Kauffmann and Paule Mink, *Idées générales sur les travaux du congrès international féministe de Londres en 1899* (Paris, 1899).

22. Wilkins, "The Paris International Feminist Congress of 1896," p. 16 (first quota-

The preparations for an International Woman Suffrage Alliance (hereafter IWSA) greatly interested Auclert, who still considered herself part of the international committee for women's suffrage to which the Americans had elected her in 1884. Despite their offer of five hundred francs, Auclert decided that she could not afford to go to Washington. She did, however, invite representatives of all French feminist groups to a meeting in mid-July 1902, at which she worked for the election of herself, Vincent, and Schmahl to the Berlin delegation. One hundred women representing nine feminist groups (Suffrage des femmes, Amélioration, the LFDF, Egalité, Etudes, Avant-Courrière, Solidarité, and two moderate groups established in 1901, the UFF and the Union de pensée féminine) participated. Leaders of the CNFF declined to attend because they were not yet prepared for suffragist activity; those of the Groupe féministe socialiste boycotted the meeting and criticized women's suffrage as a bourgeois preoccupation, although Elisabeth Renaud gave Auclert her personal encouragement. After heated discussions, in which Pognon protested against Auclert's right to organize the meeting, the participants elected Auclert, Vincent, and Schmahl to represent them.[23]

Despite the excitement of this beginning, Auclert's notes reveal that the French role in the IWSA was impaired from the start. No French woman attended the Washington meeting; Schmahl volunteered to go, but the Americans rejected her on the ground that she was English and the representative must be a French woman. When Auclert reported the results of the Paris meeting to Catt, she received a patronizing answer calling on French feminists to unite into a single "national suffrage council" because their division into nine groups "needlessly dissipates" the movement. This revealed how little the American understood French politics; it also angered Auclert, but she continued to correspond with Catt. Auclert remained excited about the Berlin meeting, but she pointedly lectured the members of Suffrage des femmes on the subject of international comparisons: French feminism was actually more advanced than American or British feminism because the French had been developing the doctrine for much longer. For her part, Catt did not forget that there was no French representative in Washington, although

tion); manuscript, "The History of the Origins of the International Alliance of Women," Carrie Chapman Catt Manuscripts, Box 7/Folder 10, New York Public Library, New York; police report, 12 July 1902, Dossier Auclert, APP.

23. Auclert to *Le Français*, 16 July 1903; Auclert to all feminist groups, Auclert Papers, 3/701; Auclert to (unknown), 14 March 1911, ibid., 3/512; Renaud to Auclert, 11 July 1902, ibid., 3/699; notes on the Washington congress, ibid., 6/68 and 6/69; police reports, 15 February 1902 and 12 July 1902, Dossier Auclert, APP; Auclert, "Elections féministes," *Le Radical*, 16 July 1902.

women came from Russia, Chile, and Turkey, nor a report on French suffragism, although reports came from Italy, Switzerland, Persia, Cuba, and the Philippines.[24]

The preparations of 1901–1902 to found the IWSA helped to revitalize Auclert's suffragism, but the Berlin meeting was a fiasco for the French movement. Preparations for the meeting of the International Council of Women in London went smoothly. The CNFF organized French participation and made arrangements for a twelve-member delegation that included Bogelot, Monod, Sainte-Croix, Oddo-Deflou, Martin, and Durand. Four members of the French council prepared reports for the international council, led by Bogelot, who spoke on peace and arbitration and stressed women as a moral force. Three other members of the CNFF held official positions in the congress, led by Monod, who had been elected to the permanent committee. The international council, facilitated their participation by paying for the travel of six of the CNFF delegates. The French militants, who were going to Berlin to organize the IWSA, had a more difficult time. Most of them were not members of either the CNFF or the international council, so they were ineligible for financial assistance, although they needed it more than the women of the national council. The IWSA offered no aid this time. And the French militants had to cope with secondhand and delayed announcements of the plans.[25]

Auclert assumed the responsibility for organizing the French suffragist deputation to Berlin. She arranged for a leading German suffragist, Anita Augspurg, to speak at a meeting of Suffrage des femmes, but Augspurg found little enthusiasm. As the congress approached, most feminists prepared for the international council and shied away from the IWSA. Auclert did not even have the reliable delegation of three militants elected in 1902, because Schmahl had undergone surgery and could not attend the meeting. When Auclert convened another meeting of French suffragists to choose a substitute for Schmahl, she discovered how much enthusiasm had waned since the elections of 1902; attendance was half of that at the original election. The boycott by Catholic feminists and the socialists had been joined by moderate groups affiliated with the CNFF, as well as the LFDF, which was then changing its

24. Notes on the Washington congress, Auclert Papers, 6/69 (quoted); minutes of SF meeting, 22 May 1903, ibid., Carton 4; police report, 15 February 1902, Dossier Auclert, APP; Catt, "Origins of the International Alliance."

25. Bogelot's speech to the international council is reprinted in Raoul Froger-Doudement, ed., *Que veulent donc ces féministes?* (Paris, 1926), p. 44; police reports, 26 April and 14 May 1904, Dossier "Le Mouvement féministe," APP; *Le Journal des femmes*, full issue on the congress, July 1904; *Bilder von Internationalen Frauen-Kongress 1904* (Berlin, 1904), copy in the Allen Manuscripts, Box 1/Folder 5, Schlesinger Library; Avril de Sainte-Croix, scrapbooks, vol. 1 (1901–1910), Musée Social; *La Fronde*, 1 May 1904.

leadership and was still displeased with the 1902 meeting. Thus only five groups participated: Suffrage des femmes, Egalité, Solidarité, Etudes, and the UFF. Caroline Kauffmann of Solidarité was elected to replace Schmahl and the delegation was expanded to four members to include Marguerite Belmant, in gratitude for her having brought members of the moderate UFF to the meeting. Auclert and Vincent were distressed that French feminists still hesitated to embrace suffragism. The police agent who attended the meeting concluded that moderates dominated the movement, although there was always danger in contact with foreign revolutionaries (a common police theme).[26]

Auclert next faced the challenge of financing French participation in the IWSA meeting. It was difficult for the delegates to pay for travel to and residence in Berlin, so they planned the shortest possible visit, covering exactly the dates of the International Council of Women meeting. Even Auclert considered herself poor because the periodic redemption of her bonds to finance feminist causes had reduced her capital, and her income had fallen behind the cost of living. (She was not poor, of course. Poverty, like her self-depictions of timidity, ugliness, ineloquence, and incompetence, forms part of the negative image with which Auclert explained her difficulties.) The delegates appealed to wealthier feminists, such as Feresse-Deraismes, for help, but they received only a few small contributions. In desperation they applied to the Municipal Council of Paris for a subvention; to their surprise and delight they obtained a promise of fifty francs each, although the paperwork was not completed until the last minute before the congress. With aid from their individual societies and personal sacrifice, money was obtained for Auclert, Kauffmann, and Belmant; Vincent was wealthy enough to cover her own costs without difficulty. In the midst of this effort to raise a few francs for trainfares, however, a shocking letter arrived from America. Catt and the organizing committee of the IWSA had decided that each nation joining the alliance must pay $50 in dues, or about 250 francs. The total budget of Suffrage des femmes for 1904, including the gifts and subvention for the Berlin meeting, was 288.10 francs. Even if Auclert bankrupted Suffrage des femmes, even if she paid for not a single letter to a deputy that year, she could not afford both to go to Berlin and to inscribe Suffrage des femmes in the IWSA. Indeed, neither Suffrage des femmes nor Solidarité could spare one-fifth of the dues. Auclert decided to go to Berlin and negotiate.[27]

26. Notes, "Les femmes ennemies (hostiles au vote des femmes)," Auclert Papers, Carton 11; minutes of SF meetings, 22 January 1904, 8 and 22 April 1904, 13 and 27 May 1904, ibid., Carton 4; note on the Berlin congress, ibid., 6/68; Henri Schmahl to Auclert, 3 April 1904, ibid., 2/381; police reports, 26 April and 14 May 1904, Dossier "Le Mouvement féministe," APP.

27. Financial records, Auclert Papers, Carton 4; minutes of SF meetings, 8 and 22 April 1904, 27 May 1904, ibid.; Durand, "Le Congrès de Berlin," *La Fronde*, 1 July 1904.

Auclert prepared for Berlin by writing the speech that she would deliver recounting her long battle for women's suffrage and her commitment to international suffragism. But the wrong muse was looking over her shoulder—Melpomene, not Polyhymnia, was guiding events. For the fourth time in her career, Auclert crafted phrases that a congress would not hear. She arrived in Berlin on schedule, to learn that the IWSA organizational meetings had already taken place, with no French participation, before the meeting of the international council. The French leagues had not been notified of this plan because they had not paid dues. Nor did the shock end there. Catt ruled that, despite Auclert's years of correspondence with her and with Anthony, France had no representatives in the alliance. The IWSA adopted the policy that France was a country with an undeveloped suffrage movement and assigned the task of tutoring the backward French to foreign suffragists. Auclert's horror was complete when she learned that the task of organizing a French suffrage alliance had been assigned to a German, Käthe Schirmacher—an even more remarkable decision when one recalls that the Americans had rejected Schmahl as the French delegate in 1902 because she was foreign-born. Auclert, with her Latin learning and sense of persecution, must have thought that the Furies had winged from the depths to attend each congress, there to torment her. Naturally, she was furious.[28]

Carrie Chapman Catt's explanation of the exclusion of Auclert, Suffrage des femmes, and French suffragism from the IWSA was consistent with a strict reading of the facts. France did not have a nationwide suffrage society; no French delegates had participated in the Washington meeting; no French group had paid dues to the IWSA. Her attitude was correct, but remarkably insensitive; it was also, it should be noted, affected by some prejudice against the Catholic countries of "Latin" Europe. Her subsequent explanation was strange: France had sent only an "auxiliary" delegation to Berlin, and "the French delegates met with an accident on their way to the station in Paris and did not reach Berlin." Auclert believed that the French were "victims of the contradictions of this lady," and she never forgave Catt or the IWSA. She refused direct invitations to subsequent IWSA meetings in Europe in 1906 (Martin went for the CNFF), in 1909 (Schmahl went, to found a French "national" league), and in 1911. When the Dutch secretary of the IWSA, Martina Kramers, urged Auclert to come to Stockholm in 1911, she received a

28. Auclert's speech for the Berlin congress, Auclert Papers, 6/110; notes on the congress, ibid., 6/68; draft letter, Auclert to (unknown), ibid., 6/114; Auclert to Martina Kramers, 14 March 1911, ibid., 3/506; notes, ibid., 11/337 and 11/339; IWSA, *Report of the Second and Third Conferences* (Copenhagen, 1906), p. 10 (copy at the Fawcett Library); Mary G. Peck, *Carrie Chapman Catt* (New York, 1944), pp. 137–39.

tart response: "After this insult by Mrs. Catt, the society Suffrage des femmes could not want to join her group."[29]

The contretemps with Catt did not prevent Auclert and the other French militants from participating in the meeting of the international council or from meeting privately with foreign suffragists. These experiences were so exciting that Auclert maintained her enthusiasm. She estimated the attendance at the assembly to be eight thousand (an overestimate) and she reported to Suffrage des femmes that she was enraptured by participating in it. It gave her great pleasure to see the international council adopt a resolution calling for "strenuous efforts" to win the vote, despite the opposition of most of the CNFF delegation. Auclert, Kauffmann, and Vincent particularly enjoyed their meetings with foreign suffragists. Details of these discussions are lacking, but Auclert's notes conclude that French suffragists must attempt more forceful demonstrations.[30]

Auclert's experiences in international suffragism from 1902 to 1904 thus led her toward greater militancy in several ways. She was angry and determined to prove that Catt's insulting verdict was wrong. She was enthusiastic after seeing the strength of international suffragism and determined to share in the progress. She was stimulated by conversations with militants who had already acted more daringly than she. The result was to be a vigorous suffrage campaign in France during the next four years.

29. For Catt's attitudes, see her manuscript on the founding of the IWSA, Catt Manuscripts, Box 7/Folder 10, New York Public Library (quoted). For her anti-Catholicism, see Evans, *The Feminists*, pp. 204, 251; for a discussion of such attitudes in American feminism, see Aileen S. Kraditor, *The Ideas of the Woman Suffrage Movement, 1890–1920* (Garden City, N.Y., 1971), ch. 6. Notes, Auclert Papers, 11/339 (second quotation); Kramers to Auclert, 27 February 1911, ibid., 3/506; Auclert to Kramers, 14 March 1911, ibid., 3/506 pièce-jointe (third quotation); minutes of SF meeting, 10 June 1904, ibid., Carton 4; IWSA, *Report of the Second and Third Conferences*, p. 12.

30. Minutes of SF meetings, 27 May and 27 June 1904, Auclert Papers, Carton 4; Auclert to Durand, 17 June 1904, Dossier Congrès 1904, BMD; Auclert, "Congrès de Berlin," *Le Radical*, 5 July 1904. For the events of the congress, see the dossier on it at the BMD; see *Le Journal des femmes*, July 1904, and *La Fronde*, late June and early July 1904, for Martin's and Durand's reactions; and see the heavy coverage in German feminist publications, esp. the *Zentralblatt des Bundes deutscher Frauenvereine* and *Die Frauenbewegung* (copies in the Gilman Manuscripts, Box 1/Folder 7, Schlesinger Library).

CHAPTER TEN

The French Suffragette,
1904–1908

B efore going to Berlin, Auclert had already contemplated forceful
protests for women's rights. She and Eliska Vincent led Suffrage
des femmes in a discussion of the subject in April 1904. The Berlin
meeting confirmed their thinking: public demonstrations were needed
to publicize their cause. During the next four years, Auclert edged closer
to using violent tactics, although she abhorred such behavior. She was
seconded in her strategy by Vincent and Kauffmann at first, then by
Madeleine Pelletier and Kauffmann; they acquired a reputation in the
Parisian press as "the French suffragettes"—a term borrowed from the
British press's descriptions of the much more militant behavior of the
Pankhursts and the Women's Social and Political Union.[1] When Auclert committed the first act of violence in the French suffrage campaign, in 1908, the French feminist movement utterly repudiated her
tactics.

THE CIVIL CODE DEMONSTRATION OF 1904

Auclert's first demonstration after returning from Berlin was a protest against the Napoleonic Code. The Chamber of Deputies had appro-

1. For use of the term "suffragettes" by French militants during this period, see police
reports of 10 February 1911 and 14 March 1913, Dossier Auclert, APP. Oddo-Deflou used
the term for Auclert; see her "Suffragettes françaises et anglaises," *La Femme de demain*,
March 1914. Auclert used the term in court to describe herself and those who supported
her demonstration of 1908 (see below and n. 34).

priated credits for a celebration of the centennial of the Civil Code in October 1904. Two days of ceremonies were to culminate in an assembly of dignitaries at the Sorbonne and a state banquet. This outraged the entire women's movement, as they considered the code to be the principal instrument of the oppression of women. Auclert, Vincent, Oddo-Deflou, and Kauffmann sent a protest to parliament and the newspapers. They printed it on posters: "French women can only believe that the oppression and injustice of which they are the victims will persist under the Third Republic." They circulated it on handbills: "The Code crushes women. We protest against its glorification." Auclert devoted her column in *Le Radical* to this subject in August 1904, warning that feminists might consider a vehement protest.[2]

Although the celebration of the Civil Code offended women of all political opinions, they disagreed on how to protest it. Most of the feminist leagues ultimately subscribed to a plan proposed by Marguerite Durand. They would organize a countercelebration at which women would tell the world that the code was "a shame to the republic." This meeting attracted nearly a thousand women, more than had attended any of the sessions of the congresses of 1900.[3]

Radical feminists considered this protest insufficient; polite complaints made in lecture halls had won few victories. They desired some action more public, more vehement, more proportionate to their indignation. In mid-September, Auclert and Kauffmann persuaded Suffrage des femmes to demonstrate in the streets on October 29, the first day of the centennial festivities. Subsequent meetings, attended by thirty to sixty-five militants, discussed specific ideas. They agreed to picket the Palais Bourbon with messages such as "Long Live Justice! Down with the Code!" Auclert and Kauffmann, however, also wanted "avenging gestures." They proposed burning a copy of the code at some appropriate site, such as the Palais de Justice or the Napoleonic column on the Place Vendôme. Some members of Suffrage des femmes and Solidarité thought this "undignified," "grotesque," or "impractical"; others worried about the police reaction. Vincent and Oddo-Deflou suggested burning the code on a table in a meeting hall.[4]

Militants continued to debate their plans at meetings of Suffrage des femmes and Solidarité throughout October 1904, Auclert and Kauff-

2. Minutes of sf meeting, 22 April 1904, Auclert Papers, Carton 4; protest handbills and posters, ibid., 13/45 and 10/20 (second quotation), and in the Dossier Auclert, bmd (first quotation); Auclert, "La Glorification du code," *Le Radical,* 29 August 1904.

3. For more on the moderate protest of 1904, see Hause with Kenney, *Women's Suffrage and Social Politics,* pp. 75–76.

4. Police reports, 15 October 1904, Dossier Auclert, app, and 15 October 1904 (2), Dossier "Le Mouvement féministe," app; Kauffmann to Auclert, undated, Auclert Papers, 3/662.

mann still insisting upon a public burning. Members of Solidarité met on October 18 but could agree only upon a resolution stating their general intention: "To express in a vehement fashion their indignation and their protest against the glorification of the code." Similar reluctance made it difficult to find outside support. Auclert's and Kauffmann's hopes to attract several women's trade unions collapsed when Blanche Schweig of the cashiers' union called the burning a "ridiculous" gesture. Efforts to win the support of the socialist "popular universities" also failed.[5]

Auclert and Kauffmann persisted in spite of the reluctance of their followers and the unpopularity of their ideas. To placate the hesitant, they devised a two-stage protest. They would publicly advertise a demonstration that all militants could accept at the Palais Bourbon on October 29. There, hired men wearing sandwich boards and feminists carrying placards would denounce the code and the expenditure to celebrate it. In private, they would organize an additional demonstration at the Place Vendôme, where the most daring among them would burn a copy of the code. All feminists would be invited to assemble at the Place de la Concorde, where they would proceed to the Napoleonic column for the burning, if they wished, or wait for the march to the Chamber of Deputies. The organizers expected 150 women to join them.[6]

Auclert and Kauffmann divided the risks of their demonstration. Auclert would lead those willing to burn the code because Kauffmann was in poor health; although she had been a pioneering advocate of sports and physical fitness for women, Kauffmann was now too frail to wrestle with police if they tried to prevent the burning. Instead, she would deposit the ashes of the code at the head table of the state banquet on October 30. To avoid forewarning the police, Auclert sent a "confidential" invitation to all feminist groups. She underestimated the disapproval of other feminists. Within hours, a member of the LFDF, Diane-Gabrielle Rony, had gone to warn the Prefecture of Police of Auclert's intentions. While her action may have galvanized the police, her information was redundant; police agents had attended most of the planning meetings and already knew of the forthcoming protest in the Place Vendôme.[7]

Fifty women from Suffrage des femmes, Solidarité, Egalité, Etudes,

5. Minutes of Solidarité meeting, 18 October 1904, Dossier Kauffmann, CP 4248, BHVP (quoted); police report, 27 October 1904, Dossier "Le Mouvement féministe," APP.

6. Police report, 27 October 1904, ibid.; financial records, Auclert Papers, Carton 4.

7. Kauffmann to Auclert, undated, ibid., 3/662; draft of Auclert's confidential invitation, ibid., 12/43; police memorandum, 27 October 1904, Dossier "Le Mouvement féministe," APP.

and the UFF assembled for the avenging gesture of October 29, 1904. Auclert led them on the short walk to the Place Vendôme, but police blocked their path before they reached the Napoleonic column. Although Auclert urged the group forward to burn the code, only a couple of women would accompany her; the others stopped on the rue Castiglione and chanted "We spit on the code!" Auclert tore several pages from a copy of the code and attempted to burn them, but the police prevented her. Accounts of this event differ sharply. According to the police, "they tried to burn the pages of the code; but the officers, who did not behave too rudely, intervened and made them move along." Auclert told the next meeting of Suffrage des femmes that she had been "repulsed by the brutal police" and printed the graphic details in *Le Radical:* the police "surrounded us, and, by squeezing hard on the hands holding matches, by bruising our arms, by bullying us, by hurting us, they dispersed us and brutally drove us back to the rue de Rivoli."[8]

The marchers were badly shaken by the realization that someone had betrayed their plans and by the reality of police repression. Their spirits collapsed when they crossed the Seine to the Chamber of Deputies and found more police awaiting them. A few militants tried to form a march, but again the police interfered. Few women had enough enthusiasm afterward to picket the banquet; even Auclert did not. Kauffmann did, even without her memorial ashes. She interrupted the speeches at the banquet and was arrested for "injurious disturbance."[9]

The Civil Code demonstrations of 1904 were an important moment in the development of feminist tactics in France. One thousand women followed Marguerite Durand; fifty followed Hubertine Auclert. The radical government showed that it would use force against women. The press gave little of the publicity Auclert sought. And several accounts considered the demonstration ineffective because the Chamber of Deputies was on vacation for All Saints' Day, and because it took place on a Saturday when few would notice it. The government of Emile Combes gave the most emphatic evidence that the demonstrations had changed few minds. Early in December 1904, when the minister of justice, Ernest Vallé (radical, Marne), chose a commission to consider revisions of the Civil Code, he refused to name women to the commission despite a pointed letter from Auclert. These events did not convince Auclert that

8. Minutes of SF meeting, 11 November 1904, Auclert Papers, Carton 4 (second quotation); police report, 30 October 1904, Dossier Auclert, APP (first quotation); Auclert, "Vers le but," *Le Radical,* 5 November 1904 (third quotation).

9. Minutes of SF meeting, 11 November 1904, Auclert Papers, Carton 4. For more details on Kauffmann's demonstration, see Hause with Kenney, *Women's Suffrage and Social Politics,* p. 77.

militant demonstrations were wrong, merely that the dedicated few had to try harder and to choose their times more carefully.[10]

Auclert did not attempt another dramatic demonstration until the spring of 1908. With Suffrage des femmes, Solidarité, and the UFF, she helped organize a demonstration during the parliamentary elections of May 1906, but this action can best be described as a parade: a feminist "cortege" of rented cars and flatbed trucks bedecked with banners circled central Paris while feminists passed out handbills. Suffrage des femmes spent more time and money on its electoral posters than on the cortege. Vincent, Schmahl, and Oddo-Deflou, had told Auclert that they refused to support vehement demonstrations. The result was a procession that *La Temps* described as "timid." Auclert's columns in *Le Radical*, however, indicated that she still believed in the need for "propaganda of the deed."[11]

THE CNFF SUFFRAGE SECTION AND REPUBLICAN MODERATION

Auclert did not behave with greater militancy in the elections of 1906 because she believed that moderate feminists might be ready to rally to her side. She had awaited that moment for thirty years and did not want to jeopardize her prospects by rashness. This optimistic belief arose from an overture made by the CNFF. Auclert had, in the words of one moderate, "stayed aloof" from the council in 1900–1901, despite Oddo-Deflou's efforts to enlist her, because it was not suffragist and scarcely seemed feminist. The CNFF, like many republican politicians, endorsed the eventual enfranchisement of women but declined to work for that goal until women had become better educated. The annual General Assembly of the council did not discuss women's suffrage in the years 1902–1906, nor did it create an administrative "section" on the ques-

10. Auclert to Vallé, 12 December 1904, Auclert Papers, 9/1. For press accounts of the demonstrations, see the clippings, ibid., Carton 9, esp. *L'Intransigeant*, 20 October 1904. For feminist recollections of them, see Auclert, *Le Vote des femmes*, p. 120; Oddo-Deflou, "Suffragettes françaises et anglaises" and "Instantané," *L'Entente*, May 1906; and esp. Kauffmann to Arria Ly, 28 May 1913, CP 4249, BHVP.

11. For an account of the feminist cortege of 1906 and other demonstrations, see Hause with Kenney, *Women's Suffrage and Social Politics*, pp. 77–81; Auclert, "Bulletin pondérateur," *Le Radical*, 25 May 1906. See *Le Temps*, 23 May 1906, for an analysis of French timidity in comparison to English suffragism. For Auclert's stress on posters in 1906, see Auclert, *Les Femmes au gouvernail*, p. 71; financial records, Auclert Papers, Carton 4. For her continuing thought of aggressive demonstrations, see her "Propagande par le fait," *Le Radical*, 11 June 1906.

tion to work alongside the sections on charity, education, and legislation. This confirmed Auclert's judgment that the CNFF was a genteel feminine coalition which included a few feminists. But she could not ignore its growth: the organizations in the CNFF numbered seventy-three thousand members in 1906–1907. This size suggested the national movement that Auclert had dreamt of since 1883.[12]

The CNFF decided to establish a suffrage section in June 1906, under pressure from suffragists in the International Council of Women. The contrast between CNFF policy and the international policy stood out when the international council met in Paris that month. Auclert participated in that congress and underscored the contrast. She raised the issue of women's suffrage at every opportunity, including a reception at the Hôtel de Ville, where she interrupted the speech of a municipal official who had proclaimed himself a feminist to ask him why he did not introduce a suffrage motion in the municipal council.[13]

The CNFF's overture to Auclert came in a letter from the secretary-general, Avril de Sainte-Croix, in April 1906. Sainte-Croix, one of the suffragists in the council, explained that the IWSA had repeatedly tried to obtain a French delegate from the CNFF. After the fourth request, the French council decided to change its suffrage policy. "We thought," Sainte-Croix wrote, "that more than any other feminine personality you were qualified to fulfill this mission. . . . We can create the place due to you as one of the doyennes of our movement." Auclert had not amended her feelings about the IWSA, but she could not resist the opportunity to lead seventy-three thousand women to suffragism. She risked the 70 francs in dues for Suffrage des femmes to join the CNFF, even though this cut her group's 1906 propaganda budget to 96.60 francs.[14]

The CNFF established its suffrage section in November 1906 and invited Auclert to preside over it. She eagerly accepted the post and urged those attending the first meeting to forget partisan political feelings and collaborate for the common goal. Early in 1907 she outlined her strategy to the group: the vigorous application of legalistic tactics,

12. Jane Misme, "Les Grands figures du féminisme. Hubertine Auclert," *Minerva,* 19 October 1930 (quoted). For the development of the CNFF suffrage policy, see Hause with Kenney, *Women's Suffrage and Social Politics,* pp. 87–89.

13. Auclert, "Conseil international des femmes," *Le Radical,* 19 June 1906; Isabelle Bogelot, "Les Femmes qui agissent," *L'Echo de Paris,* 14 June 1906; clippings in the Sainte-Croix scrapbooks, vol. 1, Musée social; *Bulletin municipal officiel,* 25 June 1906; *Le Matin,* 17 June 1906; *Le Figaro,* 17 June 1906; *L'Aurore,* 17 June 1906. For other factors affecting the CNFF decision, particularly the development of Catholic suffragism, see Steven C. Hause and Anne R. Kenney, "The Development of the Catholic Women's Suffrage Movement in France, 1896–1922," *Catholic Historical Review* 67 (1981): 11–30; Hause with Kenney, *Women's Suffrage and Social Politics,* pp. 81–89.

14. Sainte-Croix to Auclert, 23 April 1906, Auclert Papers, 2/395; financial records, ibid., Carton 4; Auclert's membership in the CNFF, ibid., 10/87.

specifically an immense national petition combined with a letter-writing campaign directed to the leaders of each parliamentary faction. Moderates now accepted such efforts, so Auclert's first weeks at the head of the national suffrage campaign went smoothly. That did not last long. Auclert pressed her luck by asking the suffrage section to organize a march to the statue of Maria Deraismes in the Square des Epinettes in northern Paris. After a few days of arguments, Auclert resigned the presidency of the suffrage section, citing her poor health and the many demands upon her energy. She reassured Sainte-Croix that she would still try to participate in the section meetings, as her health and time permitted, without presiding ("I do not attach any importance to titles"). Sainte-Croix accepted her resignation "with profound regret" and gave Auclert the title of honorary president of the section—which may have been what the CNFF wanted in the first place.[15]

Auclert was in fact ill early in 1907 (her affliction is unknown) and missed several meetings of Suffrage des femmes, but that was not why she resigned the presidency. "When I saw," she wrote in a private note, "that I was only a president without independence who had to obey opportunist orders, I resigned." She concluded correctly that women like Bogelot, Monod, Siegfried, and Sainte-Croix were not going to give her carte blanche to stage demonstrations in the name of the CNFF; the notion had been wishful thinking from the start. Auclert was incorrect, however, in asserting that "the presidency offered to me had only one goal: to absorb the society Suffrage des femmes and to claim its accomplishments." Her insecurity, her painful memories of La Citoyenne, her impetuousness wrote that sentence. The women of the CNFF were sincere in founding a suffrage section, and they acted according to their standard of etiquette in offering its presidency to the founder of the suffrage movement. But they intended to make suffragism compatible with the respectable standards of the council. Auclert would not wear this bridle. Had she chosen to devote her energy to the CNFF petition that she inaugurated she could have presided longer, for the council genuinely worked for it. But her revolutionary zeal was not at home in the CNFF, and everyone knew it.[16]

The broken rapprochement with the moderates did not immediately lead Auclert back to militant demonstrations. Instead, she pressed her

15. Notes on the CNFF suffrage section, ibid., 8/129 and 11/333; UFF, Le Petit almanach féministe illustre—1908 (Paris, 1907), p. 13; Le Journal des femmes, February, April, and May 1907; Auclert to Sainte-Croix, 5 March 1907, Auclert Papers, 3/435; Sainte-Croix to Auclert, 11 March 1907, ibid., 3/437.

16. Notes on the CNFF, Auclert Papers, 11/333 (quoted). For the CNFF petition, see the text in Froger-Doudement, ed., Que veulent ces féministes, p. 46; L'Entente, February 1908; Le Journal des femmes, May 1907; Le Petit almanach féministe illustré—1908, p. 12.

own petition campaigns, to show that even without the resources of seventy-three thousand members she could succeed. In November 1907, she singlehandedly scored the greatest success of her petitioning career. In mid-1906, Auclert had decided to try another petition to the general council. As she reminded her readers in *Le Radical*, she had approached the council in 1885 but had received "all the old masculine cliches" and eleven votes. Her new petition was simple: "The society Suffrage des femmes, which has fought for twenty-nine years to make you admit French women to the exercise of their political rights, earnestly begs you to propose to parliament to confer on women the rights to vote and to stand for office on the same conditions as men." And, *mirabile dictu*, the council accepted her plea. The reporter for Auclert's petition, the Comte d'Aulan, personally believed that "the fair sex should not mix in political battles," but he delivered a report stating that women "have the right to give their opinion." The council adopted a motion in November 1907 calling for women to receive the vote in local elections.[17]

This resolution went to the Commission of Universal Suffrage, where it supported both Auclert's petition already lodged there and the third women's suffrage bill, the Dussaussoy Bill of 1906. The committee read the motion and promptly buried it with other feminist irritants. Minutes of the committee meetings indicate that not a single debate on women's suffrage occured in the period 1906–1908. Until they realized how thoroughly ineffectual a motion by the general council actually was, Auclert and other feminists rejoiced in the victory of November 1907. "This is progress, a landmark," Auclert wrote in *L'Eclair*; "feminists, we see here the beginnings of motion [*un acheminement*]." In an autobiographical note of 1908, she considered the motion her first tangible accomplishment. Feminists praised Auclert's persistence, and even *Le Figaro* admitted that, while "a tiny victory, entirely platonic," it was a flattering accomplishment.[18]

Auclert similarly pressed her petitions on the Radical and Radical-Socialist Party, founded in 1901, in the hope that they too would send a

17. Auclert, "Voeu à émettre," *Le Radical*, 9 July 1906; Buisson, *Le Vote des femmes*, pp. 30–31 (first quotation); Auclert, *Le Vote des femmes*, pp. 122, 179–80; Conseil général du département de la Seine, *Procés-verbaux des délibérations*, vol. 106 (second session, 1907), p. 119, AD XIX¹1, AN (quoted).

18. For the Dussaussoy Bill and the Chamber of Deputies, see Hause with Kenney, *Women's Suffrage and Social Politics*, pp. 94–100. Minutes of the Commission du suffrage universal, Archives de la Chambre des députés, C 7375, AN. Auclert, "Le Vote des femmes," *L'Eclair*, 23 November 1907 (first quotation); see also her "Voeu du conseil général," *Le Radical*, 24 November 1907. Autobiographical fragment, Auclert Papers, 14/47; Auclert, *Le Vote des femmes*, pp. 182–83 (second quotation); *L'Entente*, December 1907.

message to the Commission of Universal Suffrage. Her political credo had not altered significantly since the 1870s; had the party accepted women, she would have joined the radical-socialists. She still began her speeches with the words, "I, a good republican. . . ." Her letters to radical politicians stressed her affinity for their beliefs: "I am profoundly republican, and when there is a battle to win a right, you will always find me in the first rank." Yet she still insisted that radicals were not yet "true republicans": "Opinion for or against women's suffrage is a criterion which permits us to distinguish the true and the false republicans." The Radical and Radical-Socialist Party already shared Auclert's complex blend of Jacobin nationalism and pacifist idealism and her combination of socialist concern for the working class with distrust of collectivism. But she could not persuade them to add republican feminism to their republican nationalism and republican socialism. The founding congress flatly rejected women's suffrage in 1901 while reiterating their "suffrage falsely called universal."[19]

The radical program of 1906 encouraged Auclert to believe that the party could be led to republican feminism. This was the party's first draft of a comprehensive democratic program after years of concentration upon the separation of church and state. Radicals sought an ideological identity as "a party of justice and social solidarity," an identity that would distinguish them from collectivist socialists by maintaining the principle of private property, yet one that would simultaneously separate them from liberal republicans by attacking "the egoist school of laissez-faire." To find this identity, the program of 1906 enunciated a broad promise: "The Radical and Radical-Socialist Party intends to seek tomorrow, with the same firmness, the same spirit of method, the same discipline, and the same devotion [that was shown in the church-state question], the realization of new political, social, and economic reforms which create democracy." The precise terms of these reforms were to be stated at the next congress of the party, to be held at Nancy in 1907.[20]

Auclert began her campaign to incorporate republican feminism in the radical program by using her column in *Le Radical.* She praised the party and the newspaper for their high principles and congratulated them for their triumph in separating church and state. Then she pointed out the new target: "On the morrow of your victory, republicans, remember that the exclusion of women from common rights by our fathers during the revolution means that we must still apply their

19. Untitled speech, Auclert Papers, 6/223 (first quotation); draft letter to M. Angevin, *Le Radical,* ibid., 13/12 (second quotation); *pensée,* ibid., 8/137; untitled speech, ibid., 6/228 (third quotation); minutes of SF meeting, 14 June 1901, ibid., Carton 4.

20. "Déclaration-Programme du parti radical et radical-socialiste," *Le Radical,* 22 April 1906.

program to them." Auclert could easily explain republican feminism in this context—she need only quote prominent radicals. She reprinted part of a speech by Clemenceau in her column, approving of his words: "The principle of universal suffrage does not permit any compromise, it gives the same right to the learned and the ignorant, and it gives it by virtue of natural right." She merely asked the party to act on its rhetoric, asking eloquently:

> In this country, where the word *equality* is written on so many walls and tumbles out of so many mouths, can one hesitate to give women the political rights that men enjoy?
> If the French republic is not yet capable of raising herself up to the heights of Finland, which has made women electors and deputies, at least she must raise herself up to the level of Norway, which has accorded the vote to women who pay taxes. . . . Any restrictions made upon the exercise of political rights by French women would be preferable to their total exclusion from politics.[21]

Auclert presented republican feminism to the Radical and Radical-Socialist Party by petitioning the Nancy congress of October 1907 to include women in the *demos* of their democracy. She supported the petition with a letter describing the role of women in other democratic societies. And she waited—in Paris, because the party did not accept women members or women delegates to Nancy. The Nancy congress heard several reports on democratic suffrage and conducted lengthy debates on the subject. It produced a new party program—the cardinal document of prewar radicalism—announcing the party's intention to revise the constitution "in the most democratic sense" and to maintain "the sovereignty of universal suffrage." And it included a commitment to "the gradual extension of rights to women." "Bravo!" proclaimed Jane Misme's *La Française*, the leading feminist newspaper since the closing of *La Fronde*.[22]

---

21. See the mixture of praise in Auclert's column during 1906–1907, for example, "Propagande par le fait," 11 April 1906; "Bulletin pondérateur," 25 June 1906 (first quotation); "Et les croyances républicaines," 17 September 1906 (second quotation); "L'Adjonction des capacités féminines," 17 July 1906 (third quotation).

22. Auclert's petition can be found in *Les Femmes au gouvernail*, pp. 158–59, or *Le Radical*, 13 October 1907; for her supporting letter, see the Auclert Papers, 6/228. For the events of the Nancy Congress, see *Le Radical* throughout October 1907; the party program was published there on 10 October 1907, and is reprinted in Claude Nicolet, *Le Radicalisme*, 2d ed. (Paris, 1961), pp. 48–53, and in David Thomson, ed., *France: Empire and Republic, 1850–1940* (New York, 1968), pp. 278–83. See also Hause with Kenney, *Women's Suffrage and Social Politics*, pp. 99–100; Auclert, *Le Vote des femmes*, p. 122; *La Française*, 27 October 1907.

Had Hubertine Auclert scored a triumph at Nancy as she had at Marseilles in 1879? Not quite. The feminism of the Nancy Program that Misme praised was in fact a paternalistic pledge that "women must be protected by the law in all circumstances of life." The radical committee on universal suffrage did not even consider Auclert's petition, and the congress did not discuss it. She received an explanation that her request had been "too late to be taken into consideration," although she had written it eleven months earlier. In truth, the Radical and Radical-Socialist Party had not the slighest intention of endorsing women's suffrage. Their commitment to anticlericalism meant the perpetuation of the argument that priest-ridden women menaced the republic. Their interest in the democratic extension of universal suffrage meant the study of proportional representation, a controversial idea that would face even greater difficulties if considered alongside women's suffrage.[23]

The delegation at Nancy in 1907, like that at Marseilles in 1879, included many men who admired Auclert's ideals, but while the socialists at Marseilles had been momentarily swept away by an idealistic proposal, the radicals brushed it aside. What explains this difference? Both groups proclaimed beliefs that implied the acceptance of women; both retained traditional masculine attitudes about women and their roles. The socialists of 1879, however, had little political power or responsibility. Their program described a future when they might attain power. Their debates were no less heated, but they had little effect on the government of France during the next legislature; ideological adjustments, such as deemphasizing the equality of the sexes by postponing it until after the revolution, could be made, for all remained theory. The radicals of 1907, in contrast, dominated the government. Their votes, although not leading directly to law, produced the blueprint that cabinets were to follow. As the party in power, they had an investment in preserving their accomplishments, especially the separation of church and state, and their individual seats in parliament or in the cabinet; women's suffrage seemed to threaten all these things. They also had acquired the conservative caution that overcomes all parties that pass from opposition to power. Hence the radicals, despite their democratic words, behaved less generously in 1907 than the socialists had in 1879.

Auclert's vision of true republicanism remained sufficiently strong for her to try a third time at the radical congress in Dijon in 1908. As soon as the Nancy meeting closed, she sent another petition, as well as letters to every officer of the party, to be certain that the congress would

23. The Nancy program (first quotation), *Le Radical*, 10 October 1907; Auclert's notes on the congress, Auclert Papers, 6/115 (second quotation) and 11/60. For the complex relationship between radicalism and suffragism, see Hause with Kenney, *Women's Suffrage and Social Politics*.

discuss her ideas. She wrote to Senator Auguste Delpech (Ariège), the new president of the party's executive committee: "We hope that the Radical and Radical-Socialist Party will conclude that it is dangerous for the Republic to keep women outside of common rights, as if they were the diseased in quarantine, and that radicals will prevent the collectivist party from taking political power by enfranchising women." She reiterated this theme in *Le Radical.* Did republicans "want to drive those who remain outcasts from the republic to listen to the appeals of revolutionaries?" Auclert suggested a compromise. Starting with the pledge at Nancy for the gradual extension of women's rights, radicals could adopt an evolutionary suffragism beginning with the municipal franchise.[24]

Auclert received some support and the debate she sought at the Dijon congress. Three prominent radicals, led by Lucien LeFoyer (a new member of the party's executive committee and a future deputy from Paris), introduced a motion asking that the Declaration of the Rights of Man be applied to woman and asserting that "the equality of rights must govern the relations of the sexes as it has governed the relations of the classes." The party's committee on universal suffrage delivered a report agreeing "in principle" with Auclert and LeFoyer but insisting that women were still insufficiently educated "to collaborate in the great work of emancipation"; the party must promise to educate them yet reserve "for the future the complete emancipation of women." The Radical and Radical-Socialist Party overwhelmingly agreed.[25]

THE ADOPTION OF SUFFRAGETTE TACTICS

What choices did Hubertine Auclert face in 1908? She might have continued to press for republican feminism within the Radical party, but their message was already clear. She wrote to another militant that she believed "our cause is winning much ground" in the party, but she concluded, "unhappily, the Radicals are not feminists." Alternately, Auclert could have turned her attention to the unified socialist party, the sfio, founded in 1905. She still considered herself a republican socialist, and she recognized that socialists maintained their historic comment (in theory) to the equality of the sexes, which they had reiterated as recently as 1907 at the meeting of the Second International in Stuttgart. But she had concluded that socialism divided women, who must unify across class lines—a key concept of republican solidarism—

24. For the Dijon congress, see *Le Radical,* October 1908. Auclert to Delpech, 16 November 1907, Auclert Papers, 6/117 (first quotation); Auclert, "Le Féminisme," *Le Radical,* 11 October 1908 (second quotation).
25. Notes and clippings on the Dijon congress, Auclert Papers, 6/118.

to seek justice for their gender: "There cannot be a bourgeois feminism and a socialist feminism, because there are not two female sexes." And she still distrusted the collectivism of the sFIO because men were planning it: "I am favorably disposed to accept all systems that lead to more equality in society. But if collectivism must come, women must help to establish it or else they will be duped by the men who do." The third direction in which Auclert might have turned was toward the women's movement, rather than the male political parties. But she had seen in her collaboration with the CNFF in 1906–1907 that a tremendous gulf still separated her from the mainstream of the bourgeois feminist movement. In short, all three of her natural alternatives appeared blocked.[26]

Auclert's ambitions seemed thwarted by French republicanism, socialism, and feminism alike. Combined with her sense of *déjà vu* and her realization that women's suffrage was not advancing in the Chamber of Deputies, this frustration might have induced the depression that she had experienced on other occasions. It did not. Her private papers reveal that her determination and enthusiasm remained high. She again felt "cloaked in sacred fire for our cause."[27] Nor did her frustration prompt a *démarche* to the right. Her acceptance of conservative support in the 1880s and her collaboration with Drumont in the 1890s had been tactical; she never considered taking up strategic residence on the right, where she obviously had even less support than on the left. Instead, her frustration and her "sacred fire" produced anger. And that anger led her to consider violent tactics.

Hubertine Auclert did not arrive easily at this position. Certainly her rhetoric had been tempestuous and frequently alluded to the possibility of violence. Her reasoning led her to acknowledge the historic role of, and the possible need for, violence. But her republican ideology included the conviction that change should evolve without recourse to extreme actions. In her private feelings, she knew that violence was wrong. Yet her personality included an irritability that had produced impetuous behavior and abrupt reactions. There thus existed a delicate balance in Auclert. She did not want to employ violent means, but the thought kept occurring to her. She wanted to be a revolutionary, and called herself one, in the sense of one who produces tremendous change. She did not want to be a revolutionary in the sense of one who participates in violent actions to precipitate change. The frustration, the anger, the "sacred fire" from thirty years of work having produced little revolutionary change, however, she began to consider revolutionary action.

26. Auclert to Arria Ly, 3 November 1909, Arria Ly Papers, Bouglé Collection, BHVP (first quotation); Auclert, "Socialistes et bourgeoises," *Le Radical*, 3 September 1907 (second quotation); *pensées*, Auclert Papers, 8/149 (third quotation).
27. Diary, 24 April 1885, Auclert Papers.

Auclert wrote about violence on several occasions. Most of her words can be read in two ways. Her motto, "Always be prepared for battle," presumably exhorted women to energetic work, not to pulling up paving stones. Her conclusion that "in feminism, as in all other matters, one must know how to be daring" probably meant being daring enough to risk ridicule and hostility by espousing unpopular ideas. Even her challenges to the members of Suffrage des femmes—"In France, we lack boldness!"—suggest a desire to stir up lethargic followers rather than to smash windows. Nonetheless, the cumulative weight of dozens of such exclamations add up to the consideration of dramatic demonstrations.[28]

She edged closer to this subject by returning to the streets in early 1908. As in 1885, she led a march to the statue of Jeanne d'Arc on the Place des Pyramides. Suffrage des femmes purchased a laurel crown and garlands of flowers to honor the woman they described as "the personification of feminism." After a short parade and ceremony, Auclert and her followers distributed tracts calling upon women to demand the vote "with the energy of Jeanne d'Arc." Presumably this did not mean scaling the walls of the Palais Bourbon with a broadsword in hand, but neither was it pacifist imagery. Approximately two dozen women joined Auclert in this demonstration. Their number contrasted sharply with another women's demonstration at the same statue a few months later. Early in 1909, Catholic women paraded to offer their own flowers to Joan, as part of a campaign that led to her canonization in 1920. Women marching for sainthood outnumbered women marching for suffrage by a ratio of two hundred to one.[29]

Such contrasts did not deflect Auclert's thinking. Her notes reveal that she followed the activities of the English suffragettes and contemplated the possibility of "direct action" in France. She did not hide her thinking from the public. She had warned republican politicians that their intransigence would drive women toward revolution; after the elections of 1906, for example, in an article entitled "Propaganda by the Deed," Auclert reminded radicals that they were ignoring women and that English women had shown a willingness to break the law in response to such treatment. She concluded that article with a question: "Will feminists be obliged to employ propaganda of the deed in order to force parliaments to acknowledge the rights of women?" The ambiguity was disappearing from her words. After two years of trying to persuade

28. Li, *La Presse féministe en France*, p. 49 (first quotation); *pensée*, Auclert Papers, 8/155 (second quotation); minutes of SF meeting, 22 May 1903, ibid., Carton 4 (third quotation).

29. Jeanne d'Arc handbills, Dossier Auclert, BMD (quoted); financial records, Auclert Papers, Carton 4; speech on Jeanne d'Arc, ibid., 6/49; Chaumont, "Hubertine Auclert," pp. 60–64; *La Française*, 30 May 1909.

radicals to be "true republicans," Auclert spoke even more directly: "For women to obtain the vote in France, are they going to be obliged to knock down the urns that contain only male votes?"[30]

Her words were premonitory. A few days after writing them, Auclert tried direct action—knocking down the urns at a polling place. This suffragette action occured during the Parisian municipal elections of 1908. Auclert had initially planned to capitalize on those elections with a major propaganda effort; Suffrage des femmes spent 115 francs (83 percent of its 1908 income) on suffragist posters and handbills. Her strategy changed when a young reporter for *Le Martin*, Jeanne Laloë, announced her candidacy for the municipal council as a feminist and began to attract considerable publicity. Auclert seized the opportunity for energetic suffragism. She participated in an electoral meeting for Laloë, attended by over two thousand people, and she spoke so vigorously that a vice president of the LFDF recalled that "she dominated the boisterous crowd by the heat of her convictions." No one, not even Auclert, found timidity or ineloquence in her speech.[31]

Several aspects of the Laloë candidacy prompted Auclert to stage public demonstrations. She reasoned that the foremost justification for action would be the publicity generated. The beautiful Laloë had captured the attention of the press; lavish coverage attended her campaign. Auclert expected this coverage to extend to any dramatic feminist activities that happened simultaneously. Furthermore, she did not consider Laloë, who had never been active in the movement, a serious feminist; militants must not allow their cause to be preempted by a publicity-seeking gimmick.

Auclert, Kauffmann, and Pelletier hurriedly organized a demonstration for election day, May 3, 1908. With forty to fifty members of Suffrage des femmes and Solidarité, they held a brief parade in rented cars, then set off on a day-long march, with placards and handbills, from poll to poll. At first they stood in the street and chanted, "We want to vote." As the march progressed, they became bolder—first penetrating a

30. Notes on demonstrations, Auclert Papers, 6/135; Auclert, "Propagande par le fait," *Le Radical*, 11 June 1906 (first quotation) and "Parias françaises," ibid., 2 May 1908 (second quotation).

31. For more detailed accounts of suffragist activities, especially the Laloë campaign, during the municipal elections, see Steven C. Hause and Anne R. Kenney, "Women's Suffrage and the Paris Elections of 1908," *Laurels* 51 (1980):21–32; Hause with Kenney, *Women's Suffrage and Social Politics*, pp. 101–5. For Auclert's early plans, see the handbill in the Dossier Suffrage des femmes, BMD; Auclert to Arria Ly, 30 March 1908, Arria Ly Papers, Bouglé Collection, BHVP; financial records, Auclert Papers, Carton 4; Georges Lhermitte, "Nécrologie: Hubertine Auclert," *Le Droit des femmes*, April 1914; police reports, 2 May 1908, Rapports quotidiens de la Préfecture de police, 1908, F⁷ 12557, AN (which gives the attendance at the Laloë meeting as fifteen to eighteen hundred).

polling hall, then grabbing an urn containing ballots. They debated pouring acid over the ballots, or smashing the urn, but at three successive polls the police arrived in time to escort them outside. By late afternoon, only Auclert and Kauffmann remained. They succeeded in entering the polling place at the *mairie* of the Fourth Arrondissement. There, Auclert seized the urn, threw it to the ground, and defiantly stamped on the evidence of unisexual suffrage (see illustration 10) while officials stood as frozen as if Auclert had been Medusa. She managed to shout, "These urns are illegal! They contain only masculine ballots!" before police arrived to arrest her.[32]

The police treated Auclert's actions as "not serious" (*peu graves*). They held her in custody only until the polls closed and filed misdemeanor charges for violating a decree of February 1852 governing election procedures. (The prefecture did take the precaution of sending a squad of police to the poll where Laloë's ballots were to be counted that night.) Auclert stated during her interrogation that she sought "to protest against the illegality of which woman is the victim, in not being allowed to give her opinion, like man, by voting." She told her questioners that the demonstration had succeeded because of "the publicity that will be given" to it.[33]

Auclert was mistaken in her expectations. When reporters interviewed her, she dramatized her actions. She spoke of the pleasure of holding "an urn, that urn of lies which is an outrage to the equality of the sexes." And she elevated her demonstration into the beginnings of a revolution: "We have not obtained the vote by legal means, so we are taking revolutionary means; we shall obtain by noise and force that which has been refused, in spite of all justice and legality, to sweetness and reasoning." The press response, however, disappointed Auclert; for once, Parisian papers eschewed sensationalizing the news. Of course, many papers, even the staid *Le Temps*, dubbed her a "suffragette." Some showed the anticipated righteousness; *Le Matin* described her crime as a "sacrilege." Several made the obvious comparison; *L'Eclair* called her protest "an imitation of the suffragettes of London." But in general the press mentioned the event only briefly and did not make an issue of it. Many papers, led by *Le Radical*, dismissed it as insignificant: "For a few seconds they disturbed the regular course of the voting." Worse yet, they

32. In addition to the accounts cited above and the Parisian daily press, see Dossiers Auclert and Jeanne Laloë, BMD; Auclert, *Le Vote des femmes*, p. 123 (quoted); police report, 4 May 1908, Rapports quotidiens de la Préfecture de police, 1908, F⁷ 12557, AN; police report, 5 May 1908, Dossier Auclert, APP.

33. Police report, 4 May 1908, Rapports quotidiens de la Préfecture de police, 1908, F⁷ 12557, AN (first quotation); Procès verbal transmis au Tribunal correctionnel, 6 May 1908, Dossier Auclert, APP; police report, 5 May 1908, ibid., (second and third quotations).

suggested that Auclert had merely acted "in a bad humor," nettled by the gallant attention paid to Laloë.[34]

Auclert's trial in correctional court took place one month after her arrest. She did not hesitate to admit her actions or to use the term *suffragette* to describe herself. She was neither apologetic nor defiant, but she spoke with regret and firmness. She talked about violence, using the word. For someone so often called rowdy and disreputable, she spoke with a surprising calm and lonely dignity. Only twelve feminists attended her trial and heard the testimony that summarized a complex career:

> Yes, I demonstrated on election day. . . . Yes, I upended on the floor an urn containing the ballots.
>
> It is regrettable that I committed this act which brings me before you; regrettable because I am strongly opposed to [*très ennemi de*] violence. But I acted this way because I have been pushed to the limit—as all of my suffragette comrades have been—by the egoism of men.
>
> Please consider that for many years I have tried in vain to claim the political rights of women, in a lawful manner. [Here, Auclert summarized her career.] Unfortunately, Parliament has not wanted to ratify women's rights.
>
> I am very respectful of legality, I am not a violent person. But I believe that there are moments in life when violence is excusable.
>
> Driven to desperation by seeing my legal efforts lead to nothing, I bore in mind that when men were excluded from politics, as women are today, they built barricades. . . . They cannot be surprised that women, in their turn, revolt. . . .
>
> I do not regret having committed this act, but being obliged to commit it.

To the applause of the audience and the dismay of some conservatives ("an atmosphere of great indulgence ruled," *Le Soleil* reported), Auclert's judges immediately sentenced her to the minimum fine of sixteen francs and suspended the sentence contingent upon her good conduct for five years (*condamné avec sursis*). Members of Suffrage des femmes then distributed handbills and the society's postcards to the audience.[35]

34. *L'Eclair*, 4 May 1908 (quoted); *Le Temps*, 4 June 1908; *Le Matin*, 2 June 1908; *Le Radical*, 4 May 1908.

35. Auclert's speech given here is a close paraphrase rather than a verbatim text. The complete text is not available in the court records. The text given is compiled from police records and a dozen daily newspapers for 4 June 1908. Some sentences appeared in all

The French government clearly had chosen not to make a martyr of Auclert, just as the press had decided not to make a sensation of her. What effect, then, had her action had? The protest had been very difficult for her. In an autobiographical fragment, Auclert repeated her words: she had been "driven to desperation" but remained "strongly opposed to violence." Her sister Marie described her violence as "a true sacrifice for her cause, because she was so timid of character."[36] There was tragic irony in this situation. The woman who saw herself as a martyr had publicly fulfilled that role, but the government and the press had declined to accept it. Stunned to find that she could be rejected even as a martyr, Auclert withdrew into her feelings of timidity and inadequacy.

What had Auclert achieved? One answer soon came from the feminist movement. Although one other militant, Madeleine Pelletier, committed a similar act of violence, no others copied Auclert—there was to be no suffragette movement in France. Another militant, Camille Bélilon, publicly defended Auclert ("Some will say this is violence. Pardon, these are reprisals"), but the overwhelming majority of French feminists renounced such demonstrations.[37] Her colleagues, like the government and the press, simply turned their backs on Auclert. Nonetheless, one must conclude that Auclert's demonstration had two important effects on the women's suffrage movement in France. First, she helped to define the boundaries of the movement by posing the question of what tactics, what behavior, would be acceptable. Second, and more important, by pushing militant behavior so far, she made legalistic suffragism seem moderate and respectable by comparison; women who had hesitated to join a suffrage organization could now do so, reassuring themselves of respectability by disavowing the French suffragette as they had once made themselves respectable feminists by disavowing the French suffragist.

accounts, some in only a few; the wording varies somewhat from report to report. See Procès-verbal transmis au Tribunal correctionel, 6 May 1908, Dossier Auclert, APP; police reports, 3 and 4 June 1908, ibid.; *L'Eclair* and *Messidor* (both giving long reproductions of Auclert's speech), *Le Temps, La Liberté, La Petite république, Le Figaro, Le Soleil, Le Petit parisien, La Libre parole, Le Petit journal, L'Action,* and *L'Autorité,* all for 4 June 1908.

36. Autobiographical fragment, Auclert Papers, 14/47; Chaumont, "Hubertine Auclert," p. 77.

37. For Pelletier's demonstration, see Hause with Kenney, *Women's Suffrage and Social Politics,* pp. 103–4. Camille Bélilon, "Conseillères municipales," *Le Journal des femmes,* May 1908.

CHAPTER ELEVEN

Rejection and Triumph
1908–1914

Hubertine Auclert was sixty years old when she smashed a ballot box in May 1908. That act firmly established the word *suffragette* in the lexicon of French journalists. It won Auclert the esteem of some English suffragettes, who now expressed a desire to meet her.[1] But French suffragists hastened to repudiate Auclert's behavior. Their movement grew rapidly in the years before World War I. One suffrage union alone claimed twelve thousand members in 1914; one demonstration in that year involved over five hundred thousand women. The women who presided over this expansion considered themselves suffragists, not suffragettes, and they emphatically distinguished themselves from Auclert. They held ambivalent attitudes about the mother of their movement. She was an embarrassment as well as a heroine to bourgeois feminists. They could not ignore her importance, but they would not follow her ways. She belonged in the Pantheon but not in the streets. French suffragists left no doubt that they rejected Auclert's militancy; they considered violence utterly unacceptable and wished to avoid any form of undignified behavior. When Auclert died in the spring of 1914, she was still directing Suffrage des femmes and its cadre of fewer than fifty militants in the midst of a French suffrage movement of twenty thousand to twenty five thousand.

1. See the correspondence in the Auclert Papers, Carton 3.

THE SUFFRAGIST CONGRESS OF 1908

French suffragists enunciated their moderate, legalistic principles in June 1908, a few days after Auclert's conviction in correctional court. The occasion for their pronouncement was the Congrès national des droits civils et du suffrage des femmes, the first assembly of the French feminist movement since the congresses of 1900. Auclert declined an invitation to join the organizing committee, composed of Vincent, Oddo-Deflou, and Durand. Although she again cited her poor health, poor relations were more important. Auclert again acted with unforgiving judgment of those who opposed her, again chose adamancy instead of conciliation. She may indeed have been ill, but she undertook the arduous marches and protests of May 3 a few days after refusing the invitation.

The committee adopted two goals: to unite the bourgeois-republican feminist movement—that is, not the Catholic right or the socialist left—and to proclaim women's suffrage its first priority. All feminist leagues except the most militant adhered to this program. Auclert and Pelletier, feeling like pariahs, kept their societies out of the preparations. This produced yet another poignant irony in the career of Hubertine Auclert. The congress that marked the victory of suffragism within the women's movement named two honorary presidents—Bogelot and Feresse-Deraismes—who had opposed seeking enfranchisement for most of their lives. Had they honored Auclert, she would have accepted; a few days after her demonstration, and six weeks before the congress, she reexamined her isolation and wrote to Oddo-Deflou that Suffrage des femmes would join the meeting. The decisive events between her refusal to join the organizing committee and her decision to participate, of course, were her demonstration and the reactions to it. Before these events, Auclert still felt stubborn strength in her militancy; after, she felt rejected and without self-confidence.[2]

The congress of 1908 gave great attention to women's suffrage. The organizing committee drafted appeals to Ferdinand Buisson, the Commission of Universal Suffrage's reporter on the Dussaussoy Bill for municipal suffrage, and to the parliamentary group for the defense of women's rights; they urged the former to deliver his report to the Chamber of Deputies and the latter to organize support for it. The committee saturated the program with seventeen separate speeches on

2. See the Dossier Congrès national des droits civils et du suffrage des femmes, BMD. In addition to many clippings on the congress, it contains printed documents, manuscripts, and 117 pages of Durand's notes. For Auclert's late decision to participate, see Vincent to Durand, 18 May 1908, ibid. See also Oddo-Deflou's perspective in "Congrès national des droits civils et du suffrage des femmes," *La Liberté d'opinion*, May–June 1908.

women's suffrage. Vincent delivered one of three reports on the history of the question in France. Oddo-Deflou explained the need for women's suffrage in terms of the slow legislative progress made on feminist interests. Durand spoke on the attitudes of French political parties, followed by three deputies and one senator who reported on parliamentary prospects. Maria Vérone, the new head of the LFDF, examined the municipal franchise as a starting point. Vincent delivered a second report on women's suffrage in professional situations, especially the Conseil des prud'hommes (board of labor arbitrators). One report surveyed foreign suffragism and four others studied the English and Swedish movements. These discussions led to a unanimous resolution in favor of the Dussaussoy Bill.[3]

All these speeches faded in importance next to the brief address delivered by Auclert, who had waited thirty years to deliver a suffrage report to a feminist congress. Now, after being blocked by Richer and Deraismes in 1878 and 1889, locked out in 1896, and preempted by Viviani in 1900, she could speak; indeed, she could speak to an audience that unamiously favored women's suffrage. But this hour of vindication became another painful experience. Auclert came as a misdemeanant among the lawful. If she defended her activism, she would divide a congress unified in support of the idea to which she had devoted her life, and she would win the support only of a tiny minority. To recant was not her style—especially before those who had opposed women's suffrage and her leadership, yet now presumed to speak for the movement she had founded. Auclert chose to abandon violence as a tactic, but she said *nolo contendere* rather than *mea culpa*. In a brave speech, similar to her testimony in court, she managed to concede without capitulating.

Auclert began by reviewing the tactics that she and a few comrades had used for decades. "For a long time," she said, "we have limited ourselves to completely legal demonstrations." But what victories had they won? She had submitted more than fifty petitions: "They are put in the wastebasket." Her one successful petition, to the General Council of the Seine, had produced a resolution that the Chamber of Deputies had simply ignored: "They cannot hear out of that ear." For this reason she had reconsidered her lifelong opposition to violence. She explained this as she had in *Le Radical* in 1906–1908: "To obtain the vote, men built barricades." Auclert then described the demonstration that she and a few "very determined women" had made, lamenting that they were "not numerous enough." This drew scattered applause from her supporters, still not numerous. Auclert showed her less radical listeners

3. In addition to the sources listed above, see the official report of the congress, edited by Oddo-Deflou: *Congrès national des droits civils et du suffrage des femmes. Tenu . . . les 26–28 juin 1908* (Paris, 1910).

the same amount of contrition that she had shown the court: "It was a great pity that we used this violent method, but it was quite simply to protest our exclusion from electoral rights."

Auclert reserved the announcement of her intentions for the end of her speech. The minutes of the congress do not record a collective sigh of relief, but her words surely produced one. Auclert did not say that she had been wrong or directly repudiate violent behavior. She announced that she would shift tactics and resume a lawful approach: "Having done all that [in May], ladies and gentlemen, and still not getting our legislators to deign to pay attention to our interests, I am going to propose a motion to you." The audience of eight hundred then listened to Auclert describe one of her wishful readings of the law. Since parliamentary constituencies were determined by population, Auclert wanted to challenge the legality of counting women in establishing electoral districts. Excluding women would reduce the number of seats in the Chamber of Deputies by half; theoretically, this would make politicians recognize their interest in women's rights.

Auclert's proposal was not a dazzling idea, nor was it stated as her audience would have chosen. She was altering course because she had learned that her militant actions did not succeed, not that they were wrong. Nonetheless, the ineluctable fact was that Auclert had said she would try lawful behavior again. Her relieved listeners would have adopted any motion that she set before them, however implausible it seemed. They did not pause to debate. They sprang to their feet for one of the few standing ovations of Auclert's life and adopted her motion by acclamation.[4]

Auclert's return to legalism facilitated a historic, if predictable, decision by the congress of 1908. French suffragists voted explicitly to reject violence as a means of seeking their goal.[5] The rejection of violence remained a permanent characteristic of the French suffrage campaign that was reiterated at subsequent congresses. This produced the dramatic contrast between French suffragists and English suffragettes in the years before World War I, a contrast that both feminists and journalists in Paris enjoyed pointing out.[6]

From Auclert's perspective, the congress of 1908 had mixed results. After all, she had participated in the rejection of her own behavior. Although she talked about violence again, she avoided it for the rest of

4. Ibid., pp. 216–17.

5. See Durand's notes in the Dossier Congrès national des droits civils et du suffrage des femmes, BMD, and the discussion of this vote in interviews given by Durand, *La Liberté*, 1 July 1908, and by Oddo-Deflou, unidentified clipping, Dossier Oddo-Deflou, BMD.

6. For the development of this comparison see Hause with Kenney, *Women's Suffrage and Social Politics*, pp. 108–9 and passim; for further analysis of the French rejection of violence, see Hause and Kenney, "The Limits of Suffragist Behavior," 781–806.

her life. Yet the congress was also a great victory for her idea, and one must not miss the principal issue by focusing on the subquestion of tactics. The entire bourgeois feminist movement had adopted women's suffrage as its highest priority. Auclert's moment of victory did not bring the recognition that she deserved because she had always been too radical in politics and too obstreperous in personality for her colleagues. She had been a suffragist in an age of moderate feminism; she became a suffragette in an age of moderate suffragism; she remained a rebel who alienated colleagues even as time converted them to her ideas.

THE FOUNDING OF THE UFSF

The juxtaposition of rejection and triumph characterized the last years of Auclert's life. Just as the congress of 1908 saw the victory of her plans for the congress of 1878, the foundation of the Union française pour le suffrage des femmes (hereafter UFSF) in 1909 represented the success of her plans for the Société nationale du suffrage des femmes of 1883. The UFSF, with branches in seventy-five departments by 1914, became the national society that Auclert had dreamt of, its statutes resembling those she had written a generation earlier (see appendix 2). Between the idea and the reality had fallen a shadow. The dreamer of 1878 and 1883 inhabited that shadow, darkly watching her ideas succeed in ways she had not anticipated. Even their success entailed personal rejection by a new generation of feminists.

The UFSF was the creation of Jeanne Schmahl and Jane Misme. Schmahl had disbanded Avant-Courrière in 1907 after winning the adoption of the Married Women's Earning Law (the *loi Schmahl*), to which it had been exclusively devoted. Misme, a moderate who edited the weekly *La Française* and had previously opposed suffragism, was one of Schmahl's strongest supporters in Avant-Courrière. Schmahl "conceived the idea" of the UFSF as a national society, nonpartisan and strictly legalist, which would join the IWSA. The international alliance had met in 1906 in Copenhagen and in 1908 in Amsterdam without a French league having joined. Schmahl intended to apply for IWSA membership for the UFSF at the London congress of 1909.[7]

Schmahl began corresponding with Auclert about a national suffrage league shortly after the French congress of 1908. As Misme put it, "No one could dream of creating anything for suffrage without offering her the first place." This sentiment is dubious. It had not given Auclert the

---

7. Grinberg, *Historique du mouvement suffragiste*, p. 91 (quoted). Grinberg was an officer of the UFSF. For a detailed examination of the creation of the UFSF, see Hause (with Kenney), *Women's Suffrage and Social Politics*, pp. 109–14.

honorary presidency of the congress of 1908. Nor had it produced a working rapprochement when the CNFF made Auclert founding president of its suffrage section in 1906–1907. "Offer" is the key word, of course, because Misme and Schmahl envisioned an organization with which Auclert would be temperamentally incompatible. Schmahl, however, admired Auclert. Her financial support had helped to recreate Suffrage des femmes in 1900, and she remained a dues-paying member. Schmahl was virtually the only feminist leader to address Auclert in her letters with "Chère Amie." She knew that Auclert felt the effects of age and ill health; she knew that Auclert would not direct a group that stressed dignity and respectability, committing its members not "to disturb the order nor to disturb anyone's legitimate susceptibility." Misme was curter; she found Auclert unacceptable as the head of the union because of her "particularism" (apparently this meant that Auclert represented a small segment of feminist opinion). She agreed to offer Auclert the presidency because she would certainly reject it.[8]

Schmahl invited Auclert to preside over the national suffrage union, and Auclert refused, as Schmahl and Misme expected, citing her health. She gave Schmahl her public blessing and a letter to read to the organizational meeting, but her private feelings were less gracious. She disliked Misme and her friends, whom she considered too interested in their social life and bourgeois comforts and too tepid in supporting feminism. They were women of sincere belief but not of Auclert's revolutionary zeal; she could not imagine them writing, "I must separate myself from joy just as I am separated from rights." Auclert also considered Misme a sloppy journalist and poorly informed about women's history; she frequently wrote to correct items that appeared in *La Française*, such as an article that portrayed Auclert as an active communard in 1871. Her notes on the founding of the UFSF excoriated Misme and "the new suffragists." They joined the movement only "after studying the weather-vane for a long time," but they "pretended that they invented the movement."[9]

Auclert's notes show that the formation of the UFSF wounded her. If Schmahl and Misme sincerely wanted her to head a national suffrage organization, she asked, why did they not join Suffrage des femmes and

8. Misme, "L'UFSF et Madame Hubertine Auclert," *La Française*, 28 March 1909 (first quotation); Grinberg, *Historique du mouvement suffragiste*, p. 91; financial records, Auclert Papers, Carton 4; Schmahl to Auclert, undated (early 1909), ibid., 3/709 (second quotation); Schmahl to Auclert, 4 February 1909, ibid., 3/482; statutes of the UFSF, 13 February 1909, Dossier UFSF, BMD (third quotation); Misme, "Les Grands figures du féminisme: Hubertine Auclert," *Minerva*, 19 October 1930; Misme, "Les Grands figures du féminisme: Jeanne Schmahl," ibid., 26 October 1930 (fourth quotation).

9. Auclert to Misme, 18 July 1908, Auclert Papers, 13/1; Auclert, circular letter, ibid., 13/13; notes on the UFSF, ibid., 11/335 (quoted) and 11/337.

work with her to expand it? Instead, they took her idea and even her organization's name, just as Richer had done before them. Auclert knew why moderates would not join Suffrage des femmes: "they cannot domesticate me." She realized that the UFSF would be a domesticated society when she read Schmahl's series of articles, "Propos d'une suffragiste," in *La Française.* Schmahl explicitly identified herself as a suffragist, not a suffragette. "Educated" and "civilized," the suffragist would follow an "essentially bourgeois" course. "She will instinctively avoid everything that could shock or hurt those whom she hopes to win." The suffragette, according to Schmahl, was essentially proletarian and fought for her rights with the roughness of that class. Neither Auclert nor anyone else in the women's movement could doubt what this meant.[10]

Further proof of the simultaneous triumph of Auclert's cause and rejection of her behavior can be found in Misme's report on French suffragism presented to the IWSA in London. France joined the IWSA, Auclert did not. Misme even mentioned Auclert by name and disparaged her radicalism. Auclert understood. Misme, succeeding the Sisters of St. Vincent, Richer, Hardouin, the laundrywomen's cooperative, Fauché, Mink and Michel, Epailly and Lasserre, Barberouse and Allix, Martin, Durand and Viviani, Catt, and a troop of lesser figures, became her *bête noire* of the moment, the personification of her ostracism. Auclert feuded with Misme for the rest of her life, writing angry letters to *La Française* and circulating corrections of Misme's stories to all feminist groups. (Auclert would not have been surprised to find her obituary in *La Française* repeating errors that she had written to correct, such as identifying her as one of the founders of Amélioration in 1867.) Misme continued to esteem Auclert as the champion of women's suffrage but spurned her for her extremism. She restated the case the week that Auclert died, invoking the "innate caution of the French temperament" as a barrier to "harmful" militancy.[11]

So Hubertine Auclert worked in the isolation that she had felt so profoundly since the early 1880s, while a mass suffrage movement developed in France. The UFSF reached one thousand members by the spring of 1910; Suffrage des femmes received dues from twenty-six women that year. Auclert devoted herself to another petition campaign

10. Notes on the UFSF, ibid., 11/335 (quoted); minutes of SF meeting, 11 May 1911, ibid., Carton 4; "Propos d'une suffragiste," *La Française,* 24 and 31 January 1909, 7 (quoted), 21, and 18 February 1909, 14 March 1909.

11. IWSA, *Report of the Fifth Conference* (London, 1909), pp. 96–98; Misme, "L'UFSF et Madame Hubertine Auclert," *La Française,* 28 March 1909; "Encore Madame Hubertine Auclert," ibid., 18 April 1909; "Les Françaises et les démonstrations de la rue," ibid., 4 April 1914 (quoted); "Les Disparus: Madame Hubertine Auclert," ibid., 18 April 1914; circular letters to feminist groups (1909), Auclert Papers, 13/13 and 12/111.

for women's suffrage. She decided to ask for "integral suffrage" rather than the municipal rights that the UFSF sought; why worry about offending moderates by seeming more radical than they? Once again she exhausted herself seeking signatures, supported by an exceptional effort by Arria Ly in Toulouse. At the opening of the fall 1909 session of the Chamber of Deputies, Auclert presented the Commission of Petitions with more than four thousand signatures. That committee surprised even Auclert by voting unanimously to send her petition, and Louis Marin's (republican, Meurthe-et-Moselle) report recommending its adoption, to the Commission of Universal Suffrage. This resolution, of course, went into the folder containing the report that Auclert had won from the general council in 1907 and the petition that she had sent directly to the Commission of Universal Suffrage in 1908. That folder accomodated two more petitions that arrived from her in the following months and a resolution she soon won from the Municipal Council of Paris. The committee still hesitated. It agreed to prepare a report favorable to women's suffrage, the Buisson Report, but not to submit it to the chamber until the question of proportional representation had been resolved.[12]

Auclert's persistence impressed even Jane Misme. She praised the petition in *La Française* but took the opportunity to reiterate her rejection of Auclert's militancy: "If we have disapproved of certain demonstrations of Madame Hubertine Auclert, it could not be so with her petition. The Petition is one of the great pacific instruments." Such jibes still hurt but no longer surprised Auclert. She answered in kind. Early in 1910, for example, she wrote an article on women's suffrage for *Le Matin* in which she took pride in her victory: "The political rights of women have become the axis of feminism. The number of partisans is increasing every day." And she relished the opportunity to assault the moderates who had rejected her leadership: "Union is not possible between the feminists who struggle to make their idea triumph and those who only seek aggrandizement for themselves and their shops." Her gusto for battle and her vigorous prose had not been beaten. Auclert finished that article by suggesting that feminists who attack each other "have the instincts of dogs" who fight over a bone.[13]

12. For the growth of the UFSF, see Hause with Kenney, *Women's Suffrage and Social Politics*, pp. 133–42. For the size of SF, see financial records, Auclert Papers, Carton 4. For the petition of 1909, see Commission of Petitions records, C 7936 and C 7938, AN; Auclert to Arria Ly, 6 May 1909, 5 August 1909, and 3 November 1909, Arria Ly Papers, Bouglé Collection, BHVP; Marin to Auclert, 23 October 1909, Auclert Papers, 3/480; Marin manuscript, undated, ibid., 10/78; JO, Chambre des députés, documents, 5 April 1910 (petition 1945). For the Commission of Universal Suffrage, the Buisson Report, and proportional representation, see Hause with Kenney, *Women's Suffrage and Social Politics*, pp. 128–31, 157–61.

13. Misme, "Le Vote des femmes," *La Française*, 14 November 1909; Auclert, "Les Femmes ont de la peine à se mettre d'accord," *Le Matin*, 23 March 1910.

THE ELECTIONS OF 1910

Auclert's last great suffrage effort came in the spring of 1910 when she stood as a candidate for the Chamber of Deputies in the Eleventh Arrondissement. She had not planned to run. Early in February 1910 Durand announced her own candidacy, telling the press that she would campaign for feminism, "but not rowdy feminism in the manner of the English suffragettes. Such a campaign is impossible in France; it would quickly be stopped by the ridicule." She repeated this theme in several interviews and added that she hoped Auclert would follow her example.[14]

Auclert still considered Durand an "insincere feminist" who risked nothing for the cause and adopted it only when it became respectable. In 1907, she had criticized Durand in *Le Radical* for refusing to endorse women's suffrage. When Durand changed her mind, Auclert judged her harshly in a private note: "There is a fashion for ideas, just as there is for dresses. . . . Some fear to stand out by thinking anything different from what everybody else does." According to Auclert's notes, when she had congratulated Durand on her conversion to suffragism, Durand had answered, "How could you expect me to be a suffragist when no one else was?"[15]

These attitudes did not predispose Auclert to join Durand in running for the Chamber of Deputies; Jeanne Laloë's success of 1908 did. Laloë's publicity, official recognition, and impressive vote total tantalized her. She did foresee problems, however. She told the press that it was premature to make a decision in February about a demonstration in April. She told a meeting of Suffrage des femmes that the problem was resources. Auclert would make personal sacrifices to enable Suffrage des femmes to finance a campaign, which would be costly because women lacked the advantages of male candidates. *Their* well-organized parties had permanent headquarters, campaign treasuries, and volunteer labor to mount posters or distribute ballots outside the polls. They would get free meeting halls in public buildings and exemption from the required tax stamps on posters. They had enough money to buy votes for three, five, or even ten francs each. "That is why," Auclert told Suffrage des femmes, "one can be a deputy if one is rich enough, however stupid one might be." She shocked her followers by adding that she would be willing to buy votes if she could afford masculine politics, but, to be realistic, they had to concentrate on the basic costs. Durand was popular

14. For Durand and the other feminist candidates in 1910, see Hause with Kenney, *Women's Suffrage and Social Politics*, pp. 145–51; for details of Durand's effort, see Dossier Marguerite Durand Candidate aux élections législatives de 1910, BMD. *L'Intransigeant*, 6 February 1910 (quoted) and 15 February 1910; *Le Matin*, 14 February 1910.

15. Auclert, "Le Travail féminin," *Le Radical*, 2 April 1907; notes, Auclert Papers, 6/177 and 6/252 (quoted).

with the press and could afford to rent her own hall; could Suffrage des femmes match her resources?[16]

Auclert decided to run early in March 1910 after seeing the reaction of other suffragists. The LFDF, which had become more militant under the direction of Maria Verone, agreed to oversee feminist races in all twenty arrondissements of Paris. Pelletier and Kauffmann both decided to run. Moderates opposed these decisions. Misme denounced the races on behalf of the UFSF. The union would undertake "vast propaganda for women's suffrage," she wrote, but "readers who know its program will not even suppose that it could include . . . feminine candidacies." Given a choice of running with Durand or boycotting with Misme, Auclert did not vacillate. She immediately announced her candidacy and invited friends to do likewise. Few volunteered. Oddo-Deflou declined to run, but two members of Suffrage des femmes joined Auclert in the other districts of the Eleventh Arrondissement.[17]

Suffrage des femmes financed seven hundred copies of three different posters and one thousand copies of their program to blanket the quartier. In addition to Auclert, the society sponsored Gabrielle Chapuis (see illustration 7), a leader of the group since its reestablishment, and Renée Mortier, a young postal employee who had turned to Suffrage des femmes in exasperation at the obstacles men had created to her athletic career as a swimmer. To sustain their races, Auclert formally announced them to the prefect of the Seine and requested the privileges to which candidates were entitled. She told the press that the candidates would certainly obtain meeting places because a precedent had been set in 1908.[18]

Auclert's campaign encountered difficulties almost as soon as it had begun. Chapuis fell ill and had to withdraw. Newspapers paid great attention to Durand, comparatively little to Auclert. The prefect flatly refused to grant Auclert the privileges of a legal candidate, "because you do not qualify as a citizen." One of the minor male candidates in her district threatened to sue Auclert because she posted her program in the official spaces "reserved for men only." She had to replace posters that were torn down, or plastered over, eleven times, including one depressing morning when she discovered that all of the posters mounted the previous night had been covered. Each time this happened, she had to

---

16. *L'Intransigeant,* 15 February 1910; *Le Temps,* 12 February 1910 (quoted).

17. Misme, "Le Vote des femmes: UFSF," *La Française,* 20 February 1910; Oddo-Deflou to Auclert, 15 March 1910, Auclert Papers, 3/501.

18. Financial records, Auclert Papers, Carton 4; notes, April 1910, ibid., 9/163; Mortier to Auclert, 6 March 1910, ibid., 3/499; Auclert to Prefect of the Seine, 31 March 1910, ibid., 3/488; Chaumont, "Hubertine Auclert," pp. 72–77; *Le Journal des femmes,* May 1910; *Le Matin,* 1 April 1910.

pay for tax stamps again. All of this redoubled her determination. She raised over 120 francs in special contributions, rented a meeting room in a restaurant, and continued to post her program.[19]

Auclert predicated her appeal for votes on the legal principle of *consensus facit legem* (consent makes law). The courts might rule that women were illegal candidates, but if the voters chose otherwise, their choice would force a reinterpretation of the law. The popular will could create the true republic. "You are sovereign," she told electors; *"your will has the force of law."* Her program (see illustration 12) outlined other characteristics of her republic. The equality of women included equal civil and political rights, equal education and training, "equal salary for equal production," and equality within marriage. Mothers, married or not, should receive the same state support given to men in the army: food, housing, clothing. Beyond republican feminism, Auclert appealed for the support of workers. They should receive "the total value" (*prix*) of their labor; their unions, rather than management or middlemen, should control access to day labor. Access to the judicial system should be free. Essential foods should not be taxed.[20]

Auclert's campaign did not receive the great publicity that she sought. Most newspapers portrayed her as a suffragette and concentrated on Durand—a distinction that Durand encouraged with interviews deploring the suffragettes. Auclert denounced "the conspiracy of silence" and tried to capitalize on her few opportunities. Drumont supported her, recalling her collaboration at *La Libre parole* in favorable terms and reassuring his readers that she was not "a Vesuvian of 1848," whatever the headlines said. "It was Hubertine Auclert," he wrote, "who made me understand the importance that the ballot can have for women." Only *L'Eclair*, however, gave Auclert the opportunity to explicate her theory that electors could revise the law. In an interview, she insisted that a candidate need not possess full citizenship in order to be elected; Blanqui had been elected to the Chamber of Deputies from Marseilles while deprived of civil rights because of his conviction. Auclert pressed harder: if possession of all civil rights was a precondition for sitting in the chamber, the courts should oust all military officers from that body because they lost the vote while in the service. *L'Eclair* heralded Auclert as "Polyeucte in skirts." Auclert approved of

19. Minutes of SF meetings, 14 April and 12 May 1910, Auclert Papers, Carton 4; Prefect of the Seine to Auclert, 3 April 1910, ibid., 3/501 (quoted); manuscript on the 1910 elections, ibid., 6/162 (second quotation); financial records, ibid., Carton 4.

20. Several forms of Auclert's program can be found in her papers: poster, Carton 1; programs, 7/5, 10/10, and 10/16. For more on her legal argument, see her interview in *L'Eclair*, 15 April 1910.

the comparison to Polyeucte, whose martyrdom converted others to Christianity, and kept several copies of the article in her papers.[21]

The results of the polling were also disappointing. A ruling from the prefecture again forbade the reporting of ballots cast for women, and women who tried to attend the counting were expelled by force, so all counts were unofficial. According to sympathizers present as members of the staff of legal candidates, Auclert finished fifth, behind the victorious socialist and three radicals but ahead of two conservatives, with 590 votes. This was approximately 4 percent of the fourteen thousand votes cast. Laloë had obtained 22 percent in the municipal elections; nonetheless, Auclert put a favorable interpretation on her small figure, insisting that those who deprecated her result must have expected a miracle. The proper perspective, Auclert told Suffrage des femmes, was to remember that the socialists, who had just won the seat she contested, had first entered a candidate in that constituency in 1885, and he had received only thirty-two votes. Privately, she took added pleasure in winning more votes than any other feminist candidate in Paris, especially Durand, who had been "seconded by the press and a regiment of lovers." This pride in personal accomplishment notwithstanding, it also pleased Auclert that she had not stood alone. Misme had stressed that "neither the CNFF, nor the UFSF, nor *La Française* are in favor of this manoeuver." She compared the races to the activities of the English suffragettes, for using "all means that will strike the public's attention." "The great feminist leagues," she claimed, would use "only rational means of action." But there had been nine feminist candidates in Paris and provincial candidates at Amiens, Toulouse, and Vienne. Thus Auclert could bask in the realization that for once she was not alone in offending the moderates.[22]

THE FINAL YEARS

Auclert never retired from feminist activity, but she grew tired. As the noiseless foot of time gained on her, she suffered periodic illnesses. Her papers provide no hint whether these were common ailments exac-

---

21. Minutes of SF meeting, 12 May 1910, Auclert Papers, Carton 4 (first quotation); Drumont, "Les Femmes candidates," *La Libre parole*, 18 April 1910; *L'Eclair*, 15 April 1910.

22. Notes on 1910 elections, Auclert Papers, 7/3 and 6/(unnumbered); "La Réforme électorale et les femmes," ibid., 6/147; minutes of SF meeting, 12 May 1910, ibid., Carton 4 and 9 June 1910, ibid., 6/186; Auclert to Arria Ly, 27 April 1910, Arria Ly Papers, Bouglé Collection, BHVP (first quotation); Misme, "Le Role des femmes pendant les élections," *La Française*, 10 April 1910 (second quotation). For the campaigns of Durand, Kauffmann, Pelletier, and Renaud (who received 2869 votes in Vienne), see Hause with Kenney, *Women's Suffrage and Social Politics*, pp. 145–51.

erbated by age or a serious affliction. She endured no prolonged confinement, but autumn had crept over her. The meetings of Suffrage des femmes declined to monthly instead of fortnightly gatherings, and her summer vacations stretched to four months. She lost her column in a change of management at *Le Radical* but lacked the stamina to accept invitations to begin a new column at *Les Nouvelles*, Durand's paper, or to assume the directorship of Pelletier's *La Suffragiste*. Thoughts of death reappeared in her *pensées*, accompanied by the dread that her work would be forgotten.[23]

She slowed, but Auclert was not the sort to stop for death, despite her words on the subject. She continued to direct Suffrage des femmes. She submitted five more petitions to parliament, including one that stated that she had already experienced "political death." She repeated her traditional poster campaign during the municipal elections of 1912, but she decided that she lacked the resources for any greater demonstration. She worked to prepare a final book, based on her speeches and articles, to be entitled *Les Femmes au gouvernail* (Women at the Rudder). She even undertook a few brief demonstrations of a new type, leading feminist delegations on a short march to the Chamber of Deputies to meet with sympathetic deputies. Auclert and Pelletier had tried this tactic in 1908–1909, and Auclert fondly remembered the delegation of 1909 which had given her petition to Louis Marin with such good results. These marches passed without incident—*sans tapage* in press reports. Auclert did not seek another confrontation with authorities, but she wanted to remind the UFSF that she considered activities in the streets an appropriate form of propaganda. Her meetings with deputies did not produce any important results, although she stimulated a socialist deputy, Marcel Sembat (Seine), to defend women's suffrage on the floor of the chamber; she also won a new supporter for Suffrage des femmes, the maverick radical deputy Louis Andrieux (Alpes-Basses), who became its first honorary president since de Gasté.[24]

23. For Auclert's infirmity, see her correspondence and papers: Auclert to Arria Ly, 3 September 1909, Arria Ly Papers Bouglé Collection, BHVP; C. Bélilon to Auclert, 1 February and 2 March 1914, Auclert Papers, 3/551 and 3/553; note, ibid., 11/348. For the diminution of SF's activities, see the minutes for 1911–1914, ibid., Cartons 4, 5, and 6. For the end of her column at *Le Radical*, see Auclert to M. Angevin (director of *Le Radical*), no date, ibid., 13/12.

24. Petition, "La Peine de mort et les femmes," Dossier Auclert, BMD (quoted); Auclert, *Les Femmes au gouvernail*, pp. 77–80; "Les Suffragettes au Palais Bourbon," *Le Journal*, 26 October 1909 (quoted); minutes of SF meeting, 9 March 1911, Auclert Papers, Carton 4; "Démarches au plusieurs députés (1912)," ibid., 12/2; Auclert to Andrieux, n.d., ibid., 14/34, 13 and 17 November 1913, ibid., 3/582; notes on deputies, ibid., 11/71, 11/74, and 11/75; Andrieux to Auclert, 13 and 29 July 1912, 9 and 15 November 1913, ibid., 3/511, 3/513, 3/530, and 3/532; Chéron to Auclert, 12 February 1912, ibid., 3/521; Sembat to Auclert, ibid., 3/525.

Auclert's political thought did not undergo any significant changes in her last years. She continued to describe herself as a republican feminist and to believe that the true republic would accept woman as *citoyenne.* The events of 1907 and 1908 had soured her feelings for the Radical and Radical-Socialist Party, however; she attacked the party for its "sabotage of republican principles." When Gabrielle Moyse, a member of Suffrage des femmes, created a women's league to support the party in 1913, the Fédération des femmes radicales et radicale-socialistes, Auclert refused Suffrage des femmes' endorsement on the pretext that the society must remain nonpartisan. It would have been more truthful to say that she again perceived republican socialism as the best ally. She no longer had the energy to seek a socialist affiliation, as she had in 1879 and 1885, and she distrusted both wings of the SFIO—the Guesdists were not feminists and the Jauresians were too timid in their support. She believed that most socialists would "dupe" women with false promises, but she told Suffrage des femmes that "the spirit of justice" was stronger in the SFIO than in the Radical and Radical-Socialist Party, and she hinted that she would seek a rapprochement with socialists, if anyone.[25]

Nor did Auclert modulate her rhetoric or diminish her militancy. Slaves, martyrs, and sheep still strode through her phases. In a heated speech to Suffrage des femmes in 1912, she spoke with her old fire: "We no longer have a king in France, but we have 897 potentates" creating laws "which rape justice." In 1913, when *Gil Blas* sought her opinion as "one of the most notorious feminists" on the subject of the English suffragettes, the newspapers quoted Auclert's belief that direct action "would not have any success" in France. In fact, she told Suffrage des femmes the same year that the English militants had gone too far: "French suffragettes cannot approve of them." But *Gil Blas* also portrayed Auclert as advocating "mildness." She immediately wrote a letter to the editor insisting that she was still "dangerous" and was already considering "direct action at the next elections."[26]

Auclert did not live long enough to fulfill this threat. She died at her apartment on the morning of April 8, 1914, two weeks before the parliamentary elections, at the beginning of the largest suffrage campaign in France since her founding effort in 1880–1881. According to

25. Minutes of SF meetings, 12 May 1910 (third quotation), 10 November 1910, 9 March 1911, 8 December 1912 (first quotation), and undated, Auclert Papers, Carton 4; notes on the 1910 elections, ibid., 6/162 (second quotation); "Les Ouvriers et les femmes," ibid., 7/20; "Un Miracle socialiste," ibid., 6/168; notes, ibid., 6/171; "La Réforme électorale et les femmes," ibid., 6/147; *La Française,* 29 November 1913.

26. Partial minutes of SF meeting, undated (1912), Auclert Papers, 5/6 (first quotation); "L'Action directe et les plus notoires féministes françaises," *Gil Blas,* 26 February 1913 (second quotation); police report, 14 March 1913, Dossier Auclert, APP (third quotation); Auclert to *Gil Blas,* 28 February 1913, Auclert Papers, 12/67 (fourth quotation).

Camille Bélilon, Auclert suffered constantly during the months of her final illness. Nonetheless, she presided over occasional meetings of Suffrage des femmes at her apartment. As late as mid-March she persuaded the group that the time had come to organize "a monster demonstration in the streets." Although she died with this idea an improbable dream, *pallida Mors* had arranged another irony in a life so filled with them. Fench suffragists staged an unprecedented public demonstration in 1914, the Condorcet demonstration of July 5, in which five to six thousand women marched from the Tuileries gardens to lay a wreath at the statue of Condorcet on the Left Bank. Jane Misme herself cautioned readers of *La Française* to behave because "this is the first demonstration in the streets that French feminists have organized"![27]

Auclert's final response to such treatment by her contemporaries appeared in her will, written in September 1913. For thirty years, she had unequivocally criticized French women for refusing to support feminism financially, specifically complaining that the well-to-do did not leave bequests to sustain the movement. She bemoaned the parsimony of her wealthy followers who died. In the unfinished manuscript of *Les Femmes au gouvernail*, she asked, "Why do all rich women depart without thinking of their sex?" Auclert had directly criticized Maria Deraismes for leaving her entire estate to her sister, but Auclert did exactly the same thing herself: 57,933.80 francs to Marie, nothing to the movement. Auclert certainly knew what she was doing, so one must assume that her Parthian shot contained a message. She had several alternatives: to endow Suffrage des femmes, to sustain Pelletier's *La Suffragiste*, to aid poorer colleagues (especially Kauffmann or Bélilon) who had stood with her, to fund a feminist prize. A legacy of ten thousand francs would have been a huge amount for a society accustomed to an annual budget of less than five hundred francs, and it would have set the precedent for others. It seems unlikely that her sister was in desperate straits; she too had inherited an independent estate from their father, and she had married a middle-class professional. Thus, one must assume that Auclert chose to show her feminist colleagues that she could reject them, too.[28]

Auclert was interred at Père Lachaise, in the tomb she had fought to obtain for Lévrier. The funeral announcement sent by her family re-

27. Death certificate no. 1242, 8 April 1914, Etat civil, Mairie du XIe Arrondissement; C. Bélilon to Auclert, 1 February 1914 and 2 March 1914, Auclert Papers, 3/551 and 3/553; unidentified clipping, Dossier Auclert, BMD (second quotation); Misme, "Manifestation du 5 juillet," *La Française*, 27 June 1914; Dossier Manifestation Condorcet, BMD. For the demonstration and other activities of 1914, see Hause with Kenney, *Women's Suffrage and Social Politics*, pp. 169–90.

28. Auclert's will, notarized 18 April 1914, Ministère des finances, Archives des direction de l'enregistrement. Auclert, *Les Femmes au gouvernail*, pp. 203–5.

vealed the persistence of the traditional forms that Auclert had com-
bated; it identified her as "Madame Veuve Antonin Lévrier. Née Marie
Anne Hubertine Auclert." A large crowd of feminists, representing
every group except the UFSF, gathered at her tomb—an indication that
Auclert had not been as alone as she thought, particularly when her
funeral, with its front-page newspaper coverage, is compared to the sad
and solitary passing of some colleagues during the next two decades.
More than a dozen people spoke over her grave, including Durand,
Bonnevial, Vérone, and Kauffmann (Vincent had died a week earlier and
Oddo-Deflou was away from Paris). None of them bettered the epitaph
that Auclert had written for the burial of Feresse-Deraismes in 1911: "In
this city of the dead, you will at last be the equal of the men who
despoiled you of your rights and made you their inferior in the city of the
living. When the republic becomes the government of everyone . . .
feminists will remember that you . . . labored for the emancipation of
French women. . . . Adieu."[29]

Marie Chaumont, who had been a devoted follower but never an
activist, kept Suffrage des femmes alive after Auclert's death with help
from Chapuis, who died in 1916, and Bélilon. She fended off a remarkably crude effort by Madame Remember, a recent convert to suffragism,
to take over the group, but she could not preserve her sister's militancy.
Wartime patriotism, which she correctly insisted Auclert would have
shared, and emphasis upon social feminism, which Auclert would have
opposed, actually increased the society's membership to 150 by the time
of the armistice of 1918, but new statutes left it a pale shadow of the
past. Chaumont organized annual convocations to honor the memory of
her sister; with the women of Etudes she secured the installation of a
memorial tablet on the facade of Auclert's residence at 151, rue de la
Roquette in 1924. Her greatest work of commemoration, however, was
to complete the editing of *Les Femmes au gouvernail,* which finally
appeared in 1923. That project kept Suffrage des femmes together after
World War I until the society collapsed in 1926 when the city of Paris
demanded rental for meeting rooms. Marie died in 1934 and was buried
in her sister's tomb under the name "Veuve Lucien Chaumont." (Had
no one in the family read Auclert's *Le Nom de la femme?*) One of Marie's
final acts was the preservation of her sister's private papers, essential to
the reconstruction of Auclert's life and thought.[30]

29. Invitation to interment, Auclert Papers, folder "divers," Carton 14; obituaries,
ibid., folder "Articles nécrologiques," Carton 13; "Sur la tombe de Madame Feresse-
Deraismes," ibid., 6/52.
30. For the final years of SF, see Chapuis' program for SF, ibid., 3/616; minutes of SF,
1916–1924, ibid., Carton 5; folder, "Documents convocations" (1914–1929), ibid., Carton
10; Chaumont correspondence, 1914–1928, ibid., Carton 3; Remember to Chaumont, 13
April 1914, ibid., 3/561; Chapuis to Chaumont, 9 June 1914, ibid., 3/557; Camille Bélilon

Hubertine Auclert had lived between two worlds, one dying, the other powerless to be born. She awaited her idealistic true republic, which would bring social justice and human rights. It would bring them to workers, exploited as a class, and to Arabs, exploited as a race, but most of all it would bring the equality of women. Auclert conceived of this equality as an integral feminism, by which term she meant a revolution much larger than the acquisition of civil and political rights, a revolution that transformed attitudes, behavior, even the words to describe them. Portions of her vision were naive (that "the natural parsimony" of women would conquer "masculine diseconomy," or that "women's suffrage will guarantee peace"), but they do not diminish the force of the premise that summoned women to her revolution: "Any society organized without the participation of women will be organized against the interests of women."[31]

Auclert never elucidated integral feminism as a systematic doctrine, although she expressed it in the enormous range of women's issues that she wrote about. Instead, she concentrated upon republican feminism as the route to the future: women must seek their revolution by first obtaining political equality within the republic. "To vote is not a goal," she wrote, "it is a means." The ballot represented "the basis of emancipation," and Auclert dedicated her life to obtaining it. As one of her obituaries put it, "her ardor and perseverance were extraordinary." Although an idealist in her general conception, she became a pragmatist in this combat. Thus Auclert collaborated at *Le Prolétaire*, at *La Libre parole*, at *Le Radical*. She sought a lasting political alliance, but never found more than gestures without motion. Consequently, she denounced the discrepancy between republican principles and republican practices, between socialist theories and socialist actions.[32]

Papers, Dossier 2, Bouglé Collection, BHVP; speeches and notes, ibid., Dossier 5; Chaumont to Arria Ly, April 1918, Arria Ly Papers, Bouglé Collection, BHVP; Chaumont–C. Bélilon Correspondence, 1915–1926, Dossier Marie Chaumont, CP 4247, BHVP; Chapuis–Arria Ly Correspondence, 1913–1914, Arria Ly Papers, Bouglé Collection, BHVP; Chaumont manuscripts, 1919–1926, Auclert Papers, Carton 14; police reports, October 1918, Police générale files, F⁷ 13266, AN; police reports on SF, 2 July 1915, and on Chaumont, 14 May 1917, Dossier "Le Mouvement féministe," APP; Durand's speech at the installation of Auclert's memorial tablet, 28 December 1924, Dossier Auclert, BMD.

31. The summary of Auclert's thought in these paragraphs draws heavily on the *pensées* that she jotted down in her final years. For her use of "the true republic," see the minutes of the SF meeting, 14 April 1910, Auclert Papers, Carton 4; for "integral feminism," see her fragmentary autobiography, ibid., 14/47. The quotation of parsimony is from "L'Avarice des femmes," *La Citoyenne*, December 1884; on peace, from the minutes of the SF meeting, 14 June 1901, Auclert Papers, Carton 4 (see also illustration 4, above), final quotation, notes, ibid., 11/331.

32. *Pensées*, ibid., 8/137, 8/138 (first quotation); Auclert, "Le Nom et l'argent," *La Citoyenne*, August 1889 (second quotation); Arria Ly, "Hubertine Auclert," *Le Combat féministe*, July 1914.

Auclert recognized the unpopularity of her ideas, but she believed that they would be accepted in the future. "New ideas," she wrote, "are like the green fruits which everyone rejects, but which everyone loves when the sun has ripened them." This thought led to her realization that single individuals do not produce great revolutions, that *mentalités* only change over the *longue durée:* "At the society Suffrage des femmes, we have tried to force the development of feminist ideas as gardeners try to force the flowering of plants; but . . . forcing does not produce new convictions. It takes, alas! time to make flowers bloom, as it does to change *mentalités.* But time is long and life is short!" When depressed, Auclert feared that her efforts in political horticulture had been "absolutely sterile"; but she reluctantly realized that her role had been to plant the seed of women's suffrage in France and to prepare others to cultivate it, even if they scorned her personally.[33]

The subject of Auclert's relations with her contemporaries, like biography itself, offers an enriching perspective on the past because it examines the connections between the individual's personal existence and the larger issues of her epoch. Auclert's contemporaries never quite accepted her, either as a political leader or as a person. The rejection of her politics can be explored profitably without much reference to her private life because equality for women and resistance to it are best understood in terms larger than an individual life. But as Auclert's career vividly shows, there is a constant interplay between the human being and her politics; this reciprocal relationship demands an understanding of the person involved in the politics.

Hubertine Auclert did not live a happy personal life, buoyed with exhilaration from heroic combat or stabilized with private joys. She lived with torment and insecurity, seeing herself as a martyr, lonely and rejected as a person just as she was in politics. Her life illustrates the price that a person pays for challenging the established order and rejecting traditional roles; it is also the story of conscious choices that an unhappy and mercurial person made. Auclert thought that she faced a "formidable colossus of hate, of spitefulness, of human ingratitude."[34] She exaggerated, but such feelings shaped her politics, creating a vicious circle of further rejection. "God tries each man," Yeats wrote, "according to a different plan." Auclert's trial was a small tragedy of an individual caught in that brief transit where dreams cross reality. She possessed a personality superbly suited to opening a historic debate, and she earned her place in history by doing so; equally ill-suited to the closing

---

33. *Pensées,* Auclert Papers, 8/129 (first quotation); notes, ibid., 11/340 (second quotation) and 8/126 (third quotation).

34. Diary, 31 December 1884, Auclert Papers.

of this debate, she yet devoted her life to finding a finish worthy of the start.

The most striking human characteristic to emerge from this dialectic between career and personal life is Auclert's extraordinary strength of will. But will alone does not change history; Hubertine Auclert died thirty years before French women obtained the right that she demanded. Roman law, whose effects on women she fought to eradicate, provides an ironical dictum for evaluating this fact and her life. The law says that sometimes we must conclude *Voluntas habetur pro facto:* The will is taken for the deed.

APPENDIX ONE

Auclert's Newspaper Articles, 1876–1911

This inventory omits many articles found as clippings in the Auclert Papers because complete citations are not available. It also omits letters to the editor, published documents, and unsigned articles.

I. *L'Avenir des femmes,* 1876

1. "Les Ouvrières," February 1876
2. "Les Ouvrières," March 1876
3. "Aux femmes!", November 1876

II. *La Citoyenne,* 1881–1891

[* indicates articles reprinted in Taïeb]

A. Articles signed "Hubertine Auclert"

1. "La 'Citoyenne,'" 13 February 1881*
2. "L'Habit fait l'électeur," 20 February 1881
3. "La Puissance du vote," 27 February 1881
4. "Une Objection banale," 6 March 1881*
5. "Les Mères peuvent voter," 13 March 1881
6. "Faut-il se battre pour voter," 20 March 1881
7. "Les Hypocrites," 27 March 1881
8. "Ceci remplacera cela," 3 April 1881
9. "Les Femmes ne peuvent s'instruire," 10 April 1881
10. "Les Femmes et la guerre," 17 April 1881
11. "Une Loi stérile," 24 April 1881*
12. "Impératrices et citoyennes," 1 May 1881

13. "Malheur aux absentes!", 8 May 1881*
14. "La Question n'est pas mûre," 16 May 1881
15. "Que fait le Conseil d'état," 22 May 1881
16. "55 députés de plus," 29 May 1881
17. "Pourquoi les femmes veulent controler les budgets," 5 June 1881*
18. "Réponse d'un député," 12 June 1881
19. "L'Arrêt du Conseil d'état," 19 June 1881
20. "Les Femmes juges," 26 June 1881
21. "La Politique n'interesse pas les femmes," 3 July 1881*
22. "La Bastille des femmes," 10 July 1881
23. "Les Femmes voient trop clair," 17 July 1881
24. "La Situation économique des femmes," 24 July 1881
25. "Femmes! Vous allez prendre notre place!", 31 July 1881*
26. "L'Education des souverains," 7 August 1881
27. "Programme logique," 14 August 1881*
28. "Le Coup du 21 août," 21 August 1881
29. "Les Marquis de Sennecy," 28 August 1881
30. "Pourquoi l'on s'abstient de voter," 4 September 1881
31. "Les Bulletins volés," 11 September 1881
32. "Le Bagne conjugale," 19 September 1881
33. "La Loi d'harmonie," 26 September 1881
34. "Le Service militaire des femmes," 3 October 1881
35. "Ecoles normales d'institutrices," 10 October 1881*
36. "Le Réveil de la conscience publique," 17 October 1881*
37. "Ce que valent les ennemies du droit des femmes," 24 October 1881
38. "Qui veut la fin veut les moyens," 31 October 1881
39. "La Nouvelle chambre," 7 November 1881
40. "Les Maris assassins," 14 November 1881
41. "L'Avocat général Florichon," 21 November 1881
42. "Les Déclassés," 28 November 1881
43. "Les Contrats de mariage," 5 December 1881
44. "Les Femmes et le recensement," 12 December 1881
45. "La Dot," 19 December 1881*
46. "L'Union libre," 26 December 1881
47. "L'Année," 2 January 1881
48. "Le Scandale," 9 January 1881
49. "28,000 Francs de dot," 16 January 1882
50. "La Femme est destituée de la tutelle," 23 January 1882
51. "Nos Petits maîtres," 5 February 1882
52. "Les Alphonses brevetés," 12 February 1882
53. "La Sphère des femmes," 19 February 1882*
54. "Le Jargon du palais," 26 February 1882
55. "Virtue de Chrusocale," 5 March 1882
56. "Les Monopoleurs du témoignage," 12 March 1882
57. "Le Somerville-Club," 19 March 1882*
58. "Le Divorce," April 1882
59. "Pour faire triompher son opinion," 6 May 1882*
60. "Les Judiths modernes," 5 June 1882

61. "La Fête des hommes," 2 July 1882
62. "Féodaux du XIXe siècle," 6 August 1882
63. "Faites donner les femmes," 4 September 1882
64. "Les Tireuses de marrons," 1 October 1882
65. "L'Abdication nécessaire," 6 November 1882
66. "Les Hommes cléricaux," 4 December 1882
67. "La Chasse interdite aux femmes," 7 January 1883
68. "Le Suffrage des femmes," 5 February 1883*
69. "Les Sénateurs criminels," 5 March 1883
70. "Comment on doit reviser la constitution," 2 April 1883
71. "Les Hommes mères de famille," 7 May 1883
72. "La Vote des femmes au Canada," 4 June 1883
73. "La Séparation du budget des fêtes," 2 July 1883
74. "16 Voix à déplacer," 6 August 1883
75. "La Femme en voyage," 3 September 1883
76. "La Femme vivisectée," 8 October 1883
77. "L'Obstacle supprimé," 15 November 1883
78. "La Femme imprimeur," 3 December 1883*
79. "Les Femmes juges-consulaires," January 1884
80. "Les Députés," February 1884
81. "Les Hommes seuls," March 1884
82. "Pour être belle," April 1884
83. "La Pilule politique," May 1884
84. "Les Conseillères municipales," June 1884
85. "La Fête des femmes," July 1884
86. "Le Mariage et les cordons de la bourse," August 1884*
87. "Un Juge et une joli femme," September 1884
88. "La République menacée par le cabaret," October 1884
89. "Des Femmes à la caisse," November 1884
90. "L'Avarice des femmes," December 1884
91. "Trop ou pas assez de rois," January 1885
92. "La Femme bouc émissaire," February 1885
93. "Delpit—L'Apostolat," March 1885
94. "La Loi électorale et les femmes," April 1885
95. "Lutte de classes, lutte de sexes," May 1885*
96. "Budget de 1885," June 1885*
97. "La Liberté," July 1885
98. "Programme électoral des femmes," August 1885
99. "Femmes députées," September 1885
100. "La Royauté," October 1885
101. "Les Femmes capables," November 1885
102. "Le Vote des célibataires," December 1885
103. "Le Serment devant l'urne," January 1886
104. "Les Femmes dans l'armée," February 1886
105. "La Femme diplomate," March 1886
106. "Pharmacienne," April 1886
107. "Les Femmes non représentées au parlement," May 1886
108. "L'Homme est trop grand," June 1886

109. "Les Lois d'exception et les femmes," July 1886
110. "Les Privilégiés," August 1886
111. "A bas le monopole électoral," September 1886
112. "Des Prud'femmes," October 1886
113. "Des Prud'femmes," November 1886
114. "La Peur du progrès," December 1886
115. "Une Femme élue," January 1887
116. "Le Mariage de demain," February 1887
117. "La Femme chassée de la cuisine," March 1887
118. "Des Femmes à l'Hotel de Ville," April 1887
119. "Les Femmes en cas de guerre," May 1887
120. "L'Autonomie communale et les femmes," June 1887
121. "L'Incurie masculine," July 1887
122. "La Fédération de 1889 et les femmes," August 1887
123. "Féminisez," September 1887
124. "Le Pouvoir d'abolir la Police des moeurs," October 1887
125. "Une Leçon," December 1887*
126. "Eh bien! Marchons-nous?", February 1888
127. "Un Mot de marche," March 1888*
128. "M. Michelin et les femmes," December 1888
129. "Voile et viol," January 1889
130. "Vote interdit; vote imposé," February 1889
131. "Doux aux voleurs, durs aux femmes," March 1889
132. "La Femme arabe," April 1889
133. "Le Mariage arabe," May 1889
134. "Le Quatre-vingt-neuf des femmes," June 1889*
135. "Le Nom et l'argent," August 1889*
136. "Les Votants de demain," September 1889
137. "Les Déshéritées de la République," October 1889
138. "La République des femmes," November 1889
139. "Le Traffic du vote," January 1890
140. "Les Femmes officiers de l'état," February 1890
141. "En puissance," March 1890
142. "Affameurs de femmes," April 1890
143. "Les Parias françaises," May 1890
144. "Masculinisme international," June 1890
145. "Le Devoir du vote," July 1890
146. "Des Jugesses," August 1890
147. "Sensiblerie masculine," September 1890
148. "La Cantinière," October 1890
149. "Ma Gazelle Yzette," October 1890
150. "*La Citoyenne* en Afrique," November 1890
151. "Ma Gazelle Yzette," December 1890
152. "Campagne Lavigerienne," 1 February 1891
153. "Les Maisons centrales de femmes," 15 February 1891
154. "Arabophobes-Arabophiles," 15 March 1891
155. "La Polygamie en France," 1 April 1891
156. "Françisons l'Algérie," 15 April 1891

157. "L'Avis des musulmanes," 1 May 1891
158. "La Journée de vingt heures," 15 May 1891*
159. "Une Libre-penseuse au Pape Léon XIII," 1 June 1891
160. "Les Sauterelles," 15 June 1891
161. "Plus de licou!", 1 July 1891
162. "Le Partage du travail," 1 July 1891
163. "Les Hommes tortue," 15 July 1891
164. "Commission fainéante," 1 August 1891
165. "Wagons de dames seules," 15 August 1891
166. "Esclaves d'amour," 1 September 1891
167. "Organisatrice de la victoire," 15 September 1891
168. "Leçon des femmes aux hommes," 1 October 1891
169. "Comédie masculine," 15 October 1891
170. "Sages-femmes d'Algérie," 1 November 1891
171. "Ministre et Mauresque," 15 November 1891

B. Articles signed "H. A."

1. "La Dernière grimace du singe Littré," 12 June 1881
2. "Un Député provisoire," 3 July 1881
3. "Au Ministre de la guerre," 12 December 1881
4. "En Bourse," 29 January 1882
5. "M. Thomas," April 1882
6. "La Prostitution," 6 May 1882
7. "Le Banquet de l'Hôtel de Ville," 2 July 1882
8. "L'Impôt sur les hommes-femmes," 6 August 1882
9. "L'Associée," April 1884
10. "La Bastille des femmes," July 1887
11. "Des Femmes au gouvernail," December 1887
12. "Huitième année," January 1888

C. Articles signed "Liberta"

1. "Le Prix Botta," 19 June 1881
2. "Académie des femmes," 26 June 1881
3. "Babylone assainié," 31 July 1881
4. "Un Homme rôti," 21 August 1881
5. "La Morale masculine," 4 September 1881 (attribution unverified)
6. "L'Homme prise la main dans le sac," 17 October 1881
7. "Liberté," 16 January 1882
8. "Le Divorce," 2 July 1882
9. "Histoire d'hier et d'aujourd'hui," January 1884
10. "Le Divorce est voté," June 1884
11. "Mme Clovis Hugues sera acquittée," December 1884
12. "Les Dames seules," March 1885
13. "La Guerre," April 1885
14. "L'Etat civils des canards," May 1885
15. "Bibliographie," July 1885
16. "Les Femmes et le Franc-maçonnerie," October 1885

17. "La Loi sur les faillités et les femmes," November 1885
18. "Les Femmes ne reçoivent rien," December 1885
19. "Juges complices des maris-assassins," February 1886
20. "Les Compositrices pour aveugles," March 1886
21. "Femmes d'épée," May 1886
22. "L'Injustice à l'Hôtel de Ville," August 1886
23. "Les Hommes sages-femmes," September 1886
24. "Le Drapeau de Paul Soleillet," October 1886
25. "L'Epingle de M. Scholl," April 1887
26. "L'Influence française compromise à Madagascar," May 1887
27. "Mme Paul Bert," September 1887
28. "Pas d'aumones du travail," October 1888
29. "M. de Gasté, président," 1 February 1891

D. *Articles signed "Jeanne Voitout"*

1. "La Malpropreté des administrateurs de Paris," 6 May 1882
2. "Les Logements de femme," 5 June 1882
3. "Les Manants de Bordeaux," 1 October 1882
4. "Les Secours publics," 6 November 1882
5. "Correspondance," 4 December 1882
6. "M. de Gasté, 5 March 1883
7. "Matinées et concerts," 7 May 1883
8. "Revue de la presse," 4 June 1883
9. "La Recherche de la paternité," 2 July 1883
10. "Revue de la presse," 8 October 1883
11. "Explication nécessaire," January 1884
12. "Les Justicières," February 1884
13. "M. de Gasté au Sénat," June 1884
14. "La Presse et l'élection des femmes," July 1884
15. "*Cri du peuple, Figaro, Soleil,*" August 1884
16. "Le Vote des femmes au congrès," September 1884
17. "Le Célibat de nos compatriotes," October 1884
18. "Le Nom," December 1884
19. "Le Péril," May 1885
20. "Une Loi à refaire," July 1885
21. "Les Moeurs anglais," August 1885
22. "Candidatures féminines," September 1885
23. "Voix volées," October 1885
24. "Mouvement féministe," November 1885
25. "Mouvement féministe," December 1885
26. "Séverine," January 1886
27. "La Recherche de la paternité admise," February 1886
28. "Les Femmes électrices et éligibles aux conseils départmentaux d'enseignement," March 1886
29. "Les Femmes et l'exposition," April 1886
30. "Le Règne de la fille," May 1886
31. "Les Navigatrices," July 1886

32. "La Prostitution," August 1886
33. "Nos insulteurs corrigés," September 1886
34. "Les Femmes et l'exposition," November 1886
35. "Un Homme gifflé," February 1887
36. "Une Victoire," March 1887
37. "L'Exclusion des femmes du gouvernement," April 1887
38. "L'Unisexificaton des vêtements," June 1887
39. "Partialité masculine," August 1887
40. "Frappez la déloyauté masculine," September 1887
41. "Disons déléguée," October 1887
42. "Aveux et regrets," November 1887
43. "Françaises non électrices, Prussien électeur," December 1887
44. "Plus de prions de femmes," February 1888
45. "Les Jeunes filles conscrits," March 1888
46. "Les Républicaines orléanistes," April 1890

III. *La Libre parole*, 1894

[All articles headed "Les Droits de la femme"]

1. 24 March 1894
2. 19 April 1894
3. 3 May 1894
4. 10 May 1894
5. 17 May 1894
6. 26 May 1894
7. 11 June 1894
8. 7 July 1894
9. 14 July 1894
10. 15 August 1894
11. 22 August 1894
12. 10 September 1894

IV. *Le Radical*, 1896–1909

1. "Russes et françaises," 4 October 1896
2. "Diplomate officieuse," 12 October 1896
3. "La Sans patrie," 18 October 1896
4. "Les Ménagères nationales," 24 October 1896
5. "Un Cercle des femmes," 31 October 1896
6. "La Femme dans la commune," 15 November 1896
7. "La Femme et l'Algérie," 22 November 1896
8. "Les Femmes et la budget," 28 November 1896
9. "Les Femmes artistes," 6 December 1896
10. "Indemnité maternelle," 13 December 1896
11. "Madame ou mademoiselle," 22 December 1896
12. "Le Choix d'un mariage," 4 January 1897
13. "Les Femmes et l'exposition," 10 January 1897
14. "Organisation du mouvement," 17 January 1897

15. "Emplois aux colonies," 24 January 1897
16. "Justiciables, pas juges," 1 February 1897
17. "Le Salaire du mari," 8 February 1897
18. "L'Education politique," 14 February 1897
19. "La Loi de la femme," 23 February 1897
20. "Le Mari de la compositrice," 1 March 1897
21. "Les Femmes témoins," 9 March 1897
22. "Mannequin pour modes," 14 March 1897
23. "Les Doctoresses et le service médical de l'exposition," 22 March 1897
24. "Et les anciennes?", 29 March 1897
25. "La Dot," 6 April 1897
26. "Les Placeuses," 15 April 1897
27. "Les Doigts blancs," 18 April 1897
28. "L'Esclave est morte!", 25 April 1897
29. "1er mai des femmes," 3 May 1897
30. "La Femme riz-pain-sel," 10 May 1897
31. "La Galantrie," 17 May 1897
32. "La Proposition blachette," 23 May 1897
33. "L'Ennemie de la femme," 30 May 1897
34. "La Femme en état de légitime défense," 8 June 1897
35. "L'Emmigration des femmes," 15 June 1897
36. "L'Influence électorale des femmes," 22 June 1897
37. "Les Dégradées d'origine," 28 June 1897
38. "Matriarcat," 6 July 1897
39. "Les Employées du commerce," 11 July 1897
40. "La Bastille des femmes," 20 July 1897
41. "Le Divorce pour cause," 25 July 1897
42. "Députés et chapeaux de fermiéres," 2 August 1897
43. "Les Vacances des vieilles parisiennes," 9 August 1897
44. "La Femme et la science," 15 August 1897
45. "Pacte proposé à la femme," 22 August 1897
46. "La Table et le marché," 29 August 1897
47. "Les Gardiens de 'La Poigne,'" 5 September 1897
48. "Des Prud'femmes," 12 September 1897
49. "La Braconnière," 19 September 1897
50. "Le Souverain des corporations," 27 September 1897
51. "Polygamie," 30 September 1897
52. "Le Nom de la femme mariée," 3 October 1897
53. "La Compétence des sages-femmes," 11 October 1897
54. "L'Autorité maritale," 17 October 1897
55. "Hors le droit," 24 October 1897
56. "Logements de femmes," 1 November 1897
57. "Le Thé et la liberté," 8 November 1897
58. "Elles voteraient demain!", 15 November 1897
59. "L'Exploitation des religieuses," 23 November 1897
60. "Le Passe-partout," 29 November 1897
61. "La Payeuse de plaisirs," 7 December 1897
62. "Les Frondeuses," 12 December 1897

63. "Les Epoux et le témoignage," 19 December 1897
64. "Cartes de visite de femmes," 28 December 1897
65. "Souhaits des femmes," 3 January 1898
66. "Les Belles 'premières,'" 11 January 1898
67. "Emancipation et vertu," 17 January 1898
68. "Directrices de prisons," 25 January 1898
69. "Commerçantes électeurs," 30 January 1898
70. "Le Cours de M. Flach," 7 February 1898
71. "Fraudes électorales," 15 February 1898
72. "Taxes sur les écrins," 20 February 1898
73. "Responsables d'ève," 27 February 1898
74. "Un Nouveau mystère," 8 March 1898
75. "Colonisatrices," 13 March 1898
76. "Les Précurseurs," 20 March 1898
77. "Les Croque-institutrices," 29 March 1898
78. "Candidats," 4 April 1898
79. "Professeur de politesse," 10 April 1898
80. "L'Académie et la langue," 18 April 1898
81. "Les Florifères," 25 April 1898
82. "Les Candidates," 1 May 1898
83. "La Femme muselée," 8 May 1898
84. "Voix données aux femmes," 17 May 1898
85. "La Future du citoyenne," 22 May 1898
86. "Curateur au ventre," 29 May 1898
87. "Les Conciliatrices," 7 June 1898
88. "L'Union libre," 12 June 1898
89. "M. Jaluxot et le tabouret," 21 June 1898
90. "Les Jeunes filles," 26 June 1898
91. "Maria Deraismes," 3 July 1898
92. "Michelet et les femmes," 12 July 1898
93. "Hommes dames de charité," 17 July 1898
94. "Pseudonymes," 26 July 1898
95. "Femmes de prisonniers," 3 August 1898
96. "Lire! Hériter!", 9 August 1898
97. "Le Referendum et les femmes," 15 August 1898
98. "Le Travail des femmes," 21 August 1898
99. "Contrat de mariage," 29 August 1898
100. "Les Hommes nourrices," 4 September 1898
101. "Les Patentées," 15 September 1898
102. "Tueurs de femmes," 27 September 1898
103. "Honneur et l'amour," 4 October 1898
104. "La Doyenne des lingères," 9 October 1898
105. "Place aux femmes!", 17 October 1898
106. "Les Electeurs-prêtres," 25 October 1898
107. "La Séparation de biens," 31 October 1898
108. "Un Cercle de femmes," 1 November 1898
109. "Cléricales et snobisme," 7 November 1898
110. "Interdite et responsable," 13 November 1898

111. "La Liberté de divorcer," 21 November 1898
112. "Doctoresses de l'état-civil," 27 November 1898
113. "Les Femmes artistes," 7 December 1898
114. "L'Eau de cologne surtaxée," 14 December 1898
115. "La Loi du nombre," 19 December 1898
116. "Une Correction," 26 December 1898
117. "Les Barbiers politiques," 5 January 1899
118. "L'Exemption du bâtard," 9 January 1899
119. "La Bureaucrate," 17 January 1899
120. "Le Cambrioleur légal," 24 January 1899
121. "Il n'y a pas de patriotes," 30 January 1899
122. "Terrifiante fécondité," 7 February 1899
123. "Beau sexe," 13 February 1899
124. "Doctoresse oculiste," 23 February 1899
125. "Elles sont les nègres," 6 March 1899
126. "Désarmement primordial," 14 March 1899
127. "Les Chats de Saint-Ambroise," 21 March 1899
128. "Leux égale," 31 March 1899
129. "L'Epargne des femmes," 5 April 1899
130. "La Défense et les femmes," 10 April 1899
131. "La Mort-aux-hommes," 16 April 1899
132. "Un Mari d'aujourd 'hui," 25 April 1899
133. "L'Age et le sexe," 2 May 1899
134. "Les Risques de la maternité," 10 May 1899
135. "Un Conseil d'Alexandre Dumas," 15 May 1899
136. "Notre Jeanne," 25 May 1899
137. "La Loi des sièges," 30 May 1899
138. "Epoux sauvés par leur contrat," 4 June 1899
139. "Un Art féminin," 19 June 1899
140. "Nids désertés," 26 June 1899
141. "La Prostitution est un sacerdoce," 3 July 1899
142. "Femmes avocats," 11 July 1899
143. "Rubans honorifiques," 18 July 1899
144. "Les Piétons parisiens," 24 July 1899
145. "Une Chaise pour trois," 2 August 1899
146. "Mlle Maitre, pharmacien," 8 August 1899
147. "Lycées mixtes," 15 August 1899
148. "L'Eau et les femmes," 22 August 1899
149. "Les Veuves," 29 August 1899
150. "Tireuses de marrons," 5 September 1899
151. "L'Internat du lycée Lamartine," 11 September 1899
152. "L'Obligation alimentaire," 18 September 1899
153. "Les Femmes en or," 24 September 1899
154. "Un Défenseur pour l'épouse accusée," 5 October 1899
155. "L'Empreinte du ventre," 9 October 1899
156. "Bachelières," 18 October 1899
157. "Les Congrès de l'exposition," 23 October 1899
158. "La Demande en mariage," 31 October 1899

159. "L'Inquisition contre les filles-mères," 10 November 1899
160. "L'Homme des femmes," 13 November 1899
161. "Nourrices et préfets," 28 November 1899
162. "Prix Botha," 4 December 1899
163. "Vous n'êtes pas militaires," 12 December 1899
164. "Pas de cabines! Des femmes!", 21 December 1899
165. "La Robe," 26 December 1899
166. "Des Femmes maires," 2 January 1900
167. "L'Institutrice aux sept enfants," 8 January 1900
168. "Le Vote des célibataires," 16 January 1900
169. "La Femme dentiste," 23 January 1900
170. "Et la majorité?", 28 January 1900
171. "Misères de femmes," 6 February 1900
172. "Le Droit de s'asseoir," 12 February 1900
173. "La Joie des vendeuses," 28 February 1900
174. "Mariage d'amour," 2 March 1900
175. "Le Suffrage des célibataires," 7 March 1900
176. "La Présomption de service," 12 March 1900
177. "Le Mariage des officiers," 20 March 1900
178. "L'Influence des femmes," 26 March 1900
179. "Les Littératrices éligibles," 3 April 1900
180. "Bête à plaisir," 9 April 1900
181. "L'Or libérateur," 17 April 1900
182. "Les Parisiens japonais," 22 April 1900
183. "Remercions les édiles," 1 May 1900
184. "Les Principes," 26 May 1900
185. "La Peur des mots," 28 May 1900
186. "L'Enfant des divorcés, 3 June 1900
187. "Des Femmes jurées," 12 June 1900
188. "Les Femmes à l'exposition," 19 June 1900
189. "Arrière les biens avisés," 26 June 1900
190. "Et les Parisiennes?", 5 July 1900
191. "La Force morale," 10 July 1900
192. "L'Initiative d'une lettre," 16 July 1900
193. "Un Boxer," 24 July 1900
194. "Droit de petitionner," 30 July 1900
195. "Féminisez la langue," 12 August 1900
196. "M. le Curé n'aime pas le divorce," 17 August 1900
197. "Requête à l'académie," 24 August 1900
198. "L'Aristocrate en la société," 2 September 1900
199. "L'Encensoir," 13 September 1900
200. "Les Mairesses," 25 September 1900
201. "Les Présidentes," 27 September 1900
202. "La Probité et la paix," 5 October 1900
203. "M. Jonnart et les mauresques," 23 October 1900
204. "Victimes expiatoires," 28 October 1900
205. "Les Sans-tickets," 6 November 1900
206. "Tactique," 13 November 1900

253. "Le Nom des nés hors mariages," 11 December 1901
254. "Gardez votre nom," 21 December 1901
255. "Les Féministes et les élections," 3 January 1902
256. "Baptiseurs et débaptiseurs," 14 January 1902
257. "Le Prix de Chicago," 21 January 1902
258. "Elles créent des sièges législatifs," 14 January 1902
259. "Pourquoi les timbres coloniaux," 18 February 1902
260. "Victor Hugo féministe," 7 March 1902
261. "Recompensez la maternité," 18 March 1902
262. "Elles sont laissées en otage à la réaction," 1 April 1902
263. "L'Affiche des femmes," 15 April 1902
264. "Faites nommer des républicains," 26 April 1902
265. "Enseigneurs rétrogrades," 20 May 1902
266. "Le Casier civil," 4 June 1902
267. "La Première réforme," 16 June 1902
268. "Comité international du suffrage," 25 June 1902
269. "L'Exposition des arts et métiers féminins," 1 July 1902
270. "Elections féministes," 16 July 1902
271. "Mentir est une habitude," 21 July 1902
272. "La Sympathie des épouses de France," 5 August 1902
273. "Congrès du travail féminin," 14 August 1902
274. "Un Noir à l'auréole," 23 August 1902
275. "L'Obstacle au progrès," 3 September 1902
276. "Deux hygiènes," 12 September 1902
277. "Le Meilleur auxiliaire," 19 September 1902
278. "Réformatrices," 29 September 1902
279. "Jean Macé féministe," 9 October 1902
280. "Il faut choisir," 28 October 1902
281. "Une assurance contre le divorce," 17 November 1902
282. "Droit et devoir," 2 December 1902
283. "Le Féminisme" (no subtitle), 9 December 1902
284. "Juge et partie," 22 December 1902
285. "La Conscience publique et la loi," 9 January 1903
286. "Là est la solution," 21 January 1903
287. "La Première bachelière," 4 February 1903
288. "Le Prix de Rome," 24 February 1903
289. "Par décret," 17 March 1903
290. "Elles se méprisent," 31 March 1903
291. "Sentiment et systèmes," 21 April 1903
292. "Le Féminisme" (no subtitle), 26 April 1903
293. "La Vignette féministe autorisée," 3 May 1903
294. "Le Corps social amputé," 23 May 1903
295. "La Matrie," 4 June 1903
296. "Cheffesses de districts," 23 June 1903
297. "Des Femmes dans les commissions d'hygiène," 7 July 1903
298. "En Australie," 24 July 1903
299. "Des Inspectrices primaires," 18 August 1903
300. "La Base de la laïcité," 30 August 1903

301. "Un Renfort," 12 September 1903
302. "Une Amorce," 26 October 1903
303. "La Première présidente," 2 November 1903
304. "La Dotation des mères françaises," 30 November 1903
305. "Les Préjugés entretenus à l'école," 8 December 1903
306. "Assurances sur les réformes à accomplir," 27 December 1903
307. "Au-dessous du concile de Mâcon," 6 January 1904
308. "Les Femmes et les comités électoraux," 29 January 1904
309. "Emile Deschanel féministe," 9 February 1904
310. "Amour filial," 27 February 1904
311. "L'Empreinte cléricale de la loi," 2 April 1904
312. "Arts domestiques," 14 April 1904
313. "Amnistiez les victimes de la théologie," 3 May 1904
314. "L'Argent préféré au capital," 24 May 1904
315. "Le Forçage des idées," 21 June 1904
316. "Congrès de Berlin," 5 July 1904
317. "Elles ont intéret à voter," 20 August 1904
318. "La Glorification du code," 29 August 1904
319. "Attentat à la liberté de la femme," 7 September 1904
320. "Son rôle est à aimer," 4 October 1904
321. "Vers le but," 5 November 1904
322. "Précieux concours," 8 November 1904
323. "Légitimation des naturels," 5 December 1904
324. "M. Vallé et les femmes," 8 January 1905
325. "La Retraite des mères," 19 February 1905
326. "La Loi de neuf mois," 4 April 1905
327. "La Marque du maître," 25 April 1905
328. "Les Commandements de l'homme," 23 May 1905
329. "L'Indispensable pondératrice," 14 June 1905
330. "La Pièce d'identité pour les femmes," 22 June 1905
331. "Mme Curie et l'Institut," 9 July 1905
332. "Doctoresses," 30 July 1905
333. "Gros lot," 17 August 1905
334. "L'Impôt paternel," 12 September 1905
335. "La Politique et le mariage," 29 September 1905
336. "Péril féminin," 7 October 1905
337. "Mode outrageante," 13 November 1905
338. "Propriété de rapport," 5 December 1905
339. "Retraite pour les mères," 11 December 1905
340. "Hétaïres et Cendrillons," 25 December 1905
341. "Le Mariage et l'église," 2 January 1906
342. "Un Succès," 22 January 1906
343. "Argument péremptoire," 12 February 1906
344. "Sexualisme," 11 March 1906
345. "Qu'y a-t-il de commun entre vous et nous?", 17 April 1906
346. "Bulletin pondérateur," 25 May 1906
347. "Propagande par le fait," 11 June 1906
348. "Conseil international des femmes," 19 June 1906

349. "Voeu à émettre," 9 July 1906
350. "Vers l'égalité," 31 July 1906
351. "L'Arbitrage pour les différends intersexuels," 13 August 1906
352. "Pas de repos pour les femmes," 29 August 1906
353. "L'Aristocrate en la société," 2 September 1906
354. "Et les croyances républicaines?", 17 September 1906
355. "La Maison des femmes," 8 October 1906
356. "Exposition d'économie domestique," 20 October 1906
357. "Une Ministère des femmes," 12 November 1906
358. "Les Restaurants," 3 December 1906
359. "Proposition de loi accordant aux femmes le droit de voter," 17 December 1906
360. "Bulletin affranchisseur," 7 January 1907
361. "Manque d'argent," 2 February 1907
362. "Les Rênes de l'état," 4 March 1907
363. "Le Travail féminin," 2 April 1907
364. "19 Femmes députés," 30 April 1907
365. "Gains et revenus," 27 May 1907
366. "L'Avoir des femmes," 29 June 1907
367. "L'Adjonction des capacités féminines," 17 July 1907
368. "Mariages d'intelligences," 1 August 1907
369. "Les Personnes et les immeubles," 22 August 1907
370. "Socialistes et bourgeoises," 3 September 1907
371. "Polygame," 30 September 1907
372. "Le Féminisme" (no subtitle), 13 October 1907
373. "Les Ménagères nationales," 24 October 1907
374. "Les Réformes et les femmes," 2 November 1907
375. "Voeu du conseil général," 24 November 1907
376. "L'Edifice fragile," 17 December 1907
377. "Présent à faire aux femmes," 1 January 1908
378. "Curateur au ventre," 27 January 1908
379. "Jury mixte," 10 February 1908
380. "Loi violée," 5 March 1908
381. "Les Non-votants feront des rentes aux électeurs," 22 March 1908
382. "La Digue," 21 April 1908
383. "Parias françaises," 2 May 1908
384. "L'Abstention provient de l'exclusion," 25 May 1908
385. "Une Grande femme," 16 June 1908
386. "Congrès des droits de la femme," 1 July 1908
387. "L'Impôt sur l'estomac," 13 July 1908
388. "Progrès suprème," 26 July 1908
389. "Modifiez la majorité électorale," 13 August 1908
390. "Prostitution," 25 August 1908
391. "Les Lois pas appliquées," 15 September 1908
392. "23 Femmes députés," 29 September 1908
393. "Le Féminisme" (no subtitle), 11 October 1908
394. "Des Greffières," 16 October 1908
395. "Durs aux femmes," 26 November 1908

396. "Le Prix Botta," 13 December 1908
397. "Le Piédestal des hommes est de l'or des femmes," 2 January 1909
398. "Bagne à portes ouvertes," 20 January 1909
399. "La Représentation intégrale," 8 February 1909
400. "L'Autorité des électeurs," 4 March 1909
401. "Le Fait important," 29 March 1909
402. "Gouvernement direct," 18 April 1909
403. "Du Danger d'ajourner les réformes," 4 May 1909
404. "Notre ancêtre," 30 May 1909
405. "Une Donation enlevée aux femmes," 20 June 1909
406. "Les Femmes interjettent appel," 1 July 1909
407. "L'Impôt sur l'estomac," 22 July 1909
408. "La Royauté d'un sex prépare la royauté d'un homme," 11 August 1909
409. "Elles n'ont que le droit de singulariser," 31 August 1909
410. "Les Braconnières," 21 September 1909
411. "Les Femmes doivent-elles etre représentées au parlement?", 1 October 1909
412. "Les Femmes doivent-elles etre représentées au parlement?", 13 October 1909
413. "Les Femmes doivent-elles etre représentées au parlement?", 1 November 1909

V. Individual articles, 1880–1911

1. "La Question des femmes," *La Fédération*, 16 January 1880
2. "Le Suffrage des femmes," *La Vérité*, March 1883
3. "Les Femmes," *Le Matin*, 7 March 1884
4. "La Mère égale du père," *La Quatrième état*, 28 February 1885
5. "Affameurs de femmes," *Le Radical algérien*, 26 March 1890
6. "Les Femmes électrices," *Le Radical algérien*, 28 February 1892
7. "Industries des femmes arabes," *La Petite république française*, 28 May 1892
8. "Le Mouvement féministe," *L'Eclair*, 11 June 1893
9. "Les Femmes," *Cocarde*, 23 September 1894
10. "Le Vote des femmes," *La Fronde*, 13 December 1897
11. "Le Couvert des vieux," *La Fronde*, 30 January 1898
12. "Le Suffrage des femmes," *L'Abeille*, 20 January 1901
13. "L'Actualité. La Révision des listes électorales et l'inscription des femmes," *L'Abeille*, 1 February 1901
14. "Le Suffrage des femmes," *La Petite république*, 27 May 1901
15. "Le Vote des femmes," *L'Eclair*, 23 March 1907
16. "Le Vote des femmes," *L'Eclair*, 23 November 1907
17. "Les Femmes ont de la peine à se mettre d'accord même contre les hommes," *Le Matin*, 23 May 1910
18. "La Rubrique des droits," *Le Matin*, 18 March 1911

APPENDIX TWO

Auclert's Programs, 1877–1910

I. The Program of Droit des femmes, April 1877

The ultimate objective of Droit des femmes is: *The perfect equality of the two sexes before the law and in morality.*

Program:

Droit des femmes will seek, from the beginning and by all means in its power:

1. The accession of women, married or not, to full civil and political rights, on the same legal conditions as apply to men.
2. The reestablishment of divorce.
3. A single morality for men and for women; whatever is condemned for one cannot be excusable for the other.
4. The right for women to develop their intelligence through education, with no other limitation than their ability and their desire.
5. The right to knowledge being acquired, the free accession of women to all professions and all careers for which they are qualified at the same level as applies to men (and after the same examination).
6. The rigorous application, without distinction by sex, of the economic formula: Equal Pay for Equal Work.

[Published in *Le Radical*, 3 April 1877]

II. The Statutes of Suffrage des femmes, February 1883

1. There is founded at Paris—outside of partisan religious and political opinions—a society named Société nationale du suffrage des femmes.

237

2. This society is administered by a Committee of twelve persons (this number can be increased to twenty-four).

3. The seat of the society is in Paris. . . .

4. The society is composed of active members and honorary members. All must be sympathetic to the sole goal of the society: *claiming the political rights of women.* The obligatory annual dues are three francs.

5. Given that everyone who is liable to taxation and the legal system possesses a natural right to a voice in legislative and administrative assemblies, and given that "peace, social harmony, and human well-being only exist when women help men to make the laws," the society proposes that women be given the municipal and legislative franchise on the same conditions as they are given to men.

6. All members receive, upon payment of their dues, a receipt that permits them to participate in the annual assembly of the society, held in a rented hall in Paris, and to vote for the members of the Committee. The general assembly of the society will be announced in an annual report. The annual report will be sent to all members of the society, its supporters, and its donors. A monthly report of the society will be sent, without charge, to report the decisions of the Committee, its activities, the results of meetings held under its auspices, and news from France and abroad concerning the cause.

7. Members are expected to use all means in their power to win the vote for women. Those who live in the provinces are expected to form local committees with the same statutes as the Parisian society, and to maintain relations with the Parisian society. All male members are expected to call for women's suffrage in private and public electoral meetings.

8. The powers of the Bureau and the Committee are valid for one year. The Committee cannot make any commitments beyond the duration of its term. At the annual general assembly, after the members have heard the annual reports of the treasurer and the secretary, the members will elect by secret ballot a new committee, which will meet immediately to name its Bureau. Former members of the Committee are eligible for reelection.

9. The reports of the society will be edited by the secretary and printed with the approval of a majority of the Committee. There will be three separate treasuries for dues, donations, and legacies: (1) the treasury for the expenses of the Bureau, which will receive dues payments; (2) the treasury for propaganda publications; (3) the treasury for propaganda lectures and travel. *Note:* It is understood that the first treasury will have the right to draw on the other two, in equal proportions, in order to meet expenses, and that the society will only be expected to execute its program as far as finances permit.

10. The treasurer is expected to give a receipt for all amounts above one franc.

11. Publications will be anonymous and will bear the heading "Société nationale du suffrage des femmes."

12. The society cannot contract any debt, and each member is responsible only for annual dues of three francs, which must be paid in advance.

13. All issues other than that of obtaining the vote and eligibility for office for women are firmly banned from the discussions and the publications of the society.

14. In all deliberations, the president for that meeting has the deciding vote in case of a tie.

15. The Committee will meet every month; the minutes of the meeting will list the members present.

16. If any reasons necessitate the expulsion of a member of the Committee, that expulsion will be ordered by a majority vote, after debate, without mention being made in the minutes of the reasons for the expulsion.

17. No expulsions can take place without a special meeting of the Committee for that purpose.

18. No modification can be made in the statutes except by a vote of the general assembly. In no case can Article Thirteen, stating the exclusive goal of the society, be abrogated.

[Published in *La Citoyenne*, February 1883]

III. Auclert's Electoral Program of 1885

1. All French adults, men and women, are equals before the law and enjoy civil and political rights.

2. Suffrage exercised by men and women replaces suffrage restricted to men.

3. The revision of the constitution, and of the laws of marriage, by an assembly elected by the nation, an assembly composed of women as well as men.

4. Equal opportunity for intellectual and professional development for all of the children of France, and free access without distinction by sex to all employment and public positions.

5. The Minotaur State, which manifests itself to extract taxes on blood and money, is replaced by the Maternal State, charged with assuring, by its prudent solicitude, security and work for all French people and support for children, the aged, the sick, and the injured.

6. Equitable rewards for labor and, for equal production, equal payment for men and women.

7. Taxation proportional to means; suppression of taxes on food, increase of taxes on luxury goods.

8. Questions of war and peace, and questions of the national budget, to be submitted to a vote of Frenchmen and Frenchwomen.

9. Obligatory military service for men. Obligatory humanitarian service for women. Defense of the territory assigned to men; aid to children, the aged, the sick, and the injured assigned to women.

10. Individual human autonomy. Absolute liberty to think, to say, and to write ideas.

11. Justice without charges. Tribunals and jurys composed of men and of women.

12. The same opportunities for women as for men. In short, affirmation of the egalitarian spirit of our institutions by giving preference to utility and necessity which profits everyone. . . .

[Pulished in *Le Rappel*, 15 August 1885]

IV. Statutes of Suffrage des femmes, 1900

1. A society is founded at Paris under the title Le Suffrage des femmes.

2. It is established outside of partisan political and religious opinions, and its goal is to claim the political rights of women by all means within its power.

3. It is composed of active members and adherents. All members must support the sole aim of the society: political rights for women.

4. Its efforts are devoted to incessant written and spoken propaganda, to the distribution of writings, to petitioning, to posting its program, to the circulation of the feminist stamp—in short, to proselytizing in public and in private, even in the street.

5. Its resources are composed of the dues of the members and donations made to establish true Universal Suffrage.

6. Anybody of either sex may join Suffrage des femmes.

7. To join the society, one must accept its statutes, be prepared to teach the program of feminism, pay at least three francs in dues each year, and be admitted by the Committee.

8. The society has no president. It is administered by a Committee of ten members, elected at a general assembly of the members.

9. The Committee is renewed by thirds every year. Retiring members are eligible for reelection.

10. The Committee chooses from its members a Secretary-General, a Secretary, and a Treasurer.

11. An Auditing Committee of three members is named every year to control the society's finances.

12. At the death of a member of the society, all adherents will assemble for the burial.

13. Any member who compromises the society can, after deliberation, be expelled by a majority vote in the Committee.

14. The seat of the society is fixed at Paris, 151 rue de la Roquette, at the home of Hubertine Auclert.

[Copy of statutes in the Dossier Suffrage des femmes, BMD]

V. Auclert's Electoral Program, 1910

1. Men and women, being equally liable to criminal law and tax law, should be equal before the law and should enjoy the same civil and political rights.

2. Suffrage restricted to men will become truly universal only in extending its universe to women.

3. The entire nation, composed of men and women, should be represented in all administrative and legislative assemblies.

4. Only voters should be counted in determining electoral constituencies. If women, who are not represented, were not counted, there would be 310 fewer deputies, or almost five million francs in savings.

5. Men and women should receive the same physical, moral, intellectual, and professional preparation.

6. All careers, occupations, and public functions should be accessible to women as they are to men.

7. For equal production, equal salary for the two sexes.

8. All persons should obtain the total value (*prix*) of their labor. Responsible unions, instead of middlemen, should receive the job listings from the bosses and assign them to workers.

9. Man and woman should associate as equals in marriage, remaining masters of their persons and their possessions.

10. Maternity is the foremost of social functions. Mothers, deprived of the means of survival while they perpetuate the nation, should be treated like soldiers who defend the territory—fed, housed, and clothed by society.

11. All nonluxury foodstuffs should be exempted from taxation.

12. There should be no charge for justice. Tribunals and juries should be composed of both men and women.

13. Electors should delegate their powers to representatives for only one year, during which they retain sovereignty.

[Copy of program in the Auclert Papers, Carton 1]

Bibliography

In the interest of brevity, this bibliography does not list all materials cited in the notes. The principal omissions are: Parisian daily newspapers, feminist periodicals, rare pamphlets, complete listings of individual dossiers in each manuscript collection, and some works used for background such as studies of French socialism or psychobiography.

MANUSCRIPT AND ARCHIVAL MATERIALS

Archives départmentales
Allier (Yzeure). Esp. Series 2E and 3Q (Etat civil) and 6M (census). Seine (Paris). Esp. Series D (elections).

Archives nationales (Paris)
Esp. Series B^8 and BB^{30} (justice), C (Chamber of Deputies), F^7 (interior and police), and F^{18} (press).

Archives du Préfecture de Police (Paris)
Series B^a contains many helpful files, esp. those on Auclert, Deraismes, Mink, Séverine, congresses, elections, and feminism.

Bibliothèque historique de la ville de Paris (Paris)
The huge Bouglé Collection has now been classified into subseries of papers. In addition to the Auclert Papers, see the sous-fonds for Arria Ly, Camille Bélilon, Marie-Louise Bouglé, Ferdinand Buisson, Caroline Kauffmann, Madeleine Pelletier, Léon Richer; the series on groups, congresses, and biographies. See also Série 83 (féminisme) and the fichier for manuscripts.

Bibliothèque Marguerite Durand (Paris, Mairie of 5th Arrondissement)
An extremely important collection, containing hundreds of dossiers composed of clippings and documents. Series 091 contains important correspondence. Also the best source for rare pamphlets and periodicals.

243

Bibliothèque du Trocadéro (Paris)
  The Jane Misme collection contains some pamphlets but no manuscripts.
Fawcett Library (London, Calcutta House)
  The Millicent Fawcett papers provide little about France, but her collection contains useful articles and pamphlets, particularly on the IWSA.
Institut français d'histoire sociale (Paris, Archives nationales)
  The collections on socialism contain little on Auclert; for feminism, see the Fonds Hélène Brion.
International Instituut voor Sociale Geschiedenis (Amsterdam)
  The Pankhurst and Guesde collections contain little on Auclert, but the library has some rare pamphlets and brochures of value.
Ministère des finances. Archives des directions de l'enregistrement (Paris)
  Auclert's will.
Musée social, Bibliothèque du Cédias (Paris)
  Sainte-Croix scrapbooks (uncataloged).
New York Public Library (manuscripts)
  Carrie Chapman Catt Papers.
Schlesinger Library. (Cambridge, Mass.)
  Dillon Collection, Catt and Shaw manuscripts; Gilman Papers; Andrews Papers; Allen Papers.
Ville de Paris. Mairie du XIe arrondissement.
  Etat civil (birth, marriage, and death certificates).

OFFICIAL AND SEMI-OFFICIAL GOVERNMENT PUBLICATIONS

Annuaire de l'Allier. Moulins, 1848.
Chambre des députés. *Journal officiel.* Paris, 1876–1914.
Le Code civil. Textes antérieurs et version actuelle. Edition à jour au 30 juin 1981. Paris, 1981.
Conseil général du département de la Seine. *Procès–verbaux des déliberations.* Paris, 1885–86, 1906–08.
Conseil municipal de Paris. *Bulletin municipal officiel de la ville de Paris.* Paris, 1912.
Conseil municipal de Paris. *Procès-verbaux.* Paris, 1912.
Ministère du travail (ministry varies). *Annuaire statistique.* Paris, 1876–1914.
Dalloz, M. and A. et al., eds. *Jurisprudence générale: Recueil périodique et critique de jurisprudence, de législation et doctrine en matière civile, commerciale, criminelle, administrative et de droit public.* Paris, 1876–1914.
Duvergier, J. B. et al., eds. *Collection complète des lois, décrets, ordonnances; réglements, avis du Conseil d'état.* Paris, 1876–1914.
Gazette des tribunaux. Journal de jurisprudence et des débats judicaires. Paris, 1885, 1893, 1904, 1908.

COLLECTIONS OF REPRINTED SOURCES

Albistur, Maïte, and Daniel Armogathe, eds. *Le Grief des femmes: Anthologie de textes féministes du second empire à nos jours.* 2 vols. Paris, 1978.
Anderson, Frank M., ed. *The Constitutions and Other Select Documents Illustrative of the History of France, 1789–1907.* Minneapolis, 1908.

Bell, Susan G., and Karen M. Offen, eds. *Women, the Family, and Freedom: The Debate in Documents.* 2 vols. (Stanford, 1983).

Hellerstein, Erna O., Leslie P. Hume, and Karen M. Offen, eds., *Victorian Women: A Documentary Account of Women's Lives in Nineteenth-Century England, France, and the United States.* Stanford, 1981.

Riemer, Eleanor S., and John C. Fout, eds. *European Women: A Documentary History, 1789–1945.* New York, 1980.

Thomson, David, ed. *France: Empire and Republic, 1850–1940.* New York, 1968).

PUBLISHED DEBATES AND REPORTS OF CONGRESSES

Amélioration. *Assemblée générale du . . . 26 avril 1890.* Paris, 1890.

CNFF. *Première assemblée générale publique. 17 mai 1903.* Dole, 1903.

Congrès international de la condition et des droits des femmes . . . 1900: Procès-verbaux. Edited by Marguerite Durand. Paris, 1901.

Congrès international du droit des femmes. 25 juillet 1878: Actes et compte rendu des séances plènières. Paris, 1878.

Congrès national des droits civils et du suffrage des femmes. Edited by Jeanne Oddo-Deflou. Paris, 1908.

Deraismes, Maria. *Société pour l'amélioration du sort de la femme et la revindication de ses droits. . . . Rapport adressé au congrès des femmes représentantes tenu à Chicago, 1893.* Paris, 1893.

Deuxième congrès international des oeuvres et institutions féminins. . . . 1900. 4 vols. Edited by Marie Pégard. Paris, 1902.

Dixième congrès international des femmes: Oeuvres et institutions féminines, droits des femmes . . . tenu à Paris le 2 juin 1913. Edited by Avril de Sainte-Croix. Paris, 1914.

IWSA *Report of the Fifth Conference.* London, 1909.

———. *Report of the Second and Third Conferences.* Copenhagen, 1906.

Kauffmann, Caroline and Mme [Paule] Mink. *Idées générales sur les travaux du congrès international féministe de Londres en 1899. Rapport fait au Conseil municipale de Paris, en qualité de déléguées du groupe de la Solidarité des femmes.* Paris, 1899.

Séances du congrès ouvrier socialiste de France. Troisième session. Marseilles, 1879.

Vincent, Eliska. *Congrès général des sociétés féministes.* Paris, 1892.

———. *Rapport à la VIe Conference of the International Woman Suffrage Alliance, à Stockholm, 1911* [sic]. Paris, 1911.

Voeux adoptés par le congrès féministe international, tenu à Paris en 1896. Paris, n.d.

REFERENCE WORKS

Bluysen, Paul, ed. *Annuaire de la presse française.* Paris, 1881, 1884–85, 1890, 1900, supplément 1891.

James, Edward P., ed. *Notable American Women, 1607–1950: A Biographical Dictionary.* 3 vols. Cambridge, Mass., 1971.

Jolly, Jean, ed. *Dictionnaire des parlementaires français: Notices biographiques sur les ministres, députés, et sénateurs français de 1889 à 1940.* 8 vols. Paris, 1960–1977.

Maitron, Jean. *Dictionnaire biographique du mouvement ouvrier français.* 21 vols. Paris, 1964–   .

Robert, Adolphe, Edgar Bourloton, and Gaston Cougny, eds. *Dictionnaire des parlementaires français: Comprénant tous les membres des assemblées françaises et tous les ministres français depuis le 1er mai 1789 jusqu'au 1er mai 1889.* 5 vols. Paris, 1891.

NEWSPAPERS AND PERIODICALS

Most of the Parisian newspaper citations here are based on clippings in the Auclert Papers and in dossiers at the APP, the BHVP, and the BMD. The newspapers consulted are:

Le Figaro
La Libre parole
Le Prolétaire
Le Radical
Le Temps

A huge listing of feminist periodicals may be compiled by consulting the notes. The most important for this subject are:

L'Avenir des femmes (Richer)
Bulletin (Amélioration)
La Citoyenne (Auclert)
Le Combat féministe (Arria Ly)
Le Droit des femmes (Richer)
L'Entente (Oddo-Deflou)
La Femme (Monod)
La Femme socialiste (Renaud and Saumoneau)
La Française (Misme)
La Fronde (Durand)
Le Journal des femmes (Martin)
La Revue féministe (Dissard)
La Suffragiste (Pelletier)

SELECTED WORKS BY FEMINISTS

Anthony, S. B., and Ida Harper. *The History of Woman Suffrage.* 6 vols. Rochester, 1881–1922.

Auclert, Hubertine. *L'Argent de la femme.* Paris, 1904.

———. *La Citoyenne: Articles de 1881 à 1891.* Edited by Edith Taïeb. Paris, 1982.

———. *Le Droit politique des femmes: Question qui n'est pas traitée au congrès international des femmes.* Paris, 1878.

———. *Egalité sociale et politique de la femme et de l'homme: Discours prononcée au congrès ouvrier socialiste de Marseille.* Marseilles, 1879.

———. *Les Femmes arabes en Algérie.* Paris, 1900.

———. *Les Femmes au gouvernail.* Paris, 1923.

———. *Historique de la société le droit des femmes, 1876–1880*. Paris, 1881.
———. *Lettre-préface*. In Léon Giraud, *Le Roman de la femme chrétienne, étude historique*. Paris, 1880.
———. *Le Nom de la femme*. Paris, 1905.
———. *Le Vote des femmes*. Paris, 1908.
Audouard, Olympe. *Guerre aux hommes*. Paris, 1866.
Bogelot, Isabelle. *Trente ans de solidarité, 1877–1906*. Paris, 1908.
Brunschwicg, Cécile. "Féminisme: Le Suffrage des femmes en France." In *Les Documents du progrès*, pp. 229–300. Paris, 1913.
———. *Le Suffrage des femmes en France*. Leiden, 1938.
Chaumont, Marie. Preface to Hubertine Auclert, *Les Femmes au Gouvernail*. Paris, 1923.
Chéliga, Marya, ed. *Almanach féministe, 1899*. Paris, 1900.
Daubié, Julie. *La Femme pauvre au XIXe siècle*. Paris, 1866.
Deraismes, Maria. *Ce que veulent les femmes: Articles et discours*. Edited by Odile Krakovitch. Paris, 1980.
———. *Discours contre la vivisection*. Paris, 1884.
———. *Eve contre Monsieur Dumas fils*. Paris, 1872.
———. *Eve dans l'humanité*. Paris, 1891.
———. *France et progrès*. 2d ed. Paris, 1874.
———. *Lettre au clergé français*. Paris, 1879.
Etrivières, Jehan des [pseudonym of Marie-Rose Astié de Valsayre]. *Les Amazons du siècle*. Paris, 1882.
Ferrer, Mme C. L. *Pourquoi voteraient-elles?* Paris, 1910.
Giraud, Léon. *Le Roman de la femme chrétienne, étude historique*. Paris, 1880.
Grinberg, Suzanne. *Historique du mouvement suffragiste depuis 1848*. Paris, 1926.
International Council of Women. *Histories of Affiliated Councils, 1888–1938*. Brussels, 1938.
Laguerre, Odette. *Qu'est-ce que le féminisme?* Lyons, 1899.
Laloë, Jeanne. "Les Deux féminismes." In *La Nouvelle revue*, May–June 1908.
Lévrier, Antonin. *Discours prononcé par le citoyen Antonin Lévrier à la réunion des travailleurs indépendants: Capitalistes-commerçants-producteurs*. Paris, 1879.
———. *Histoire des Deux-sèvres*. Niort, 1886.
LFDF. *Cinquante ans de féminisme, 1870–1920*. Paris, 1921.
Martial, Lydie. *Action du féminisme rationnel. Union de pensée féminine*. Paris, 1905.
Martin, Marguerite. *Les Droits de la femme*. Paris, 1912.
Mink, Paule. *Communarde et féministe (1839–1901). Les Mouches et les araignées . . . et autres textes*. Edited by Alain Dalotel. Paris, 1981.
Mirtel, Héra. "Nous n'aurons pas encore législatrices en France." In *Les Documents du progrès*, July 1910.
Misme, Jane. *Les Dernières obstacles au vote des femmes*. Paris, n.d.
———. "Les Grands figures du féminisme: Hubertine Auclert." In *Minerva*, 19 October 1930.
———. "Les Grands figures du féminisme: Jeanne Schmahl." In *Minerva*, 26 October 1930.

———. "Les Grands figures du féminisme: De Maria Deraismes à Maria Vérone." In *Minerva*, 12 October 1930.

———. "Madame la Duchesse d'Uzès." In *Revue bleue*, 17 August 1897.

———. *Pour le suffrage des femmes: Le Féminisme et la politique*. Paris, n.d. [c. 1910].

Oddo-Deflou, Jeanne. "Les Congrès national des droits civils et du suffrage des femmes tenu . . . 1908." In *Liberté d'opinion* 2, 1908.

———. *Le Sexualisme: Critique de la préponderance et la mentalité du sexe fort*. Paris, 1906.

Pelletier, Madeleine. *Admissions des femmes dans la franc-maçonnerie*. Paris, n.d.

———. *L'Education féministe des filles et autres textes*. Edited by Claude Maignien. Paris, 1978.

———. "Le Féminisme et ses militants." In *Les Documents du progrès*, 1911.

———. *La Femme en lutte pour ses droits*. Paris, 1908.

———. "French Feminism." In *The Freewoman*, 25 April 1912.

———. "Ma Candidature à la députation." In *Les Documents du progrès*, July 1910.

———. *Philosophie sociale: Les Opinions, les partis, les classes*. Paris, 1912.

———. *La Question du vote des femmes*. Paris, 1909.

———. "La Tactique féministe." In *La Revue socialiste*, April 1908.

Potonié-Pierre, Edmond. *Historique du mouvement pacifique*. Berne, 1899.

Potonié-Pierre, Eugénie. *Un Peu plus tard*. Paris, 1892.

———. *L'Union libre*. Liège, 1902.

Rebour, Pauline. *Pourquoi les françaises doivent et veulent voter*. Paris, 1923.

Remember, Madame. *Le Féminisme intégral*. Paris, 1919.

Richer, Léon. *Le Code des femmes*. Paris, 1883.

———. *Le Divorce: Projet de loi*. Paris, 1873.

———. *La Femme libre*. Paris, 1877.

———. *Lettres parisiennes: La Politique en 1873*. Paris, n.d.

———. *Lettres d'un libre-penseur à un curé de village*. Paris, 1869.

———. *Le Livre des femmes*. Paris, 1872.

———. *Réforme du code civil: Pétition à l'Assemblée nationale*. Paris, n.d.

Roussel, Nelly. *Derniers combats: Recueil d'articles et de discours*. Paris, 1932.

———. *L'Eternelle sacrifiée*. Edited by Daniel Armogathe and Maïte Albistur. Paris, 1979.

———. *Paroles de combat et d'espoir*. Paris, 1919.

———. *Quelques discours*. Paris, 1907.

———. *Quelques lances rompues pour nos libertés*. Paris, 1910.

———. *Trois conférences*. Paris, 1930.

Rouzade, Léonie. *Les Classes dirigéantes et les travailleurs jugés par une femme*. Nancy, n.d.

———. *Connais-toi toi-meme* (Paris, 1871).

———. *Développement du programme de la Société l'Union des femmes par la citoyenne Rouzade: Discours prononcé 13 avril 1880*. Paris, 1880.

———. *La Femme et le peuple*. Paris, 1896.

———. *Petit catéchisme de morale laïque et socialiste*. Meudon, 1895.

Sainte-Croix, Avril de. *Le Féminisme*. Paris, 1907.

————. "Les Françaises et le droit du suffrage." In *The Englishwoman* 2, 1909.

————. *Une morale pour les deux sexes*. Paris, 1900.

————. "Une nouvelle puissance: Le Conseil national des femmes français. In *La Contemporaine*, 10 November 1901.

Saumoneau, Louise. *Principes et action féministes socialistes*. Paris, n.d.

Schmahl, Jeanne. *Le Préjugé de sexe*. Paris, 1895.

————. "Progress of the Women's Rights Movement in France." In *The Forum*, September 1896.

————. *La Question de la femme*. Paris, 1893.

————. "Women's Suffrage in France." In *Englishwoman's Review*, 1902.

Séverine. *Choix de papiers*. Edited by Evelyne Le Garrec. Paris, 1982.

Stanton, Elizabeth Cady. *Eighty Years and More: Reminiscences, 1815–1897*. 1898. Reprint. New York: Schocken, 1971.

Stanton, Theodore, ed. *The Woman Question in Europe: A Series of Original Essays*. New York, 1884.

UFSF. *Le Suffrage des femmes en France*. 3d ed. Paris, 1912.

————. *L'Union Française et l'alliance internationale pour le suffrage des femmes*. Paris, 1910.

Uzès, Duchesse d'. *Souvenirs*. Paris, 1930.

————. *Le Suffrage féminin au point de vue historique*. Meulan, 1914.

Vérone, Maria. *Appel à la justice: Addressé par le CNFF à la Chambre des Députés et la Sénat*. Paris, n.d. [1909].

————. *La Femme devant la loi, autour du monde*. Paris, n.d.

————. *Maria Vérone parle du féminisme*. Paris, n.d.

————. *Résultats du suffrage des femmes*. Paris, 1914.

————, and Georges Lhermitte. *La Séparation et ses conséquences*. Paris, 1906.

————, Chrystal MacMillan, and Marie Stritt. *Woman Suffrage in Practice*. London, 1913.

Villermont, Marie, Comtesse de. *Le Mouvement féministe: Ses Causes, son avenir, solution chrétien*. Paris, 1904.

Vincent, Eliska. *Electorat et éligibilité des femmes aux conseils des prud'-hommes*. Autun, 1907.

————. *La Répression de la traité des blanches et la préservation de la jeune fille: Rapport*. Paris, 1905.

Witt-Schlumberger, Marguerite de. *Une femme aux femmes*. Paris, 1909.

CONTEMPORARY BOOKS AND ARTICLES

Adam, Juliette. "The Position of Women in France." *The Humanitarian* 10 (1897):81–87.

Barthélemy, Joseph. *Le Vote des femmes*. Paris, 1920.

Bashkirtseff, Marie. *Journal of Marie Bashkirtseff*. Chicago, 1890.

Benoist, Charles. *Pour la réforme électorale*. Paris, 1908.

————. *Souvenirs, 1883–1933*. 3 vols. Paris, 1932–1934.

Blum, Léon. *Du Mariage*. Paris, 1907.

Bolo, Abbé Henry. *La Femme et la clergé*. Paris, 1902.

Bourgeois, Léon. *Les Applications sociales de la solidarité*. Paris, 1904.

————. *La Solidarité*. Paris, 1897.

Broda, Rodolphe. "Le Mouvement en faveur du vote des femmes." *Les Documents du progrès*, July 1909.

———. "Le Vote des femmes." *Les Documents du progrès*, July 1909.

Breuil de Saint-Ermain, Jean du. *La Misère sociale de la femme et le suffrage.* Suresnes, 1911.

Buisson, Ferdinand. *La Politique radicale.* Paris, 1908.

———. *Souvenirs, 1866–1916. Conférence faite . . . le 10 janvier 1916.* Paris, 1916.

———. *Le Vote des femmes.* Paris, 1911.

———. "Le Vote des femmes." *Les Documents du progrès*, 1913.

Choquency, Antonin. *L'Emancipation de la femme au commencement du XXe siècle.* Lyons, 1902.

Clemenceau, Georges. *La "Justice" du sexe fort.* Paris, 1907.

Cone, Ada. "The Feminist Movement in France and its Leaders." *The Humanitarian* 12 (1898):5–12.

Crouzet-Benaben, Jeanne. "Une Assemblée des femmes en 1913: Le Congrès international de Paris (2–7 juin)." *La Grande revue*, 10 July 1913.

Dawbarn, Charles. "The French Woman and the Vote." *Fortnightly Review*, August 1911.

Dumas (*fils*), Alexandre. *Les Femmes qui tuent et les femmes qui votent.* Paris, 1880.

———. *La Question du divorce . . . 6 décembre 1879.* 16th ed. Paris, 1882.

———. *La Recherche de la paternité: Lettre à M. Rivet, député.* 2d ed. Paris, 1883.

Durkheim, Emile. *Suicide: A Study in Sociology.* 1897. Reprint. New York: Free Press, 1951.

Faguet, Emile. "L'Abbé féministe." *Revue bleue* 17 (1902).

Finot, Jean. *La Charte de la femme.* Paris, 1910.

———. *Problems of the Sexes.* London, 1909.

Flach, Jacques. "La Souveraineté du peuple et les suffrage politique de la femme." *Revue bleue*, 1910.

Fouilée, Alfred. *La Démocratie politique et sociale en France.* Paris, 1910.

———. *La Propriété sociale.* Paris, 1909.

Froger-Doudemont, Raoul, ed. *Que veulent donc ces féministes?* Paris, 1926.

Grémy, Gaston. *A propos du vote des femmes: La Femme éligible mais non électrice: Opinions et interviews.* Paris, n.d.

Hire, Marie d'Espie de la. "Le Féminisme en France et les sociétés féministes." *La Revue des lettres*, August 1907.

Joran, Théodore. *Au Coeur du féminisme.* Paris, 1908.

———. *Autour du féminisme.* Paris, 1906.

———. *Le Féminisme à l'heure actuelle.* Paris, 1907.

———. *Les Féministes avant le féminisme.* Paris, 1910.

———. *Le Mensonge du féminisme.* Paris, 1905.

———. *Le Suffrage des femmes.* Paris, 1913.

———. *La Trouée féministe.* Paris, 1909.

Joseph-Renaud, J. *Le Catéchisme féministe: Résume de la doctrine sous forme de réponse aux objections.* Paris, 1910.

Koppe, Louise. "Le Droit politique des femmes." *La Femme*, May 1880.

Lamy, Etienne. *La Femme de demain.* Paris, 1901.

Le Bon, Gustave. *The Crowd: A Study of the Popular Mind.* 1897. Reprint. New York: Viking, 1960.

Lecointre, Comtesse Pierre. *Etat de la question féministe en France en 1907.* Paris, 1907.

Lees, Frederic. "The Progress of Woman in France." *The Humanitarian,* February 1901.

Lemaitre, Jules. *Opinions à répandre.* Paris, 1901.

Levray, Mlle. *L'Alcoolisme et le vote des femmes.* Paris, n.d.

Maret, Henry. *Pensées et opinions.* Paris, 1903.

Michel, Louise. *The Red Virgin: Memoirs of Louise Michel.* Edited by Bullitt Lowry and Elizabeth E. Gunter. University, Alabama, 1981.

Michelet, Jules. *Le Pretre, la femme, et la famille.* 1845. Reprint. Paris, 1890.

Naudet, Abbé Paul. *Pour la femme: Etudes féministes.* Paris, 1903.

Neera, Anna Z. *Les Idées d'une femme sur le féminisme.* Paris, 1908.

Novicow, Jacques. *L'Affranchissement de la femme.* Paris, 1903.

Poirson, S. *Mon féminisme.* Paris, 1905.

Pottecher, Thérèse. "Le Mouvement féministe en France." *La Grande revue,* January-February 1911.

Renaudot, M. *Le Féminisme et les droits publics de la femme.* Niort, 1902.

Sembat, Marcel. "L'Accession des femmes aux fonctions publiques." *Les Documents du progrès,* January 1909.

"Société pour l'amélioration du sort des femmes." *Englishwoman's Review* 20 (1874):246–49.

"Suppression of the Association pour l'amélioration du sort des femmes." *Englishwoman's Review* 33 (1876):13–14.

Templiez, Ida. "Les Féministes françaises et le mouvement anti-parlementaire." *Les Documents du progrès,* August 1911.

Turgeon, Charles. *Le Féminisme français.* 2 vols. 2d ed. Paris, 1907.

Viviani, René. "La Femme." *La Grande revue,* 1 February 1901.

SECONDARY STUDIES

Ageron, Charles-Robert. *Les Algériens musulmans et la France, 1871–1919.* 2 vols. Paris, 1968.

Albistur, Maïte, and Daniel Armogathe. *Histoire du féminisme français.* 2 vols. Paris, 1977.

Ariès, Philippe. *The Hour of Our Death.* New York, 1981.

Bachrach, Susan D. *Dames Employées: The Feminization of Postal Work in Nineteenth-Century France.* New York, 1984.

Bardèche, Maurice. *Histoire des femmes.* 2 vols. Paris, 1968.

Barrows, Susanna. *Distorting Mirrors: Visions of the Crowd in Late Nineteenth-Century France.* New Haven, 1981.

Beauvoir, Simone de. *The Second Sex.* 1949. Reprint. New York: Vintage, 1974.

Bellanger, Claude, Jacques Godechot, Pierre Guiral, and Fernand Terrou, eds. *Histoire générale de la presse française.* Vol. 3, *De 1871 à 1940.* Paris, 1972.

Bernstein, Samuel. *Auguste Blanqui and the Art of Insurrection.* London, 1971.

————. *The Beginnings of Marxian Socialism in France.* 1933. Reprint. New York, 1965.

————. "Jules Guesde: Pioneer of Marxism in France." *Science and Society* 4 (1940).

Betts, Raymond F. *Assimilation and Association in French Colonial Theory, 1890–1914.* New York, 1961.

Bidelman, Patrick K. "The Feminist Movement in France: The Formative Years, 1858–1889." Ph.D. diss., Michigan State University, 1975.

————. "Maria Deraismes, Léon Richer, and the Founding of the French Feminist Movement, 1866–1878." *TR/TR* 3–4 (1977):20–73.

————. *Pariahs Stand Up! The Founding of the Liberal Feminist Movement in France, 1858–1889.* Westport, Conn., 1982.

————. "The Politics of French Feminism: Léon Richer and the LFDF, 1882–1891." *HR/RH* 3 (1976):93–120.

Bonnefous, Georges and Edouard. *Histoire politique de la IIIe République.* 7 vols. Paris, 1956–1967.

Boxer, Marilyn J. "French Socialism, Feminism, and the Family." *TR/TR* 3–4 (1977):128–67.

————. "Socialism Faces Feminism in France, 1879–1913." Ph.D. diss., University of California at Riverside, 1975.

————. "Socialism Faces Feminism in France: The Failure of Synthesis in France, 1879–1914." In *Socialist Women,* edited by Marilyn J. Boxer and Jean H. Quataert, pp. 75–111. New York, 1978.

————. "When Radical and Socialist Feminism Were Joined: The Extraordinary Failure of Madeleine Pelletier." In *European Women on the Left,* edited by Jane Slaughter and Robert Kern, pp. 51–74. Westport, Conn., 1981.

Boxer, Marilyn J. and Jean H. Quataert, eds. *Socialist Women: European Socialist Feminism in the Nineteenth and Early Twentieth Centuries.* New York, 1978.

Brault, Elaine. *La Franc-maçonnerie et l'émancipation des femmes.* Paris, 1954.

Bridenthal, Renate, and Claudia Koonz, eds. *Becoming Visible: Women in European History.* Boston, 1977.

Brown, Frederick. *Père Lachaise: Elysium as Real Estate.* New York, 1973.

Byrnes, Robert F. *Antisemitism in Modern France.* Vol. 1, *The Prologue to the Dreyfus Affair.* New Brunswick, N.J., 1950.

Campbell, Peter. *French Electoral Systems and Elections since 1789.* London, 1958.

Clark, Linda L. *Schooling the Daughters of Marianne: Textbooks and the Socialization of Girls in Modern French Primary Schools.* Albany, 1983.

Clarke, J. A. "French Socialist Congresses, 1876–1914." *JMH* 31 (1959).

Collins, Irene. *The Government and the Newspaper Press in France, 1814–1881.* Oxford, 1959.

Confer, Vincent. *France and Algeria: The Problem of Civil and Political Reform, 1870–1920.* Syracuse, 1966.

Decaux, Alain. *Histoire des françaises.* 2 vols. Paris, 1972.

Dansette, Adrien. *Religious History of Modern France.* 2 vols. London, 1961.

Derfler, Leslie. "Reformism and Jules Guesde." *IRSH* 12 (1967).

Deschamps, Hubert. *Méthodes et doctrines coloniales de la France*. Paris, 1953.

Dommanget, Maurice. *Auguste Blanqui au début de la Troisième République, 1871–1880: Dernière prison et ultimes combats*. Paris, 1971.

Dudit, Suzanne. "Le Nom de la femme mariée?" *Minerva*, 10 April 1932.

Elwitt, Sanford. *The Making of the Third Republic: Class and Politics in France, 1868–1884*. Baton Rouge, 1975.

———. "Social Reform and Social Order in Late Nineteenth-Century France: The Musée Social and Its Friends." *FHS* 11 (1980):431–51.

Evans, Richard J. "Feminism and Anticlericalism in France, 1870–1922." *Historical Journal* 25 (1982): 947–52.

———. *The Feminists: Women's Emancipation Movements in Europe, America, and Australasia, 1840–1920*. New York, 1977.

Fleming, Marie. *The Anarchist Way to Socialism: Elisée Reclus and Nineteenth-Century European Anarchism*. London, 1979.

Forstenzer, Thomas R. *French Provincial Police and the Fall of the Second Republic: Social Fear and Counterrevolution*. Princeton, 1981.

Garrec, Evelyne le. *Séverine: Une rebelle, 1855–1929*. Paris, 1982.

Gaudemet, Yves-Henri. *Les Juristes et la vie politique de la Troisième République*. Paris, 1970.

Goldberg, Harvey. *The Life of Jean Jaurès*. Madison, 1962.

Goliber, Sue H. "The Life and Times of Marguerite Durand: A Study in French Feminism." Ph.D. diss., Kent State University, 1975.

Guibert, Madeleine. *Les Femmes et l'organisation syndicale avant 1914: Présentation et commentaire de documents pour une étude du syndicalisme féminin*. Paris, 1966.

Hause, Steven C. "The Failure of Feminism in Provincial France, 1890–1920." *PWSFH* 8 (1982):423–36.

Hause, Steven C., with Anne R. Kenney. *Women's Suffrage and Social Politics in the French Third Republic*. Princeton, 1984.

Hause, Steven C., and Anne R. Kenney. "The Development of the Catholic Women's Suffrage Movement in France, 1896–1922." *Catholic Historical Review* 67 (1981):11–30.

———. "The Limits of Suffragist Behavior: Legalism and Militancy in France, 1876–1922." *AHR* 86 (1981):781–806.

———. "Women's Suffrage and the Paris Elections of 1908." *Laurels* 51 (1980): 21–32.

Heinzely, Hélène. "Le Mouvement socialiste devant les problèmes du féminisme, 1879–1914." Ph.d. diss., Paris, 1957.

Howorth, Jolyon. *Edouard Vaillant. La Création de l'unité socialiste en France: La Politique de l'action totale*. Paris, 1982.

———. "The Myth of Blanquism under the Third Republic." *JMH*, on-demand supplement to 48 (1976).

Hunt, Persis C. "Revolutionary Syndicalism and Feminism among Teachers in France, 1900–1921." Ph.D. diss., Tufts University, 1975.

———. "Teachers and Workers: Problems of Feminist Organization in the Early Third Republic." *TR/TR* 3–4 (1977):168–204.

Hunter, John C. "The Problem of the French Birth Rate on the Eve of World War I." *FHS* 2 (1962):490–503.

Hutton, Patrick H. *The Cult of Revolutionary Tradition: The Blanquists in French Politics, 1864–1893*. Berkeley, 1981.

———. "The Role of the Blanquist Party in Left-Wing Politics in France, 1879–1890." *JMH* 46 (1974):277–95.

Joughin, Jean T. *The Paris Commune in French Politics, 1871–1880: The History of the Amnesty of 1880*. 2 vols. Baltimore, 1955.

Kraditor, Aileen S. *The Ideas of the Woman Suffrage Movement, 1890–1920*. Garden City, N.Y. 1971.

Larkin, Maurice. *Church and State after the Dreyfus Affair: The Separation Issue in France*. London, 1974.

Lacache, Bernard. *Séverine*. Paris, 1930.

Landauer, C. "The Origin of Socialist Reformism in France." *IRSH* 12 (1967).

Lasswell, Harold. *Power and Personality*. 1948. Reprint. New York: Compass, 1962.

———. *Psychopathology and Politics*. 1930. Reprint. New York: Viking, 1962.

Leclère, André. *Le Vote des femmes en France: Les Causes de l'attitude particulière de notre pays*. Paris, 1929.

Lefranc, Georges. *Le Mouvement socialiste sous la Troisième République, 1875–1940*. Paris, 1963.

Leguai, André. *Histoire du Bourbonnais*. 2d ed. Paris, 1974.

Lejeune, Paule. *Louise Michel l'indomptable*. Paris, 1978.

Li Dzeh-Djen. *La Presse féministe en France de 1869 à 1914*. Paris, 1934.

Ligou, Daniel. *Histoire du socialisme en France, 1871–1961*. Paris, 1962.

Logue, William. *From Philosophy to Sociology: The Evolution of French Liberalism, 1870–1914*. DeKalb, Ill., 1983.

Loménie, E. Beau de. *Edouard Drumont, ou l'anticapitalisme national*. Paris, 1968.

Loubère, Leo. *Radicalism in Mediterranean France: Its Rise and Decline, 1848–1914*. Albany, 1974.

McLaren, Angus. "Abortion in France: Women and the Regulation of Family Size, 1800–1914." *FHS* 10 (1978):461–85.

McMillan, James F. "The Character of the French Feminist Movement, 1870–1914." In *Actes du colloque franco-britannique tenu à Bordeaux du 27 au 30 septembre 1976: Sociétés et groupes sociaux en Aquitaine et en Angleterre*. Edited by Fédération historique du sud-ouest. Bordeaux, 1979.

———. *Housewife or Harlot: The Place of Women in French Society, 1870–1940*. New York, 1981.

Machin, Howard. "The Prefects and Political Repression: February 1848 to December 1851." In *Revolution and Reaction: 1848 and the Second French Republic*, edited by Roger Price, pp. 280–302. London, 1975.

Margadant, Ted W. *French Peasants in Revolt: The Insurrection of 1851*. Princeton, 1979.

Marichy, Jean-Pierre. *La Deuxième chambre dans la vie politique française depuis 1875*. Paris, 1969.

Marrus, Michael R. *The Politics of Assimilation: A Study of the French Jewish Community at the Time of the Dreyfus Affair*. Oxford, 1971.

Martin, Benjamin F. *Count Albert de Mun: Paladin of the Third Republic*. Chapel Hill, 1978.

Maurois, André. *Olympio: The Life of Victor Hugo.* New York, 1956.

Mazlish, Bruce. *The Revolutionary Ascetic: Evolution of a Political Type.* New York, 1976.

Merriman, John M. *The Agony of the Republic: The Repression of the Left in Revolutionary France, 1848–1851.* New Haven, 1978.

Merriman, John M., ed. *Consciousness and Class Experience in Nineteenth-Century Europe.* New York, 1980.

Monnerville, Gaston. *Clemenceau.* Paris, 1968.

Moody, Joseph N. *French Education since Napoleon.* Syracuse, 1978.

Moon, S. Joan. "Feminism and Socialism: The Utopian Synthesis of Flora Tristan." In *Socialist Women,* edited by Marilyn J. Boxer and Jean H. Quataert, pp. 21–50. New York, 1978.

———. "The Saint-Simonian Association of Working-Class Women, 1830–1850." *PWSFH* 5 (1977):274–81.

Moses, Claire G. *French Feminism in the Nineteenth Century.* Albany, 1984.

———. "Saint-Simonian Men/Saint-Simonian Women: The Transformation of Feminist Thought in 1830s France." *JMH* 54 (1982):240–67.

Moss, Bernhard H. *The Origins of the French Labor Movement, 1830–1914.* Berkeley, 1976.

Mullaney, Marie M. "Gender and the Socialist Revolutionary Role, 1871–1921: A General Theory of the Female Revolutionary Personality." *HR/RH* 11 (1984):99–151.

Nicolet, Claude. *Le Radicalisme.* 2d ed. Paris, 1961.

Offen, Karen. "Aspects of the Woman Question during the Third Republic." *TR/TR* 3–4 (1977):1–19.

———. "Depopulation, Nationalism, and Feminism in Fin-de-Siècle France." *AHR* 89 (1984):648–76.

———. "The Second sex and the Baccalauréat in Republican France, 1880–1924." *FHS* 13 (1983):252–86.

Payne, Howard C. *The Police State of Louis Napoleon Bonaparte, 1851–1860.* Seattle, 1966.

Peck, Mary G. *Carrie Chapman Catt: A Biography.* New York, 1944.

Perrot, Michelle. "Les Guesdistes: Controverse sur l'introduction du Marxisme en France." *Annales* 22 (1967).

———. "Le Premier journal marxiste français: *L'Egalité* de Jules Guesde, 1877–1883." *L'Actualité de l'histoire* 28 (1959).

Price, Roger. *The French Second Republic: A Social History.* Ithaca, 1972.

Price, Roger, ed. *Revolution and Reaction: 1848 and the Second French Republic.* London, 1975.

Puget, Jean. *La Duchesse d'Uzès.* 2d ed. Uzès, 1972.

Rabaut, Jean. "1900, tournant du féminisme français." *Bulletin de la Société d'histoire moderne* 16 (1983):5–16.

Rafferty, Frances. "Madame Séverine: Crusading Journalist of the Third Republic." *Contemporary French Civilization* 1 (1977):185–202.

Rebérioux, Madeleine, Christiane Dufrancatel, and Béatrice Slama. "Hubertine Auclert et la question des femmes à 'l'immortel congrès' (1879)." *Romantisme* 13–14 (1976):123–42.

Robertson, Priscilla. *An Experience of Women: Pattern and Change in Nineteenth-Century Europe.* Philadelphia, 1982.

Ronsin, Francis. *La Grève des ventres: Propagande néo-malthusienne et baisse de la natalité en France (19e–20e siècles).* Paris, 1980.

Sauna, Louli. *Figures féminines, 1900–1939.* Paris, 1949.

Savy, Nicole. "Victor Hugo féministe." *Pensée* 245 (1985):5–18.

Seager, Frederic H. *The Boulanger Affair: Political Crossroads of France, 1886–1889.* Ithaca, 1969.

Sewall, William H., Jr. *Work and Revolution in France: The Language of Labor from the Old Regime to 1848.* Cambridge, 1980.

Slaughter, Jane, and Robert Kern, eds. *European Women on the Left: Socialism, Feminism, and the Problems Faced by Political Women, 1880 to the Present.* Westport, Conn., 1981.

Smith, Bonnie G. *Ladies of the Leisure Class: The Bourgeoisie of Northern France in the Nineteenth Century.* Princeton, 1981.

Soltau, Roger. *French Political Thought in the Nineteenth Century.* New Haven, 1931.

Sowerwine, Charles. *Les Femmes et le socialisme.* Paris, 1978.

———. "Le Groupe féministe socialiste, 1899–1902." *Le Mouvement social* 90 (1975):87–120.

———. "The Organization of French Socialist Women, 1880–1914." *HR/RH* 3 (1976):3–24.

———. *Sisters or Citizens? Women and Socialism in France since 1876.* Cambridge, 1982.

———. "Women and the Origins of the French Socialist Party." *TR/TR* 3–4 (1977):104–27.

———. "Workers and Women in France before 1914: The Debate over the Couriau Affair." *JMH* 55 (1983):411–41.

Spengler, Joseph P. *France Faces Depopulation.* Durham, North Carolina, 1938.

Spitzer, Alan B. *The Revolutionary Theories of Louis Auguste Blanqui.* New York, 1957.

Stafford, David. *From Anarchism to Reformism: A Study of the Political Activities of Paul Brousse within the First International and the French Socialist Movement, 1870–1890.* London, 1971.

Stephens, Winifred. *Madame Adam (Juliette Lamber): La Grande Française: From Louis-Philippe until 1917.* 2d ed. New York, 1917.

Sternhell, Zeev. *La Droite révolutionnaire, 1885–1914: Les Origines françaises du fascisme.* Paris, 1978.

Suarez, Georges. *Briand: Sa vie, son oeuvre, avec son journal et de nombreaux documents inédits.* 6 vols. Paris, 1938–1952.

Sullerot, Evelyne. *La Presse féminine.* Paris, 1963.

Sumler, David E. "Domestic Influences on the Nationalist Revival in France, 1909–1914." *FHS* 6 (1970):517–37.

Thibaudet, Albert. *Les Idées politiques de la France.* Paris, 1932.

Thibert, Marguerite. "Le Féminisme dans le socialisme français de 1830 à 1850." Ph.d. diss., Paris, 1926.

Thiébaux, Charles. *Le Féminisme et les socialists: Depuis Saint-Simon jusqu'à nos jours.* Paris, 1906.

Thomas, Edith. *Louise Michel, ou la velléda de l'anarchie.* Paris, 1971.

――――. *The Women Incendiaries.* London, 1967.

Tilly, Louise A. "Women's Collective Action and Feminism in France, 1870–1914." In *Class Conflict and Collective Action,* edited by Louise A. Tilly and Charles Tilly. Beverly Hills, Calif., 1981.

Tilly, Louise A., and Joan W. Scott. *Women, Work, and Family.* New York, 1978.

Toulemon, André. *Le Suffrage familial ou suffrage universel intégral: Le Vote des femmes.* Paris, 1933.

Toutain, J.-C. *La Population de la France de 1700 à 1959.* Paris, 1963.

Vidalenc, Jean. *La Société française de 1815 à 1848: Le Peuple des campagnes.* Paris, 1970.

Watson, David R. *Georges Clemenceau: A Political Biography.* London, 1974.

Weber, Eugen. *Peasants into Frenchmen: The Modernization of Rural France, 1870–1914.* Stanford, 1976.

Weston, Elisabeth A. "Prostitution in Paris in the Later Nineteenth Century. A Study in Politics and Social Ideology." Ph.D. diss., State University of New York at Buffalo, 1979.

Wilkins, Wyona H. "The Paris International Feminist Congress of 1896 and Its French Antecedents." *North Dakota Quarterly* 43 (1975):5–28.

Willard, Claude. *Les Guesdistes: Le Mouvement socialiste en France, 1893–1905.* Paris, 1965.

Winock, Michel. "Les Allemanistes." *Bulletin de la société des études jaurèsiennes* 50 (1973).

――――. *Edouard Drumont et Cie: Antisémitisme et fascisme en France.* Paris, 1982.

Wolfenstein, E. Victor. *The Revolutionary Personality: Lenin, Trotsky, Gandhi.* Princeton, 1967.

Wright, Vincent. "The Coup d'état of December 1851: Repression and the Limits to Repression." In *Revolution and Reaction: 1848 and the Second French Republic,* edited by Roger Price, pp. 303–33. London, 1975.

Zeldin, Theodore. *France, 1848–1945.* 2 vols. Oxford, 1973–1977.

Zylberberg-Hocquard, Marie-Hélène. *Femmes et féminisme dans le mouvement ouvrier français.* Paris, 1981.

Index